A HISTORY OF CHRISTIAN THOUGHT

A HISTORY OF CHRISTIAN THOUGHT

(From Apostolic Times to Saint Augustine)

John R. Willis, S.J.

θ

An Exposition-University Book

Exposition Press   *Hicksville, New York*

NIHIL OBSTAT:
James L. Monks, S.J.
Leo A. Reilly, S.J.
Censores Deputati

IMPRIMATUR:
Humberto Cardinal Medeiros
Archbishop of Boston
April, 22, 1976

FIRST EDITION

© 1976 by John R. Willis, S.J.

Copyright © under the Universal Copyright and Berne Conventions

Library of Congress Catalog Card Number: 76-16237

ISBN 0-682-48583-7

Printed in the United States of America

For Ruth, Vic, and Ted

Contents

7

Contents   9

Introduction

Anyone who writes any sort of book today must show just cause why he has added still another item to the mountain of literature which already exists in the world, and anyone who writes a history of Christian thought must show why the numerous works on this subject already in circulation should admit still one more to their growing number. In defense of such an effort, (and this is, I hope, the first of several volumes directed to that end), it is my belief that we are in a period which needs to be reminded that history did not begin yesterday, and cannot be swept away as a major obstacle to the progress of and advance toward tomorrow. We are what we are today largely because of our past history, and although history may be somewhat poor cargo to lug into the future, it can serve as very good ballast. So much passes for novelty in our time which is actually quite old that it needs to be unmasked for what it really is. It is well said that those who do not know history are forced to repeat it, and nowhere may this be truer than in the field of historical theology.

There are several histories of Christian thought available, but their point of view is often quite at variance with this writer's and that of the readers he has in mind. To adopt any stance at all may seem to some to surrender all historical objectivity and unbiased presentation of facts. But if there is to be any meaningful selection of material, and if the course of historical thought is to eventuate in a comprehensive synthesis of leading ideas, some vantage point must be adopted at the outset. Otherwise we are left with a jumble of facts with little attempt to evaluate their overall significance. What would we think of an author who allotted an equal amount of space to Saint Augustine's doctrine of grace and Saint Paul's ideas on women's hats in church?

This book has been written from the standpoint of catholic Christianity in the very large sense of the term, and is primarily for students and others interested in the development of both traditional Catholic and Protestant Christianity. The author tries in broad outlines to lay down the belief of the People of God in the famous formula of Saint Vincent of Lerins, *quod ubique, quod semper, quod ab omnibus creditum est.* To focus on what has been believed by everyone at all times everywhere is not to ignore variant or heterodox points of view, but such have

11

been dubbed variant or heterodox because they have not met acceptance with the teaching church nor of the classical position of the Reformation. The point of view of this writer is that those who correctly interpreted the true meaning of the Gospel were the ones who subsequently received the approval of the church. Hence, while trying to be fair and understanding to all parties, his sympathies will lie with Polycarp rather than with Marcion, with Athanasius rather than Arius, with Augustine rather than Pelagius. But a proper comprehension of the history of early Christian thought requires that we know what all parties believed and taught, even though some were closer to the truth than others. Yet in all cases the writer has striven for historical objectivity, and has tried always to separate the impartial scholar from the man of faith. He has attempted to interpret the facts without prejudice, while at the same time placing them in a broad and meaningful pattern which shows the developing mainstream of traditional Christianity.

I call this *A History of Christian Thought,* using the word *thought* as somewhat broader than either *doctrine* or *dogma. Dogma* has an unpleasant connotation in the minds of many moderns (we don't like people who are dogmatic) and *doctrine* suffers from some of the same disabilities (doctrinaire is related to it). *Thought* may seem somewhat vague and undefined, but is meant to include what was taught and at the same time believed. It also seems to me the least pretentious, and thus fits better in the idea and spirit of this book.

The emphasis is placed squarely on individual writers, and the attempt has been made to summarize their general point of view, rather than to single out and focus on their peculiarities. This has necessitated some repetition, but the aim has been to show similarities as well as differences of viewpoint. By keeping individuals very much in the foreground, there may seem to be some neglect of general trends or climates of opinion, but there are numerous church histories which supply ample background for the general reader and encompass material which is more properly Church History than Christian Thought.

In my concentration on primary sources with the intention of having each writer speak for himself as far as that was feasible, I have tried not to minimize the importance of secondary material, but to mention even the most valuable works would require a volume in itself. I have therefore appended a short list of suggested books which deal with overall surveys, and made further indications, in the Notes, of books which are particularly helpful at various given points. This seems to me more useful to the average reader than a long bibliography.

New Testament studies occupy a field all their own, and many would claim that Christian thought must begin with the writings of the "apostles" not included in the New Testament canon. But the ultimate source of historical theology must be Jesus of Nazareth himself—his Person and his message, and so the New Testament writers have a special claim also in the history of Christian thought. Therefore, I have included a brief synopsis of New Testament teaching, fully realizing that many would exclude this area from a proper history. There is precedent for including it, however, and to omit it would seem to some to concentrate on the river and ignore its source.

I need to express a deep debt of gratitude to three former teachers: Plato Ernest Shaw (Hartford Seminary Foundation), Ernest Findlay Scott (Union Theological Seminary), and Robert Lowry Calhoun (Yale University). I am also indebted to Father Leo A. Reilly, S.J., and Father James L. Monks, S.J., of Boston College and to Ms. Muriel Vitriol who painstakingly read the manuscript and offered invaluable suggestions, as well as to President J. Donald Monan, S.J., of Boston College, Rev. Francis J. Nicholson, S.J., and Rev. Edward J. Gorman, S.J., for indispensable material aid. I need to thank others for their kind encouragement, especially Helen Fitzgerald for her secretarial expertise, and finally Paul W. Frost, who literally drove me to the whole enterprise.

I

THE NEW TESTAMENT WITNESS

The Synoptic Gospels

A history of Christian thought might appear incomplete if it did not take some account of the New Testament writings, even though this may seem to be trespassing in an area which more properly belongs to Biblical studies. Still, Jesus of Nazareth is nonetheless the font of all thinking about him, Christian and non-Christian, and so, if only to satisfy a sense of completion as well as subsequent historical thought, we are bound to take some notice of what his contemporaries and other writers of the first century have to say about him.

Jesus is an eminently mysterious Person who somehow always manages to elude our grasp. Since he seems to have written nothing himself, we are bound to rely on reports about him, virtually all of which reside in the narrow limits of the New Testament. This means that we are dependent on what others have said about him, and consequently we have to take into account their own particular environment, their peculiar historical situation, and the culture, mores and religion of first-century Palestine. It is not surprising that some have averred that the historical Jesus has disappeared completely and all that truly remains is the Christ of faith.

No one today can be unaware, much less indifferent, to the mountains of scholarship and archaelogical research that have occurred in this present century alone, but one thing is certain: we know far more about Jesus and his times than scholars of the preceding centuries did. And it is equally certain that the life of Jesus will continue to fascinate future scholars long after all the indefatigable workers from David Strauss to Oscar Cullmann have receded into ancient history.

Our task in this chapter is to review the witness of the Synoptic Gospels to see what three writers, in substantial agreement, had to say about an extraordinary man whom their friends had come to call God's chosen Messiah. Who was he? What did he teach and do? How did he live and die? And what was the significance of it all?[1]

Jesus, the son of Mary and (putatively) Joseph, was a pious Jew living in Galilee, a carpenter by trade who was about thirty years old when he came into public prominence. He must have been rugged, attractive, and possessed of great charm, a charismatic figure to the nth degree. The common people flocked to hear him gladly, and not a

17

few were cured by his healing powers. He soon attracted a sizeable group of some seventy disciples, and a more intimate band of twelve of whom Peter, James, and John seem to have been his closest friends. Much of his teaching was cast into parables and, at first, directed to whoever would hear him, but toward the end of his ministry he concentrated on private teaching for the intimate group gathered around him. After approximately three years of a ministry based in Galilee, he determined to make a decisive trip to Jerusalem to announce his messiahship. The Jewish authorities arrested him as a troublemaker and turned him over to the Romans on the charge of political sedition. The Roman governor, Pontius Pilate, intended to release Jesus after having him whipped, but finally yielded to public pressure by ordering his crucifixion. Three days later some of his followers claimed that he had risen from the dead and was still alive in Galilee.

It used to be thought that the teachings *of* Jesus could be separated from the teachings *about* Jesus and that a sharp distinction existed between the Jesus of history and the Christ of faith. But it is now obvious that the teaching and the life cannot be separated, and, indeed, what Jesus teaches is the life that he led. It is sometimes supposed that Jesus was mainly interested in ideas, but actually he was much more of a leader and a man of action. There is surprisingly little originality in his teachings as such, nor did Jesus seek to be particularly original. Much less was he a social reformer or interested in building a better society. Clearly he was no political revolutionary. So it is very dangerous to judge Jesus from one vantage point only, although each generation is tempted to view him through its own specially colored glasses.

Jesus chose his disciples that they might be with him. He hoped they would be able to absorb from him new attitudes, new approaches, new ways of looking at God and the world, which they could learn in part from his teaching, but more by just being with him. His teaching really has no meaning apart from his life, for it is his life which endorses his teaching as true; in fact, if this were not so, his teaching would be useless—beautiful, no doubt, but hopelessly impractical.

Jesus' message centers around the principal theme of the Kingdom of God (or, in Matthew's words, the Kingdom of Heaven). Men are to repent, for the Kingdom of God is at their very doors. Precisely what does Jesus mean by this expression? Does he mean the church? Does he mean the life hereafter? Does he mean the perfect society of the future which is just around the corner? Surely all of these are meant, but Jesus was no doubt using an apocalyptic idea which was quite familiar to his listeners. Only once does he seem to offer an actual definition of the Kingdom—it is that state in which God's will is done perfectly on earth, just as it is carried out in heaven.

John the Baptist had based his message on the same idea, and Jesus repeated John's message in much the same words. With the advent of the Kingdom there will be drastic changes in the moral order. The will of God will occupy men's minds, and earthly possessions, honor, and glory will cease to be of concern. There will be a tremendous reversal of values, the last will be first and the first last, and those who do not count for much in the present society will press forward to occupy important places in the Kingdom. Will the Kingdom come suddenly, catastrophically, or will it be the result of a long evolution? And did he think of it as wholly in the future, or in some manner already present?

The usual apocalyptic view was that the Kingdom would come suddenly and was still in the future. Its arrival would be totally unexpected just as in the days of Noah when the flood came. Two men would be in a field, one taken and the other left; two women would be together, and one taken while the other is left behind. The principal petition of the Lord's Prayer is that the Kingdom will come, and yet, in some sense, the Kingdom is already present. It is present where two or three are gathered together to seek the will of God; it is in the future, but it is already here insofar as you are doing God's will.

The Beatitudes mark the contrast between two types of character, those of the present and those of the coming age. Jesus pronounces a blessing on those who are becoming meek, humble, and peaceable, for when the Kingdom comes, they will find themselves in their natural element. But to enter the Kingdom, one must undergo a great change of mind ($\mu\epsilon\tau\alpha\nu\omega\alpha$), which Jesus calls repentance. This requires a conversion to the fullest extent, a new outlook on life, a new standard to judge by. It means ridding one's self of all the old prejudices, attitudes, and biases of the past, and looking at life with the wonderment of a small child. It means a complete facing-about, and it is paradoxically both hard and easy. Along with repentance goes renunciation, a surrendering of one's possessions and earthly interests. This is not always to be taken in the literal sense—the larger number of followers stayed where they were and some were even men of wealth and position—but in order to assert one's freedom from the present age some kind of sacrifice is necessary in order to enter the future life. On the disciples, however, Jesus laid a special obligation to give up everything and devote their entire lives to his cause.

A considerable part of the Synoptic Gospels is taken up with the debates between Jesus and the scribes and Pharisees, who were the representatives of the official religion. Not infrequently Jesus contrasts his position with theirs, and so it is necessary to understand why some of them opposed him so bitterly. In fact, it was they (some of them) who brought about his death. The Pharisees were those who obeyed God's will as contained in the Law. They were actually a small group of religious leaders, but they had an enormous influence. In the Gospels the scribes are always coupled with the Pharisees, although they might belong to any party; they were exponents of the system which the Pharisees set about to practice. The Law included both the written record and the oral tradition for the Pharisees, while the Sadducees were more fundamentalist and lacked the liberalizing influence of the Pharisees. Many of the more enlightened members of the group were unquestionably exemplary. Paul himself was a Pharisee and Jesus declared that some of them were not far from the Kingdom of God; Christianity drew some of its converts from this group.

When Jesus condemns the Pharisees, he is not condemning individuals so much as types, and it is the entire system which comes under attack from him. He felt that they had made religion mechanical and that their obedience to God depended more on outward rules than on inward spirit. Since all the rules could be obeyed (if one had sufficient leisure), then Phariseeism led to a kind of smugness and self-righteousness, thus opening the door to a sort of self-satisfaction in the idea that God now no longer required anything of the person. This in turn led to pride, toward both God and one's fellowman—it resulted in a superiority complex which despised the common man who knew not the Law, and was therefore cursed. Service to God likewise became a show, the object being to impress others and to reap a little personal credit. Since there was a good deal of emphasis on externals, the temptation was only natural to want to gain a bit of recognition; thus it was easy to corrupt the inner motive.

Jesus' object was to create in men a new and better will, which would put them in a right relationship to God, making his will their own. If the tree is made good, the fruit will be good because men will know how to act in any given situation. While there is indeed an occasional stress on this or that particular virtue, it is really virtue as a whole which concerns him, and this new type of character he tries to convey as much by example as by teaching. Unlike the Pharisees with their rules and regulations, Jesus tries to impart a new way of life to characterize those who belong to the coming Kingdom.

First-century Palestine was strongly influenced by apocalyptic ideas which had been in circulation since about 200 B.C. It had been a time of distress for the Jews: things had been going from bad to worse, and people were beginning to look for a special act of intervention on God's part. The present age was given over to Satan and his evil rule, but in the coming age God would establish a new order. Change was coming soon and it would be announced by a miracle, but before it came there would be a time of great crisis; the present evil would build up to a climax and then God would intervene and inaugurate a new day. This new day would mean glory and deliverance for Israel, and a humiliation of Israel's enemies. And so we have a profound pessimism with regard to the present age, which would soon be ending in a triumphant burst of optimism.

The new era would be ushered in by God's chosen representative: the Messiah. The Messiah might be a "warrior-king," who would lead the Jews to victory in a kind of Napoleonic whirlwind campaign which would establish his rule in all directions. The less military- minded often believed that the Son of God would appear in glory in the clouds, and once he manifested himself, all opposition would simply crumble. There were innumerable variations on this Messianic concept, but most of the opinions fell in one of these two categories. There was also the tradition that Elijah or one of the prophets would appear to announce the Messiah, and get things ready for the final showdown. It was natural for many people to wonder if John the Baptist or Jesus might not be either Elijah or perhaps the Messiah himself.

The aim of Matthew's Gospel is to show that Jesus is indeed the expected Messiah, and Matthew does this by demonstrating how a large number of texts from the Old Testament have been fulfilled by the life of Jesus. This was certainly the view of the early church, and it was also the keynote of much evangelical preaching, and especially that of Peter and Paul. But how did Jesus himself view the matter? Did he deliberately set out to fulfill Old Testament prophecy and thus claim to be the Messiah? Setting aside the second question for discussion later, Jesus seems certainly to have considered himself in the line of the Old Testament prophets. They are quoted with approval; Moses and Elijah actually appear in one scene, Isaiah prophesied well about the Jews, and Jonah is used to illustrate Jesus' death. On at least one occasion Jesus set out to fulfill a prophecy in Zechariah by riding into Jerusalem astride a donkey to effect a triumphal entry. And yet the fulfillment of prophecy was not convincing to many Jews. Luke, writing to Gentile converts, does not emphasize it, and Mark lays less stress on prophetic fulfillment than Matthew, who goes so far as to have Jesus fulfill a prophecy not specifically recorded in the Old Testament at all (Matt. 2:23).

The Synoptic Gospels also testify to the fact that Jesus worked miracles. Many of these were miracles of healing, and were usually performed when Jesus required some act of faith and made a personal contact. The primary purpose in working the miracle was to show God's love for men rather than to prove a claim to divinity. There is no question about the miracles themselves, for even his opponents never denied them; they simply said that he cast out demons by the prince of demons, Beelzebub. Some of the miracles show that Jesus had control over nature and could walk on water, cause trees to wither, or food to be multiplied for the benefit of a large group of people. In virtually every instance the miracle occurs to illustrate some truth in the moral or spiritual realm. Jesus seems to work a miracle only with reluctance and actually considers them occasionally misleading; toward the end of his life the miracles are fewer, and in specific cases when a miracle would have been highly advantageous, it is not performed at all.

Even though there are instances of people dying and then being restored to life, the greatest miracle of all is reserved for the end of the Gospel: Jesus rose again from the dead. After a detailed account of Jesus' last hours on earth, this most tremendous event of all was proof that death simply could not hold him. In view of this, the other miracles reported by the Evangelists become quite credible, but like the prophecies, they never crowd out the central theme of Jesus' message—the announcement that the Kingdom of God is at hand.

Did Jesus somehow think of himself as the Messiah who would usher in the Kingdom? His most frequent reference to himself is the Son of Man, which in Aramaic simply means *man*. People who referred to him in more glowing terms were not infrequenly rebuked. Was he afraid that an open declaration of Messiahship would be misunderstood and have disastrous consequences? Or had the suspicion or conviction of being Messiah only come upon him in later days?

The early church held that Jesus was always conscious of somehow being the Messiah, although a clear announcement of this did not come until the conversation with Peter and the disciples at Caesarea Philippi. Here he definitely adopts the posture of Messiahship, but proceeds to change the disciples' concept by declaring that rather than being a victorious Messiah, the Messiah will have to die. The prediction tolls like a knell three times in Mark's account (8:31, 9:30, 10:33) and causes such surprise among the group that Peter positively rejects it. The Master upbraids his disciples for slowness of understanding and hardness of heart, and then hurries on to Jerusalem for a final confrontation with the authorities. Even though he might think of himself as a suffering servant type of Messiah, so ably described in Isaiah 53, there would surely be many who would read this as a political move as well as a direct challenge to Roman hegemony. Jesus' declaration would sooner or later force Rome to intervene.

Matthew tells us that Peter was the first to blurt out the true identity of the Son of Man, and that as a result of his perception Jesus granted him a primacy of position in the church. In a passage which has always been highly controversial (Matt. 16:16-18), the early church did believe that one of Jesus' aims was to gather together a group of believers of whom Peter was somehow spokesman and leader. Since Peter's later life was spent at Rome, this afforded prestige to the congregation at the empire's capital. All of this will soon be reflected in Clement's famous letter to the Corinthians.

What was the political attitude of Jesus himself? The autocracies of different times and places have found their sanction in the teachings of Jesus, but now we are told he favored democracy, socialism, communism, and even anarchy. However, the Synoptic Gospels leave us little if anything that can be construed in a political fashion. Only once does Jesus seem to touch on duties to the state, and this was extorted from him by his enemies: "Render unto Caesar the things that are Caesar's . . ." The actual question was whether it was right for the Jews to obey a foreign power or not, and it was a trick question because an affirmative answer would cause him to lose many of his more zealous supporters, while a negative one would have at once branded him as a revolutionary. Jesus puts the question on a higher plane, but before answering it he says, "Show me a coin." Usually this is taken as a dramatic gesture, but its effect was to have everybody shell out a penny. If people were all using tribute money they were availing themselves of the benefits of the government while having doubts about its laws. Outside of this particular incident, Jesus is silent about diverse forms of political government. His deliberate purpose was to keep clear of the stormy political issues of his day, because the new kind of world which he envisioned would be created solely by an act of God; the present arrangements, being faulty, would be superseded. God himself, if only men would keep their hearts on the Kingdom of God, would solve many of the problems in the New Order. For the present, Jesus bids men to obey, but he contents himself with only a passive obedience; men are to submit because the state is necessary, beneficent, and soon to disappear. Jesus' concern is with the inward principle of man's life, not with the framework of society. Men must respect other men and deal with them justly; social systems can always be reorganized and political systems can always be changed. And so, Jesus avoids drawing up concrete plans, knowing that any scheme would only have been for the time in which he lived. Men must prepare their hearts for the coming Kingdom; all else would then follow.

A great many of Jesus' best-known sayings are concerned with the subject of possessions and wealth. Some have argued that he was out to secure an economic change and effect a redistribution of goods. From the Gospels we learn that he had been a carpenter—a highly respected trade—and had given up comfort, good prospects, good position, and the like. Hence, he could make similar demands on his followers. Jesus thinks of wealth as being the chief hindrance to obtaining higher blessings; the poor are blessed because of their poverty. The rich man's stake in this world is so large that he cannot see his way into another; the best Christian athletes are those who travel light. Even apart from the apocalyptic note—and Jesus certainly has this in mind in his teaching about money—worldly goods are a real hindrance to the spiritual life. The note of poverty is especially stressed by Luke, whereas

Matthew emphasizes spiritual poverty and detachment. For Jesus, wealth is the unrighteous Mammon and it belongs to the realm where evil prevails, but if wealth is used rightfully, it can bring about real good for its owner. Jesus is really concerned about good stewardship of wealth, but because of the immanence of God's Kingdom the truly wise will let nothing stand in their way (and money can be a chief obstacle) of their entrance into it. Every man is accountable for the way he uses his time, his talents, and his possessions.

First-century Palestine was characterized by a strong family life, which had a religious as well as a social unity, and in the Jewish family the father occasionally took on a quasi-priestly function. The family bond was considered sacred and Jesus' use of the word Father for God shows that he held the family in high esteem, as does the fact that he referred to all men as brothers. Yet, when Jesus speaks of the family in the Synoptic writers he seems to disparage it. He regards it as one of the institutions which belong to the present age, but in the Kingdom of God all divisions will be done away; there will be no marrying or giving in marriage—all souls will depend immediately upon God. Even in the present order Jesus declares that the family must necessarily come second. Do God's will! If family ties interfere, they must be sacrificed. A man must be prepared to leave father, mother and brethren, wife, houses and lands for the sake of the Kingdom. Jesus could readily see that families counted for a very great deal, but he insisted that there is something which must rank even higher. However, Jesus does enhance the family in his prohibition of divorce, or perhaps it would be better to say he forbids remarriage after separation. So he recognizes a sanctity in the marriage relationship which prevents its union from being infringed upon; in this particular instance, Jesus lays down a hard and fast ruling which has caused no end of discomfort ever since.

One of the objections to Jesus was that he associated with people he shouldn't have, and had some friends and connections who were more than a little open to suspect. Many people with whom he spoke were simply *people of the land (Am ha-aretz)*, worthy and pious souls, no doubt, but careless of and disobedient to the requirements of the Jewish Torah because of the conditions of their life. To have dealings with such "indifferentists" contaminated those who were zealous for the Law. Jesus also numbered publicans and sinners among his friends, those who were out for worldly gain and who worked for the heathen over-lords; they handled unclean money and included not merely tax collectors but those involved in shady financial dealings. Then there were real moral offenders, such as harlots. With the first group of people Jesus was most sympathetic and resented the stamp of inferiority placed upon them; he declared they could understand his message better than those who were allegedly superior socially. The second class of people he never tried to defend, and the third class he frankly acknowledged to be great sinners. "Your sins which are many are forgiven." He implies the need for forgiveness on the part of every one, and this is precisely why people should be quick to forgive those who offend them. In his relations with the outcasts, Jesus acted on his belief in the value of human personality as such, but he had special care for the disinherited because they were the objects of God's love. He recognized the kernel of goodness which is in all men and worked hard to cultivate it.

Each of the Synoptic writers begins his account of the life of Jesus by drawing from different material and starting from a different point of view. But when they reach the last week of his life, they march harmoniously together with a surprising degree of agreement. The teaching of Jesus gains its validity from his life during his final hours upon earth.

Following the triumphal entry into Jerusalem, Jesus taught daily in the temple, and successfully eluded a number of trick questions posed by his enemies. Every one of these encounters with the scribes and Pharisees he won, and yet he left the scene a defeated man. Sensing that his political foes were closing in on him, he decided to have a final supper together with his inmost disciples, which the Synoptic writers declare was a Passover meal. He washed his disciples' feet, declared that one of them would betray him, and enacted a simple rite in which he took bread and said, "This is my body," and declared of a cup of wine, "This is my blood." Then he retired to a garden for agonizing prayer, leaving his three most trusted friends to stand watch. Before long, a motley rabble had gathered to arrest him and take him to the house of the high priest for questioning. An interrogation (rather than a trial) before the Sanhedrin declared him worthy of death for claiming to be the Messiah. He endured house arrest for the remainder of the night, and was shuffled off to Pilate in the morning, who claimed that the case really fell under the jurisdiction of King Herod. However, Herod returned the prisoner to Pilate, who thereupon tried to wash his hands of the whole affair. After a vicious beating, the Roman procurator announced his intention of releasing the prisoner, but the malice of the crowd, stirred up by the principal religious leaders, shouted for Jesus' crucifixion. He was led away, carrying at least the cross bar on his shoulders, with the charge against him of claiming to be "King of the Jews." Criminals had been known to last for several days upon the cross; Jesus was dead in less than three hours, so short a time that Pilate was astonished. He was laid in a borrowed tomb, and his body prepared for burial prior to the Sabbath, while a large stone was placed at the entrance of the tomb to guard it.

On the first day of the week three women went to the tomb to anoint the body, but found the sepulcher empty and the large stone rolled away, which fact they reported to Peter, who likewise made an investigation. Soon reports were circulating that Jesus was alive and had been seen by his disciples traveling to Emmaus, as well as by Mary Magdalene, and eventually (in spite of initial disbelief) the inner group of eleven apostles became convinced that Jesus had actually risen from the dead. In spite of seeming discrepancies in the narrative, it is obvious that something tremendous occurred, and whether one chooses to believe the resurrection event or not, what we must stress here is that the early Christians gambled their very lives on the fact of its being true. The conviction of the early church with regard to Christ's resurrection must precede the writing of the Synoptic Gospels themselves. In fact, it is this event that the Gospel writers are giving primary testimony to, otherwise there would be no sense in recording the life of Jesus at all.

Following his resurrection, Jesus did not long remain on earth. Giving his apostles a final commission to go into the whole world and preach the Gospel to every creature and to baptize those who would believe (Matthew says, "In the name of the Father, Son and Holy Spirit"), he ascended into heaven to be with his heavenly Father.

This is the barest outline of the life and teachings of Jesus as reported by the Synoptic Gospels. Only the highlights can be mentioned in such short compass, and such important topics as prayer, fasting, almsgiving, self-denial, and a host of other subjects merely alluded to in passing. The "Simple Gospel" turns out to be many-sided and far more complicated than the most sophisticated theological system; the difference between the two is the difference between a living organism and a machine, between the human body and a typewriter. The early church was to interpret this message, now from the philosophical, now from the moral, now from the mystical side—only to discover that each of its interpretations was in the main correct but inadequate. The whole object of Jesus' life and teachings was not to lay down rules, but to offer men salvation. He offered men a few great principles which they were to apply to themselves as citizens of the Kingdom of God. He laid emphasis on the new will or the new nature in man, rejuvenated by his teaching and Person. This was the Good News which he came to proclaim to all men; this was the Gospel of Our Lord and Savior Jesus Christ.

The mission and message of Jesus had been almost wholly confined to the Jews in Palestine. Very soon, however, it was to be adopted by a brilliant Jew of the Diaspora, and addressed to non-Jews living in Hellenistic cultures outside of Palestine. Some have declared that this was to result in an alteration of the very essence of the Gospel tidings, while others have claimed that, on the contrary, the Good News was freed from narrow parochialism to become a worldwide religion addressed to all mankind. The man most responsible for this was Paul of Tarsus, and it is to his interpretation of the message of Jesus that we now turn.

NOTE

1. Commentaries and studies on the Synoptic Gospels will be found listed in the bibliography. I am particularly indebted to my former professor Ernest Findlay Scott, who was one of the first to interest me in New Testament studies, and whose influence was lasting.

Saint Paul

The central teaching in the Synoptic Gospels is Jesus' idea of the Kingdom of God. In Saint Paul, the central idea is God's salvific will for mankind in the death and resurrection of Jesus the Christ. It used to be thought that Paul had totally distorted the message of the Synoptic writers and had supplied a new interpretation of Christianity which was altogether his own. But a closer reading shows that this is not true, that Paul has interpreted the Gospel for Jews of the Dispersion and pagan converts with Hellenistic backgrounds. Although cast in different terms to make more of an appeal to his hearers, Paul's message is fundamentally the same as that of Jesus.

Paul was primarily a missionary and man of action; his letters are almost incidental to his main work of founding churches and spreading the Good News. He was not a systematic theologian, nor always altogether clear or careful in his thinking, which soars from the poetic inspiration of the thirteenth chapter of First Corinthians to the question of women wearing hats in church. Furthermore, Paul's literary output is quite small, making it impossible to extract an entire systematic theology from such scant material; this is important because too often arguments have been settled by appeals to what Paul did not say, rather than to what he explicitly stated. These arguments from silence have often loomed large in the history of theological controversy, but the fact that Paul does not deal with every religious question relevant for a later age does not mean that he was unable to, or did not think it important.

Paul developed his theology mainly from his own personal religious experience. Born outside of Palestine, trained in the Jewish Law, he was a rabbi who earned his living making tents. His conversion to Christianity was sudden, but because he had always been a Pharisee of the Pharisees, his Judaism never quite left him. One of his major concerns was to show that Christianity was the fulfillment of the Jewish hope and the Jewish Law. All of this is summed up in the idea of redemption, for to know Christ personally is to be free from legalism, from sin, from the spirit of the world, and from the evil one. His thinking is both very complex and very profound; all we can do here is to examine some of its multifaceted aspects.

The earliest followers of Jesus were Jews who observed the Mosaic Law. But when Gentiles in increasing numbers entered the church by accepting Christ by faith, the Law came to be regarded as superfluous and even inconsistent. What part, then, did the Law play in the new divine economy; was it to be kept, or was it a positive evil? Of course, in Paul's time, the Law embraced not merely the Ten Commandments and the moral law delivered on Sinai, but ceremonial law as well, to say nothing of the centuries of traditional interpretation which had grown up around it. Since Paul considers the entire Law as something imposed on man from outside, he fails to make the necessary distinctions between types of law. And so he views it as both something good and something bad. It is good because it has a divine value, and is therefore holy, "and the commandment holy, and just, and good" (Rom. 7:12). Since God had inspired it, it could not lightly be put aside. And yet, the Law is also hostile because it stands over man, making demands on him which are quite impossible to satisfy; it demands a righteousness which man finds impossible to fulfill. So the Law has this twofold ambivalent nature which Paul attempts to resolve in some manner.

He does so by declaring that Christ himself has satisfied the demands of the Law by fulfilling it perfectly, and thus superseding it. The Law contains a curse for those who do not keep it, but Christ has taken this curse upon himself and blotted out the handwriting which was against us (Col. 2:14). Christ cancelled the Law by nailing it to his cross and satisfying it by his death. Is this to say that the Law is somehow evil in itself? No! God forbid (Gal. 3:19)! It was an interim measure enacted between the time of Abraham and that of Christ because of sin. But while it stated the will of God, it gave no power to obey it, with the result that the estrangement between God and man was greater than ever before. The Law might be all very well for angels, but its demands on human nature of flesh and bones only made man feel all the more impotent. For the Law made man more conscious of lust and sinful concupiscence, and linked this with a conscious feeling of guilt. In fact, it increased sin to more vigorous action by its very prohibitions. So what was God's purpose in giving the Law, which Paul (being always a good Pharisee at heart) declares is actually good? The Law makes man conscious of the need for deliverance by acting as a sort of restraining governor (Gal. 3:24). When a child went to school he was often accompanied by a kind of male nurse, a confidential servant who looked out for him and disciplined him if the occasion arose. It was the sort of thing a child would hate. So the Law, like a governess, held him in check, making him more aware of sin, but giving him no power to overcome it.

As a Jew, Paul revered the Law. As a Christian, he was aware that the Law had no further claim, but he could not grant that the Law had been abrogated. He continually had to wrestle with the problem of reconciling his new position as a Christian, with the one he had held as a Jew.

In Christianity, Paul had discovered a power which, unlike the Law, was able to break the dominion of sin. Sin was rather more like an outward power (instead of something inward) which had invaded man and had corrupted the entire human race. Like death, it was almost the personification of an evil force which had seized all of humanity. Paul views all men as forming a single whole; there is individual sin, to be sure, but there is also a corporate sin by which every living person is tainted. This is due in part to Adam's fall by which sin entered the world (Rom. 5:12), but it is also due to the fact that man has a fleshly nature. By fleshly nature Paul means everything that is related to the body, as opposed to man's immaterial component, and, indeed, the flesh actually wars against the spirit in man, and his spirit against the flesh (Gal. 5:17). At times he appears to be almost saying that the flesh is somehow intrinsically evil (Rom. 8:7, 8). It is this weak side of human nature which sin takes advantage of to bring into slavery, and so, sin and the flesh are somehow allied against God and man's spirit. Now, to win a victory over sin man must strike at the flesh, but by the very fact that he is a creature of the flesh, man is powerless. How can he escape this dilemma? Christ solves the problem for us by winning victory over the flesh through his death (Rom. 8:3). On the cross, the flesh was crucified, and in this way men gained liberty from its slavery. Christ adopted the disguise of sin by taking on flesh so that he could deal the enemy the death blow (2 Cor. 5:21).

What Paul is really driving at is that with Christ a new and higher power has entered the world, the power which makes it possible for men to overcome sin. Christ communicated to man a power to do something which he could not do for himself. Through Christ we have access to this higher power because he himself has taken on our humanity, while at the same time being sinless; he thus does for us something which for ourselves would have been impossible.

This brings us to Paul's doctrine of justification by faith, a teaching which Protestantism has fastened upon as being the core of Paul's message. In spite of the great emphasis which Luther placed upon it, it is discussed only in Galatians and Romans, for in the other letters Paul introduces different ideas to highlight the Gospel message. Justification by faith certainly does not comprise the whole nor even the most significant part of Paul's message, yet it is tied to two very important notions: grace and faith. By grace, Paul means a free gift of God which is given to man quite apart from any merit of his. It is God's nature to give, and he makes his sun to shine on the just and unjust alike. Faith is the receptivity on man's part of God's gift; it is the willingness to receive what God freely bestows.

It is at this point that so much modern religion fails. It too often conceives of Christianity as a kind of activism, a do-goodism quite apart from God. It tries to reduce everything to a love of one's neighbor; it refuses to recognize human and social limitations; it becomes frenetic activism. This is not to argue for a modern quietism, but too often people fail to realize that the essence of religion is to accept with humble faith and thanksgiving what God sends our way. Everything that we receive, everything that happens to us is a gift of God, which only requires that we be receptive to its proper use and acknowledge his love in the giving of it.

Paul is saying that faith is simply belief. Jesus is the Christ, the Messiah of God, who has proved his love for us by dying on the cross. Jesus loved men so much that he was willing to do anything to prove it, even to die upon the cross. It is through the cross that we partake of the fellowship of Christ's sufferings. And we do this through faith in God's redemptive power, a faith which justifies us, makes us no longer subject to sin but holy unto God. Justification actually means acquittal before God; it is a legal term by which the culprit is declared exempt from guilt. What makes us no longer guilty in the eyes of God is our faith in the redeeming work of Christ. It is our faith by which God now imputes to us righteousness, a righteousness which is not our own, but is the gift of God. But a mere imputation of righteousness does not satisfy Paul; somehow man is made righteous; the sinner is touched by God's goodness and so is led to enter upon a new life by means of the Holy Spirit.

The doctrine of justification must be supplemented by Paul's other conception, that is, by union with Christ a man loses his own nature and is changed from a carnal being into a spiritual man. By faith we are united with Christ, so that his nature becomes our nature. And yet, man can do nothing of himself to attain this justification before God. He must throw himself on the mercy of God, and let God's grace do for him what his own actions, deeds, works, could not achieve. When this happens, there is no longer any condemnation for those who are in Christ Jesus (Rom. 8:1).

Redemption is therefore the keynote of Christianity. Man is in bondage to the powers of darkness from which he cannot escape, but God has interposed his grace for man's deliverance by sending a Redeemer. Paul's theology thus centers on the work which Christ has achieved. Since he had never known Jesus during his earthly life, it might seem at first sight that this was of no concern to Paul, and that he actually makes a dichtomy between the Jesus of history and the Christ of faith. But nothing could be further from the truth, for it is precisely the crucifixion, death, and resurrection of Jesus the Christ upon which Paul lays the greatest stress. Probably he never tried to state to himself in metaphysical terms the nature of Christ's relation to God. He distinguishes between the two, but he brings them into such close relationship that Christ is far more than any created being. Every one of Christ's actions carries a divine significance, and this is all summed up in the idea that God was in Christ reconciling the world to himself (2 Cor. 5:19).

Christ was the Son of David and thus fulfilled the Messianic hope of the Jews (Rom. 1:3, 4). He was declared to be the Son of God with power by his resurrection from the dead. There was something divine in his inner nature which resulted in his resurrection. But in a celebrated passage in Philippians (2:6-9), Christ pre-existed in the form of God, but considered this not a prize to be equal to God but rather took upon himself the form of a servant—he assumed human life—and as a reward for this humiliation of himself he was raised to an even higher dignity than he had had at first; he received a name above every name, "that at the name of Jesus every knee would bow" (Phil. 2:10). So, before his life on earth Jesus preexisted in heaven, a spiritual being related in some way to God; He appeared on earth in the fashion of a man; and he arose as the exalted Lord and so lives forever, attaining to a higher dignity than he had before. Paul thus combines the traditional Jewish idea of the Messiah with the apocalyptic conception of the heavenly Messiah and certain ideas derived from the mystery religions with philosophical ideas connected with the Logos doctrine.

All of this is succinctly summarized in the letter to the Colossians, where Paul tells us that Christ "is the image of the invisible God, the firstborn of every creature. For in him were created all things in the heavens and on the earth, things visible and things invisible, . . . For it has pleased God the Father that in him all his fullness should dwell, and that through him he should reconcile to himself all things, whether on the earth or in the heavens, making peace through the blood of his cross" (Col. 1:15-20).

By laying stress on the preexistence of Jesus in heaven, Paul relegates the earthly life to the background. In numerous passages Paul ascribes a divine value to Christ; in fact, the term he uses is the Lord Jesus Christ, and sometimes just "the Lord." It is occasionally not clear whether "the Lord" refers to Christ or God, but in either case universal homage is meant. Now, since the Jewish Messiah was never equated with God (angelic status was the highest ever accorded to the Messiah), Paul's language is more reminiscent of the mystery cults, with their notion of a dying and rising god. Yet the cults were always polytheistic in character, and Paul is a strict monotheist—no Jewish rabbi could have been otherwise. So neither the Messianic concept nor the mystery cults offer satisfactory analogies to Paul's theological formulation of the person of Christ. Christ is worthy of worship because he is somehow external to the believer, but he is also an inward presence, a person, who at the same time dwells within the individual Christian (Rom. 8:10, Gal. 2:20). In later New Testament writings, both Messianic concepts and mystery cults give way to the Logos doctrine of the preexistent Word.

Paul conceives of the Christian life as a life in the Holy Spirit. Because our natural condition is one of flesh, we are at the mercy of sin and death. But to be in Christ means that his spirit takes possession of us, and by it we become no longer subject to sin. So the doctrine of the Spirit holds an important place in Paul's thought, for faith in Christ carries with it the gift of the Spirit, and that means a real change occurs in man's condition. The working of the spirit is supernatural; *naturally* man lives like an animal because a good life is something which nature has not provided for; life in the Spirit is above nature and, therefore, supernatural.

The early church, which believed strongly that the Spirit was operative within it, lived in a kind of continued excitement. Working of miracles, gifts of prophecy, speaking in tongues—all signified that the age of the Spirit had truly come. Paul never denies this, but he enriches and transforms the primitive notions of spirit in very real and profound ways. Under the idea of the Spirit he brings in the whole concept of the Christian life, thus relegating the more spectacular manifestations of the Spirit to the periphery. He also conceives of the Spirit as something more or less permanent, and not something that came and went haphazardly and spasmodically. He saw in the Spirit an abiding reality, a power that was always present and was a normal not an abnormal condition permeating all Christian activities. Most important, he connected the Spirit with a higher ethical life and thus prevented Christianity from turning into a religion of emotion or mere rapture. The distinctive thing about the Spirit is that it gives rise to a new moral life; it has its real root in faith, hope, and love and manifests itself most clearly in ordinary Christian life. Paul saw in higher morality the highest function of Christianity; the apocalyptic note was still there, but it receded in importance as time went on.

How does Paul conceive the nature of the Spirit? It is like the mind of God, a source of revelation (1 Cor. 2:11), and just as there is mind in man, so in God there is Spirit; no man knows God unless he has the Spirit of God. Sometimes he speaks of this power in almost personal terms (Rom. 8:16, 26), and the doctrine of the Trinity is at least implicit in Paul (1 Cor. 6:11; 2 Cor. 13:13). It is certainly remarkable that when one of the Persons of the Trinity is referred to, the other two not infrequently come to mind; whenever the Spirit is mentioned, mention is also made of God and Christ. Spirit enters human nature through Christ, thus making it possible for the Christian to live the higher ethic which is impossible for the natural man. Between the Christian and the best man there is this essential difference, for apart from Christ it is impossible to have the Spirit which is exactly what makes it possible to aspire to the higher life.

How are Christ and the Spirit related? Usually Paul holds that it is in baptism that the Spirit is imparted through Christ. Often the two seem to be equated: it is Christ who dwells within you as well as the Spirit who dwells within you. Paul is actually trying to balance two facts which for him are ultimately the same. The Spirit is the source of revelation, of peculiar gifts, of the new life which manifests itself in believers. It is a power that belongs to the new age, the heavenly world, and the special possession of Christians; and yet, all of this merges with Christ himself.

The Christian nature in all of its facets is transformed by the Spirit. It is the Spirit which makes us capable of higher knowledge putting us in touch with the mind of God; it is the Spirit that strengthens and renews the will in man, and it is the Spirit that purifies and changes the emotional nature, causing a higher affection to spring up within us. To "walk in the Spirit" is to no longer fulfill the lust of the flesh (Gal. 5:16; Rom. 13:14).

One of the fundamental ideas in Paul is the idea that redemption depends upon a call or election upon the part of God, who has already determined beforehand who would enter the Kingdom, and it is by virtue of the divine call that men respond to Christ. This concept of predestination was to have an enormous effect on men like Augustine and Calvin, as well as many other lesser theologians. In the minds of not a few people it seems like a dreadful doctrine which makes the whole Christian Gospel of no effect; it seems to make the universality of the message meaningless by limiting it to a select few. God turns into a senseless tyrant by offering love and pardon to everybody and then having the majority of people condemned. Yet Paul assumed that all who were in Christ, all who had entered the Christian church, were by that very fact numbered among the "elect" of God. In this way, he accounted for one of the mysterious facts of life: that while many might hear the Gospel message, far from everyone would accept it. Most of the Jews rejected it, and a large number of Gentiles as well. Not many wise, not many mighty, not many noble accepted it (1 Cor. 1:26) because it was too often a stumbling block, or sheer foolishness. And so Paul simply had to conclude that God had somehow put limitations to his work. One may view predestination as a theological dogma if one likes, but it is only Paul's attempt to solve one of life's profound mysteries: the great gift of salvation was freely offered to all men, yet only a few accepted it.

The fullest discussion of this doctrine is in Romans 9, 10 and 11. Paul is well aware of the difficulties which this teaching presents: that it seems to make God unjust (Rom. 9:14), and, again, that it makes God responsible for the sins he punishes (18, 19), and that man must not question God's will (20). God's purposes are often too deep for men's comprehension, but his eternal love is always seeking to effect good. Since the predestination of God is not arbitrary but is determined by love, Paul finds this a very consoling doctrine. It means that it is God, not man, who takes the initiative in salvation and that faith in Christ is actually a free gift on God's part. If God were to deal with men solely on the basis of their merits, no one would be saved because no one would be truly worthy to receive God's grace. In fact, Paul holds that men are predestined by God before they even exist as human beings, and in this he takes great comfort. If we see that everything depends on our own efforts we may easily get discouraged, for even the saints are profoundly aware of how weak they are. The point of Paul's doctrine of predestination is not a matter of holding on to God, so much as God's holding on to you! Paul's doctrine of predestination is in fact an answer to the fatalism of the age, which declared that life was ruled by blind, mechanical forces of relentless tyranny. Through confidence in God we can defy the powers of fate and feel ourselves elevated to a plane where the love of God lifts us beyond hostile, mechanical forces.

Christianity delivers us from all the powers inimical to man, the last of which is death. Paul appears to hold two different and inconsistent views on the nature of death; on the one hand, it is intrinsic to all things living which are temporal by their very nature, and yet to man death seems like something alien which is the result of sin. Paul speaks of death as punishment provided by God for sin, and indeed death is inherent in sin. Death entered the world as an alien power, thanks to the sin of Adam. Paul conceives of it in almost personal terms, it is a single power which has secured a hold on man, and it could only be destroyed by the coming of Christ himself.

Paul's view, therefore, is that death had a rightful hold over men because as sinners they had laid themselves open to death. But Christ was without sin, and therefore death had no hold over him. The assault which death made on Christ recoiled on death itself; thus death slew itself on the cross of Christ. Paul never alludes to the human factors in the crucifixion, assuming that they were merely instruments used by principalities and powers. These saw Christ come to earth and saw an opportunity to destroy him once and for all, not knowing the plan of God that through the destruction of Christ they would destroy themselves. Christ's death and resurrection were two sides of the same coin to Paul; the resurrection brings to light what had been achieved by the death. The destruction of death involves a new life (Rom. 6:8-11).

But if it be true that Christ by dying destroyed death, why is it that even Christians still die? Instead of disappearing from the world as it should have, death continues as before. One answer is that the power of death has been broken, but its effects are still operative, just as an illness may continue for a while, even after the cause of the illness has been successfully treated. Another answer is that while the outward man continues to perish, the inward man is renewed day by day. But Paul adopts another position and declares that the real freedom from death comes when we are united to Christ in a spiritual union which begins at the moment of faith. After death, this union is merely completed, for death makes no essential change in the Christian; the real dividing line is between the time of faith and the time of unbelief. So the future life is a fuller realization of the life of the spirit which is begun on earth by union with Christ.

Since the life of the individual Christian must conform to the life of Christ, this means that each person is to undergo a resurrection. There are three main passages in which Paul discusses the nature of the resurrection. To the Thessalonians he writes that when the Lord gives the command, the dead will rise, and those who are still living will be caught up together to meet the Lord in the air (1 Thess. 4:13-18). To the Corinthians he writes an assurance that the resurrection will involve some sort of physical body. We are not to think of it as merely the immortality of the soul (as the Greeks would have it), but as somehow also involving the body (as Jewish tradition maintained). Therefore, the resurrection involves the body as well as the soul (1 Cor. 15). In a second letter to the Corinthians (2 Cor. 5:1-10), he deals with the specific problem: What becomes of the soul during the interim between death and the resurrection? Paul declares that it enters a new habitation immediately at death; a new eternal house is waiting for it (2 Cor. 5:1).

But Paul's greatest utterance on immortality is in the eighth chapter of Romans, especially in the closing verses. Here he starts by declaring that Christ rose from the dead, and that this is a pledge that Christians will do likewise. From the fact of the resurrection he passes on to its nature: with what body are the dead raised? He closes by forecasting the circumstances of the resurrection: it will come suddenly, the first event in the new age; and it will mark the final overthrow of death. In all of this two things stand out clearly: there can be no immortality without the body, and the new body will be different in kind from the earthly body—it will be spiritual. In Philippians 3:21 he describes this body as one of glory; it will be similar to that which Jesus now wears and which all Christians will wear eventually.

And so, for Paul, the great change takes place not at death but at the moment when we are united with Christ by faith—it is then that we cease to become carnal and become spiritual. Our life afterward continues what has been started. Under earthly conditions we are never revealed in our true selves; this occurs when our nature is clothed in a spiritual body and this change takes place at death, when the soul is clothed in a body which truly represents it. Thus the future life will give complete realization to life in the Spirit which had been begun on earth.

Since Paul is the great representative of personal religion, it may seem surprising that he is also the New Testament author who has the most to say about the church. He is at once both a personalist and an ecclesiastic. Finding the church, or perhaps it would be better to say a group of Christians, followers of the Way, Paul's real contribution was to make the church conscious of itself. He was a born organizer, and in his missionary journeys one of his prime aims was to collect individual Christians into a group and thus found a church. He could readily see that unless this were done, the Christian fervor would soon evaporate, and believers would soon be reabsorbed into the world. Where there was much spiritual fervor but less order, Paul imposed a certain discipline and order into the believing community; this was absolutely necessary if the church was to survive.

In some mysterious way, the church represents Christ on earth. Just as Jesus was incarnate in a physical body while among men, the church is also the body of Christ since Jesus no longer appears in physical fashion. But Jesus is somehow the head of this body called the church (Eph. 1:22), and as such he continues to direct its destiny. The church is one with Christ, even though it is made up of a diversity of people, all with differing practical and spiritual gifts (1 Cor. 12:27). Paul also insists that the church must be separate, distinct from the world; indeed, since our citizenship is in heaven, it would be accurate to describe the church as a sort of colony of heaven. Men are to be drawn out of the world and into the church. But while the church is distinct from the world, it must also live in the world. It became increasingly clear to Paul that the Parousia might not come so soon as he had anticipated, and this is one of the reasons for his insisting not only on order and organization, but also that the church and its members live as blamelessly as possible. He therefore insists that Christians do everything possible to avoid scandal and to give edifying example to their neighbors. Occasions for friction between believers and pagans should be kept at a minimum; otherwise, the hostile world might soon put the church out of existence.

Paul clearly saw that the Christian life could never be lived in isolation; to accept the person and work of Christ was also to accept his brethren whom the Master loved dearly, as a bridegroom loves his bride, and so all must love the church. The church was already in existence before Paul arrived on the scene. He enlarged it, organized it, disciplined it, but most important of all, made it conscious of herself and her great destiny.

Incorporation of the individual into the Christian church comes through the rite of baptism, which is man's response to the gift of faith. Baptism symbolizes for the Christian the death, burial, and resurrection of Christ himself; through baptism we are buried with Christ in death, and then rise to newness of life (Rom. 6:5). This may indeed allude to the rite of immersion, although Professor Fitzmyer thinks this is hard to establish for the first century.[1] At any rate the Christian dies like Christ, but in this case to sin and the Law, and then shares a new life with the Christ who rose from the dead, and imparts his spirit. Thus, baptism is not an individual affair, but is the gateway to the corporate Christian life, for all are baptized in one spirit to form one body (1 Cor. 12:13). Just as Israel passed through the waters of the Red Sea, so also must the new Israel pass through the waters of baptism (1 Cor. 10:1, 2). There is no explicit reference to a Trinitarian formula, but perhaps it is implicit insofar as mention is invariably made of the Spirit and of God the Father (1 Cor. 6:11, 19). The Trinitarian formula used in the rite of baptism is not so much heard, as overheard.

Paul is the earliest writer to give us an account of the Last Supper and the institution of the Eucharist (1 Cor. 11:23-25), although his main purpose is to criticize the corrupt Corinthian practice. The celebration of the Eucharist is for the Apostle a sign of Christian fellowship and symbolizes the unity of Christians with Christ. One is to eat and drink worthily of the Eucharistic bread and wine, because these are equated with the body and blood of Christ; Paul does not say how, but neither does he mean a mere symbolic equation. Therefore, a decorous following of the ritual is called for because of its obviously sacred character. It is in this way that the Lord's death is proclaimed until the time of his second coming, when all such sacramental actions would be rendered obsolete. The sacramental meal also has a sacrificial implication, because it is the blood of the new covenant which is shed for the remission of the sins of many. All of this is reminiscent of the Exodus story, which itself is a type or symbol of Christ, the sacrificial Passover Lamb.

The letters of Paul are never mere abstract theological treatises, but invariably conclude with quite specific ethical and social teachings. The Christian Gospel sets a man free, but this is not to say that we may do anything we wish; freedom also implies very specific responsibilities, and Paul mentions not a few. Very explicit ideas with regard to marriage, divorce, and virginity are directed to the Corinthians, while the Romans are to observe certain behavior toward the state and all those who are in authority. Prayer, almsgiving, and other pious practices are urged, as well as appropriate conduct between masters and slaves. Despite his profound theology, Paul always has very practical ends in view, and it is his theology which serves to underscore his Christian ethics. For this reason, his profound understanding of the Christian message is all the more amazing, since his aim is never to systematize it as such, but rather to draw upon it for the practical daily life of the churches. Had he sat down to present an elaborate and complete synthesis of the newly revealed Gospel, what might the result not have been![2]

The Letter to the Hebrews seems to be of an early date, possibly before the year A.D. 70 because of its seeming implication that the temple at Jerusalem was still standing; its author (Apollos, Stephen?) is anyone's guess, but the weight of evidence is against a Pauline authorship. Strongly influenced by Alexandrian theology, and particularly by Philo's doctrine of the Logos, the whole thought of the letter rests on the conception of a higher, ideal world over against this present material one. Thus, the object of the writing is to demonstrate that through Christ we have the substance of absolute religion where previously we had only shadow.

Taking Judaism as the highest religion known up to that time, the author shows that the entire Jewish religion existed in order to make it possible for the High Priest to enter the Holy of Holies once a year and to renew the covenant between God and His people. But what Judaism attempted to do through symbols, Christianity does in reality. Christ is greater than the agents through which the old covenant was given (Heb. 1:2). He is also greater than Moses to whom the covenant was given, and he is greater than the High Priest through whom the covenant operates, for in Christ we have the once sufficient High Priest of whom the Levitical priesthood was only a symbol. Proof of this is based on Psalm 110, which speaks of Melchizedek as being both King and Priest by virtue of his personality; Christ is the true High Priest, not by virtue of his descent but by virtue of his intrinsic nature—who he really is.

On the Day of Atonement, the High Priest did two things: he offered sacrifice for the sins of his people, and he passed through the veil of the Holy of Holies, and stood for a moment in the presence of God. Likewise, Christ offered a sacrifice, not of an animal victim, but of himself, and after his death he passed into the sanctuary of heaven, thus affording his people real access to God. But whereas the Jewish sacrifice effected only a symbolic cleansing, Christ's sacrifice effected an inward, real purging of the sins of the believer, and whereas the High Priest stood only for a moment in God's presence, Christ entered and sat down to stay. So Christ was freed from this world of transitory phenomena and entered the world of higher reality, and it is to this higher world that he beckons his followers. All of this is very Platonic, and very familiar to those acquainted with Philo's teaching on the Wisdom of God.

The whole argument comes to a head in the eleventh chapter, which contains a paean to faith. From the outset, the password of Christianity had been faith, which meant not merely intellectual assent to the fact that Jesus was the Messiah, but trust and obedience to him as well. But in Hebrews, faith is defined as the substance of things hoped for— enabling us to grasp future things as if they were present realities; and it is the evidence of things not seen—proving that invisible things exist which are not evident to the senses. Numerous examples are cited from the Old Testament of people who through faith were able to re-charter the future, and also to apprehend reality which did not testify to their senses. These people knew their hopes would come to pass because they grasped eternal realities which were inaccessible to other men. But faith is not so much a matter of knowledge (as in Philo) as it is a principle of action; nor is it the quality of a philosopher (as in Philo) so much as it is a principle in the religious life of God's chosen people. And in Hebrews it is connected with fulfillment in Christ, for even in the Old Covenant, Abraham and others looked forward to the time of the New Covenant.

And so, faith is the power of grasping invisible realities, and for this reason Christianity is the final religion, because it is concerned with unseen realities. But it is also faith which links the new religion with the old, so that the heroes of former times belong in the same company with Christians today because all live by faith. What is distinctive, then, about Christianity? It claims to present not the shadow of unseen things, but the reality of the invisible world itself. Abraham, for instance, was not so much looking for Palestine as he was a city with foundations, eternal in the heavens. What he sought by faith, Christ now offers to us in substance. What Christ has done, the writer holds, is to bring us into full view, for the first time, of the true goal. He endured the cross in the knowledge of the supreme attainment that lay before him, and so through Christ we can set our hearts on the ideal world because he has perfected faith in the sense that he has made faith fully conscious of itself. God's purpose has been the same in all ages; those who went before us strove, but did not receive the reward until we came along to share the reward with them, since they could not be perfected without us.

The writer thus attempts to appeal to both Jewish and Hellenistic readers. Borrowing the idea of Platonic, unseen realities through Philo's symbolic interpretation of Judaism in Alexandria, the author of the Hebrews puts the Christian stamp on the heroic which has inspired men of all ages. Through faith, we have insight into the invisible world which is none the less real, and through faith in Jesus, who both begins and consummates this faith in us, we are able to run, with patience, the race which is set before us.

NOTES

1. Joseph A. Fitzmyer, "Pauline Theology" in *The Jerome Biblical Commentary* (Englewood Cliffs, N.J.: Prentice-Hall, 1968) p. 822.
2. Commentaries and studies on Saint Paul will be found in the bibliography.

The Johannine Literature

The Johannine literature embraces the Fourth Gospel, the three letters very likely by the same author, and the Book of Revelation. Our focus of concern will be with the Gospel, which reached its final form sometime near the end of the first century, and which is substantially the work of the apostle John, plus the work of a redactor(s), one of whom may also have been named John. Problems of dating, integrity, and authorship belong to the field of New Testament studies and need not detain us here.

The purpose of the Gospel is "that you may believe that Jesus is the Christ, the Son of God, and that believing this you may have life through his name" (Jno. 20:31). The author is thoroughly acquainted not only with the geography and topography of Palestine, but with Jewish customs and practices as well. A strong effort is made to set off Christianity from Judaism by showing that Christ not only fulfilled the Law, the liturgy, the Messianic expectation, but by fulfilling these brought them all to an end. Likewise, there appears a real attempt to subordinate John the Baptist and his following; no actual baptism of Jesus is recorded at all, for it is Jesus (not John) who is God's Anointed. Similarly, there are anti-Gnostic indications in the Gospel for the author wants to make Christianity intelligible to all men, not a select few, and it is a way of life for all, not merely Jews; Jesus has a universal appeal because he was both with God, and yet human, approachable to all men.

It is to Philo of Alexandria that we owe the development of the Logos philosophy, which attempted to take Jewish ideas and clothe them in Greek thought. It is through the Logos, the Word, the Wisdom of God that he makes contact with the world of matter. But the Logos is also God's Son, through whom all things were made and who is the culmination of all things, for he brings grace and truth. But the Word, the Wisdom, the Logos of God now makes a bold, unheard-of move: he becomes flesh and dwells with men! Men behold simultaneously the glory of God's only-begotten Son as well as his genuine humanity. The first witness to this is John the Baptist himself, who immediately directs his followers to the Nazarene, for it is he who baptizes not with water but with the Holy Spirit, which proves that he is the Lamb, and the Son of God.

41

The Gospel now divides roughly into two parts: chapters 2 through 12 have been appropriately named by Professor Dodd *The Book of Signs*.[1] The remaining chapters 13 to 21 deal with the Passion narrative, and subsequent events following the death of Jesus.

Sign and symbol play a large part in the Fourth Gospel, a sign being that which points to something else, while a symbol stands for something else. Often the two meanings merge.[2] The first miracle which Jesus performs—a sign that a new dispensation is breaking forth—takes place at a wedding feast in Cana. Quite apart from the historical incident, the entire affair is meant to symbolize something much deeper than the mere transformation of water into wine. What Jesus really does, the author implies, is to take the water of Judaism and transform it into the wine of Christianity. Jesus also, by his presence, sanctifies the sacrament of marriage, but most important of all, perhaps, is the word which is put into the mouth of Mary his Mother who says to the attendants: "Do whatever he tells you." And what Jesus is saying, not only here but in the story which follows of the Cleansing of the Temple, is that the Old Dispensation is finished, is through, and you are to align yourself with the New Dispensation which Jesus is inaugurating.

The discussion with Nicodemus in the third chapter is on the necessity for rebirth into eternal life, but this is only possible because it is offered by the Son of Man who descends from heaven and then ascends back to heaven. What he brings is life and light, for the Logos of God stands in contradiction to the earthly world of matter which is below. The man who believes in the Son of God receives light and life, whereas the man who does not believe is already condemned, since he prefers darkness because of his evil deeds, which will bring him only death. The figure of John the Baptist is reintroduced to fortify this idea at the end of the chapter. He who believes in the Son has everlasting life; he who is unbelieving toward the Son shall not see life, but the wrath of God rests upon him (Jno. 3:36).

Water is the symbol under discussion once again in the conversation with the woman of Samaria, but this time it is not the water of Judaism or the water connected with the bestowal of the Holy Spirit, but the water of life which the Messiah gives to those who ask him. The new religion will worship the Father not by the Temple, but in Spirit and in Truth, for that is the way God now wants to be worshiped (Jno. 4:23, 24). The predominant symbol of water is contrasted subtly with a subordinate symbol of food, for the Messiah does the will of the Father and is bringing his work to a conclusion and this is the food which sustains him. The Samaritan woman may also be said to symbolize the Gentile world, just as Nicodemus stood for the Jewish. These conversational encounters are all summarized by the Samaritan villagers when they declare: "We no longer believe because of what you have said, for we have heard for ourselves and we know that this is in truth the Saviour of the world" (Jno. 4:42).

The cure of the official's son and the healing at the pool of Bethsaida center around the idea of the Word. The second incident arouses a storm of protest from the Jews; not only does Jesus break the Sabbath, but he makes himself equal to God. This sets the stage for a discourse on the divinity of the Son, whose program of activity tallies exactly with that of the Father. The Son equates himself with the Word of the Father, and he who hears and believes has life everlasting, and does not come to judgment. In fact, the time has already arrived when even the dead will hear the voice of the Son of God, and hearing, will live (Jno. 5:25). Voice, word, witness, are all connected with the idea of speech; John the Baptist has already witnessed to Jesus, just as Jesus now witnesses to the Father. The Father also witnesses to Jesus, as do also the Scriptures, but belief is lacking because the listeners are earthbound; they failed to believe Moses, so how can they believe the Word who speaks to them, who desires above all to give them life?

The feeding of the five thousand centers around the symbol of bread, and ends with a discourse on Jesus as the Bread of Life. It is an explication of the Christian sacrament of the Eucharist, and makes not only a reference to the Passover season, but contrasts the Eucharistic bread with the manna in the wilderness which sustained the Israelites only temporarily. To the question, How can this man give us his flesh to eat? the suggestion is hinted that only by death, and a death of violence at that, will Jesus be able to feed his people with the Bread of Life. The drinking of blood was abhorrent to the pious Jew, and as a result, many of his followers drew back. The manna of Old Testament times might have mysteriously descended from heaven, but the Jews cannot accept the parallel which Jesus draws between this and himself. The discourse in the synagogue ends with the somber prediction that one of the twelve will turn traitor. The discourse on the Bread of Life also serves to sift the multitude, and from this point on, Jesus concentrates on the disciples as those who acknowledge that he has the words of eternal life.

A Feast of Tabernacles acts as the backdrop to a series of encounters with the Jews that express the irreconcilable conflict which has now developed between his new teaching and the traditional religion. The symbolic idea here is that of judgment, or irreconciliation between light and darkness, what is above and what is below, the new theophany and the old religion. Judgment by appearances must give way to just judgment, just as light illumines everything, or throws it into shadow. The various dialogues centering around this theme show that the hostility to Jesus is increasing, and the end of it will be his death, but his death specified at a distinct time in the future. The symbol of the Good Shepherd helps to distinguish between the lambs and the wolves; it is the shepherd who can tell the true from the false, it is he whose judgment is infallible. Not only is he a shepherd, but he symbolizes the door to the sheepfold, which is the only legitimate access to security. The story of the adulteress again illustrates the righteous judgment which Christ executes, a judgment not based on false appearances. And the cure of the man born blind brings out further the idea of light and darkness, and the need to judge from Christ's deeds themselves with respect to the validity of the claim he is making. But it is also Christ who judges those who disbelieve; those who are against him cannot believe because they have already given their allegiance to that which is below.

The Raising of Lazarus (in the eleventh chapter) highlights the idea of life, which had been introduced previously in the section on the Good Shepherd. But this is not merely abundant life, so much as the victory of life over death. The symbolism here is of the resurrection, for Lazarus actually typifies what is about to happen to the Master himself; Lazarus symbolizes the resurrection to new life, while Jesus *is* the resurrection and the life. But a resurrection is impossible without a previous death, and so we are brought to the gateway of the Passion narrative with the information that the Jewish authorities have decided on Jesus' death. He is aware of this, and allows the anointing of his feet with oil, in preparation for his burial. A triumphal entry into Jerusalem affords him the opportunity of addressing the people for the last time, and the arrival of some Greeks upon the scene symbolizes the end of the ministry to the Jews and the beginning of preaching to the Gentiles. There is a summing up of Jesus' mission of having been sent by the Father, and the key ideas of light-darkness, life-death, and belief-judgment for unbelief are reiterated once again as the public ministry comes to a close.

Five chapters cover the events of the Last Supper, and it is here that John has collected a number of "farewell discourses" whose object is to explain the coming events of Jesus' death and resurrection, and also to instruct the church which is about to come into existence. The first incident is the washing of the disciples' feet, which evokes a discussion of cleansing—outward and inward—with Peter as the foil to bring out the symbolism of cleansing, inasmuch as water is always the sign of regeneration. Christ washes his disciples' feet dressed as a servant, for this is the slave of God who will be obedient unto death for the sake of those whom he loves. Next, the betrayal of Judas is predicted, and the traitor goes out into the darkness—the commentator making the pungent observation that it was now night (Jno. 13:30). As if betrayal were not enough, there would also be a threefold denial on the part of the very chief of the apostles himself.

A word of comfort to the disciples leads to the symbolism of Jesus as the Way, as well as the Truth and the Life. The latter two have repeatedly been discussed before, and in the discourse about the Good Shepherd, reference is made to Jesus as the Way; these three ideas are now brought together in summary fashion, and lead to the emphasis placed on love. It is the Father who has loved the Son, and the Son has loved his own, with the result that they must now love one another. Love means keeping the commandments of him who is the Way, so that the Father will also love them as he does the Son. It is in love that the Father and the Son dwell in the disciple, while the Holy Spirit reminds him of all things. Love begets peace, not a worldly peace, but a heavenly peace which is impervious to the turmoil of the world. The fact that the Father and Son make their abode in the disciple is symbolized by the vine with its branches; the branches are fruitful only insofar as they are connected to the vine, which is purged by the vine-dresser in order to make the branches even more fruitful. But if a branch is separated from the vine, it withers and is of no further use than to be burnt up. Union is possible only through love, as love is possible only through union which together bring joy, which like peace is not of worldly origin. The disciples are always to remember that their love is the result of first being loved by the Father and the Son. It is God who has chosen *them,* and they have only chosen God because they were enabled to do so by God. This hint of predestination has already turned up before, especially in the Bread of Life discourse, and now the Evangelist states it quite succinctly.

Love will not be answered by love in the world, for persecution will be the lot of Christ's disciples. The love-hate syndrome undergoes exploration, with the conclusion that the world will hate the believer because it has already been convicted by the Advocate and no longer has a cover-up for its sin. The third member of the divine Godhead cannot arrive until the Son has departed, so for a little while he must go away. But all will be well in the end, for joy and love will abound, overcoming all obstacles.

A prayer for unity concludes the Farewell discourses, and it re-capitulates some of the ideas in the previous chapters. The central idea here is the apartness of the disciples from the world; they are in it but not of it, for their goal is eternal life through love of the Son and the Father, while the world is already condemned for not knowing God. That is why there must always be enmity between the world and the church, for world and church represent two entirely different orders, always incompatible, never reconcilable. Church and world now continue the pairs of opposites: light and darkness, life and death, truth and lies, and so forth.

While the Synoptic Gospels seems to regard the Last Supper as a Paschal meal, the Fourth Gospel places the Supper a day earlier, when the Paschal lamb was killed. Hence the crucifixion would tally with the slaughter of the Paschal lamb, whereas in the Synoptics the Supper would tally with the Passover. In either case the symbolism would be most striking, and indeed there was a tradition in the early church which favored the Johannine contention that Jesus died on 14 Nisan rather than on the following day. In the Johannine account of the Passion, Jesus seems to be fully in command of the situation at the time of his arrest (there is no agony in the garden recorded), and he allows himself to be taken only after safe-conduct has been granted to the disciples. The principal charge against Jesus is political, making Pilate indubitably responsible for the execution, which would not be by stoning but by crucifixion, in order to fulfill the prophecy of "being lifted up and thus drawing all men to himself." In the trial scenes, Jesus has a good deal more to say in defense of himself than is recorded by the Synoptics, and the utterances from the cross are different. The Fourth Gospel alone records the story of the Mother of Jesus and the disciple whom Jesus especially loved. And after Jesus dies, special attention is called to the fact that water and blood issued from the spear wound inflicted in his side. These, as we have seen, symbolize the life-giving water which quenches the thirst of the spirit, and the blood which one must drink to have eternal life. Tradition says that these symbolize the birth of the church, and the text invokes witnesses that these phenomena actually did take place, whatever their symbolic import.

The Resurrection stories emphasize the fact of the empty tomb, and then add some post-resurrection incidents with considerable detail. An encounter with Mary Magdalene commands her to relay the good news to the disciples before Jesus ascends to his Father. The Holy Spirit is breathed upon the disciples, collected fearfully together in the upper room, but in the absence of Thomas, who is nonetheless present a week later. Thomas confesses to the divinity of Jesus, who uses the incident to bless those who likewise will believe, even though nonparticipatory to the actual event. The Evangelist also declares that Jesus worked many other signs in the sight of his disciples which were not written in his book; he has written in order that he may, through the material he presents, excite belief in Jesus, the Christ, the Son of God (Jno. 20:31). And it is for this, after all, that the Gospel has been written; its purpose is to promise an abundant blessing on all who in future countless ages will believe.

The Johannine use of symbolism is continued in the three letters to which John's name is attached, especially in the first and most important of the three. The Life of God which always was with God has been actualized in the flesh, and has lived among us in such a way that it can be seen and handled. The symbol presently shifts to light, or rather the opposition between light and darkness. Sin is darkness to be found in all men, but confession effects a cleansing with the blood of Jesus. This results in a realization of God's love for us and the necessity to love one another. To love means to abide in the light, with the result that light and love are contrasted now with darkness and sin, and presently with the couplet God and the world, or permanence and impermanence.

A note of urgency now enters; it is the last hour, it is the time of Antichrist, and this means that the Parousia is just around the corner. To be safe from coming disaster means to abide in the Father and the Son, or rather that They should abide in the believer, bringing him to everlasting life. But persecution will be his lot because the children of the devil hate the children of God, just as Cain hated his brother. Wickedness and disbelief characterize the world with its pride and its lust, while the children of God act through love and belief. But it is easy to be trapped; one must test the spirits and carefully distinguish between the spirit of truth and the spirit of error.

The remainder of the letter is a strong exhortation to charity, and it is all very reminiscent of the Farewell discourses in the Gospel. The predominant symbols of light, life, and love, with their opposites are drawn out, and the letter concludes with the note of hope and encouragement. The same exhortation to love and to love the truth make up the content of the second letter, written to an unknown lady, and the third letter makes specific reference to the church as a body of believers.

The Book of Revelation is the best example of several instances of apocalyptic literature which circulated in the first century, and had their prototypes in Jewish literature, of which the best example is the Book of Daniel. The thirteenth chapter of Mark is sometimes called the "Little Apocalypse" and even Paul was given to ecstasies, prophecies, and visions (1 Cor. 15; 2 Thess. 2) of things to come. Indeed, there is something of a revival of this in our own day of Pentecostal fervor with its speaking in tongues. Christian Apocalyptic usually flourishes when times are disastrous and ordinary events seem to portend the end of the world; it always has a popular appeal, especially for ordinary men and women, for whom abstruse theology is best left to professional theologians.

On first reading, the book appears to be a "chinoiserie" with little relevance for the modern world, but it must be remembered that the work was expressly written for its own time, the end of the first century. It is highly symbolic, even cryptic in character, but that is true of all apocalyptic literature of the age, which in general does not deal with the distant future, but rather "those things which are shortly to come to pass." So the predictions which the book describes are already taking place at the very moment.

At first sight the book seems to be a unity, but closer inspection would indicate that several sources have been put together by the author, who has then imposed a unity upon his material. But who is the author? Is it the apostle John, or someone else? Probably, the man who gave final shape to the writing was the presbyter John, who himself had been associated with the apostle John. Books written by disciples were not infrequently associated with their masters, and since Ephesus was the city of both Johns, it is not hard to see how (in time) there could easily have arisen a confusion. Whoever the author, he was certainly a genius, for his book was to have an enormous effect not only on the church, but on Christian art and poetry as well. The etchings of Dürer, the frescoes of Michelangelo, and the requiems of a Berlioz or a Verdi, would be a few among many examples.

After the destruction of Jerusalem in A.D. 70 the early church attempted more and more to distinguish itself from a Judaism which had fallen on very hard times indeed. But in so doing, the church also cut loose its mooring with the toleration extended to the Jewish religion. Toward the end of the century, the cult of emperor worship was insisted upon during the reign of Domitian, and those who would not comply were subject to fierce persecution. The island of Patmos had already received John in exile, and the deliberate assault on the nascent Christian church seems to indicate that the end was nigh. Hence, the main purpose of the book is an exhortation to stand fast. The rulers of this world may attempt to do their worst, but deliverance is just around the corner. It we can manage to hold out just a little longer, Christ will come triumphant; times are indeed bad, but to suffer for Christ is to reign with Christ.

The Almighty, He who is and was and is to come, sends special messages to seven churches in Asia Minor, after which there is a description of various "woes," or rather cataclysmic disasters. After Christ has broken the seventh seal of the book, seven angels with trumpets appear, and the blowing of each trumpet sets off a new woe (Apoc. 8-10). The central portion of the book is devoted to the mysterious figure of Antichrist, who may be Domitian or Vespasian, but more probably stands for the emperor Nero, the first and most vicious of the persecutors. At any rate, the mark of the beast (666) may be added up to spell out his name, and legend had it that Nero had not really died but would come back in the latter day to wreck fearful revenge on the world, and especially the church. The city of Babylon symbolizes all the wickedness of Rome, the city of this world which is pitted against the city of God, symbolized by the heavenly Jerusalem with its earthly counterpart.

So the Book of Revelation is dealing with actual accounts of its time, and predicts the speedy overthrow of the powers of this world. Yet, its fantastic imagery is not to be understood too literally because what is important is the triumphant end which awaits every Christian who is faithful even unto death. It is when things seem most hopeless that victory is most assured; things may look black but God is standing hidden in the wings, and at a given signal He will intervene to set everything right. The martyrs are exhorted to be patient a little longer, for they will soon be speedily avenged as the number of the elect is filled and God is about to wipe away every tear from every eye. A splendid vision of the New Jerusalem indicates that it will be of surpassing beauty and value (gold does not rust; pearls are priceless) and will endure throughout all eternity.

Critics carp at the seemingly unchristian ethics of the Apocalypse: Let him who is unjust be unjust still (Apoc. 22:11), but the work is not primarily concerned with ethics, and has little to say about love, mercy, forgiveness, or even the Kingdom of God, for that matter. It is a far cry from Saint Paul. Its primary purpose is to steel the will, and it is addressed to ordinary men and women of mediocre intelligence who were about to undergo a fiery trial similar to the one Polycarp was to meet. They were to keep their eye on the Lamb who was slain in sacrifice such as theirs, but it was to be a somewhat militant Lamb who was to overcome his enemies, and to rule in his everlasting Kingdom.

E. F. Scott says, "The religious value of the Book of Revelation is not to be sought in its theology, but in the great convictions which lie behind it. The writer believes with his whole heart that God is ruling the world, that material power, however strongly intrenched, is only for a time, that the service of Christ leads to eternal life. These were the beliefs that sustained the early church, and though they were commonly held in a crude, unreasoned fashion, as they have been in most times since, they were intensely realized. The religion which finds expression in the book may not have been profound and spiritual, but it was a living one, and drew its vitality from truths that were central in the message of Christ. There was ground for John's confidence that the church which held to it would, in the end, 'overcome the world.' "[3]

The twenty-seven books or writings of the New Testament, despite their very real differences in style, method, and approach, form a single volume, an integral whole. They all deal with the Good News which has come to man through Jesus Christ. This good news of reconciliation between man and God may be dealt with in quite different ways, but the kaleidoscopic treatment of the different authors is unified with the single theme of God's appearance to men in Christ Jesus, thus reconciling the world unto himself. It is an error to suppose that there are many differing theologies which have somehow been brought together by the church to serve as a manual of devotional readings. The New Testament has but a single purpose, to announce the New Covenant between God and man which has been effected through the life, death, and resurrection of Jesus of Nazareth. This great fact of history may have innumerable facets, but the facets are all related to an integral whole. And it will be this, and some of its facets that will occupy the attention of the so-called Apostolic Fathers, to whom we now turn.[4]

NOTES

1. C. H. Dodd, *Interpretation of the Fourth Gospel* (Cambridge: The University Press, 1953) p. 133ff.
2. *Ibid.*
3. E. F. Scott, *The Literature of the New Testament* (New York: Columbia University Press, 1936), p. 284.
4. Commentaries and studies on the Johannine literature will be found in the bibliography.

II
THE
APOSTOLIC FATHERS

A collection of brief writings, written near the end of the first and beginning of the second centuries, in Greek, by authors who were thought to be apostles of Jesus, or at least represented the thinking of apostles, goes to make up the corpus usually entitled "The Apostolic Fathers"—although the label itself is from the eighteenth century. There is no general agreement with regard to the precise membership of this motley group, but there are some general characteristics underlying the quite surprising variety to be found among individual authors. The writings are usually addressed to churches, or members of the church, and treat of rather specific needs or problems. They are quite practical in nature, while the moral teachings generally predominate over the theological. They make frequent reference to Scripture, and invariably insist that they are in complete harmony with the Gospel teaching. Their literary style ranges from excellent to poor, but in no case is style their main concern; all have a strong piety which addresses itself to specific problems or situations. As a witness to early Christianity, their value is inestimable in an age which relied more on the oral tradition and preaching of the Word than on literary production. No doubt much has been lost, and that is a pity, but what survives has never ceased to intrigue scholars both Catholic and Protestant. Many translations and editions of the "Fathers" testify to their continued popularity in our own time.

Saint Clement of Rome

The *First Epistle of Saint Clement of Rome to the Corinthians* was written about the year A.D. 96 and is therefore possibly the oldest writing we have which is not included in the New Testament. Eusebius cites Dionysius, bishop of Corinth, as saying that Clement is its author.[1] Whether this Clement is the same as the one mentioned in Philippians 4:3, or is Domitian's cousin Titus Flavius Clemens or one of his freedmen, or the same Clement mentioned in Hermas is still open to conjecture.

The fascination of this epistle rests in the occasion for its writing. Strife had broken out in the Church of Corinth with the result that certain esteemed leaders had been deposed by a younger faction. Possibly the Church at Rome was asked to intervene; at any rate it did so by sending a fatherly reply couched in at least implicit terms of authority. This raises the intriguing question of the relationship of the Roman church to other churches of the empire. Did Clement write with all the authority claimed later by the Papacy? Or was this simply a friendly letter coming from one church to another? Scholars generally agree that the truth lies somewhere between. While Clement of Rome is listed as the third successor of Saint Peter and no doubt enjoyed some authority in his own church, the evidence does not show that this authority extended to the Church of Corinth. On the other hand, neither can it be argued that each Christian church was independent of every other, but rather that each local church thought of itself as a branch of one larger fellowship, sojourning at a particular spot. It is therefore easy to see why an appeal might be made to the Church at Rome, not merely because this was the capital of the empire but also because of its connection with Peter and Paul. Nor does Clement apologize for interfering in Corinthian affairs, but gracefully assumes the power to do so. In all of this, then, there seems to be at least an indirect testimony to the primacy of the leader of the Roman church.

It is not until we are two-thirds of the way through the epistle that Clement comes to grip with the question at hand. Those who have participated in the schism must acknowledge their fault because it has subverted the faith of many, and caused disedification to everyone.[2] The authors of the schism must make submission to the presbyters and

53

repent of their folly; only in this way will God continue to bless the church and shower his gifts upon it. And the messengers from Rome, Claudius Ephebus and Valerius Bito with Fortunatus, are to be sent back speedily, to announce that peace and harmony have once again been restored.[3]

To emphasize the need to restore harmony, Clement appeals to the nature of God himself. He is the Creator and Lord of all and he rules his universe in peace and harmony.[4] All creation testifies to his goodness, and man is the most excellent of his creatures and the express likeness of God's own image; man is great because God has given him understanding.[5] Christ, who is called the Scepter of the majesty of God, appeared among men in a lowly condition and gave his blood for us[6] but he was also raised by God from the dead.[7] With God and Christ, Clement also associates the Holy Spirit whose grace is poured out upon all of them.[8] Just as he had spoken through the Old Testament prophets he now speaks to the church to reestablish good order.[9] All of this language has a very Pauline flavor to it, but Clement is not the ecstatic mystic that Paul could be, but rather the sober admonitor and perhaps even the diplomatic administrator!

It is a mistake to suppose, however, that Clement took a free and charismatic Christianity and imposed a legal structure on it. Both Clarke and Lawson agree that tradition was already important for first-century Christianity.[10] In all likelihood the organization of churches was very much the same. Clement likens the church to an army, with Christ as the leader and his people soldiers.[11] Or perhaps the well-known illustration of the people as members of a body whose head is Christ is a better example. The church is ruled by those who were appointed by the apostles, sent by Christ, who had himself been sent by God.[12] The church gives its consent to be ruled by such eminent men, and therefore they cannot be justly dismissed. The righteous never cast off the holy, but one of the functions of the wicked is to vex the just.

There is a considerable amount of moral teaching in Clement; in fact, the ethical note is far more prominent than the theological. Great emphasis is placed on humility, since that will solve the Corinthian schism. The pursuit of peace in genuine sincerity is also enjoined, but all things are to be governed by love. One way to show love is to be hospitable. We are to foresake wicked works and evil desires and to serve God in purity of heart. We are to admonish and correct one another and above all to avoid discord. Patience and meekness characterize the true believer. The stress is on order, harmony, and tranquillity, and in all of this there is an echo of Stoicism. But this is also the sort of emphasis that one would expect to come out at Rome.

One fascinating aspect of Clement's epistle is reflected in its attitude toward the state. The end of the first century saw a persecution, under the Emperor Domitian, which produced real tension between the church and the state. This persecution is clearly reflected in other literature of the period; it is not discernible in Clement. Rather there seems to be an admiration of the secular government and a desire to imitate its order, and there is even the prayer of obedience to governors and rulers on earth![13]

How far does Clement re-echo the teaching of Saint Paul with regard to grace, justification by faith, and good works? We are said to be "justified not through ourselves or through our own wisdom or understanding or piety or works which we have wrought in holiness, but through faith."[14] Yet we are not to give up the practice of good works and love, for God himself is an example to us of good works. So we may say that Clement follows the Pauline doctrine, but flavors it with the Epistle of Saint James.

The *Epistle of Clement* is a valuable jewel from apostolic times. Its stylistic appeal may not be of the highest, but it is a sober, sincere, and earnest appeal for unity and harmony in a church torn by factions. It ranks high in its value for a glimpse of the church at the end of the first century, and the great Harnack esteemed it to such an extent that he made a translation of it and wrote a commentary. The epistle was widely read in the early church and enjoyed almost a canonical status.

NOTES

The text is that of F. X. Funk, revised by K. Bihlmeyer, "Die apostolischen Väter," 1 Teil, Tübingen, 1924, in *Ancient Christian Writers* (*see* Bibliography).

1. Eusebius of Caesarea, *Ecclesiastical History,* The Fathers of the Church Series, vol. 19 (Washington D.C.: The Catholic University of America Press, 1948), 4. 23. 11.
2. *Klemensbrief* 51. 46.
3. Ibid., 56. passim.
4. Ibid., 22. passim.
5. Ibid., 33. 5.
6. Ibid., 21. 6.
7. Ibid., 24. 1.
8. Ibid., 46. 6.
9. Ibid., 45. 1.
10. W. H. L. Clarke, *First Epistle of Clement to the Corinthians* (New York: Macmillan Co., 1937), p. 23; and John Lawson, *A Theological and Historical Introduction to the Apostolic Fathers* (New York: Macmillan Co., 1961), p. 23 ff.
11. *Klemensbrief* 37. 1.
12. Ibid., 44.
13. Ibid., 40. 4.
14. Ibid., 32. 4.

The Didache

The *Didache,* or *The Teaching of the Twelve Apostles,* was long
thought to be a document forever lost to the modern world, but in 1873
it was discovered by Philotheos Bryennios in Constantinople and published ten years later. Its existence is mentioned by Eusebius in his
celebrated *Ecclesiastical History,*[1] and so its discovery caused a considerable stir matched only by the present century's unearthing of the Dead
Sea Scrolls. At first sight the document seems very primitive and a number
of competent scholars would date it as early as some portions of the
New Testament, between A.D. 70 and 90. Other experts consider it a
much later work falling in the second century, perhaps in the year
120 or 150 or even later than Justin Martyr's *Apology,* say between
A.D. 155 and 250.[2] References in the text to a lack of running water
and grain scattered on the hills have suggested Syria as a possible
place of composition; other evidence favors Egypt.

The first six chapters comprise a moral instruction clustered around
the Two Ways, the Way of Life, and the Way of Death. The Way of
Life is summed up with the injunction to love God, who is our Maker,
and our neighbor as ourself. The Golden Rule is stated in its negative
form, after which there follows a detailed elaboration of these general
principles, much of which is a paraphrase of the Sermon on the Mount.
Special emphasis is placed on the importance of sharing with the needy,
and being openhanded with those who request material aid. One is to
accept as blessings the casualties which may occur, confident that nothing
happens apart from God. And, in summary, the commandments of the
Lord are not to be neglected, nor are the traditions, which must be
fastened on to, neither adding or subtracting anything.[3]

The Way of Death embraces a formidable list of sins: murders,
adulteries, lustful desires, fornications, thefts, idolatries, magical arts,
sorceries, robberies, false testimonies, hypocrisy, duplicity, fraud, pride,
malice, surliness, covetousness, foul talk, jealousy, rashness, haughtiness,
false pretensions, absence of the fear of God.[4]

Baptism is to be administered, preferably in running water which is at
the same time cold, and the Trinitarian formula is expressly enjoined.
Candidates for baptism are to fast one or two days previously. Lacking

cold running water, one may baptize by pouring, although there is a clear preference for immersion.[5]

Chapters 9 and 10 of the *Didache* deal with the Eucharist, and represent the heart of the book's teaching. Only those who have been baptized are allowed to take part in the Eucharist. What we have preserved for us here is a series of prayers which were offered at different points in the rite.

First, there is a thanksgiving prayer which accompanies the partaking of the cup, and specifically refers to Jesus as the Holy Vine of David and the Servant of the Father. A similar prayer accompanies the breaking of the bread. A third prayer is for the church which has been gathered from the ends of the earth into the Father's Kingdom, just as the broken bread which was formerly scattered over the hills has been gathered together into one mass. The regular meal now follows, and after it there are several more prayers, all ending with a sort of congregational response: "Glory be to thee forever and ever." The fourth prayer thanks the Father for the knowledge and faith and immortality made known through Jesus, a fifth gives thanks for all created things, and a sixth is again for the church which has been gathered from the four winds. The prayers conclude with the ejaculation "Lord, Come!"[6]

These brief passages in the *Didache* obviously do not represent a developed theology of the Eucharist. The central meaning of the rite is not clearly spelled out, the actual words of institution are lacking, there is no mention of a presiding officer, nor any mention of confession or forgiveness of sins. But it may well be that all of these essential matters are assumed and require no specific mention; indeed, the mystery is so arcane that it is deliberately not mentioned. What is recorded is actually supporting material for the Eucharist, the essentials being self-evident and so well-known to the participants that they are deliberately not recorded. Thus the *Didache* preserves a reticence regarding the Eucharist, as almost too esoteric to set down in writing.[7]

The concluding chapters of *The Teaching of the Twelve Apostles* (11 to 16) deal at some length with various types of church officers. There are apostles or itinerant missionaries, better described as "hit-and-run" preachers, who are to stay no more than a day or two at the most; there are prophets who speak in ecstasy and whose genuineness can be tested by some practical rules of thumb; and there are teachers or catechists whose message must tally essentially with the norms set down in the *Didache*. All of these emissaries of Christ must be welcomed, and if they are not impostors they are worthy of their hire. Finally, men who are an honor to the Lord are to be elected as bishops and as deacons, since they too render you the sacred service along with prophets and teachers.[8]

The tract concludes with the warning to be ready for the Lord's coming. The last days may not be far away when the Deceiver of this world appears, claiming to be the Son of God and giving striking exhibitions of power. Humanity will be put to a fiery test, and many will lose their faith and perish. Stand firm, for the proofs of the truth will appear—an opening in the heavens, the sounding of the trumpet, the resurrection of the dead—so that when the Lord comes and all his saints with him, his own will rejoice to see him riding the clouds in the sky.[9]

The *Didache* is a kind of enchiridion of church practice and liturgy which in all probability gives us a very early glimpse into the life of late first-century Christianity. Although it is brief, it is informative and affords a valuable supplement to the literature of this period. It is more suggestive than highly developed in its theological thinking, but as an insight into the primitive church it is a Christian classic of inestimable value.

NOTES

The text is that of Theodor Klauser, "Doctrina duodecim apostolorum," translated by James A. Kleist, in *Ancient Christian Writers (see* Bibliography).
1. Eusebius *Ecclesiastical History* 3. 25. 4.
2. F. E. Vokes, *Riddle of the Didache,* (London, 1937).
3. *Didache,* 4. 13.
4. Ibid., 5. 1.
5. Ibid., 7.
6. Ibid., 10. 6.
7. Cf. Lawson, *An Introduction to the Apostolic Fathers,* pp. 87-91.
8. *Didache,* 15. 1, 2.
9. Ibid., 16.

Saint Ignatius of Antioch

The most charming writer of all the apostolic fathers is clearly Ignatius of Antioch, who was put to death some time during the reign of Trajan, probably in the year 107. Seven of his letters are considered authentic, although during the Middle Ages some spurious writings circulated under his name. He is also called Theophorus, or "God-bearer," and there used to be a legend that he was the little child set in the midst of the Master's disciples when he had to teach them a painful lesson. The letters of Ignatius seem to echo the Johannine literature and they are written to various churches in Asia Minor—to the Ephesians, Magnesians, Trallians, and Philadelphians. The letters take the form of greetings to those churches which Ignatius was unable to visit since they were not on the route by which he was traveling to martyrdom in Rome. The communication to the Romans serves a different purpose; it is to warn them not to seek to secure his release. The letter to the Smyrnaeans deals specifically with the false teachings of Docetism, and a final letter to Polycarp treats of various matters of episcopal administration.

The great longing of Ignatius to achieve complete union with Christ by embracing martyrdom is apt to evoke both admiration and suspicion on the part of today's Christian. We admire the man who desires to be the food of wild beasts, who calls himself God's wheat to be ground into Christ's pure bread.[1] We understand at least inchoately why he feels that complete unity with Christ is possible for him in only this way. But we are afraid that modern psychology might label this masochistic, or at least mentally unhealthy. In short, Ignatius excites our admiration, but not our imitation!

The seven genuine letters are primarily of a pastoral nature, and it is difficult to extract a systematic theology from material which was not so intended. Yet one idea pervades his entire thinking, the necessity of *unity,* whether this be his own personal union with Jesus Christ which is about to culminate in martyrdom, or the unity of believers in the one true faith preached by the apostles, or the unity of the church under its bishop. All else is but a variation of this single theme of union and unity found in all seven of the letters.[2] Symphony, concord, and harmony are other words which express the underlying unity of Christ's church.[3]

Ignatius employs traditional language with reference to the attributes of God, but in the letter to the Ephesians he speaks of God's silence which was broken by three mysteries loudly proclaimed to the world— the virginity of Mary, the birth of her Son, and his death.[4] These mysteries were accomplished in the stillness of God but their revelation to the ages resulted in the incipient destruction of evil, ignorance, malice, and death. God made his appearance in human form in the person of Jesus Christ who now gives us true knowledge of what God is really like. This revelation has confounded the philosopher, the controversialist, the so-called intellectual. Jesus is of the Davidic line, yet conceived by the Holy Spirit and born of the Virgin Mary.[5]

Against the Docetists, Ignatius insists on the humanity of Jesus, who was really of the line of David according to the flesh, really born of a virgin, really nailed to the cross in the flesh, and really raised himself from the dead with real flesh and real blood.[6] Those who say that Christ's suffering was but a make-believe are in reality only make-believe themselves.[7] What is worse, they make the personal testimony and witness of Ignatius about to be sealed with his death, only a lie about the Lord.

But if Ignatius emphasizes Christ's humanity by saying that he truly did this and that, he likewise insists on the divinity of Christ against the Judaizers. Christ underwent his sufferings that we might be saved, and we must either believe in the Blood of Christ which is our resurrection, or else face damnation.[8] The ancient prophecies as well as the Law of Moses anticipate the Gospel, and, indeed, those who in former times hoped for Christ and waited for Christ were saved by their belief in him, for thus they were one with him.[9]

Errors with regard to Christ's human and divine nature Ignatius considers as noxious weeds not planted by God the Father, and not having Christ as their Gardener.[10] To follow after schismatics is to forfeit the Kingdom of God. For this reason we must adhere closely to the bishop because he actually holds the place of Christ. Nothing can be done apart from the bishop, and where he appears, there must the people be, just as where Christ is, there is the Catholic church.[11] So there is a definite hierarchical order of bishop, elders, and deacons, and unity in the church is to be found in communion with them and in subordination to them. The expression "the Catholic church" occurs for the first time (anywhere) in the letter to the Smyrnaeans, and by it Ignatius means "the church universal"—universal applying to both its monarchical government and its unity of doctrine.[12] Thus the church is bound together by a kind of ecclesiastical chain: people, diaconate, presbytery, bishop, apostle, Christ, God.

The great symbol of unity is the Eucharist, which must be presided over by the bishop or someone authorized by him. The Eucharist is the Flesh of the Saviour who suffered for our sins and was raised from the dead.[13] The Ephesians are asked to make an effort to meet more frequently to celebrate God's Eucharist and to offer praise;[14] the Trallians are to renew themselves in faith, which is the Flesh of the Lord, and in love, which is the Blood of Jesus Christ;[15] the Philadelphians are to partake of one Eucharist, for one is the Flesh of Our Lord Jesus Christ, and one the cup to unite them in his Blood, and there is one altar just as there is one bishop assisted by the presbytery and the deacons.[16]

And so, by faithful adhesion to these various signs of unity, Christians become like stones in the Father's temple, set in place by the hoisting engine of the Cross of Christ; the Holy Spirit serves as a rope, faith is our spiritual windlass, and love the road which leads up to God. Thus it is we become fellow travelers, God-bearers, temple-bearers, Christ-bearers, bearers of holiness, with the commandments of Jesus Christ as holiday attire.[17]

These brief letters of Antioch's third bishop offer a priceless insight into the life of the church in the early second century. While they offer little factual material about the author himself, they reveal much of his personality. Obsessed with the coming glory of his martyrdom, he cannot insist too strongly on a personal relationship with Christ Jesus, to be accomplished by a strong adherence to right belief and a hatred of both schism and heresy. The key man is the bishop who, as head of the episcopacy, enables the faithful to avoid all the pitfalls surrounding the itinerant church. The Eucharist is the heavenly food which nourishes the Christ-bearer in supernatural manner and hastens him away from the world and on to God. Though they are separated from us by almost two thousand years, yet the letters of Ignatius sparkle with a freshness and enthusiasm which make them seem almost to transcend their own time and place. They will long remain on the best-seller list of early Christian devotional literature.

NOTES

Texts are presented and fully discussed in *The Ante-Nicene Fathers*, vol. 1, American reprint of the Edinburgh edition (*see* Bibliography)
1. Romans 4:1
2. *Ephesians* 4. 1; 5. 1; 8. 2; *Magnesians* 1. 2; 7. 1; 13. 2; *Trallians* 11. 2; *Roman Salutation* 4. 3; *Philadelphians* 2. 1, 2; 4. 1; 6. 2; 8. 1; *Smyrnaeans* 7. 2; 12. 2; *Polycarp* 1. 1, 2; 8. 2.
3. *Ephesians* 4. 1, 2; 5. 1
4. *Ephesians* 19. 1
5. *Ephesians* 18. 1, 2.
6. *Smyrnaeans* 1. 1, 2.
7. *Trallians* 10; *Smyrnaeans* 7
8. *Smyrnaeans* 6. 1

9. *Philadelphians* 5. 2; *Magnesians* 10.
10. *Philadelphians* 3. 1.
11. *Smyrnaeans* 8. 2.
12. Cf. Kleist, *Ancient Christian Writers,* p. 141
13. *Smyrnaeans* 7. 1.
14. *Ephesians* 13. 1.
15. *Trallians* 8. 1.
16. *Philadelphians* 4. 1.
17. *Ephesians* 9. 1, 2.

The Letter to Diognetus

Of all the writings that have come down to us under the category of "Apostolic Fathers" perhaps the most delightful is the *Letter to Diognetus,* written by an unknown writer to an unknown recipient at an unknown date. Diognetus was a pagan of the upper class, possibly even Emperor Hadrian himself, and so he is addressed as "Most excellent Diognetus," and what follows is a persuasive address of sophistication and polish. Andriessen[1] suggests that what we actually have is the long-lost *Apology* of Quadratus, who is the real author of the letter rather than Justin Martyr, Clement of Rome, Aristides, or several other possibilities. Scholars favor a date some time during the second century, or possibly even later, so the best we can say is that the letter was written possibly around the year A.D. 150.

The aim of the writer is to describe the "third world" of Christians, who are not to be confused with the Jews, on the one hand, or pagans on the other. Why is it that Christians have just lately arrived upon the scene? What is the secret of their love for each other, and why are they willing to undergo torture and death for what they believe? To enlighten Diognetus in these matters is also to solicit and, it is hoped, to enlist his support.

Paganism cannot really appeal to the intelligent mind, because its worship of many gods requires the manufacture of numerous and various idols, some made of cheap material as well as those fashioned out of silver or gold. That these objects are not worshipped for their own sake, but rather those deities whom they represent, the author is not willing to admit.

Jewish worship offers a sharp contrast to pagan idolatry. It is correct in offering worship to only the one true God, but errs by being fussy about burnt offerings, the matter of special foods, Sabbath regulations, circumcision, fast days, and new moons. All of this is a lack of understanding rather than a proof of religion.[2] For these reasons Christians are right in separating themselves from the senseless practices which characterize both groups.

It must always be remembered that the early Christian church considered Judaism a real threat to its survival. At first it was easy for the outside world to confuse both groups, and this was not altogether inconvenient for Christians who wished to profit from various exemptions granted to Jews. Later on, when the hand of the state fell heavily on Judaism, Christians insisted that theirs was a new religion not to be confused with the Mosaic Law or its Judaic homeland. Today's ecumenical spirit may find the "anti-Semitism" of the apostolic fathers somewhat embarrassing, but we need to remember that many felt the survival of the early church to be at stake, a survival based on the clear delineation of why Christianity among all the religions was unique.

But their uniqueness did not consist in a special homeland, customs, or speech; the manner of their life is ordinary and conforms to the particular place in which they happen to find themselves. They indeed share their food, but not their wives. They obey the established laws, but rise above them since their true citizenship is in heaven. They love all men, but in return they are hated, reviled, dishonored, calumniated, insulted, and penalized as evildooers, but in every case they return good for the malice they must endure. Then comes the telling remark: "Those who hate them are at a loss to explain their hatred."[3]

Christians are in the world just as the soul is in the body. In a famous passage the author elaborates this simile (which must not be pushed too far) in which the world wars on Christians just as the body (the flesh) makes war on the soul. But just as the soul holds the body together, Christians hold the world together. And why has God assigned to them such an important role? Because they have firmly established in their hearts the holy, incomprehensible Logos. The Designer, the Architect of the universe, has come in person to save them, to persuade and to invite men to a higher way of life, to a personal fellowship with the Lord of the universe. God has been revealed through his beloved Son. Up to the present time God has exercised patience in allowing men to be mis-led by inane philosophical concepts and unruly passions, but now that our past conduct has shown us to be unworthy of life, we are made worthy by the goodness of God and enabled by the power of God to enter the Kingdom of God formerly closed to us and inaccessible through our own efforts. The Son of God acts as a ransom for sinners—the Saint for sinners, the Guiltless for the guilty, the Innocent for the wicked, the Incorruptible for the corruptible, the Immortal for the mortal.[4] God wants us to consider his Son as Savior, Nurse, Father, Teacher, Counselor, Physician, Mind, Light, Honor, Glory, Strength, Life.

This is the faith which Diognetus is looking for—a knowledge of God the Father which will bring him great joy when he understands how much God loves men, and how much he has done for them in establishing his kingdom through his only-begotten Son. This makes it possible for Christians to practice a high ethic, since they realize that heaven is their true home, and they are able to endure a fire which lasts but for a while because they are more terrified of the eternal fire which will torment the wicked forever, and is the real death reserved for those who are condemned.[5]

The last two chapters of the letter are generally thought to be by another hand, someone who felt that the letter needed a more clinching conclusion, and who claims to be a disciple of the Apostles. There is an elaboration of the idea of Christ as the Logos, who for Christians is the Way and Source of life. Life means the full realization and knowledge of the Logos, who resides in the hearts of Christians, enabling them through obedience to him to become fruitful trees. If Diognetus does this he will always harvest the blessings desirable in the sight of God.[6]

The *Letter to Diognetus* actually belongs to the apologetic literature of the second century and, unlike the writings of the apostolic fathers, is addressed not to the church, but to the pagan world. The style of the letter, if not casual, is light and moves easily from one idea to the next, but nonetheless its tone is quite serious and very earnest. Its literary style makes pleasant reading, and it avoids theological subtleties by emphasizing the line of reasoning best calculated to appeal to a sophisticated pagan. Of all the literature we have encountered so far, it makes the happiest appeal to the modern mind.

NOTES

The text is that of F. X. Funk, revised by K. Bihlmeyer, "Die apostolischen Väter," 1 Teil, translated by James A. Kleist, in *Ancient Christian Writers* (*see* Bibliography).
1. P. Andriessen, "L'Apologie de Quadratus, conservée sous le title d'Epître a Diognète," in *Recherches de theologie ancienne et médiévale*, 13, 1946.
2. *Epistle to Diognetus* 4. 5.
3. Ibid., 5. 17.
4. Ibid., 9. 2.
5. Ibid., 10.7.
6. Ibid., 12. 8.

The Fragments of Papias

Only a dozen or so fragments have survived as the literary remains of Papias, bishop of Hierapolis in Phrygia, Asia Minor. The church historian Eusebius tells us that he was a hearer of John, a friend of Polycarp, a man of the primitive age.[1] It is generally believed that he was born some time during the sixties of the first century, but how long he lived and where and how he died remain a mystery. He wrote five books with the title *Exegesis of the Lord's Gospel,* which in all likelihood was a kind of commentary on the Gospel, and he took great care to run down all the firsthand source material which was still available by the end of the first century. Finding the written Gospels apparently too brief or lacking in sufficient detail, Papias was the diligent scholar-reporter who desired to make full use of living or still-surviving voices while there was yet time. His best source was the apostle John as well as those who had been associated with Andrew, Peter, Philip, Thomas, or James. All of this is discussed in the fragment generally numbered No. 2 and quoted by Eusebius; indeed, this fragment is far and away the most valuable and interesting of them all since it bears so directly on the composition of the Gospels. While this is of interest for textual criticism and church history, it has little relevance for a history of Christian thought.

One theological point may detain us for a moment: Papias was a believer in chiliastic or millenarian expectations—Christ would soon return in bodily form and set up an earthly kingdom of a thousand years. He employs vivid imagery to describe this coming time and quotes the Lord as saying, "These things are believable to believers. . . . Those will see who will then be living."[2] This particular idea, however, found little favor with better minds than that of Papias.

As in the case of Polycarp we cannot make an adequate judgment with regard to Papias from these few surviving quotations. There is no doubt that he enjoyed considerable prestige in his own time, and he is to be commended highly for attempting to collect and record authentic traditions with regard to Christ's life and the Gospel record. Certainly he did not consider the written documents of Scripture the sole source of faith. While he does furnish us with a considerable amount of incidental and some important information, Eusebius may well be correct in saying that he appeared to have been a man of very meager intelligence, judged by his own words, but for all that, he is also partly responsible for the fact that ever so many ecclesiastical writers after him, on the plea of Papias's antiquity, held the same opinions as he did.[3]

NOTES

The text is that of F. X. Funk, revised by K. Bihlmeyer, "Die apostolischen Väter," 1 Teil, translated by James A. Kleist, in *Ancient Christian Writers* (*see* Bibliography).
1. Eusebius, *Ecclesiastical History* 3. 39. 1.
2. *Fragments* 1.
3. *Fragments* 2.

Saint Polycarp

Venerable is the word for Polycarp, who was at least eighty-six years old at the time of his martyrdom, probably in the year A.D. 155 or 156. He enjoyed immense prestige in the second century church, although his writing does not show him to be an original or brilliant thinker. Scholarship today inclines toward the idea of two letters rather than one to explain the passages regarding Ignatius, one of which apparently anticipates his martyrdom, the other referring to it as an accomplished fact.[1] Whether there be one letter or two to the Philippians, we are certainly indebted to Ignatius's letters for shedding light on the person of Polycarp himself and the churches of Asia Minor in the second century. Polycarp was bishop of Smyrna, located on the central west coast of Asia Minor and hence on the highway to Europe and to Rome. His name means "fruitful."

Since he may have been born as early as A.D. 70, Polycarp knew at first hand many of the figures associated with New Testament times, particularly John, and, therefore, he forms an invaluable link between the first and second centuries.

For these reasons the contents of his letter(s) (the "earliest" is generally dated about the year 107) may come as something of a disappointment. Its purpose is to deal with a specific problem, the financial mismanagement of certain funds on the part of the presbyter Valens. There is consequently the admonition to shun avarice, and this particular admonition is repeated several times.[2] Christians must keep themselves detached from the world and unspotted by it. This requires a purity of behavior not merely with regard to chastity but all aspects of human living as well. But while the Christian keeps himself unsullied by worldly temptations his personal living must be chaste and beyond reproach. Lust of any kind makes war upon the spirit; only he who possesses love is entirely out of the reach of sin.[3]

After stressing various moral commandments in which avarice and impurity are condemned especially, Polycarp turns to doctrinal matters. Like Ignatius, he insists on the earthly life of the Lord, for whoever does not acknowledge that Jesus Christ has come in the flesh is Antichrist; whoever does not admit the testimony of the Cross is sprung from the

Devil; whoever wrests the Lord's Gospel to suit his own lusts and denies both resurrection and judgment—such a one is the firstborn of Satan.[4] Possibly Polycarp has Marcion in mind, for in an epilogue from the Moscow manuscript, when Marcion once asked, "Do you know me, Polycarp?" the reply came back, "Yes, yes, I know very well the firstborn of Satan." The senseless speculations and false doctrines of such people as the gnostics must be rejected by adhering closely to the teaching which was delivered in the beginning, and if we endure patiently we will abide in the love of the Lord.

Mention is made of presbyters and deacons, although a bishop is not mentioned, and Polycarp's letter closes with a prayer for civil authorities, kings, magistrates and rulers, for those who persecute and hate us, as well as for enemies of the Cross.[5] This is all the more striking since Polycarp is about to seal his faith with martyrdom in the arena.

The Martyrdom of Polycarp is a sort of "church circular letter" which was sent to Philomelium (possibly upon request) but intended for perusal among all the churches of Asia Minor. It is a fascinating account of "the teacher of Asia" 's martyrdom at Smyrna along with eleven others from Philadelphia, and great care is taken to draw parallels between this and the Lord's own passion and martyrdom. When compared with other accounts of martyrs this one is singularly restrained and historically accurate, being almost certainly the account of an eyewitness.[6] With one or two possible exceptions the account has fortunately escaped later embellishments.

When "the heat was on" some Christians had rushed forward to declare themselves, but others like Polycarp had either lain low or retired to positions of safety, a course of action preferred by the narrator because some who were too eager at the start were later talked out of their generosity. "For this reason, then, brethren, we do not commend those who volunteer to come forward, since that is not the teaching of the Gospel."[7]

In Polycarp's prayer mention is made of the whole worldwide Catholic church, reminding us of Ignatius's similar expression in his letter to the Smyrnaeans. In Polycarp's defense before the proconsul he expressly tells the magistrate, "You are, I indeed consider, entitled to an explanation; for we have been trained to render honor, insofar as it does not harm us, to magistrates and authorities appointed by God."[8] The early church frequently tried to show that it was by no means hostile to the state nor was it attempting to subvert the social order.

The personality of Polycarp overshadows his writings, or at least, what little we have from his hand. Clearly he was a man of great patience, a celebrated teacher and an outstanding martyr who was a thrilling inspiration to many of his contemporaries anxious to follow his example. Some indication of the immense prestige that was his is magnificently epitomized in the simple and succinct title by which he was universally known: "Bishop of Asia."[9]

NOTES

The text is that of F. X. Funk, revised by K. Bihlmeyer, "Die apostolischen Väter," 1. Teil, translated by James A. Kleist, in *Ancient Christian Writers* (*see* Bibliography).
1. P. N. Harrison, *Polycarp's Two Epistles to the Philippians* (Cambridge: The University Press, 1936).
2. *Letter to the Philippians* 4. 1; 5. 2; 6. 1; 11. 1.
3. Ibid., 3. 3; 5. 3
4. Ibid., 7. 1.
5. Ibid., 13. 3.
6. *Martyrdom of Saint Polycarp, Bishop of Smyrna* 8.3.
7. Ibid., 4. 1
8. Ibid., 10. 2.
9. Asia in this instance means principally Asia Minor.

The Shepherd of Hermas

The *Muratorian Fragment* states that "the *Shepherd* was written quite lately in our times in the city of Rome by Hermas, while his brother Pius, the bishop, was sitting in the chair of the church of the city of Rome; and therefore it ought indeed to be read, but it cannot to the end of time be publicly read in the Church to the people, either among the prophets, who are complete in number, or among the Apostles."[1] Pius was bishop of Rome from A.D. 140 to 155. The *Muratorian Fragment* is late second century and the content of the *Shepherd* establishes Rome as its place of origin; what is not clear is whether there may not be earlier material incorporated in the work possibly coming from the Hermas mentioned in Paul's Epistle to the Romans (16:14). At any rate, the *Shepherd* is not much later than A.D. 140[2] and the balance of opinion favors a single author.

The *Shepherd of Hermas* almost captured a place for itself in the New Testament canon. It was extremely popular in its day and was read in the west almost as widely as in the east. This is hard to appreciate, since it surely falls short of the writings of Clement, Ignatius, or the *Letter to Diognetus*. But much of its appeal rested on its claim to be "prophetic"—akin to the spirit of prophecy which had characterized New Testament times and was now dying out as Saint Paul himself had predicted (1 Cor. 6:33). Visions, commandments, and parables make up its tripartite structure and the Shepherd declares it his aim to lead his people away from the excesses of Montanism, on the one hand, and worldly laxity on the other. Hermas is in need of instruction and this the Shepherd furnishes abundantly in tones authoritarian and disciplinary, which require obedience and penitence. So what we have here is the Christian Gospel interpreted in the light of fresh insights.

The first three visions are about the church eternal, portrayed first as a lady, second as a tower being built. Hermas encounters an old woman carrying a book in her hand from which she reads, rebuking Hermas for certain family sins and then telling him to carry a message to the churches. She is the church, old because she has been established from earliest times, yet she turns up in the company of four young men, representing the four Gospels.[3] In a subsequent vision the lady becomes radiant and beautiful, signifying the youthful loveliness of the church, ever old but ever young.

Hermas now sees a tower being constructed on waters, the saving waters of baptism. In the ninth parable we learn further that the tower is based on a rock very ancient, but containing a newly cut gate. Both signify the Lord, who is more ancient than any of his creatures, but who has only just recently made his appearance in the world of men. The tower rises, layer upon layer as the workmen fit the various stones into place. Some stones are a perfect fit, but others must be polished, still others chiseled down before they can be accepted, and some must be rejected as totally unsuitable. Thus, human souls are fitted into the structure of the tower, which is the church. Some are white, polished, shiny, properly cut, some must be reshaped and cleansed, but others are so hopeless that they must be thrown away completely.

All of this leads to a doctrine of penitence which is a main theme in the *Shepherd of Hermas*. Apostles, bishops, teachers, deacons and those who have lived in godly purity fit exactly into each other and into place in the tower. Stones that were dragged from the depths and fitted into place represent the martyrs; those being put into the tower are the faithful and the young in faith. Those stones cast away which yet lie not far from the tower are those who wish to repent and will be strong in faith if they repent before the tower is completed. Those however who are thrown far from the tower are the unredeemed sons of iniquity, and include the sowers of discord, the wealthy, and the unchaste. Hermas asks if repentance is possible for those who have been cast away and did not fit into the building of the tower, and learns that repentance is possible but there is no suitable place for them and they must be relegated to an inferior spot to be tormented, and thus complete the days of their sin. Adultery, apostasy, and murder were generally regarded as the three sins which put one outside the church completely. This would be true for adultery until ca. 220, for apostasy ca. 250, and for murder, some time during the reign of Constantine. But such modifications are beyond Hermas's ken; he explicitly says the tower will very soon be finished, and, after a great tribulation which is about to come (personified by a huge beast), implies that the end is already near at hand.[4] In the fifth and final vision, the Shepherd himself makes his appearance as "The Angel of Repentance." Perhaps he is Christ himself—although this is not altogether certain—but his purpose is clear: to enjoin Hermas to write down the commandments and parables which he is to hear, while always remembering to exercise penance in fearing the Lord and obeying his mandates.[5]

The second section of the book is a series of twelve commandments, beginning with the necessity for faith in God, and warning against evil-speaking, falsehood, sadness of heart, impatience, grief, and urging the necessity for almsgiving, fasting, and prayer. Of particular interest is the fourth commandment with regard to adultery; here we learn that one repentance after baptism is still allowed. But since the erring party may always repent at some future date, the innocent party is not allowed to remarry. Therefore, Hermas holds a less rigoristic position than that of the Montanists, or even possibly of the first-century church. It is interesting to see how the church felt forced to make an accommodation with ordinary Christians of less heroic stamp.

The sixth commandment is a fascinating discussion of the discernment of spirits. Every person is attended by two spirits, the one good and the other bad. They are recognized by their effects rather than directly, the good angel counseling righteousness, purity, chastity, and contentment; the bad angel suggesting wrath, harshness, delicacies, revels, and luxuries. The *Shepherd of Hermas* contains a quite developed angelology and we are made aware of the importance of the unseen world around us and the necessity for testing the spirits to see whether they be good or evil. We are to fear God, but not the devil, listen to the good angel but not the evil, and follow the various commandments set forth by the Shepherd.

The concluding third of the book is a collection of parables or similitudes, and there are ten of them. Christians should remember that they have no continuing city here but should prepare for the Kingdom which is to come. It is difficult in this world to separate the just from the wicked, but in the world to come happiness will be the lot of the first as misery characterizes the second. (In the sixth parable there is an attempt to fix the duration of punishment which must be undergone.) In the ninth parable, which is almost as long as all the others put together, we return once again to the Shepherd's favorite theme of the building of the tower which is represented by the church. Before the tower is completed, however, it must undergo a rather rigid building inspection by the Shepherd himself. Some of the stones require further modification and rearranging in the tower; then the rejected stones which have been lying around must be replaced by twelve women clothed in black whose job it is to return them to the various mountains from which they have come—the nations of the world. There is also an explanation of how the church fits into the Old Covenant; the righteous of the Old Testament are united to the church because of their virtue and because they preached the coming of the Messiah. The complicated imagery of the parable finally concludes with the Shepherd's exhortation to repent wholeheartedly so that former sins may be completely blotted out. Otherwise, the building of the tower will be completed, and we may be excluded from it.

It is always a mistake to push the details of an allegory too far. The fifth parable tells the story of a certain slave who served his master so well in the vineyard that he gained his freedom and was made a co-heir with the landlord's son. The language used here is perhaps suggestive of adoptionism, but Seeberg has shown that the view of Hermas is not essentially different from that of the New Testament. The concept of preexistence is quite clear; it is simply not worked out in detail, since the author's interests lie elsewhere.[6]

NOTES

The text is that of Hilgenfeld, based on the Sinaitic Codex, translated by F. Crombie, in *The Ante-Nicene Fathers,* vol. 2 *(see* Bibliography).
1. John R. Willis, *The Teachings of the Church Fathers* (New York: Herder & Herder, 1966), p. 41
2. Cf. Stanislas Giet, *Hermas et les Pasteurs,* (Paris, 1963).
3. *Hermas* Vision 1, chap. 4.
4. Ibid., Vision 3, chap. 8.
5. Ibid., Vision 5.
6. Ronald Seeberg, *Textbook of the History of Doctrines,* tr. Charles E. Hay (Grand Rapids, Mich., 1952) p. 57

The Letter of Barnabas

No one knows who actually wrote the *Letter of Barnabas,* although some writers in antiquity thought the author was Paul's companion mentioned in the Book of Acts. Nor are we sure where it was written, although Alexandria is a possibility because of the allegorical style of the letter, since the Alexandrians had a penchant for allegory. There is likewise considerable latitude with regard to the date of writing. It seems to be later than the destruction of Jerusalem in A.D. 70, but for various reasons earlier than the Bar Kokhba revolt of A.D. 135. Therefore it may be as early as the end of the first century, or some decades later.

The letter addresses itself to a very specific problem: the relationship of Christianity to Judaism. It has been conjectured that during the reign of Hadrian (117-138) a more lenient policy toward Judaism encouraged a proselytizing spirit among the Jews, and so alarmed the writer "Barnabas" that he set out to do two things: to show that Christianity was separate and distinct from Judaism, and that a proper allegorical interpretation of the Old Testament was necessary to show how the New Testament had fulfilled the types, allegories, and prophecies of the Old. Thus, it was necessary to avoid Marcion's error of separating the two dispensations completely from each other, but rather to insist that Christianity had fulfilled much of the Law and the Prophets, while abrogating that which was no longer binding.[1]

The writer insists that God demands a contrite heart as a true sacrifice acceptable to him, and not burnt offerings; likewise, true fasting means to practice justice and charity. The times are evil and a crisis is at hand; we must therefore be on our guard. Our covenant is not the same as the Jewish covenant, which was indeed received from Moses but has by this time become corrupted. Our covenant rests on the sufferings of Christ, whose incarnation and passion were foretold by the prophets, and through which we are redeemed from our sins. The scapegoat (Lev. 16:7-9) driven into the desert and the heifer (Num. 19:1-10) are both types of Christ, as was also the old rite of circumcision which has now been abolished. The various commandments with regard to clean and unclean foods must also be taken in a spiritual sense. Even baptism and the mystery of the cross were foreshadowed in the Old Dispensation. The Jews failed even to understand the laws regulating the Sabbath and were misinformed with regard to the temple at Jerusalem, which is not necessary for the true worship of God Who dwells in our hearts. All of

75

this means that the covenant God made with his chosen people was not the Jewish covenant; it is the Christians who are its true heirs having Jesus as their Mediator. This is proved by the fact that the three hundred and eighteen men of Abraham's household stand for Jesus Christ and his cross: 300 T the cross 10 I 8 H (IHSOUS).

The last chapters of Barnabas's letter are a discussion of Christian doctrine and authority under the form of The Way of Light and The Way of Darkness. We have already met this in the *Didache*, which means that one is copying from the other, or both are copying from a third source. The letter concludes with a "ferverino" to stand fast in the Lord because his day is not far off, and his reward is with him.[2]

The highly allegorical nature of the letter is not apt to appeal to modern minds. The abstruse gymnastics performed with Old Testament texts in a doubtful cause excites more suspicion and impatience than admiration or conviction. Yet there is an earnestness about Barnabas which shows him clearly alert to a situation which he deems may well be fatal to the Christian cause if an alarm is not sounded in time. This alarm is all the more necessary because the time is short, and the Lord may speedily return at any moment. Hence, the necessity for understanding the Old Testament in its true spiritual light, so that Christianity which is the true Judaism may resist the false catchword, "Their covenant is ours also." This is not to admit a total divorce from the two faiths, but neither must they be equated. Rather, the Old Testament Scriptures must be interpreted in their spiritual and allegorical sense, which is also their true meaning.

The *Letter of Barnabas* was highly respected in antiquity; indeed, the ancient Christians regarded it more reverentially than we do. Yet at no time was there the danger that it might find its way into the New Testament canon. It is certainly inferior to the Epistle to the Hebrews, and its highly polemic character does not make for either very satisfying or very rewarding reading. The intense effort to achieve speculative superiority and insight almost backfires, and certainly moves it perilously close to the Gnostic world. But we must remember that the author is addressing himself to a specific problem of crisis proportions, and he is summoning his entire energies to safeguard the Christian community from an irreparable disaster. It is for these reasons that the *Letter of Barnabas* enjoyed such a high rating in the early Christian communities of the ancient Near East.

NOTES

The text is that of Theodor Klauser, "Doctrina duodecim apostolorum. Barnaba epistula," translated by James A. Kleist, in *Ancient Christian Writers* (*see* Bibliography).

1. Cf. Lawson, *An Introduction to the Apostolic Fathers*, p. 193 ff., and Kleist in *Ancient Christian Writers*, p. 31 ff.
2. *Barnabas* 4. 6.

The Second Letter
of Saint Clement

Traditionally associated with Clement of Rome is a second "epistle" which is actually a homily or sermon and is generally agreed to be the work of somebody else writing some time during the first half of the second century. It is possible that the author is the Clement mentioned in *The Shepherd of Hermas* (Vis. II), but in all likelihood this is not Clement of Rome or Clement of Alexandria.

The homily is largely moral in tone and does not betray either great preaching or great literary style, but it does touch on a number of doctrinal points and is principally of interest as being the first Christian sermon that we have. Since so much preaching is "run-of-the-mill" anyhow, perhaps it is not altogether unfitting that our first example of it may best be illustrated by this "epistle."

We ought not to think that the whole matter of our salvation is "small peanuts" since we shall obtain little from Christ if we do not have a high regard for what he has done for us. His great mercy toward us should evoke on our part the response of a true confession illustrated by love, compassion, continence, and doing good. We must reject the present world for what it really is—the enemy of the future world of holiness and righteousness. So a struggle is inevitable, a struggle which begins with our repentance followed by keeping the flesh holy and observing the Lord's commandments which leads us to eternal life. We must preserve the flesh as the temple of God, because we shall be judged in the flesh in the resurrection. If we serve God with a pure heart, trusting in his promise, we shall enter into his Kingdom which far exceeds man's earthly comprehension.

The Kingdom of God embraces the living church which is also the body of Christ and has existed from the beginning of time as spiritual, but manifested in the last days in order that Christ may save us through it. Christ is related to his church just as the soul is related to the body; therefore our bodies must be temples of the Holy Spirit since Christ dwells in his church, so that those who do not practice continence shamefully sin against Christ and the church. Chapter 14 of the homily actually elaborates Paul's doctrine of the church in Ephesians,[1] and in spite of a somewhat confused imagery involving male and female, soul

77

and body, spirit and flesh, Christ and the church, the author makes here a real contribution to early ecclesiology. Hence, in spite of its generally moral tone, the author at the same time offers a significant theological dimension. The letter concludes with a general exhortation to giving alms, prayer, fasting, and the continued necessity for repentance; the author closes with an encouragement to perseverance and a final doxology.

While the whole work is no doubt boring, filled with repetitions, and not altogether clear in some of its similes, it ought not to be dismissed with a wave of the hand as a spurious letter masquerading under the protective cloak of Clement of Rome. It is a fine example of that period in the church when the treasure of the Gospel was being assimilated and inwardly digested. The so-called *Second Letter of Saint Clement* may not enjoy today the prestige it had in ancient times, but it is far from being a worthless document of little or no interest for the church of today.

NOTES

The entire letter, translated by John Keith, appears in *The Ante-Nicene Fathers,* vol. 9 (*see* Bibliography).

1. Cf. Eph. 1:22, 23; 1 Cor. 12:27.

III

MAJOR APOLOGISTS
OF THE
SECOND CENTURY

The term "apologist" is a broad one, and is used to embrace a number of writers of the second century whose purpose was to present Christianity in a favorable light to the Roman state, to pagans, to Jews, and (in the case of Irenaeus) to Gnostics. Their appeal is based on rational argument and addressed to an audience of at least average intelligence. The word *apologia* actually refers to the "last words" from the prisoner's dock of one about to be executed. The aims of the apologists are broadly twofold: to defend the new Christian faith against the charges of atheism, immorality, and treason, on the one hand, and to attack the weak points of belief in paganism, Judaism, or the cult of Caesar, on the other. The action is therefore both defensive and offensive, and characterizes a large number of writers of the second century. In fact it is hard to draw the line of inclusion or exclusion (Irenaeus, for example); it would be more accurate to apply the term to the writing rather than to the writer, the *Letter to Diognetus* (already treated in the last chapter) would certainly fall in this category. Bearing these brief comments in mind, the assortment of writers presented here as "apologists" will perhaps seem less motley than would otherwise have been the case.

Saint Justin (Martyr)

Three works of Saint Justin (Martyr) are universally considered to be genuine: the two Apologies and the *Dialogue with a Jew named Trypho;* there is doubt about the two Address to the Greeks, and *On the Sole Government of God,* as well as the *Fragments on the Resurrection.* The *Epistle to Diognetus* has been ascribed to him as well as some other works which are definitely spurious, dating from the fourth century.

Born in Flavia Neapolis, a city of Samaria, some time during the second decade of the second century, Justin studied in various schools of philosophy prior to his conversion to Christianity. In the new faith he declared that he had found the true philosophy, and thus continued always to wear his philosopher's robe. Ephesus and Rome were two scenes of his teaching activity which ultimately aroused the hostility of the Cynics and eventuated in his martyrdom some time in the reign of Marcus Aurelius (161-180), probably about the year A.D. 165.

Justin is the first writer who has left us a sizable record of his thought, and from him one can extract a fairly complete system of doctrine. In a celebrated passage in the *Dialogue with Trypho,* he relates how he first studied under a certain Stoic, who thought that any knowledge of God was unnecessary, and then under a Peripatetic, who felt that his teaching was too valuable to hand out gratis, and requested Justin to settle his bill. Abandoning him as no true philosopher, he enrolled under a Pythagorean, whose philosophical prerequisites included music, astronomy, and geometry, a kind of "core course" for philosophy majors. Finally, he sought out the Platonists with whom he made such progress that he expected any day to look on God. One day, while contemplating ideas and immaterial things in a field by the sea, he met a venerable old man who informed him that long before Plato lived there were prophets who spoke by the Spirit of God who proclaimed the coming of the Christ, God's Son. "Straightaway a flame was kindled in my soul," says Justin, "and a love of the prophets, and of those men who are friends of Christ possessed me; . . . and I found this philosophy alone to be safe and reliable."[1] Christianity, then, is the true philosophy, and the greatest profession and most honorable before God.

As purveyor of the true philosophy, Justin is the apologist par excellence, although "apologist" is not so good a word as "defender" or "propagandist." His writings are directed against two classes of people: the pagan rulers who are persecuting Christians without a hearing, usually on the charge of being atheists and subversive to the state, and the Jews who consider Christianity a nefarious heresy out to destroy Judaism altogether. The two Apologies are directed against the pagans, the *Dialogue with Trypho* addresses itself to Judaism.

In the rescript of the emperor Hadrian written to Minucius Fundanus on behalf of the Christians and generally conceded to be authentic, instructions are given not to arrest Christians on mere hearsay, but only if the plaintiff is willing to bring serious charges in a court of law with proof positive of wrongdoing; otherwise, Christians are not to be molested. It is the violation of this imperial rescript which has caused Justin to take up his pen on behalf of his fellow Christians.

The first charge which Justin must meet is the charge of atheism, which is more precisely a political-religious charge of social subversion inimical to the state. The diversity of religious belief in the Roman Empire required some unifying practices which would assure the government of the loyalty of its heterogeneous citizens. One such act was the burning of a pinch of incense on an altar dedicated to the daemon, the divine genius of the ruling emperor. The aged Polycarp had proved very stubborn on this point but what harm was there really in it, the proconsul had insisted.[2] Justin's reply to the charge of atheism is to admit it, and he then goes on to urge that the gods currently worshipped are in actuality demons! These evil demons from earliest times have struck fear and terror into people, have maliciously misused helpless women and boys, and have even gone to such lengths as to effect the death of Socrates. The folly of idol worship and the lascivious stories about Jupiter should convince us that "atheism" is the only enlightened and sensible course,[3] and yet Christians cannot really be called atheists since they worship God, the Father of righteousness, His Son, and the prophetic Spirit, in reason and truth.[4]

A second charge is made, that of evil-doing, on the grounds that Christians meet in secret, and perform atrocious acts culminating in the cannibalistic eating and drinking of someone's Body and Blood. In order to refute these charges of clandestine activity, Justin feels it necessary to describe the sacraments of baptism and the Lord's Supper. Those who become convinced of Christian truth are baptized, and this "washing" illuminates them, making them good citizens and keepers of the commandments, worthy to be saved with an everlasting salvation. After the baptismal prayers are ended, the kiss of peace is given and then bread and a cup of wine mixed with water are brought to the presiding officer who gives praise and glory to the Father of the universe, through the name of the Son and of the Holy Spirit, and after a long prayer to which the people pronounce Amen, the deacons distribute the bread and wine to those present and then carry away some to those who are not there. This Eucharist (literally, thanksgiving) is reserved to believers only, and this means baptized believers whose sins have been remitted, and who, so regenerated, are living as Christ has commanded. For this is not ordinary bread and wine, but the flesh and blood of Jesus who was made flesh for their sakes.[5] This memorial service has been enjoined by the Lord himself as is clearly stated in the books called Gospels, which constitute the memoirs of the apostles. This celebration of the Eucharist occurs on the first day of the week, since on that day Christ rose from the dead. After the prayer of thanksgiving, alms are collected and distributed to orphans and widows and other needy persons, the president of the assembly acting as a sort of social service agent. The purpose of this passage is to prove to the public that Christians are good moral folk, not orgiastic cannibals of the most heinous sort. Yet Justin avoids a too minute description in order to safeguard the arcane discipline and not vulgarize Christian worship. As for the controverted passage with regard to the real or the spiritual presence of Christ in the Eucharist, we shall return to that later.

A third charge against Christians was that they were traitors. It was well known that they talked about a coming kingdom, which was clearly treasonable talk. Justin insists that this is not a human kingdom, for if it were, Christians would deny Christ in order to stay alive in it; but the thoughts of Christians are not fixed upon the present, but on eternity, and so it is of no concern to them when they are cut off, since death is a debt which must be paid anyhow. Rather, they are helpers and allies of the state in promoting peace; they practice civil obedience, they pay taxes both ordinary and extraordinary, and in paying tribute to Caesar they are doing precisely what the Lord himself taught.[6] Besides, they offer prayers for kings and rulers, praying that those who have royal power may also have sound judgment to go along with it. In all things, with the single exception of their worship, Christians are just like anyone else.

Having disposed of these charges of impiety, immorality, and political subversion, Justin goes on to present Christianity in a more positive light. Considerable attention is paid to the teachings of Christ and their high ethical quality. His aim is always to show that Christianity is a reasonable religion, and its followers, far from being mere riffraff, become spiritually and morally regenerated when they decided to become followers of Christ. The real enemies of the faith, Justin insists, are actually the evil demons of the world who have fomented persecution, provoked slander and abuse, and done their utmost to mislead men from the worship of the one true God.

The *Dialogue with Trypho* is a studied attempt to show that Christianity is the true Judaism which has now become abrogated with God's revelation in Christ. Whether or not there was an actual dialogue with a real person Trypho, or whether this is simply a literary device, need not detain us here. Much longer than the two Apologies combined, this work is certainly to be regarded as Justin's opus magnum.

Moses and the prophets correctly predicted the coming of Christ, but Jewish ceremonies have arisen to obscure the real nature of God's Law. Man is not justified through rites, but by giving his heart to Christ and becoming baptized. The Law was instituted because of the hardness of men's hearts, and the Jewish ceremonies were primarily designed to atone for these acts of impiety. But with the coming of Christ all of this is useless, for only through him can the Jews be saved. So it is a case of legal work-righteousness versus the true righteousness which Christians possess in Christ.

To all of this Trypho complains that Christ has misled the Jews by coming not as the glorious Redeemer described by Daniel and the Psalmist, but in lowly guise culminating in ignominious crucifixion. Justin distinguishes two sets of prophecies, those which refer to Christ's first coming, and those referring to the more glorious, second advent. All of this boils down to the conclusion that those who were righteous before and under the Law shall be saved by Christ, but that keeping the Law now contributes northing to righteousness.

Trypho thereupon asserts that it remains to be proved that Jesus is the Christ whom the prophets spoke about, and that he really is divine. This entails an examination of a multitude of Scripture passages from the Old Testament, a collection no doubt gathered by Christians, (not haphazardly but systematically) in their polemic against Judaism. Many of the *loci classici* are found in the prophet Isaiah and here Justin focuses all his exegetical powers. A detailed analysis is made of Christ's passion and death, and an exhaustive study of the Old Testament made to prove that the first advent has indeed already taken place. Thus it is proved that Christ is truly the King of Israel, and that the Christians are the true Jews; moreover the Jews in rejecting Christ, rejected God who sent him. They must therefore become converted, for the Scriptures compel us all to assent, and pour no ridicule on the Son of God, Israel's King. The two disputants take amicable leave of one another, Trypho declaring that he and his friends had found more than it was possible to have expected!

Summarizing Justin's doctrine of God, it may well be true that he attempted to synthesize a Middle Platonist concept of the transcendent and unknowable Cause with the Biblical and Christian idea of God as a living Creator and Father of Our Lord Jesus Christ.[7] But actually he does little more than to reiterate what the Hellenistic Judaism of his day taught regarding the nature of God. The Almighty is not bound by time nor limited by spatial location. He is unbegotten ($\alpha\gamma\epsilon\nu\nu\eta\tau os$) and incorruptible ($\alpha\phi\theta\alpha\rho\tau os$)[8] and the Cause of everything else, nameless and unutterable.[9] He directs the universe through his omniscience and omnipotence. He is majestic and holy, but he expresses his love and his goodness toward men by sending them his grace and offering them his fellowship.

Inasmuch as transcendence is one of God's salient attributes, the question now arises how God is able to make contact with the created world. Justin solves this problem by invoking the doctrine of the Logos, a concept which was current coin in his day. The universe is set up on rational principles and governed by law; it is a reasonable affair, and its order and harmony are clearly evident to the reasonable man. This rational principle underlying all cosmic reality was perhaps first enunciated by Heraclitus[10] and it reappears in the "nous" of Anaxagoras.[11] Later on, the Stoics elaborated the idea and insisted that if man is to be happy, his own reason must tally with this governing or generating principle which is immanent in, active in, and pervading all of reality. In the Old Testament, this principle of reason appears as a quasi-personification of Wisdom, which is somehow equated with God, but yet is differentiated from God. In Philo it is the principle which is intermediate between ultimate or divine reality and the world of sense perception. All of this reappears in the Prologue of the Fourth Gospel where Saint John astounds his readers by declaring that "the Logos became flesh and dwelt among us" (Jno. 1:14).

But how precisely is the Logos related to God himself? Here it is useless to expect the precise and refined definition of the more sophisticated theologians of the fourth century, nor to accuse Justin of being simplistic or naive; "Adoptionist," "Subordinationist," "Arian," and "Nicene" are labels of a later time not acceptable to early thought still in the process of formation. For Justin, the Logos is a certain rational power proceding from God and sometimes called the Glory of the Lord, sometimes the Son, Wisdom, Angel, Lord, and Logos.

For Justin, Jesus Christ and the Logos of God are one; the first-begotten Word of God is also God. But to say that Christ is the first-begotten of the unbegotten God is not to imply any abscission, any separation from God. Thus, he must avoid ditheism on the one hand, and an insufficient doctrine of emanations popular with the Gnostics, on the other. To show that the Logos is one with the Father, Justin resorts to the illustration of light streaming from the sun. Light is distinct from the sun, yet it is nothing without the sun, which suffers no diminution from emitting sunlight. In similar fashion, fire is kindled from fire, without decreasing the first fire yet allowing for separate existence of both fires. Or we may use the figure of speech as it emanates from thought. Whenever we say something meaningful, we produce speech without at the same time diminishing thought but yet making a clear separation between speech and thought.[12] In this instance, the term Logos may be used for both thought and speech, for rationality is common to both. Justin has in mind the philosophical concepts of his day which distinguished un-uttered thought from the thought which was now uttered. Just as the spoken word comes forth from the rational mind with no loss of wisdom, so also Christ the Logos had come forth from God without the slightest division or diminution on the part of the Father.

What the time of origin of the Logos' begetting was, Justin does not say, and for this reason he is capable of an Arian interpretation. Certainly the Logos was in existence at the time of creation and actively participated in it. But this is not to say that he did not hold for the eternity of the Logos; his language is simply too imprecise to quote one way or the other, and it is a mistake to expect from him a sophisticated answer to a problem which was only to agitate later generations.

Borrowing a term from Stoic physiology, Justin sometimes refers to Christ as the Spermatic Logos. For the Stoics, this was a sort of creative principle represented by a very fine gas which in the male united with a similar flow in the female to produce fertility. In Philo this is spiritualized to represent the way in which God deals with creation, and since men are a part of creation they likewise have a fragment of, or participate in, the Spermatic Logos in totality. So the Logos contains this intrinsic vitality, which germinates and grows and brings God's plans to full fruition. It is represented by the Cross which can be discovered everywhere in the world—in the plow which digs the earth to sustain mankind, or in the cross bars of the ship. Even Plato recognized this in the *Timaeus* and all men now realize that the Cosmos is permeated by a world soul. But the Spermatic Logos, which is the principle of creation, is also a personal force, and it is through this personal force that God operates in his creation and conservation of the world. But at its highest level it appears as the reason which is to be found in all men, and it is the truly rational man who readily sees that Christianity is the true philosophy apart from which there is none other, and gladly embraces the Gospel, which is Christ the Logos himself.

If the doctrine of the Logos is made explicit at some length in Justin's thought, the doctrine of the Holy Spirit has not been. It must always be remembered that the second century apologists focused their attention on the revelation given by God to mankind through Christ, his only-begotten Son; it was not until later that the relationship of the Son to the Spirit had to be carefully worked out. Goodenough thinks that Justin more or less equated the Holy Spirit with the Logos, and did not address himself directly to the problem. Justin did use the Trinitarian formula, however, and he did associate the Holy Spirit with the spirit of prophecy in the Old Testament.[13] He does seem to assign an inferior position to the Holy Spirit, and in one celebrated passage introduces the angels after mentioning the Son and *before* mentioning the Holy Spirit.

It seems more accurate to say, however, that Justin simply did not bother to work out an elaborate theology of either the Third Person of the Trinity, or a sophisticated doctrine of the Trinity itself; all of this was still in the future.

With regard to the angels, the apologist declares that some are permanent while others are only temporary, and some are good, others bad. Evil is to be found on every side in the world in which we live, and this is the direct working of the malevolent supernatural forces. If the human race is ignorant and sinful, slave to its own passion, wallowing in lust and crime, reduced to misery by war, this is the hatred of the demons for the human race. They have corrupted the Scriptural prophecies, fostered idolatry, created confusion, corrupted knowledge of the Christian way, infiltrated the mystery cults, incited the rulers to a senseless persecution, and vented their fury against the followers of the Spermatic Logos. The damage which the demonic host has done, led by Satan their leader (who fell after his deception of Adam and Eve), has been incalculable. But the situation is not totally dark; through the coming of Christ, the power of the demons has been broken, and their furious activity against the sons of men indicates clearly that their complete overthrow is not far off. Christ has demonstrated power over the hosts of darkness, and therefore Christians have not only been liberated from the demons, but actually exercise control over them as well. Since he does not postulate a doctrine of original sin, Justin's ideas of demonology serve to explain the origin and continuing presence of evil in the world.

Justin accepted the Biblical account of creation much as he found it in Genesis. Two or three passages suggest that he believed that God had formed matter first, and then had imposed form upon formless matter, but at other times he is content to state simply that God created the heavens and the earth. Nowhere does he reiterate the Platonic teaching that matter is eternal, and so he seems to be quite faithful to the Christian tradition. Man himself is created out of a material and a non-material element; his physical nature is mortal, but the divine element is his soul or spirit, which is actually a part of the Spermatic Logos. In fact, Justin claims that every man actually possesses the entire Logos, who is none other than Christ himself, "who was partially known even by Socrates (for he was and is the Word who is in every man, and who foretold the things that were to come to pass both through the prophets and in his own person when he was made of like passions, and taught these things). Not only philosophers and scholars believed, but also artisans and people entirely uneducated, despising both glory and fear and death, for he is indeed a power of the ineffable Father, and not the mere instrument of human reason."[14] Barnard holds that Justin believed in a tripartite division of man: body, soul, and spirit.

thus reflecting early Christian teaching and Middle Platonism.[15] Thus, man is endowed with free will; Justin rejects any Stoic notion of cosmic fate, along with the Pauline doctrine of man as found in the Epistle to the Romans. If men have erred, have sinned, it is because they have allowed themselves to be duped and have unwittingly cooperated with the evil spirits. Justin was no Augustinian, the blame lay with him who chose, but God is blameless.

It may well be that in some of his theology Justin never quite overcame his earlier philosophical influences, but with regard to Christ's incarnation he is soundly orthodox. Christ is both divine and human, conceived by the Holy Spirit and born of the Virgin Mary. He is the whole Logos who has become (through the Incarnation) an entire man. He became man by the will of God for the benefit of the whole race of mankind; he is therefore both human and divine. How these two elements are related, Justin does not bother to explain. He summarizes in some detail for the benefit of Trypho the various events in Our Lord's life, maintaining that he is the one prophesied by the Old Testament, and whose entire life was without sin. In all of this he seems to be reflecting the common tradition in the early church.

In answer to the question, "Why did Christ die?" Justin actually held two separate theories with regard to Christ's saving death. His "philosophic" answer is that Christ has come to bless men with the truth, to save them from ignorance and folly and the malicious influence of the demons. Christ is the supreme teacher who has come to dispel the darkness and delusion of the world, and to lead all men into the fullness of light and truth. He is the supreme example whose persuasive love is a very strong force for the redemption of sinners. The emphasis here is on the incarnation of the Logos, who now shines as a beacon of light in the world. But Justin also holds that Christ actually effected the redemption of men by dying on the cross, and by so doing conquered death and made immortality possible for all men. Christ's death and resurrection somehow broke the power of demons, and thus it is not merely the person of Christ, but also what he accomplished by freely offering himself to the Father, that makes victory over sin and a new life possible for every man. This second answer to Christ's suffering and death represents the more traditional kerygma of the primitive church.

Since Justin is primarily an apologist addressing a non-Christian audience, he fails to give us a completely worked-out doctrine of the church. That the church was not only a vehicle entrusted with a saving doctrine but likewise a supernatural society stemming from Christ and his apostles, Justin seems to have accepted without question. He was also aware of various heretical sects claiming the name of Christian but to him obviously impostors because they all bore the name of their particular founders—another indication that the nefarious demons were ceaselessly at work. For him the church is one, the head of which is Christ himself, and the body, individual believers in Christ. What the internal makeup of the church is, is not altogether clear. Nowhere does Justin use the word επισκοπος in describing a ruler of the church, but his avoidance of the term may be a deliberate effort not to irritate pagans. However, in describing a Eucharistic service he does refer to the presiding official as ο προεστως των αδελφων and Jalland argues that this implies a sort of ruling authority, very possibly a bishop under another name. It is significant that Justin does refer to deacons, but never to presbyters, and his προεστως may well have had charge not only of public worship and the celebration of the Eucharist, but church financial administration as well.[16]

In order to disarm hostile critics, Justin gives a rather detailed description of both the sacrament of baptism and of the Lord's Supper. In baptism, the Trinitarian formula is used, although Justin is silent with regard to *how* the baptism takes place and where. For him, baptism signifies a new birth and with it goes a remission of sins, forgiveness for the repentant believer. Baptism carries with it a special illumination which makes it possible to lead a new life, one which is truly ethical, and this is aided by the cooperation of the indwelling Logos, thus making the newly baptized and illuminated convert a fit dwelling place for the Holy Spirit.

In the *First Apology* there are two separate descriptions of the Eucharist, one a baptismal-Eucharist and the other a typical Eucharist celebrated at an ordinary Sunday worship service. It is restricted to those who have been baptized and who are living according to Christ's precepts. Probably a strict liturgical form has not yet developed, because the presiding officer of the Eucharist offers prayers and thanksgivings more or less as the spirit moves him. After the prayers of thanksgiving have been said, the consecrated elements are no longer common food but take on a sacred character—the body and blood of Christ are present. Justin expressly states *(I Apol. 66)* that "not as common bread and common drink do we receive these; but in like manner as Jesus Christ our Savior, having been made flesh by the Word of God, had both flesh and blood for our salvation, so likewise have we been taught that the food which is blessed by the prayer of his word, and from which our blood and flesh by transmutation are nourished, is the flesh and blood of that Jesus who was made flesh." This is not to say *how* such a change takes place, much less that the change is effected by transubstantiation; Justin is only saying *that* there is such a change because the Logos itself assumed flesh, and then he leaves the whole matter right there. The Eucharist is, of course, a memorial of the Passion and carries with it a sacrificial character as foreshadowed by the prophecies of the Old Testament.[17]

Justin's description of these two important sacraments shows a strong traditional background mixed with a certain fluidity of liturgical practice. On the one hand, Justin is reporting the practice of the early church, personal innovation being the furthest thing possible from his mind. At the same time, he indicates that liturgical practice has not yet reached a fixed form identical at all times and in all places. For him, the sacraments are a vital necessity to the fruitful leading of the Christian life, yet their fruit is properly an ethical and a religious one. In Justin we have a nice balance between the sacramental and the moral; there is no attempt to view the Eucharist as a kind of magic, nor is there the notion that it is aesthetically lovely but at the same time superfluous.

Both sacraments are a real aid to living the Christian life, no easy task in a corrupt world ruled by demons which have shown their avowed hatred for Christianity. In trying to make the new religion acceptable to the state, and to clear it of the alleged charges of immorality and political subversion, Justin's avowed aim, especially in the two Apologies, is to show what a high moral standard Christians actually uphold in their daily lives. It has been suggested that perhaps he is presenting a somewhat idealized picture of the church, yet the very fact of pagan and official hostility shows that the new religion was beginning to have a marked effect on society. Even allowing for possible exaggeration, Justin is clearly proud of the contrast between Christians of a high ethical stamp, and the dissolute pagan immorality which he encountered everywhere around him.

Since men are endowed with freedom and have the power to choose either good or evil (although the demons are constantly putting pressure on him to side with *them*) it follows that a system of rewards or punishments awaits everyone. The first coming of Christ involved a general call to repentance, and the time is short for a general emendation of life since, Christ's second coming may occur at any moment, at which time it will already be too late for repentance. The fact that belief in the immanence of Christ's second coming was already on the wane in the second-century church does not seem to bother him. He dismisses the difficulty (if it is such for him) by saying that the opportunity for repentance must be given to future generations.[18] What is certain is that strict justice will be meted out, and each one rewarded or punished as he deserves.

Justin also believes that the present age is under judgment and eventually the world will be restored after suffering a prior destruction. The new Jerusalem will be the capital of an eternal kingdom to be forever enjoyed by the saints. Although details of his eschatology vary depending on the audience he is addressing, the important thing is that no man escapes the divine scrutiny and final evaluation of his destiny. In fact, this is one of the major reasons for moral behavior in this life, and since no one escapes judgment, "We are in fact of all men your best helpers and allies in securing good order, convinced as we are that no wicked man, no covetous man or conspirator, or virtuous man either, can be hidden from God, and that every one goes to eternal punishment or salvation in accordance with the character of his actions."[19]

Justin Martyr stands in the middle of the second century as one of the most appealing apologists of his time. For him, Christianity is the true philosophy, and all other systems of thought are mere caricatures fostered on ignorant men by malicious demons. The coming of Jesus Christ into the world is the incarnation of the eternal Logos, already well known through the teachings of the Stoics and their predecessors. Rather than being an enemy of the state, Christianity is really its friend and ally, as indeed it is the true Judaism already predicted in the Old Testament writings. The Gospel is for all men, and to prove this, Justin opens a window on Christian life and briefly describes for us the sacraments of baptism and the Eucharist. Attesting to the high moral character of Christians, ignorant and learned alike, he warns an immoral age that a just reckoning cannot be far off, and that all must repent in order to avoid the judgment of a just God. He is a man with a missionary purpose who has made the kerygma of the church, given it by Christ and the apostles, his very own, and he is fearless in preaching what he knows to be the truth, even though it cost him his life. Indeed, of all the many who had already died for the faith, he is the only one who absorbed "Martyr" as part of his name. His purpose is never to be an innovator (in spite of his previous philosophical training in Middle Platonism), but merely to transmit what he has learned from the Christian community. Hence, his thought is rarely brilliant, daring, or profound, but neither does he fall into occasional errors which mar the thinking of some of his successors. There has been something of a tradition in the past to dismiss him as a theological "lightweight," but more recent scholarship has brought with it a deeper appreciation of what Justin was attempting to accomplish, plus the realization that the task he set out to achieve was effected very well for his own times and contemporaries.

NOTES

The text is in *The Ante-Nicene Fathers,* vol. 1 (*see* Bibliography).
1. *Dialogue with Trypho,* ii-vii, passim. (*See also* Thomas B. Fall's translation in *The Fathers of the Church.*)
2. *The Martyrdom of Polycarp* chap. 8.
3. *I Apology* chaps. 4, 5.

4. Ibid., chap. 6.
5. Ibid., chap 66.
6. Ibid., chaps 11, 17
7. J. W. Barnard, *Justin Martyr* (Cambridge: The University Press, 1967), p. 83.
8. *Dialogue* chap. 5
9. *I Apology* chap. 61.
10. Cf. Frederick Copleston, *A History of Philosophy*, vol. 1 (New York: Image Publishing Corp., 1948), p. 59.
11. Ibid., p. 86 ff.
12. *Dialogue* chap. 61
13. E. R. Goodenough, *The Theology of Justin Martyr* (Jena, 1923), passim.
14. *II Apology* chap. 10.
15. Barnard, *Justin Martyr*, p. 114.
16. Trevor Gervase Jalland, *Studia Patristica*, vol. 5 (1962), pp. 83-84.
17. *Dialogue* chap. 70.
18. *Dialogue* chap. 28; *I Apology* chap. 28.
19. *I Apology* chap. 12.

Saint Irenaeus

It is one of the ironies of history that during the reign of Marcus Aurelius (161-180), the philosopher king of the Roman Empire, a severe persecution of Christians was launched which produced a host of martyrs in Lyons and Vienne in Southern Gaul, detailed for us by Eusebius in the fifth book of his celebrated *Ecclesiastical History*. At the time of the persecution, Irenaeus was a presbyter of the diocese of Lyons on a mission to Eleutherus, bishop of Rome. Not only did the churches have to contend with persecution from the government, but also from the insidious influences of doctrinal variations as represented by the various Gnostic systems, and from Montanism. When Pothinus was martyred at the age of ninety in the persecution of 177, Irenaeus succeeded to the episcopacy at Lyons. Considerable trade flourished between Gaul and Asia Minor, so that Irenaeus did not preside in an isolated post in the western part of the empire, but had opportunity for considerable contact with many of the churches in the East as well as in Rome itself. His name means "peacemaker," and his aim was always to draw the churches together in the unity of the faith, while at the same time warning them against hostile action and hostile doctrine. Eusebius mentions a number of his writings, but only two have come down to us: *Against Heresies* (its correct title is *A Refutation and Subversion of Knowledge Falsely So-called*), a long work in five books, and the much shorter *Proof of the Apostolic Preaching* which was discovered in 1904 in an Armenian version. Irenaeus wrote in Greek, but the *Against Heresies* has come down to us in an ancient Latin translation. This, coupled with the fact that Irenaeus does not possess the clearest of styles, sometimes makes for difficulties in translation, but while there may not infrequently be questions with regard to the meaning of particular sentences or paragraphs, there is no question whatever about the overall meaning of his thought.

The purpose of the *Against Heresies* is to elaborate with careful precision the leading Gnostic systems of his day and to expose them to ridicule (and this he does all the more effectively by showing that he has mastered their detail), and over against these various systems to present Catholic doctrine as the only *true* knowledge, all others being counterfeit. Books One and Two are devoted to a careful elaboration of the various leading Gnostic systems—that of Valentinus, Marcus, Saturninus, Basilides, Cerinthus, and a host of others, whereas the remaining three books deal more properly with a careful exposition of the Catholic faith.

Nothing could be more tedious than a minute description of the various Gnostic systems, which seem just as preposterous to us as they did to Irenaeus. These "fragments of a faith forgotten" show us what elaborations the human mind is capable of when it focuses on and is captured by religious speculation. Actually, the Gnostics begin with two very important questions in mind: How can we account for evil in the world? and How can man escape from this present evil and find the right road to salvation? In order to answer the first question, the Gnostics frequently had recourse to the idea of a Demiurge who created the messy world in which man now finds himself. Since the true God was pure spirit and capable only of good, this doctrine of the Demiurge not only absolved him from having created a world obviously imperfect, but also accounted for evil as being inextricably tied up with matter. Gnostic theology usually required an elaborate system of aeons, sometimes represented by male and female pairs of emanations linked together in an elaborate ladder of relationships. This very complicated theology helps to show how man reached his present plight, and how he can escape it by returning up the ladder of being, and back to the realm of pure spirit away from the material world of evil. Gnostic ethics generally took an ascetic turn and insisted on self-denial and a mortification of the flesh (many of the Gnostic leaders led quite exemplary lives), although some taught that unbridled licentiousness was also a valid approach, to show that the flesh was unimportant and could be disposed of as one wished.

The best approach to Saint Irenaeus, then, is to emphasize his positive teaching and at the same time to show how it is directed against certain very specific adversaries or positions which he wants to refute. Most people find the speculations of the Gnostics of little more than academic interest, yet it must be remembered that the great strength of Irenaeus lay in his complete grasp of the detail of these systems, a grasp which made his exposure all the more effective when he held them up to deserved ridicule.

The plan of salvation, Irenaeus declares, has come to us through no one else than from those through whom the Gospel has come down to us, and it has been transmitted in the Scriptures to be the ground and pillar of our faith; the apostles went to the ends of the earth proclaiming the peace of heaven to men, each one of them equally and individually possessing the Gospel of God. Matthew also issued a written Gospel in Hebrew while Peter and Paul were preaching at Rome, and laying the foundations of the church. Peter's preaching was recorded by Mark, and Luke recorded that of Paul. A fourth Gospel was published by John when he was residing at Ephesus in Asia. Four is the exact number of Gospels—neither more nor less—since there are four zones of the world and four principal winds, and so it is fitting that the Church should have four pillars breathing out immortality on every side, since her Founder has given us the Gospel under four aspects, but bound together by one Spirit.[1] Those who attempt to add or subtract to these four Gospels, accepted as genuine from the earliest of times, only condemn themselves from the very Gospel they accept as genuine. The Ebionites, who use only Matthew's gospel, are confuted from the same Gospel— for they make false suppositions with regard to the Lord, and Marcion is condemned by his own abridgment of Luke's Gospel. Those who allege that it was only Jesus who suffered but not the Christ may have their errors corrected by the Gospel of Mark if they read it with a love of the truth. To destroy the form of the Gospel is to be vain, unlearned, and also very daring, and either to pretend that more truth has been revealed than actually has, or that the dispensations of God can readily be brushed aside.[2] Saint Irenaeus makes a strong appeal to tradition, citing the practice of the bishops of Rome on the one hand and the Johannine practice of Polycarp in Asia Minor, on the other.

The genuinity of the four Gospels is therefore attested to by the very heretics themselves. And these Scriptures bear witness to the Lord, the King Eternal, the Incarnate Word, proclaimed by all the prophets, the apostles, and by the Holy Spirit himself. Jesus is no mere man, but born of the Most High Father, and also of the Virgin, thus making him truly Emmanuel. People are willing to die for this truth, and so martyrdom is just another testimony of the truth of the Christian religion. The heretics not only have nothing of this kind to point to, they even maintain that such witness-bearing is not at all necessary.[3]

Whereas the Gnostic teachers are numerous, all teaching a different system of knowledge and salvation, the preaching of the church is everywhere consistent because through it the Spirit of truth operates. For where the church is, there is the Spirit of God, and where the Spirit of God is, there is the church, and every kind of grace—for the Spirit is truth itself. And although the church is scattered throughout the whole world, yet she carefully preserves the truth as though she occupied just one house only. She believes the faith as if she had but one soul, one heart—and transmits her doctrine as if she possessed only one mouth. Churches in Germany do not hand down anything different from those in Spain, nor do the churches of Gaul anything from those in the East. The preaching of the truth, like the sun, shines everywhere, enlightening all men of good will, nor do more eloquent pastors teach different doctrines or make additions to it, anymore than the less-gifted diminish it by being less articulate. But those who do not join themselves to the church defraud themselves of life through their perverse opinions and infamous behavior.

With this unity of faith goes also a unity of government for Saint Irenaeus; the apostles committed the care of the churches to the bishops, and in case of any dispute, it is the ancient churches that enjoy a prestige of dignity. The heretics, however, are of a much later date than the bishops to whom the apostles committed the churches, and hence have been forced into various bypaths, while the path of those belonging to the church circumscribes the whole world since they possess the sure tradition from the apostles. Therefore it is necessary to obey the presbyters who are in the church, for they have received the certain gift of truth, along with the succession of the episcopate. However, those who depart from the primitive succession and assemble themselves together in any place whatsoever, are to be held suspect.

In a very celebrated and very controversial passage, Saint Irenaeus says that it would indeed be tedious to list all of the bishops of all the churches, but heretics can be put to confusion simply by indicating that tradition derived from the apostles of the very great, the very ancient, and the universally known church founded and organized at Rome by the two most glorious apostles, Peter and Paul. It is a matter of necessity that every church should agree with this church on account of its pre-eminent authority, that is, the faithful everywhere, inasmuch as the apostolic tradition has been preserved continuously by those (faithful men) who exist everywhere.[4] Some scholars have suggested that Saint Irenaeus really means that the true faith was kept at Rome by those who resorted there from all quarters of the world. Rome was a mirror of the Catholic world, owing her orthodoxy to those who resorted to Rome, not the sun dispensing its own light to others, but the glass bringing their rays into focus. Granting the difficulty of the phrase "pre-eminent authority" it seems to me that this second interpretation has much less to recommend it than the first.[5] At any rate it is clear that from early times Rome was considered as a sort of key-church or center of unity for one reason or another.

In his battle with the heretics, the bishops were key figures for Saint Irenaeus. If the apostles had known hidden mysteries which they were in the habit of imparting to "the perfect" apart and privately from the rest, they would have delivered them especially to those to whom they were also committing the churches themselves. But the bishops do not know what the heretics are raving about. Yet it is in the apostolic succession of the bishops that the distinctive manifestation of the body of Christ is evident. This is not to say that the early transmission of jurisdiction took place in all the churches at the same time and in the same way, but by the end of the second century the bishops are clearly sitting in the seat of the apostles and presiding in churches that claim to be infallible in their handing down of the Christian faith. When the apostles preached the truth in the churches, they were like rich men depositing money in a bank. Whoever wants to, may draw from her the waters of life, for she is the entrance to life and all others are but thieves and robbers. Away with them, but let us make choice of the things pertaining to the Christian church with the utmost diligence!

How did Saint Irenaeus view the Scriptures to which he had made so strong an appeal against the Gnostics? He considers them perfect because they were spoken by the Word of God and his Spirit.[6] Hence, no error could be found in them. But actually the Scriptures were also a part of a sacred tradition which had been handed down since the time of the apostles, a tradition which gave the Scriptures their authentic interpretation. In fact, if there were no Scriptures at all, one could follow the course of tradition handed down by them to the churches. After the death of the apostles, Irenaeus considers this a fixed tradition in the sense that it can neither be added to or subtracted from, like some precious deposit in an excellent vessel, which causes the vessel itself containing it to renew its youth also.

Turning now to a more careful consideration of Saint Irenaeus's idea of God, the saint insists that everyone knows there is one God, the Lord of all, because reason has revealed this truth to them. And even the created world reveals him who formed it, and the world manifests him who ordered it. God is truly perfect in all things, himself equal and similar to himself, as he is all light, all mind, all substance, and the fount of all good.[7] He contains all things, but he himself can be contained by no one. He is without beginning and without end; he is the only God, the only Lord, the only Creator, the only Father, alone containing all things, and himself commanding all things into existence. No man can see God and live, for the Father is incomprehensible, but in regard to his love, and kindness, and as to his infinite power, even this he grants to those who love him—to be seen by men, by whom he wills, and when he wills, and as he wills. God knows everything that he has made, or will make in the future, for through his providence every one of them has obtained its nature, and rank, and number, and special quantity; nothing lies outside his providence.

Early in the first book *Against Heresies,* Saint Irenaeus states that the Christian church, though dispersed throughout the whole world, believes in one God, the Father Almighty, Maker of heaven and earth and the sea, and all things that are in them; and in one Christ Jesus, the Son of God, who became incarnate for our salvation; and in the Holy Spirit, who proclaimed through the prophets the dispensations of God.[8] Again, in God were always present the Word and Wisdom, the Son and the Spirit, by whom and in whom, freely and spontaneously, he made all things, to whom also he speaks, saying, "Let us make man after our image and likeness." And again, the Father is indeed above all, and he is the Head of Christ, but the Word is through all things, and is himself the Head of the Church, while the Holy Spirit is in us all, and he is the living water which the Lord grants to those who rightly believe in him (the Lord), and love him. And so we have a clear statement of the Trinitarian formula, often set in a sort of credal context.

Granting that the Holy Trinity is a profound mystery, Irenaeus does assert that the Son eternally coexists with the Father, but unlike human words which have a beginning and an end, the Word of God does not, but is eternal. In some sense, however, the Father is greater than the Word, for he is above all, and through all, and in us all; moreover the Son expressly states that certain knowledge is reserved solely to the Father. Since the Son is not ashamed to declare himself ignorant of the very day and hour of judgment, neither should we be ashamed not to know how the Son is produced by the Father. Against the Gnostics and their elaborate theories, Irenaeus asserts that no one understands the Son's production, or generation, or calling, or revelation, or by whatever name one may describe his generation, which is in fact altogether indescribable. Neither Valentinus, nor Marcion, nor Saturninus, nor Basilides, nor angels, nor archangels, nor principalities, nor powers possess this knowledge, but the Father only who begat, and the Son who was begotten.[9] And any one who tries to describe this indescribable begetting is out of his mind.

The repeated insistence on the fact that God created the world rules out any notion of a Demiurge acting as a link between an other-worldly "good" God and a universe composed of evil matter. By the Word of the Lord were the heavens established, and all the might of them, by the Spirit of his mouth. Prior to their existence there was nothing, no primeval matter or substratum awaiting form. Nor was God influenced by any one, but of his own free will he created all things, since he is the only God—and all this because of his goodness, in order to have a way to confer his benefits. And it is the three Persons of the Trinity acting in consort who create the entire universe. In Fragment 33, Irenaeus rejects the idea that matter is somehow eternal and that God merely annexed certain qualities to matter; to say that God is merely the cause of quality resident in matter removes from God the half of his creative power.

With regard to angels, Irenaeus assures us that they do exist and that they have the power of choosing good or evil; evil angels have the power to injure men, but the devil (an apostate angel) can only deceive and lead astray men's minds into disobeying God's commandments with the hope that eventually he can command their worship—which rightfully belongs only to the Eternal. But the saint says little about angels, not because he did not believe in them, but possibly because he felt they played far too important a role in the Gnostic systems which he so vehemently opposed.

Man is made up of body and soul, the soul being incorporeal and hence immortal. God made man a free agent from the beginning, possessing his own power, even as he does his own soul, to obey the behests of God voluntarily, and not by compulsion of God. God took dust from the earth and formed man. "And surely," says Irenaeus, "it is much more difficult and incredible, from non-existent bones, and nerves, and veins, and the rest of man's organization, to bring it about that all this should be, and to make man an animated and rational creature, than to reintegrate again that which had been created and then afterwards decomposed into earth, having thus passed into those (elements) from which man, who had no previous existence, was formed. For He who in the beginning caused him to have being who as yet was not, just when he pleased, shall much more reinstate again those who had a former existence, when it is His will (that they should inherit) the life granted by Him."[10]

Of the first parents, Saint Irenaeus says only that they were endowed with the robe of sanctity from the Spirit, and that prior to their disobedience they had no understanding of the procreation of children and had not reached adult age; death resulted, however, from disobedience which was only rectified when Mary, years later, yielded obedience to become the cause of salvation both to herself and the whole human race. When Adam and Eve are mentioned, it is generally to compare the work of Christ who recapitulated Adam in himself, and the obedience of the Virgin Mary to the disobedience of the virgin Eve.

This leads us to a consideration of Irenaeus's notion of sin. Sin is always a misuse of freedom; to obey is to be found in possession of that which is good, given indeed by God but preserved by ourselves. Our walk through life must be circumspect, for we are commanded not merely to abstain from evil actions, but even from evil thoughts, and from idle words, and empty talk, and scurrilous language. Punishment— not merely temporal but also eternal—will be visited on those who do not believe the Word of God, and despise his advent, and are turned away backwards. Damnation awaits those to whom the Lord shall say, "Depart from me, ye cursed, into everlasting fire."

The sin of the first parents resulted in the loss of pristine righteousness as well as certain other gifts including the gift of continence, although not that of free will. The results of this first disobedience are to be discovered in all mankind; we offended God in the first Adam when he did not perform his commandment, while in the second Adam we are reconciled, being made obedient even unto death since we are debtors to none other than to God whose commandment we had transgressed at the beginning.[11]

Grace is absolutely necessary, therefore, for any saving act, and the necessity of such grace in order to effect man's salvation is described by Irenaeus in figurative language: "For as a compacted lump of dough cannot be formed of dry wheat without fluid matter, nor can a loaf possess unity, so, in like manner, neither could we, being many be made one in Christ Jesus without the water from heaven. And as dry earth does not bring forth unless it receive moisture, in like manner we also, being originally a dry tree, could never have brought forth fruit unto life without the voluntary rain from above. For our bodies have received unity among themselves by means of that layer which leads to incorruption; but our souls by means of the Spirit. Wherefore both are necessary, since both contribute toward the life of God."[12] The allusion is not only to baptism, but also to grace which follows from baptism. Nor does this grace nullify free will; invitations to the marriage feast were sent out to everyone, but those who did not obey deprived themselves of the royal supper. God has the power to raise up children to Abraham from the very stones, but the man who does not attain salvation is the very cause of his own imperfection. The light does not fail because some have blinded themselves to it, for while it remains the same as ever, those who are (thus) blinded are involved in darkness through their own fault. The light never enslaves anyone by necessity, nor, again, does God exercise compulsion upon anyone unwilling to accept the exercise of his skill. Those persons, therefore, who have apostatized from the light given by the Father, and transgressed the law of liberty, have done so through their own fault, since they have been created free agents and possessed of power over themselves.[13]

When, through faith, man receives the Spirit of God, he certainly does not lose the substance of flesh, but changes the quality of his deeds, just as the engrafted wild olive does not lose the substance of its wood, but changes the quality of its fruit, and receives another name, being now not a wild olive, but a fruitbearing olive tree. Those become perfect who retain the Spirit of God and preserve their souls and bodies blameless and maintain righteous dealings with respect to their neighbors. Irenaeus follows closely the Pauline teaching that the body is the temple in which the Spirit dwells. This temple is holy, and if any man defiles it, God will destroy him. Therefore, when man is made righteous he receives a permanent supernatural gift, the gift of the Spirit, or habitual grace.

Saving grace is connected with the person and work of Christ. Saint Irenaeus tells us several times that Christ is truly divine, the Son of God, whose suffering reconciles us to God. He rose from the dead, is at the right hand of the Father, and perfect in all things. He truly brought in salvation, being the Word of God and the Only-begotten of the Father, Christ Jesus Our Lord.[14] So there is no question that he is divine, nor did many of the Gnostics deny this. But Christ also took on a real human nature, and not one which was only apparent—and this is what many of the Gnostics denied. "For if He did not truly suffer, no thanks to Him, since there was no suffering at all; and when we shall actually begin to suffer, He will seem as leading us astray, exhorting us to endure buffeting, and to turn the other cheek, if He did not Himself before us in reality suffer the same; and as He misled them by seeming to them what He was not, so does He also mislead us, by exhorting us to endure what He did not endure Himself."[15] Just how the union of the divine and human nature is effected in Christ, Irenaeus does not say; what he makes crystal clear is that there are not two Persons—a suffering Jesus and a non-suffering Christ—but one and the same Person who is both the Son of God and the servant who suffered on the cross. All of this is directed against those Gnostics who postulated not one, but two Persons involved in the economy of man's salvation. It is not merely man's spirit which is to be saved but his body as well, for man is a composite of the two. For this reason the Word of God became flesh and blood, for those whom he came to save were made of flesh and blood also. He seems to be implying that if Adam had not sinned, there would have been no need at all for the Incarnation. But Christ became what we are, that he might bring us to be even what he is himself.

The purpose of the Incarnation, then, is the salvation of all men—infants, children, boys, youths and the aged, and Irenaeus states that Christ went through each one of these stages himself. This passage which has raised some eyebrows as well as discussion reads like this: "So likewise He was an old man for old men, that He might be a perfect Master for all, not merely as respects the setting forth of the truth, but also as regards age, sanctifying at the same time the aged also, and becoming an example to them likewise."[16] One may take this passage in a figurative sense, or adopt the suggestion that Our Lord was prematurely aged. It does not seem possible, however, to assume that he actually reached fifty years of age, however one interprets John 8:56, 57.

Reconciliation is possible for all inasmuch as the obedience of Mary countermanded the disobedience of Eve, and Christ's obedience unto death that of Adam's disobedience. In order that this reconciliation might be extended to everyone, the Lord descended into the regions beneath the earth, preaching his advent there also, and declaring the remission of sins received by those who believe in him. Irenaeus repeats this tradition more than once before going on to assert Christ's bodily resurrection and ascension into heaven.[17] On his return in the glory of his Father, he will judge both the living and the dead.

Saint Irenaeus has some very explicit things to say about Mary whom he refers to as the Virgin and the mother of Emmanuel. She gave birth to Christ in a special way, and the implication is that Mary remained a virgin. But her particular glory was her cooperation with the Holy Spirit in reversing the sentence of Eve, and gaining through obedience what had formerly been lost through disobedience. This reversion of the progress begun by Adam is insisted upon several times; the knot of Eve's disobedience was loosed by the obedience of Mary, for what the virgin Eve had bound fast through unbelief, this did the virgin Mary set free through faith.[18]

Saint Irenaeus seems to speak of baptism somewhat indirectly. He refers to it as the laver of regeneration, and makes it clear that all persons of whatever age are candidates for the newness of life which is thereby offered. Since he expressly includes infants, this would seem to be indirect testimony to the fact of infant baptism in at least the church of the second century. The effect of baptism is clearly a new birth in which former sins are washed away and there is an infusion of grace making it now possible for "the wild olive" to become grafted into a fruitful-bearing olive tree. Baptism and the Holy Spirit join Christians together in God. Water is for the body and the Holy Spirit for the soul, and both are necessary, since both contribute toward the life of God.[19]

That Christ is really present in the Eucharist under the species of bread and wine is a very clear teaching of Saint Irenaeus. He accuses the Gnostic heretics of being inconsistent when they hold this same teaching, but deny that the Son is begotten of the Creator of the world. Moreover, how could the Lord, with any justice, if he belonged to another father, have acknowledged the bread to be his body, while he took it from that creation to which we belong, and affirmed the mixed cup to be his blood? If the flesh is not capable of salvation as the heretics claim, what is the point of acknowledging the real presence? If there is to be no resurrection of the body, then Christ's words are pointless. "Just as a cutting from the vine planted in the ground fructifies in its season, or as a corn of wheat falling into the earth and becoming decomposed, rises with manifold increase by the Spirit of God, who contains all things, and then, through the wisdom of God, serves for the use of men, and having received the Word of God, becomes the Eucharist, which is the body and blood of Christ; so also our bodies, being nourished by it, and deposited in the earth, and suffering decomposition there, shall rise at their appointed time, the Word of God granting them resurrection to the glory of God the Father."[20]

Reference is made to the prophecy of Malachi (1:10, 11) to confirm the Eucharist as being the new pure sacrifice which would be offered among the Gentiles everywhere, and Christ's words of institution at the Last Supper prove his presence in the species of bread and wine. Again, Irenaeus is not trying to prove this against Gnostics who would deny it; he is saying that it is inconsistent to hold this doctrine and then to deny that the flesh can be saved. He frequently speaks of the "manufactured" bread and the "mingled" or "mixed" cup, and this is reminiscent of similar language in the *Didache*. So the Eucharist is a pledge or token of the resurrection and the promise of eternal life. Following Christ's example, the church has received this new oblation of the new covenant from the apostles, and now offers it throughout the world. That this is a true sacrifice the quotation from Malachi is intended to substantiate.

Saint Irenaeus has little to tell us of the penitential system. He declares that the gnostic disciples of Marcus have deluded many women, who have their consciences seared as with a hot iron. Some had indeed made a public confession of their sins, but others were ashamed to do so, and in a tacit kind of way had apostatized altogether, despairing of attaining to the life of God, while others kept hesitating between two courses.[21] Certainly there is baptismal repentance, and this is mentioned several times, but little if any mention of post-baptismal repentance. However, an argument from silence is always a dangerous one; we must remember that Irenaeus is writing against a special audience, and we would naturally expect him to discuss the points which had the greatest relevance for him in his *Against Heresies*. In the *Proof of the Apostolic Preaching,* the doctrine of penance is again more implicit than explicit, since this too is a writing polemic in character. Mention is made of the sacrament of Holy Orders; it is necessary to obey the presbyters who are in the church who possess the apostolic succession; they, together with the succession of the episcopate, have received the certain gift of truth, according to the good pleasure of the Father. One of the effects of Holy Orders therefore seems to be an increase of grace, a character, and a spiritual power involving teaching, administration, and, very likely, liturgical function.[22]

For Saint Irenaeus, death results in the separation of corporeal, composite body from incorporeal, simple soul. The body decomposes and returns to the elements, but the soul, being immortal, continues to live. Christ executes just judgment on every soul, and in the exercise of his grace may confer immortality on the righteous, the holy, and those who have kept his commandments; having persevered in his love (some from the beginning and others from the time of their repentance), those he may surround with everlasting glory. But, "spiritual wickedness," and the angels who transgressed and became apostates, together with the ungodly, unrighteous, wicked, and profane among men, he may send into everlasting fire.[23] That the fire is indeed everlasting is proved by Our Lord's own words in Matt. 25:41.

Passages in the fifth book of the *Against Heresies* seem to show that Irenaeus held a kind of millenarianism. It was fitting that the creation itself, being restored to its primeval condition, should without restraint be under the domination of the righteous. For it seemed only fair that in that very creation in which they toiled or were afflicted, being proved in every way by suffering, they should receive the reward of their suffering, and that in the creation in which they were slain because of their love to God, in that they should be revived again, and that in the creation in which they endured servitude, in that they should reign. Afterwards, the judgment would take place.[24] An allusion is made to the Papias fragment in which Saint John reports the saying of the Lord about the vines with ten thousand branches; possibly Irenaeus includes this more as a deference to the memory of Polycarp. Paragraph 61 of the *Proof of the Apostolic Preaching* seems to imply, however, that all of this has already taken place.

At any rate, the present system of things will pass away and man will be renewed and flourish in an incorruptible state and there will be a new heaven and a new earth where man can always hold conversation with God. This has been prophesied by Isaiah (66:22) and is confirmed by the presbyters who say that those who are deemed worthy of an abode in heaven shall go there, others shall enjoy the delights of paradise, and others shall possess the splendor of the city; for everywhere the Savior shall be seen according as they who see him shall be worthy.[25] The vision of God, then, makes for the incorruption of eternal life, a beatitude which is truly everlasting, and can never be lost.

NOTES

The text is that of Wigan Harvey in *The Ante-Nicene Fathers,* vol. 1 (*see* Bibliography).

1. *Against Heresies* 3. 1; 3. 8.
2. Ibid., 3. 11, 9.
3. Ibid., 4. 33.
4. Ibid., 3. 3.
5. Cf. Roberts and Donaldson in *The Ante-Nicene Fathers,* vol. 1, p. 415, col. 2, n. 3.
6. *Against Heresies* 2. 28.
7. Ibid., 4. 11.
8. Ibid., 1. 10.
9. Ibid., 2. 28.
10. Ibid., 5. 3.
11. Ibid., 5. 16; see also the stimulating study of J. T. Nielsen, *Adam and Christ in the Theology of Iranaeus of Lyons* (Assen: Van Gorcum & Co., 1968).
12. *Against Heresies* 3. 17.
13. Ibid., 4. 39.
14. Ibid., 3. 16.

15. Ibid., 3. 18; cf. Albert Houssiau, *La Christologie de Saint Irénée* (Louvain: Publications Universitaires, 1955).
16. *Against Heresies* 2. 24.
17. Ibid., 4. 27; 5. 31.
18. Ibid., 3. 22.
19. Ibid., 3. 17.
20. Ibid., 5. 2.
21. Ibid., 1. 13.
22. Ibid., 4. 26.
23. Ibid., 1. 10.
24. Ibid., 5. 32.
25. Ibid., 5. 36.

IV

MINOR APOLOGISTS OF THE SECOND AND THIRD CENTURIES

Saint Justin (Martyr) and Saint Irenaeus represent two major apologists of the second century, but they were by no means alone in their witness. Other writers have left us vivid testimony to the struggle for acceptance that engaged the church of the second century. Although they are minor figures, each brought his own particular insight or emphasis to the growing body of articulated Christian thought. Much of their writing has been lost, but what has survived affords illuminating and fascinating vignettes of the Good News which had so recently come into the Roman world. To these somewhat obscure but nonetheless important writers we now turn.

Tatian

We know very little about Tatian other than that he was a contemporary of Saint Justin Martyr and knew him when he was in Rome, possibly having been converted by him. He seems to have been a rhetorician but also had a broad knowledge of the culture of his day. He calls himself an Assyrian and a barbarian from the East which seems to betray an inferiority complex toward Greek culture and philosophy which his principal work, *The Address to the Greeks,* flays mercilessly. Following the death of his idol Justin (ca. 165), Tatian left Rome and took up residence in Antioch, where at the end of his life he fell in with the Encratites, a heretical sect practicing a strict morality. His connection with them may have been tenuous at best; however, he certainly seems to have considered marriage a corrupting influence which resulted in his having the Gnostic label plastered on him by subsequent church fathers, most of whom refer to him in a quite hostile tone. Irenaeus says that he denied the salvation of Adam, but ignored Paul's teaching that where sin abounded, grace had much more abounded.[1] Tatian's attempt to weave the four Gospels into one is the earliest that we have; his *Diatessaron,* having been lost for centuries, was rediscovered in a translation and issued at the Vatican in 1888, a jubilee year during the pontificate of Leo XIII. The discovery of the *Diatessaron* does not substantially alter the main outlines of Tatian's thought. Other works attributed to him remain lost.

The *Address to the Greeks* attempts to present Christianity as the one true philosophy by summarizing and decrying all the evil of "contemporary culture" (Greek paganism). In vain do the Greeks boast of having invented the arts; the ancients beat them to it. The Greek philosophers taught as much nonsense as they did truth and their personal lives left much to be desired. But the heathen divinities are the most reprehensible of all, for their downright immoral conduct is either laughable or disgusting. Hence the religious rites or solemnities connected with such fraudulent deities is reprehensible in the extreme. The same is true of such things as gladiatorial amusements and other such public spectacles. Even the entire educational system of the Greeks is a total waste of time. And as for Greek statuary (a great deal of which Tatian seems to have known), its main purpose seems to be a memorial to iniquity and impurity of every possible description.

Because of the black and white interpretation which Tatian puts upon paganism versus Christianity, critics have been impatient with him for his harsh judgments; but it must be remembered that as an apologist he is trying to show the pagan world how really bankrupt its highly-touted culture is, and the Christianity which the Greeks despise as barbarism is the true philosophy and culture that the world so badly needs. Culture and Christianity are two separate entities incapable of fusion (so Tatian thought) because one stood for the world's perdition and the other for its salvation. To the liberal mind which sometimes confuses Christianity with Western culture this may seem like too harsh a dichotomy, but Tatian feels that only by heightening this contrast can he show that Christianity is the only hope of a world floundering badly in ignorance and sin.

Hence, his doctrine of God is sharply delineated from the heathen polytheism of his day. God is not a body, not material, but a purely spiritual being. He is one, not many, and he can neither be seen or tasted, in a word, he cannot be known by the corporeal sense at all. Moreover, he is eternal without beginning or end, and is comparable to no one else. He is the Author only of good; no evil can come from him so that whatever proceeds from him, whatever he does, must be called good. He is Creator of both things visible and invisible and through his visible creation we apprehend his invisible power by his works. He is also the Arbiter and Judge of all human kind, just as he is the ground of all being, without whom nothing can exist. Thus we see God's love for all men, although for Tatian the love of God is more implied than expressly stated. What Tatian is doing, of course, is to emphasize the aspects of the Christian God which would be in direct contrast to the prevailing heathen notions of deity.

Like Justin, Tatian also makes use of the Logos doctrine, but without prejudice to his strict monotheism. Having denied that matter somehow contains its own life force (as the Stoics taught) Tatian shows that it is God who possesses the life-giving power which engenders the Logos. By his simple will the Logos springs forth and becomes the first-begotten work of the Father. His coming into being is not by abscission but by participation, so that there is no resultant diminution of the main source. Just as one torch can light many fires without lessening its own flame, so the Logos, coming forth from the Logos-power of the Father, has not divested him of the Logos-power, who did the begetting. The text has excited scholarly controversy because it admits of different punctuations and some of the words which Tatian used are not easily translated. Is he merely repeating the doctrine of the Logos which he had learned from his teacher Justin, or is he dangerously close to a doctrine of emanations which he would have picked up from the Gnostics? Is he suggesting that the Logos was not a personal force prior to the Father's begetting? And does he identify Christ with the Logos, for if he does the connection seems somewhat tenuous and casual.[2] At any rate, the Logos begotten in the beginning gave birth in turn to our world, having first created for himself the necessary matter; and so Tatian (in imitation of the Logos) has likewise undergone a spiritual birth, and now being possessed of the truth is trying to reduce to order the confused matter which is kindred with himself. This is not to say that matter has no beginning, it too is brought into existence by the Framer of all things. Whether God brings matter into existence first, and then creates form—or whether the two are created simultaneously, Tatian does not specify.

In spite of the difficulties of his language, there is no reason why Tatian cannot be interpreted in a perfectly orthodox sense; that his language is misleading and not clearly thought-out seems to be evident, but at the same time it is by no means evident that it should be summarily labeled heterodox.

Along with the Logos, there is also the spirit of God called by Tatian the Holy Spirit, the Perfect Spirit and the Heavenly Spirit. Man's goal is to unite his soul with the Holy Spirit and to strive for union with God. Actually there are two kinds of spirits, for in addition to the Holy Spirit, there is also the soul, and both of these existed side by side in the first men. Being associated with matter, the soul is a material-spirit which must enter into union with the divine Spirit if it is to ascend to the regions which are proper to it, and this is done by obedience of spirit to Spirit, thus reversing the downward trend which disobedience causes. The soul is not in itself immortal; if it does not know the truth, it dies and is dissolved with the body, but at the last day it rises again and receives death by punishment in immortality. If, however, it acquires the knowledge of God it only undergoes a temporary dissolution at the time of death, after which it achieves a blessed immortality thanks to its obedience to the Holy Spirit, and its acceptance of the work of the suffering God.

But the soul must be on guard against the demons of the world, who have chosen men as their special object of hatred in their own revolt against God. Their principal aim is to divert worship to themselves, and this they accomplish by falsely promising health to those who place confidence in roots and herbs. Rather than putting their trust in these material aids, men ought rather to trust to the all-powerful Spirit of God. Demons are all too ready to take advantage of man's ignorance, folly and sickness in order to turn these natural maladies to advantage for themselves. But they will be punished more severely than man is, and will "enjoy" an immortality which will be a fitting reward for their wickedness while at work on earth.

But in spite of the influence of demons in the world, and the fall of the first men through the chief of the demons, man's sin is not due to fate, but to the misuse of his own free will, which destroys him and makes him a slave to sin. He must regulate his inordinate desires and unruly passions, seeing that one death awaits everyone whether they be rich or poor, famous or obscure, of high or low birth. The wise man will die to the world and repudiate the madness which is in it; we must live to God and by apprehending him lay aside our old nature. We are created for life, to enjoy the companionship of the Spirit of God, but if we reject this it will be our own fault, and the fault of no one else.

The *Address to the Greeks* contains some interesting and puzzling omissions. In spite of his use of the Logos doctrine, Tatian never averts to the historical Jesus, nor does he do any more than allude to the incarnation and almost by accident mention the Passion. The name of Jesus does not appear once, nor any mention directly of the Christ. There is no mention of the church, nor any of baptism, and only a vague reference to the Eucharist in the twenty-fifth chapter where he refers to the persecution of Christians who allegedly ate human flesh. These are some of the reasons for suspecting that Tatian was a Docetist whose correct position was more outside the church than in it. But if his *Address* is more properly an exhortation whose aim is to dissuade the Greeks from their polytheism, and if one of his aims is not to travel the same road taken by Justin, much less present a complete system of apologetic theology, then he must be judged by how well he achieves his main purpose—the conversion of the heathen.

Perhaps little needs to be said about Tatian's ethical views, which, while not prominent, are scattered here and there throughout his *Address*. He seems to be somewhat prudish with regard to sex, and in his later life with the Encratites denounced marriage as a defilement. There is a misogynist strain in his writings which results in his praise of virgins and the excoriation of a woman of whom a statue was made for having given birth to thirty children. That is to bear off the fruits of great incontinence in imitation of a sow! One must admit that thirty does seem excessive. There are also condemnations of the licentiousness of the theater, to say nothing of the barbarity of gladiatorial combats.

Tatian's *Diatessaron* is the earliest attempt we have to weave the four Gospels into a single strand, and bears valuable testimony from the second century that the church recognized four authentic Gospels, and only four. It has important bearing on the Synoptic Problem which has intrigued New Testament scholars down to the present day.

NOTES

The *Address* is translated by J. E. Rowland in vol. 2, and the Diatessaron is an Arabic text translated by Hope Hogg in vol. 9 of *The Ante-Nicene Fathers* (*see* Bibliography).
1. Irenaeus, *Against Heresies* 1. 28; 3. 37.
2. Cf. James Donaldson, "A Critical History of Christian Literature and Doctrine," in *The Ante-Nicene Fathers,* vol. 3, p. 42 ff.; also *Recherches sur le Discours aux Grecs de Tatien* (Paris: Alcan, 1903), p. 55 ff.

Melito of Sardis

Melito, bishop of Sardis, flourished toward the end of the second century and died probably around the year 190. Eusebius lists no less than sixteen or eighteen of his writings, and we gather from other sources that he was an articulate and prolific writer. We know that he supported the Quartodeciman side of the Paschal controversy that dated back at least to the time of Polycarp and agitated the church during the second century. Melito is cited against Artemon and the Anti-Trinitarians as an upholder of the doctrine that Christ was at once God and man. Apart from a number of fragments, the only complete work we have from his hand is *The Homily on the Passion*. His last writing was his *Apology* on behalf of the Christians, addressed to Marcus Aurelius. Melito is a rhetorician and a stylist to such an extent that various literary devices which he uses tend to detract from what he has to say, but despite the ornate style (which is almost second-century baroque) there is a solidity of content and a good deal of meat and muscle to go with it. Carlyle would have enjoyed reading Melito.

The Homily on the Passion opens with a discussion of the Passover, considering it first as a historical event and then as typifying the sacrifice of Christ on the cross. The historical event visited suffering and retribution on Egypt, climaxed by the slaying of all the firstborn. Israel was protected from this holocaust by the spirit of the Lord, but in Melito's description of the horror and wailing of the Egyptians gathered about their stricken Pharaoh, the bishop of Sardis pulls out all the stops. Egypt now symbolizes the old dispensation while Israel symbolizes the new, the Chosen People who are to be God's special instruments of his grace to all the world. The argument now turns on the key idea of suffering. Because of his sin man must suffer, but from the Chosen People (and predicted by the various key figures of the Old Testament,) Christ will come, has come, to redeem man and to consummate the mystical Passover by his crucifixion and resurrection. One would have expected Israel to be grateful for this, but instead they have been complicit in the trial and death of their very own king. So they will certainly be punished for executing their greatest benefactor. In closing his Good Friday sermon Melito now turns to the Crucifixion scene itself, contrasting the shame and humiliation of the cross with the magnificent figure of Christ himself: "He who hung the earth [in its place] is hanged, he who fixed the heavens is fixed [upon the cross], he who made all things fast is made fast upon the tree, the Master has been insulted, God has been murdered, the King of Israel has been slain by an Israelitish hand."[1] The moral is plain; for this impiety Israel will be punished, and those who reject Christ and his church will in turn be rejected by God. Just as Egypt was punished for oppressing Israel, Israel will also be punished unless she accepts the new dispensation offered by her Redeemer.

It would, of course, be impossible to derive a complete theological system from a single sermon such as this, and indeed, what specific points do emerge ought well to be checked with other sources from the same author. Since we have before us a Good Friday sermon it comes as no surprise to find that the theology herein expressed is very Christocentric, emphasis being placed on the Second Person of the Blessed Trinity to an almost complete exclusion of the first and third members. There would be nothing wrong with this except for the fact that on occasion Melito uses language which is not felicitous or always precise, and for this reason he was accused by a later age of a simple modalism or monarchianism, which may help to explain why his works experienced difficulty in surviving. For instance, he speaks of Christ, "Who is all things: in that he judges—Law; in that he teaches—Word; in that he saves—Grace; in that he begets—Father; in that he is begotten—Son; in that he suffers—a [sacrificial] sheep; in that he is buried—Man; in that he arises, God."[2] Similarly, in the expression, "God has been murdered" in the previous quotation cited, there is the possibility of interpreting Melito in a Patripassian sense. Of course, one can explain these passages away as the incautious exuberance of a rhetorical preacher, but they do at least arouse suspicions.[3] We need more passages or better proof of the distinctive personality of God the Father, to keep from assuming that Melito looked upon Father and Son as simply different modes, phases, or aspects of a single Deity.

References to the Spirit of God likewise seem to suggest not so much the Holy Spirit, but the spirit of the angel which smote Egypt because she had no part in the Passover. And again, the rhetorical passage where the angel is asked: "What stayed thy hand, the sacrifice of the sheep or the life of the Lord? The death of the sheep, or the type of the Lord? The blood of the sheep or the Spirit of the Lord?" suggests that spirit is used in a general operative sense, rather than the Holy Spirit as a distinct member of the Trinity.[4]

The major emphasis in the sermon is devoted to the person and work of Christ, which is centered around the idea of the historical Passover as a mystical symbol of the redemption of man, who had been suffering under the bondage of sin. Born of a virgin named Mary, Christ is led as a lamb and slaughtered as a sheep; he ransomed us from the ruin of the world as from the land of Egypt, and freed us from the slavery of the devil as from the hand of Pharaoh, and sealed our souls with his own spirit and the members of our bodies with his own blood. Christ arose from the dead, "God who put on man, and suffered for the sufferer, and was bound for him who was bound, and judged for him who was condemned, and buried for him who was buried.[5]

There is a reference to the "harrowing of hell" at the end of the sermon where Christ announces of himself: "I am he who put down death, and triumphed over the enemy, and trod upon Hades, and bound the strong one and brought man safely home to the heights of the heavens."[6] Christ's death and resurrection altered not merely man's world, but the entire universe as well, although precisely what occurred in Hades we are not told.

Melito's ethic, then, if one may use that word, consists primarily in man's acceptance of what Christ has done. The Christian message demands first of all belief, which belief will then issue in moral behavior. The penultimate paragraph of the sermon sums up Melito's entire message which he places in the mouth of the Savior himself: "Therefore, come hither all you families of men, who are sullied with sins, and receive remission of sins. For I am your remission. I am the Passover of salvation, the Lamb that was sacrificed for you, I am your ransom[?], I am your light, I am your savior, I am the resurrection, I am your king, I lead you up to the heights of the heavens, I will show you the Father [who is] from the ages, I will raise you up by my right hand."[7]

It is a pity that we have only this one work of Melito's; it shows a vigorous preacher who may have been a colorful character as well. Other writings of his would no doubt show him in a less anti-Semitic light. Saint Jerome says that Tertullian rather sneered at Melito for what today would be called pulpit antics. In all likelihood a sneer from Tertullian would in this case be rather a compliment.

NOTES

1. Campbell Bonner, ed., *The Homily on the Passion by Melito Bishop of Sardis* (London: Christopher's 1940), p. 179.
2. *Homily* No. 9.
3. Cf. Bonner, *The Homily on the Passion,* p. 28.
4. *Homily* No. 32.
5. Ibid., No. 67, No. 100.
6. Ibid., No. 102.
7. Ibid., No. 103.

Saint Theophilus of Antioch

Our knowledge of Saint Theophilus of Antioch is quite scant. Eusebius says that he was the sixth from the apostles in the episcopacy and that he was the author of several works, including the three "elementary works addressed to Autolycus," which is the only one that has come down to us.[1] Theophilus even mentions a work of his own, *On History,* but this has been lost, along with his writings against Hermogenes and Marcion. Since he became bishop of Antioch in the eighth year of the reign of Marcus Aurelius this would be in A.D. 168 and apparently he died either in A.D. 181 or 188. Possibly he was born sometime during the second decade of the century.

The three very long personal letters which are called "books" and are addressed to Autolycus are not so much a defense of Christianity as an attack on pagan polytheism with the intention of dissuading a learned heathen from idolatry and converting him to the true faith. To do this, Theophilus will not call upon a fluent tongue or elegant style, but as a lover of truth will simply present the facts and let them speak for themselves. And he will ask his friend Autolycus to open the eyes of his soul and the ears of his heart and to cleanse himself from all impurity so that darkness will be dispelled, and beholding the light of truth, he will be able to see God. What follows is, first, a long attack on the idol worship of the heathens and a condemnation of the polytheism of the Greeks and the ridiculous stories attached to the Olympian deities. A second attack is launched against the poets and philosophers who are the vehicles of the religion and culture of his day and who propagated this nonsense from a desire of vainglory. They are all condemned, from Socrates on down, because they rely in man's erring reason rather than on God's inspiration. So, for Theophilus, while Plato and others may have attained some truth, it was so mixed up with error that it would take an inspired revelation from God to set man on the right path. This necessary inspiration Theophilus found in the Old Testament, which he could prove to be older than the Homeric writings, just as Moses antedated by several centuries the savants of the Greek culture. If he seems to us somewhat harsh and altogether too sweeping in his condemnation of the best Greek thinking, we cannot forget that a polemic of this sort required showing Christianity in its best light and its opponent in the worst.

116

To a modern reader, the lengths which the apologists adopt to refute the inane stories of ancient mythology become tiresome, long before they have sated themselves. To us it seems like beating a dead dog even as they pursue their heathen opponents to flush them out of the bushes of allegorical interpretation. But we forget that Christianity and ancient culture formed two sharp entities in strong contrast to each other; the cultural blend was not to come for years later, and Christian thinking in the second century was sharply "polarized" from the usual thinking of the ordinary man living in the reign of Commodus. Autolycus would be more impressed with the uniqueness of Christianity rather than with the attempt to identify it with all the best in ancient culture.

Over against the Homeric deities Theophilus describes for his friend the Christian God, who is ineffable and indescribable and cannot be seen by mortal eyes. "For in glory He is incomprehensible, in greatness unfathomable, in height inconceivable, in power incomparable, in wisdom unrivalled, in goodness inimitable, in kindness unutterable. For if I say He is Light, I name but His own work; if I call Him Word, I name but His sovereignty; if I call Him Mind, I speak but of His wisdom; if I say He is Spirit, I speak of His breath; if I call Him Wisdom, I speak of His offspring; if I call Him Strength, I speak of His sway; if I call Him Power, I am mentioning His activity; if Providence, I but mention His goodness; if I call Him Kingdom, I but mention His glory; if I call Him Lord, I mention His being judge; if I call Him Judge, I speak of Him as being just; if I call Him Father, I speak of all things as being from Him."[2] God is without beginning because he is unbegotten; and he is unchangeable because he is immortal. He is creator, maker, and ruler of the universe, for the heavens are his work, the earth is his creation, the sea is his handiwork; man is his formation and his image; sun, moon, and stars are his elements, made for signs, and seasons, and days, and years, that they may serve and be slaves to man. It is through his works that this invisible God is perceived to be governor or pilot of the whole universe, just as when one sees a ship on the sea rigged and in sail, and making for the harbor, he can infer that there is a pilot on board who is steering it. If this is not altogether clear to us now, it will be when we put off our mortality and put on incorruption; then we will see God worthily and as he actually is.

Now before anything came into existence, God was not alone but had residing within his heart as a counselor the Word which always existed. But when God wished to make all that he determined on, he begot his Logos, uttered, the firstborn of all creation, without emptying himself of it, but always conversing with it. Theophilus thus clearly distinguishes (and is probably the first to do so) between the Logos which was always with God and the Logos uttered by God and through whom all things were made.[3] This enables him to explain the theophanies

of the Old Testament, so that when God walked in the garden and
conversed with Adam, it was actually the Logos who took on the
person, or more precisely, the mask of the Father. Likewise, in the
creation of the world, God had the Logos as helper, and for this reason
he is called "governing principle" (αρχη) because he rules, and is Lord
of all things fashioned by him. It is this same Logos that inspired the
various prophets as well as Solomon and Moses, from whom we have
an account of the world's creation.[4]

With regard to the Spirit of God the thinking of Theophilus is less
precise. Sometimes he seems to confuse the Spirit with the Logos, but
at the same time he generally implies a personal note when speaking
of the Spirit of God.[5] The Spirit was especially present at the creation
which is sustained and nourished by it. The Spirit also inspires Holy
Scripture and speaks through Moses and the prophets, but his special
task now is to lead Christians in the way of truth. Both the Logos and
the Spirit come somehow from God and are intimately associated with
him; they are both personal, but what their relationship is each to the
other, Theophilus does not further specify.

In his description of the work of the fourth day[6] Theophilus tells
us that the first three days are types of the Trinity, of God, and his
Word, and his wisdom. In the creation of man, there is considerable
discussion of the words, "Let us make man in our image, after our
likeness." But to whom could the words be addressed by God except
to his own Word and Wisdom? It may be difficult to distinguish
between these two, but Theophilus gives each of them a personal note.
More often, the Spirit of God seems to be the sustaining power of
God's breath, without which the whole universe would collapse. While
it is certain that there is considerable confusion in his thinking, nonetheless it is clear that Theophilus did hold for a Trinity of personalized
elements, all of them in complete agreement and acting in perfect
concord.

Because he says that he has discussed the matter in another place,
Theophilus has little to say of Satan, the "demon" or "dragon" who
deceived Eve by means of the serpent. Seeing that he had failed to
secure the death of the first parents, he instigated friction between
Cain and Abel and effected the latter's murder. The demons also
inspired the nonsense put out by the Greek poets, and wherever
they could, Satan and his cohorts advanced polytheism and idolatry.
He is even the author of the cry "Eva" in the orgies of Bacchus, for
so do the frenzied cultists salute the mother of all sin!

In Bk. 2, chap. 27, Theophilus describes at some length the nature
of man. He is neither mortal nor immortal, for if he were mortal
God would seem to be the cause of his death, and if he were immortal
he would have been like God. God made man free with power over

himself, and through obedience to God, man attains immortality, just as disobedience results in his death. Adam and Eve were set in a park of delight, a paradise, after God had first created them babes (understood either in the physical sense of childhood or a state of complete innocence), but commanded them not to eat of the tree of knowledge. The tree itself was good, but the disobedience brought about Adam's expulsion and condemnation of death. For there was nothing else in the fruit than knowledge, says Theophilus, but knowledge is good when one uses it discreetly.[7] The expulsion from Paradise, however, worked to man's advantage because it allowed the punishment to be expiated within an appointed time, after which man would be replaced in Paradise after the resurrection and judgment. (That is why it is mystically written in Genesis, as if he had been twice placed in paradise.) "For just as a vessel, when on being fashioned has some flaw, is remoulded or remade, that it may become new and entire; so also it happens to man by death. For somehow or other he is broken up, that he may rise in the resurrection whole; I mean spotless, and righteous, and immortal."[8]

All of this obviously calls for a change of heart and action on man's part. The way of salvation depends on obedience to God's law and the teachings of the prophets, with the attendant renunciation of idolatry, adultery, murder, fornication, theft, avarice, false swearing, wrath, incontinence and impurity, and not to do to others what they would not wish to be done to themselves—by so acting one may escape the eternal punishments and be thought worthy of the eternal life from God.[9]

In Bk. 2, chap. 14, Theophilus compares the world to the ocean which is nourished by fresh water rivers which keep it from becoming too briny; likewise, the law of God and the prophets flows and wells up sweetness and compassion and righteousness to prevent it from going to ruin through sin and wickedness. And just as there are islands in the sea, God has given to the world assemblies or holy churches in which survive the doctrines of truth. And as there are other islands which are rocky and without water, and barren, and infested with wild beasts, serving only to wreck ships and injure navigators, so there are doctrines of error—heresies—which destroy those who approach them. This is the sole passage which makes any allusion to the Church, or churches, in Theophilus, and there is likewise a single allusion to baptism (Bk. 1, chap. 10) or possibly confirmation where he speaks of the anointing of Christians with the oil of God.

And so the Christian life must begin with *metanoia* and a firm belief in the Hebrew Scriptures, and it must be lived in faith and trust in God, and the belief that he intends to raise everyman from the dead. To those who believe already, the resurrection is being effected within them without their knowing it; God has already created them, and now intends to crown his work in the resurrection. On all sides we see the necessity for faith, for faith is the leading principle in all matters. Happy are those who believe now, for in the resurrection all will believe whether they want to or not. God has already created us out of nothing, brought us into this life with a minimal use of matter, and intends even greater things for us in the resurrection. All we need to do is to believe him, and when we have put off mortality and put on incorruption, we shall then see God worthily.

Theophilus follows in the footsteps of Justin Martyr and presents us with a chiaroscuro—all the worst in pagan culture contrasted with all the best in Christianity. To some this has seemed an imbalance, but everyone is agreed that Theophilus' style is a forceful and vigorous apologetic, or rather polemic, for the faith to which he had been converted after reading the Scriptures. The manliness of his style and the cogency of his arguments have not diminished through the centuries.

NOTES

A translation of the text, based on the Benedictine edition, is in *The Ante-Nicene Fathers*, vol. 2 (*see* Bibliography).

1. Eusebius *Ecclesiastical History* 4. 20, 24.
2. *To Autolycus* 1. 3.
3. Ibid., 22; see also Otto Gross, *Die Weltenstehungs-Lehre des Theophilus von Antiochia* (Jena, 1895), p. 20 ff; and Arno Pommerich, *Des Apologeten Theophilus von Antiochia Gottes—und Logoslehre* (an inaugural dissertation) (Leipzig, 1904), p. 36 ff.
4. *To Autolycus* 1. 10.
5. Ibid.
6. *To Autolycus* 2. 15.
7. Ibid., 2. 24, 25.
8. Ibid., 2. 26.
9. Ibid., 2. 34.

Saint Hegesippus

Brief mention should be given to Saint Hegesippus, who flourished around the year 180, and who is mentioned several times by Eusebius, in the *Ecclesiastical History*. Apparently Hegesippus was a Jewish convert, and was conversant with unwritten Jewish traditions as well as Jewish thought. He maintained that the heresies were in large part derived from Jewish rather than pagan origins. Eusebius quotes a long passage from Hegesippus with regard to the activities of James the apostle when presiding over the church at Jerusalem. The picture we derive is one of stark asceticism, an austerity which is not very appealing. The Apostle (according to Hegesippus) was in the habit of speaking about the "door of Jesus," possibly an allusion to the Way of Life as opposed to the road to destruction.

The five treatises of Saint Hegesippus have all been lost, but Eusebius states that he left a very complete record of his own opinion; more important, he traveled as far as Rome and mingled with a great many bishops, and received the same doctrine from all. He spent some days at the church of the Corinthians, during which he says they were all mutually stimulated by the true Word. When he was in Rome he drew up a list of succession ending with Eleutherus (174/6-189/91). The implication here is that not only had the apostolic succession been preserved at Rome but the true preaching as well. Eusebius seems to suggest that Hegesippus was not a systematic thinker, but rather a collector of personal memoirs interspersed with a kind of travelogue. It is a pity that his work has not survived, for it would undoubtedly have furnished us with a good deal of detail regarding the life of the church in the second century.

NOTE

References to Hegesippus are in Eusebius *Ecclesiastical History* 2. 23; 3. 11, 20, 32; 4. 8, 22, 23.

The Epitaph of Abercius

The epitaph of Abercius was unearthed in 1883 by the British archaeologist W. Ramsey in Hierapolis, and is now in the Lateran Museum. Since the epitaph of Alexander dates from the year 216 and quotes the epitaph of Abercius, the latter can be dated from some time late in the second century, probably around the year 180. Its importance lies in its testimony to the Eucharist, and although the style is quite cryptic, the epitaph refers to the Christian mysteries rather than to those of the pagan mystery religions. The highly symbolic language with its air of mystery testifies to the arcane discipline of the church in the second century. Abercius refers to the Christian community or the church at Rome which he visited (and was the great event of his life) as the queen, and the splendid seal is generally taken to refer to baptism. The entire epitaph runs as follows:

I, a citizen of the elect city, erected this tomb in my lifetime, that I might have clearly there a place for my body; my name is Abercius, a disciple of the pure Shepherd who feeds the flocks of sheep on mountains and plains, who has great all-seeing eyes; he taught me . . . faithful Scriptures. To Rome he sent me to behold sovereignty and to see a queen, golden-robed and golden sandaled; a people I saw there which has a splendid seal, and I saw the plain of Syria and all the cities, and Nisibis, crossing the Euphrates; but everywhere I met with brethren; with Paul before me, I followed, and Faith everywhere led the way and served food everywhere, the Fish from the spring—immense, pure, which the pure Virgin caught and gave to her friends to eat forever, with good wine, giving the cup with the loaf. These things I Abercius ordered to be written thus in my presence. I am truly seventy-two years old. Let him who understands these things, and everyone who is in agreement, pray for Abercius.

Saint Athenagoras

If we were to grade each of the apologists with regard to content and style of writing, we should readily give Saint Athenagoras an "A." Of all the apologists, he is the most organized, the most convincing, and the most easily read. It is therefore all the more surprising, that antiquity says so very little about him. He is mentioned by Methodius in his *On the Resurrection of the Body,* and by Philip of Side who flourished in the fifth century in Pamphylia. Eusebius seems never to have heard of him, which is quite surprising considering the excellence of Athenagoras' writings. Two works have come down to us, the *Embassy for the Christians* (or *Plea for the Christians*) written about the year A.D. 177 and *The Resurrection of the Dead* written some time after that. The *Embassy* is addressed to Marcus Aurelius and Commodus (his son associated with him in the government); Marcus Aurelius died in A.D. 180 so the *Embassy* would have been written prior to that date. Athenagoras was probably an Athenian, and he may have actually gone on an "embassy" to the Roman emperors to state the case for the Christians.

The usual charges against Christians were the familiar ones of atheism, cannibalism, and immorality, and Athenagoras sets about to answer these symtematically and cogently. Unlike Tatian and Theophilus, he views pagan culture in its best light, and asserts that the classical poets inclined strongly to a belief in monotheism. His approach, then, to the idea of God is more philosophical than theological; it was not that he did not acknowledge revelation or the Scriptures, but he felt a reasoned approach would be more acceptable to the pagan mind. Now it must be remembered that this "pagan mind" never grasped the notion of creation out of nothing and always supposed that divinity was encased in the universe, but never was to be found outside of it. Athenagoras thus proceeds to establish the fundamental point: that God and matter are totally alien from each other—God being eternal and uncreated, while matter is perishable and created—and a wide gulf exists between the two. The pagan notion that deity must be composed of stuff ($v\lambda\eta$), however rarified it might be, is simply unacceptable. But the idea of creation out of nothing was never attained by the ancient mind, it was actually a revelation to be found only in the Hebrew Scriptures.[1]

123

Using the poets and philosophers as guides, Athenagoras proceeds to establish the existence of God, using (in the main) arguments from causality. The established order, the universal harmony, the magnitude, the color, the form, the arrangement of the world are not explicable in themselves, but argue to a Designer, a Creator and Sustainer. And the best tradition of the Greek philosophers is that this God is one, unique. Nor let it be supposed that this is some sort of a corporate god, one in being, but having many parts, like Socrates. Athenagoras disposes of this objection by a curious and somewhat tortuous line of reasoning about two divinities being unable to occupy the same space simultaneously. It is therefore logically impossible for God not to be One. And this one God is also eternal, all-wise, all-powerful, all-knowing, although incomprehensible, and not only does he create the universe of matter, but he sustains it as well.

The power of God is so great that nothing is really able to oppose it—this disposes of Empedocles and his doctrine of Love and Strife—for if anything *had* placed itself in opposition to God it would have ceased to exist, its structure being destroyed by God's power and might. This suggests that even Satan may will the evil but work the good.

Athenagoras has a good deal to say about the providence of God. God preserves all things in being and superintends them by his knowledge, and since he does not need anything, it is silly to offer him holocausts or attempt to placate him with burnt offerings.[2] This providence extends to the most minute detail and especially to man's body and soul, which will be subject to judgment in the resurrection.[3] The governance of the universe is carried on by the angels who are especially appointed for that purpose. This is the basis for the Christian hope in the resurrection, the knowledge that not the slightest detail escapes the notice of God and that all things will have to render an account at the last.

Other attributes include the justice and goodness of God, although less is said about his forgiveness and mercy, albeit these can easily be inferred. Athenagoras frequently uses very inspiring language in his description of the divine attributes, and there is likewise a graciousness of style that is less prominent in the other apologists.

According to Plato, immaterial forms or ideas were eternally in the divine Mind, and this is a convenient vehicle for Athenagoras to expound his doctrine of the Logos. But for him, the Logos is invariably associated with the Holy Spirit, and he does not speak of one without reference to the other. The Logos is to be equated with the Son of God, nor let anyone think it laughable that God should have a Son![4] The Son of God is the Logos of the Father in both idea and operation—in idea, in that he is one with the Father in power, spirit, understanding, and reason; and in operation, in that he is the energizing power of all material things which lay like a nature without attributes and an inactive earth. This seems to suggest that primate matter was in existence before it received form through the mediating power of the Logos. In another passage[5] Athenagoras says that men who reckon the present life of very small worth are conducted to the future life by this one thing alone—that they know God and his Logos, the oneness of the Father with the Son and the communion of the Father with the Son. In another, he declares that the Son is the mind, wisdom, and reason of the Father,[6] and in still another: all things have been subjected to God and the Logos which comes from him, who is conceived by us as his Son inseparable.[7]

The Holy Spirit, which is most evident when prophetic utterances are being made, is an effluence of God, flowing from and being carried back, as a ray of the sun. The Spirit is in union with the Father and Son, with whom it has a fellowship of power. Just as light flows from fire, the Spirit flows from God. While nowhere does Athenagoras personalize the Spirit, the evidence is really too scant to say that he denied to the Spirit personality.

Although the relationships of Father, Son and Holy Spirit are not clearly worked out in Athenagoras, nonetheless it is clear that he held a Trinitarian conception of God. All three were united or made one with respect to power, the power of any one Person being at the command of the other Two. The Holy Spirit is a somewhat more shadowy figure than the Father or Son, but the triad is not complete until he is mentioned. Since Christians worship Father, Son and Holy Spirit they can hardly be called atheists, and while Athenagoras has thought through neither his concept of the Spirit nor the Trinitarian relationships, nonetheless his references to the Trinity are frequent and unequivocal. Yet nowhere does he equate Christ with the Logos.

God has created noetic natures or angelic intelligences to serve in the universe, or rather in specific parts of the universe. The more ethereal angels are benevolent, but the angel in charge of matter (the devil) is a malevolent foe of mankind. He is the great opponent of God insofar as we can speak of God's having any opponent at all. Evil then is the result of angelic natures who have chosen to rebel against their divine natures and to create havoc in the universe by upsetting its order. Some of the demons are merely the souls of the giants who were born when the sons of God fell in love with the daughters of men and in a lustful union produced these monstrosities. All of this is reminiscent of the apocryphal writing *The Book of Enoch,* for example; Adam and Eve, however, are not mentioned.[8] In spite of this demonic element, the universe is still an orderly place, an instrument in tune and moving in well-measured time. But if the world is such a place of harmony and beauty, all the more reason for worshipping the Creator of it.

God has created man of two component parts—body and soul.

Man's excellence is due to the fact that God has stamped his own image on him. In judging man, God brings both body and soul under judgment, since it is the entire man who is judged. In the work *On the Resurrection of the Dead,* Athenagoras affirms repeatedly that God will reunite the souls and bodies of man. If some impiously believe this impossible, they are reminded that nothing is impossible with God, who is quite able to take care of such problems arising from cannibalism or natural processes. It is impossible to deny that the resurrection is a logical possibility and since man is created for God and responsible for his deeds, a judgment of man is required in order to show that the universe is a moral affair, created to reflect the splendor of its Maker. It is to Athenagoras that we owe our first long and detailed analysis of the resurrection of the dead, and he performs a fine job in collecting all the arguments that can be adduced for this very important but likewise difficult doctrine. It is a carefully reasoned, logical, and philosophical approach calculated to be just as convincing as a more theological line based mainly upon authority.

In his address to the emperors Marcus Aurelius and Commodus, Athenagoras says very little about the distinctive features of Christianity. The Incarnation, the earthly life of Jesus, the equation of Christ with the Logos, the nature of the church, the sacraments—there is scarcely an allusion to any of these topics. All of this is no doubt played down in order to meet the specific charges leveled against Christians, which charges would have come to the notice of the emperors. But he does rest his case heavily on the Old Testament Scriptures which are from God and in which are recorded the ancient prophecies. Just as a flautist blows into his flute, the Holy Spirit made use of such men as Moses, Isaiah, Jeremiah, and the other prophets. There are a few quotations from New Testament writings, but of course the canon of the New Dispensation has not yet reached final form.

The elaborated doctrine on the resurrection of man's soul and body forms the basis of Athenagoras' ethical stance. Compared with their pagan accusers, the life of Christians is of the highest moral quality. Its fundamental base is derived from the twofold Christian precept of love of God and love of neighbor plus the acceptance of the Ten Commandments of Moses. Chapters 11, 12, 32, 33, 34, 35, and 36 of the *Embassy* are devoted to a discussion of Christian morality, for here lies the strongest weapon he has for refuting the charges of atheism, cannibalism, and indecency. Athenagoras suspects that much of the hostility against Christians is a concealed envy of their chaste behavior. "The harlot reproves the chaste," he says, and Christians are falsely accused of the actual practices of pagans. There follows a long section on the chastity of Christian marriage, and the desirability of avoiding second marriages, which he calls only a specious adultery. Virginity and celibacy are to be preferred, for they bring a person nearer to God, while the indulgence of carnal thought and desire lead away from him. There is a charming little admonition with regard to kissing. He cites the Logos as having taught that "if any one kiss a second time because it has given him pleasure [he sins]"; adding, "Therefore the kiss, or rather the salutation, should be given with the greatest care, since, if there be mixed with it the least defilement of thought, it excludes us from eternal life."[9] Abortion and infanticide are likewise condemned, as well as the cruelty of the gladiatorial encounters with wild beasts in the arena. All of this is against *reason,* and it is the reasonable man who is likewise the ethical man, for he knows that for all of his actions he must render a strict account to God.

History did not deal kindly with Athenagoras. He seems to have been overlooked by his contemporaries, and even later generations paid him extremely scant notice. Yet he was one of the most gracious and cogent apologists of the second century, and presented the world with a reasoned plea for the Christian way of life. He was preeminently a philosopher who did not reject revelation, but rather played it down in an effort to convince his contemporaries that the Christian Gospel was the only rational way to live. He can be eloquent in discussing the nature of God even though some of his logical argumentation is not acceptable.

In his doctrine of the Logos Athenagoras follows that of Saint Justin, but his explicitation of the Trinity is clearly set forth, if not worked out in detail. His view of the universe is one of harmony and order, with the stress laid on causality and purpose; its beauty argues to the loveliness of its Creator. He describes accurately the nature of man and carefully delineates the functions of both soul and body in the human composite. An entire treatise on resurrection, judgment, and immortality shows him to be a pioneer thinker in this most important area. Evil for Athenagoras was the result of demonic influence coupled with the misuse of man's free will. The Christian ethic, which contrasted so painfully with its immortal environment, was the only rational way to live, and if men were reasonable they would adopt it unhesitatingly. The case for Christianity is thus presented to the emperor by an apologist of the first rank who unfortunately suffered from a real lack of public image. Had he been read and pondered more widely, the church might have made even quicker strides in its conquest of the mind and heart of the Roman Empire.

NOTES

The text is that of Geffeken, translated by Joseph Hugh Crehan in *Ancient Christian Writers* (*see* Bibliography).
1. *Embassy* 4 (*A Plea for the Christians*).

2. Ibid., 13.
3. *On the Resurrection of the Dead* 18.
4. *Embassy* 10.
5. Ibid., 12.
6. Ibid., 24.
7. Ibid., 28.
8. Cf. Henry A. Lucks, *The Philosophy of Athenagoras: Its Source and Values* (Washington, D.C.: Catholic University of America Press, 1936) p. 55.
9. *Embassy* 32.

The Muratorian Canon

In 1740, an Italian scholar, archivist, and historian, Lodovico Antonio Muratori discovered the oldest known canon of the New Testament in the Ambrosian Library at Milan. The fragment, which seemed to be from the eighth century, apparently comes from the monastery at Bobbio. It can be dated with a fair degree of accuracy, for of the *Shepherd of Hermas* it says that this "was written quite lately in our times in the city of Rome by Hermas, while his brother Pius, the bishop, was sitting in the chair of the church of the city of Rome; and therefore it ought indeed to be read," but not as part of the accepted canon. Dates for Pius I are 142-155, so the Muratorian fragment is from the latter half of the second century.

Several suggestions have been made with regard to authorship: Clement of Alexandria, Melito of Sardis, Polycrates of Ephesus, Pope Victor, Pope Zephyrinus, or possibly the antipope Hippolytus. The poor Latin style of the fragment suggests that it is a translation from a Greek original.

The canon asserts that all the Johannine literature is from the Apostle John. The traditional Pauline letters are accepted, but the two letters to the Laodiceans and the Alexandrians are declared forgeries, since they suit the heresy of Marcion. Valentinus and Miltiades are rejected along with the Asian founder of the Cataphrygians and Marcion's new Psalm Book.

Rome seems to be as good a guess as any for the place of compilation; there is rather an authoritarian tone in the fragment, which suggests that it may be directed against such persons as the priest Caius who questioned whether Saint John had written both the Fourth Gospel and the Apocalypse. The fragment goes on to say that there is really only one Gospel after all, even though various ideas are taught in the several books of the Gospels. "Yet it makes no difference to the faith of believers, since by one sovereign Spirit all things are declared in all of them concerning the Nativity, the Passion, the Resurrection, the conversation with his disciples and his two comings, the first in lowliness and contempt, which has come to pass, the second, glorious with royal power, which is to come."

V

THE SCHOOL OF
ALEXANDRIA

Alexandria was an intellectual center of the Roman Empire, noted for its museum and libraries, and boasting a cosmopolitan culture. At an early date the Catechetical School had been established by the principal bishop of the city to aid in instructing converts, and before long the celebrated Pantaenus had paved the way for the school's two most illustrious teachers: Clement and Origen. At a later day both Arius and Athanasius presented their rival theologies against an Alexandrian background, and still later the great Cyril gave definitive form to fifth-century Christology.

The School of Alexandria was characterized by the tendency to allegorize the Scriptures and to stress the divine unity, with the express intention of making an appeal to the more thoughtful intellectuals of the great city. Here the great Philo had lived, and all took their cue from him, Jew and Christian alike. Whether one understands "school" in the institutional or in the intellectual sense, certain it is that there was a large number of people over several centuries who were inspired and guided by it. But it is with the third-century thinkers Clement and Origen that we are here principally concerned, and to whose leadership and thinking we now turn.

Saint Clement of Alexandria

Although born probably in Athens, Saint Clement spent most of his life in the bustling seaport of Alexandria, that potpourri of nationalities founded by the great Alexander himself, and which had become the second largest city in the Roman Empire by the third century. Here was located the catechetical school for Christian instruction, presided over by Pantaenus and later by Clement himself and then the celebrated Origen. Clement was born sometime during the middle of the second century and was perhaps in his middle thirties when he reached Alexandria at the end of the reign of Marcus Aurelius (180). Under Septimius Severus sharp persecution broke out against the Christians in 202-3, and Clement left the city never to return. Whether he retired to Cappadocia, and whether he is the Clement referred to as residing in Antioch in 211 by Bishop Alexander, is somewhat conjectural. His death occurred some time around the year 215.

Clement was principally a scholar and a man of letters, well read in Greek philosophy and characterized by enormous cultural erudition. This is not to say that he may not also have been a man of affairs and an activist in the Christian community, but what we know of him points rather to the former. His style of writing is disparate and frequently lacking in order—deliberately so, but it is broad in scope and cheerful in tone, elevated and dignified in style and with an originality which is peculiarly Clement's. His major works which have come down to us are four: *Protreptikós,* an apology for Christianity in the traditional manner; *Paidagogós (Christ the Educator),* a sort of pastoral and moral theology book; the *Stromateis,* a kind of anthology in eight books, the last of which is a closely reasoned treatise on logic and epistemology; and finally there is *Quis Dives Salvetur? (What Rich Man Will Be Saved?)* a sermon on how the wealthy may best enter the Kingdom of Heaven.

For Clement, the true *gnosis* is Christianity itself, it is the culmination in all the best of Greek thought and culture, as well as being the fulfillment of Moses through the divine Logos. Clement's attitude toward secular culture, then, is quite the opposite of that of Tertullian; he feels that pagan culture often adumbrates the Christian Gospel.

Clement's writings are saturated with Scriptural quotations, but these are not always accurate because not infrequently he seems to be quoting

133

from memory. Yet his copious use of Scripture also contains a difficulty— Clement was in the habit of allegorizing the literal meaning of Scripture almost out of existence. His is the scholarly mind at work, neither guided nor hampered by an authoritative interpretation of Scripture by the church. His purpose is to make Scripture acceptable to the Gnostic, and in interpreting the Old Testament he takes his cue from Philo, and for the New Testament his own imagination in exploring all the possible latent symbolism in Holy Writ. His thinking is saturated by Scripture, which he then turns to his own purpose. In *Hypotyposeis (Outlines)* of which fragments survive, Clement attempted a complete commentary on virtually all of Scripture. He says he could adduce ten thousand Scriptures of which not "one tittle shall pass away" without being fulfilled; for the mouth of the Lord the Holy Spirit hath spoken these things.[1] Scripture, therefore, was divinely inspired and through it God issued his gracious call to men. We cannot wholly adopt Clement's principles, says Tollinton, but his permanent interest lies in the fact that he exemplifies the fundamental importance of the right to interpret the Scriptures, he also illustrates the place and function of learning, as contrasted with that of authority, and he ever shows a delight and an enthusiasm for it.[2]

Genuine disappointment greets us when we turn to Clement for information about the church. The latter half of the second century saw the crystallizing of doctrine and the hardening of church discipline, and surely these tendencies would be evident in as large a city as Alexandria, visited by Saint Mark himself, according to tradition. Whether Alexandria was behind in its development or whether Clement was temperamentally disinterested in that sort of thing is hard to say. The *Christ the Educator* indicates quite clearly the hierarchical constitution of the church, and in the *Stromateis* he testifies to the unity of the church, which is ancient and true and enrolls the just person according to God's purpose.[3] In the nature of the One, then, is associated (in a joint heritage) the one church, which resists those who strive to cut it asunder into many sects. The church is like a virgin mother, a virgin because she is undefiled, a mother because she is full of love. Calling her children about her, she nourishes them with milk that is holy: the Infant Word.[4] In the sermon *What Rich Man Will Be Saved?* Clement singles out Peter as being preeminent in the establishment of the church, while John in his later life emerged from seclusion to appoint bishops.[5] But this is about the sum of it; Clement's references to the church are specific, but they are few and brief.

Turning to Clement's doctrine of God, we are told that he is a Being difficult to grasp and apprehend, ever receding and withdrawing from him who pursues. It is perhaps a truism to say that Clement's God is ontologically distant but dynamically near. The aim of philosophy, when pursued with a right course of conduct, leads through Wisdom, the Artificer of all things, to the Ruler of all.[6] But to ask for proofs for the existence of Providence is to ask for punishment; it is impious to think that the whole of prophecy and the economy in reference to a Savior did not take place in accordance with Providence. And perhaps one should not even attempt to demonstrate such points, the divine Providence being evident from the sight of all its skillful and wise works which are seen, some of which take place in order, and some appear in order.[7] And if the workings of Providence were not sufficient to demonstrate the existence of God, there is always conscience and self-knowledge, for if anyone knows himself, says Clement, he will also know God.[8] For to all men whoever they are—especially those engaged in intellectual pursuits—a certain divine effluence has been instilled, so that they must confess (even reluctantly) that God is one, indestructible, unbegotten, and that somewhere above in the tracts ($νωτα$) of heaven, in his own peculiar appropriate eminence, where he surveys all things, he has an existence both true and eternal.[9] For there was always a natural manifestation of the one Almighty God, among all right-thinking men and most of them who had not quite divested themselves of shame with respect to the truth, apprehended the eternal beneficence in divine Providence.

God is both indivisible and infinite, but it is difficult to say very much about him. If we speak of God as the One, or the Good, or Mind, or Absolute Being, or Father, or God, or Creator, or Lord, we speak not as supplying his name, but for want of it; each of these terms does not express God, but all taken together are indicative of the power of the Omnipotent. For predicates are expressed either from what belongs to things themselves, or from their mutual relation. But none of these are admissible in reference to God. Nor any more is God apprehended by the science of demonstration for this depends on primary and better-known principles, but there is nothing antecedent to the Unbegotten.[10]

Our knowledge of God rests largely on knowing what God is not, for God as First Cause is not in space, but above both space, and time, and name, and conception. God is not capable of being taught by man, or expressed in speech, but is known only by his own power. If we abstract all that belongs to bodies and things called incorporeal and cast ourselves into the greatness of Christ, and then advance into immensity by holiness, we may reach somehow to the conception of the Almighty by way of negation.

God knows all things present and future, and possesses from eternity the idea of each thing individually. In one glance he views all things together, and each thing by itself. Many things in life, says Clement take their rise in some exercise of human reason, having received the kindling spark from God. Even the thoughts of virtuous men are produced through the inspiration of God, so that God knows at a glance all things. But Clement has little to say about salvific will, predestination, reprobation or election of individual souls.[11]

Clement presents us with a clearly explicated doctrine of the three divine Persons. The Father of all is one, the Word who belongs to all is one, the Holy Spirit is one and the same for all. The loving and kind Father has rained down the Word, it is he himself who has become the spiritual nourishment of the saints. The Word of God does all things, teaches all things, uses all things to educate us, and hence he is rightly called Christ the Educator. Father and Son are Teacher and Educator along with the Holy Spirit. Yet Clement clearly distinguishes between the Son and the Father; the Father alone is the timeless and un-originated First Principle, the Remoter Cause, the most ancient and the most beneficent of all. Christ as the Logos is coeternal with the Father, generated by the Father but coexistent with him. The Logos acts as a kind of intermediary between God and the world, but if the Logos is capable of activities inconsistent with the nature of the Godhead, mediation must involve some degree and phase of subordination. Is Clement then a subordinationist? If he lived a century later, would he be in the Arian camp? Tollinton says that Clement did not anticipate the issues which divided Alexandria a century later, "nor can we be surprised if, in an age when Christianity was first beginning to think out its theology, conceptions subsequently regarded as incompatible found an equal status and acceptance in the thought of a great teacher, more generous than rigidly systematic in his outlook."[12] In a word, Clement looks both ways; a case can be made out for either side. The same holds true for the personality of the Logos. The Logos is personal, but he is more than personal. And he can also be described in impersonal terms, almost suggestive of Sabellianism. But in general, the personal terms predominate.

The Logos is denominated the Creator of the World, and its Teacher; it is he who has created man, and pours out his love upon man and appeared in the latter day, that as God he might afterwards conduct us to the life that never ends.[13] The divine power, casting its radiance on earth, has filled the universe with the seed of salvation. Assuming the character of man, and fashioning himself in flesh, the divine Word enacted the drama of human salvation. He dawned from his Father's counsel quicker than the sun, with the most perfect ease he made God to shine upon us. He showed himself to be the Herald of the Covenant, the Reconciler, our Savior, the Word, the Fountain of life, the Giver of peace, diffused over the whole face of the earth, by whom the universe has already become an ocean of blessings.[14] The Savior, is then truly most manifest Deity, Who at the same time has assumed humanity. The purpose of all this is to redeem man from sin, for the first man when in paradise succumbed to pleasure, and seduced by lusts, grew in disobedience. But the Savior clothed himself in flesh, vanquished the serpent, and enslaved the tyrant death, thus setting man free from corruption. The Lord was laid low, and man rose up; and he that fell from paradise receives as the reward of obedience something greater than paradise—namely, heaven itself.[15] So the purpose of the Incarnation was to effect the salvation of men, and this Christ does through his suffering and death. The rest of Christ's life, while not rejected by any means, is soft-pedalled; Clement seldom dwells on the earthly life of Jesus; he has virtually nothing to say about the Blessed Virgin.

What is Clement's view of the sacraments? The purpose of baptism is to enlighten us and to make us adopted sons; becoming adopted sons, we are made perfect, and becoming perfect, we are made divine. The ceremony of baptism is called "free gift," "enlightenment," "perfection," and "cleansing"—"cleansing," because through it we are completely purified in our sins; "free gift," because by it the punishments due to our sins are remitted; "enlightenment," since by it we behold the wonderful holy light of salvation, that is, it enables us to see God clearly; and finally it is called "perfection" since nothing further is needed. What more is needed beyond the knowledge of God?[16] The effect of baptism is a spiritual regeneration in which sin and its punishment are removed and there is an infusion of sanctifying grace. "We may summarise the scanty information he gives us," Tollinton says, "by saying that with Clement, Baptism is mainly for adults, after careful preparation, administered by immersion, conditional upon a confession of the faith, and followed by unction, by the sign of the Cross, by the laying on of hands, and by the tasting of the milk and honey. His references are in substantial agreement with what we know of the church's practice from other authorities for this period."[17]

With regard to the Eucharist, which by this time had probably become separated from the agape, Clement clearly indicates his belief in the Lord's real presence in the sacrament. "The Word is everything to His little ones, both father and mother, educator and nurse. 'Eat My flesh,' He says, 'and drink My blood.' He is himself the nourishment that He gives. He delivers up His own flesh and pours out His own blood. There is nothing lacking His children, that they may grow."[18] The Eucharist is a union of drink, and the Word, a very wonderful gift of great praise, and those who partake of it are sanctified in body and soul. The blood of the Lord may be understood in a twofold sense: one is corporeal, redeeming us from corruption, while the other is spiritual, with which we are anointed. To drink the blood of Jesus is to participate in his incorruption. The Spirit is the strength of the Word in the same way that the blood is of the body. Similarly, wine is mixed with water and the Spirit is joined to man; the mixture provides feasting that faith may be increased, while the other, the Spirit, leads us on to incorruption.[19]

The Eucharist was instituted for the life of the soul, real food becoming spiritual food. But Clement has little to say with regard to the sacrifice of the Mass. He says even less about penance—only a passing reference to perfect and imperfect contrition. The fear of the Lord remains forever, and therefore those who from fear turn to faith and righteousness will likewise abide forever.

We have considerable evidence in Clement of the hierarchical structure of the church. In *What Rich Man Will Be Saved?* he tells us that the apostle John left the island of Patmos and returned to Ephesus in order to appoint bishops, as well as to set in order whole churches and to ordain such as were marked out by the Holy Spirit.[20] The grades in the church of bishops, presbyters, deacons, are imitations of the angelic glory, and in one passage he adds to this list widows whom he proposes to deal with in another place.[21] So they also have a special consecration to God, even though they do not constitute a rung in the hierarchical ladder.

The sacrament of matrimony produces an indissoluble union, according to the *Stromateis,*[22] from which there is no release, says Clement, citing a number of Scripture passages from the New Testament. He adopts a position midway between the libertine free love of a Carpocrates, who would deny the necessity of marriage at all, and the Encratite position of a Tatian, who would exalt celibacy at the expense of marriage. For Clement, Christian marriage seems to be the ideal state for most people. He has a good deal to say about the model Christian family and the Christian home, and betrays a detailed knowledge of the physiological aspects of marriage, but at the same time he is never inspirational in his discussion of the sacrament of marriage. It may be questioned whether he was married himself, and while the balance of probability is in favor of his having been married, it is still possible that he is speaking from the bachelor's point of view. His picture of married life is endowed with charm, sobriety, and love, but it never reaches an exalted position of a Saint Teresa or a Saint Bernard. He is well aware of the church as the bride of Christ, but this New Testament figure never receives any developed treatment on his part.

In discussing the last things, Clement cautions his flock against hasty judgment. We are not to judge who is worthy or unworthy, we may be mistaken in our opinion. In the uncertainty of ignorance it is better to do good to the undeserving for the sake of the deserving, than by guarding against those who are less good to fail to benefit the worthy. For in trying to ascertain those who should receive meritoriously or not, it is possible for you to overlook some that are loved by God.[23]

Various signs will precede the end of the world. The dead will rise in the resurrection and their souls will return to their bodies, both joined to one another according to their peculiar nature, adapting themselves, through the composition of each, by a kind of congruity like a building of stones.[24] In the *Stromateis* Clement sums up the whole process of restoration of all things in Christ. For the man of faith, knowledge is added, and to this, love, and to love, the inheritance of the Kingdom. In this way man ascends along with Christ to where God the guardian of our faith and love is. Knowledge is committed to those fit and selected for it and leads us to the perfect and endless end, teaching us beforehand the future life that we shall lead, after we have been freed from all punishment and penalty which we undergo, in consequence of our sins, for salutary discipline. The reward and the honors are assigned to those who have become perfect, after they have finished their purification. Finally, having become pure in heart and near to the Lord, they are restored to everlasting contemplation, and are called gods, being destined to sit on thrones with the other gods already placed there by the Savior.[25] In his emphasis on knowledge as a way to life, Clement is echoing the Gnostics and borrowing from them language which would be acceptable to their peculiar position.

In *Protreptikós (Exhortation to the Heathen)* Clement exposes to ridicule, as many had done before him, the absurdities of paganism and the heathen mysteries with their absurdities of the dying and rising god. Idolatry and image worship came under special attack as well as the whole traffic of iconography that goes with it. Yet, it must be remembered that the philosophers and the poets sometimes hit upon the truth, although accidently, and if this be so, is it not an impiety to forsake the religion of our ancestors? No; the coming of Christ is of such immense value that it is like receiving gold for brass, a hundred oxen's worth for that of nine, as witness Glaucus in the *Iliad*. The *Exhortation* concludes with the admonition to abandon the erroneous old ways in favor of Christ's way, and his instructions.

The *Christ the Educator* purports to show the young believer how to improve his soul and to train it to perform a virtuous, not an intellectual life. This is a manual for all—men, women, and children alike. There is a long discourse on eating, and the gluttony which demands oysters from Abydos, the eels of the Maeander, and reddish-brown dried figs, on account of which the Persians unhappily marched into Greece. Proper drinking habits come under like scrutiny, followed by the proper dishes to serve food in at first-class feasts. Laughter and filthy speaking are subjected to comment, and then follows some rules for people who are living together. Clement becomes so explicit on these matters that most translators prefer to leave this section in the original, well aware that only scholars can transcend the suggestiveness of such delicate matters! Clothes, shoes, and excessive fondness for gold jewelry form the subject of instruction; for example, women are to be allowed a white shoe, except when on a journey, and then a greased shoe must be used.[26] All of this leads to a discussion of true beauty, and then a long disquisition against men who embellish themselves. When attending the baths, proper behavior is mandatory at all times. Clement even encourages exercise as part of the good life. Coiffures, cosmetics, rings, amusements, walking, conduct in and out of church, the government of the eyes, as well as love and the kiss of charity and religion in ordinary life come under the purview of the Instructor. The entire treatise concludes with a prayer to the divine Paedagogue, and a hymn.

The *Stromateis (Miscellanies)* is by all odds the longest of the three major works of Clement, and was perhaps only a collection of materials which he planned to weave later into an overall systematic outlook. There is again the idea that Greek philosophers were not totally wrong, and since they did attain some truth, Greek philosophy can lead us to a proper understanding of the divine. Although philosophy is in a sense the handmaid of theology, it can direct us toward moral action and even some knowledge of God himself. And so, some culture has value in its own right, and human knowledge is essential in a right understanding of what the Scriptures teach us. But a far more valuable knowledge is to be found in the Old Testament of the Jews, where Moses, the divine lawgiver quite exceeds Plato in stature. Indeed, the Greeks are but children when compared to the Hebrews. This leads to a discussion on the necessity of faith, for it is by faith that we gain true knowledge. Knowledge leads to a realization of sin and a necessity for repentance with a strict adherence to the moral law, and this is what distinguishes the true from the false Gnostic. The third book of the *Stromateis* (usually left in the original) is devoted to continence. Suffering and martyrdom occupy Clement's attention in the fourth book and give occasion to discuss the real meaning of love, and the need for true perfection which can all be summed up in the knowledge and love of God. This leads to a further consideration of the three theological virtues of faith, hope and love in the fifth book and a discussion of symbolism in the presentation of the mysteries of the Gospel. Returning again and again to his favorite theme that philosophy leads to true knowledge, there is finally a description of the true gnostic as one who possesses a right knowledge of the world but despises worldly things in his pursuit of perfection.

In the sermon *What Rich Man Will Be Saved?* it is apparent that even in the time of the martyrs there were people sufficiently affluent to require the warning that it "is easier for a camel to go through the eye of a needle than for a rich man to enter into the Kingdom of Heaven." Although the rich young man was directed to go and sell all that he had, this saying is not to be applied to everyone indiscriminately. Riches which benefit also our neighbors are not to be thrown away, but he who carries his riches in his soul instead of God's Spirit is certainly on the downward path away from the Kingdom of Heaven. The superfluity of riches is a real hindrance to the spiritual life because of the very real obstacles which they interpose, but the barrier is not insurmountable and the rich man can be saved, although with difficulty. The sermon ends with the charming story of the apostle John who braved a band of robbers to claim its chief for Christ, a young man who had formally been an exemplary Christian, but had swung to the opposite extreme. Clement's point is that continued repentance as well as detachment from riches is the best safeguard to entering into eternal life.

And so it is that Clement attempts a rapprochement between the Christianity of his day and Greek philosophy. He is well aware that for many, Greek philosophy is the same as heretical Gnosticism, and both should be avoided like the plague. And yet philosophy looms large in Clement's thinking precisely because he feels that this is the rational approach to a religion essentially mystical. It is hard to say whether the emphasis in his thought lies more with Christianity than it does with Greek philosophy; they both interact on each other to point to a truth which is the concern of each. It is philosophy freed from a false gnosis which is Clement's main concern. Hence, he stands in sharp contradiction to those who would have no traffic with the speculations of the Greeks and would with Tertullian shout "away with it." Although ordinary Christians might well live uncontaminated by the true gnosis, for Clement, the true gnosis was not the speculations of a Basilides or a Valentinus, but Christianity itself, to which philosophy was the rational avenue. Since philosophy was actually the handmaid of theology, Clement envisaged a large systematic picture which would combine the insights of philosophy with the mystical revealed truth of Christianity. It was with this end in view that he wrote his three major works, and it is a pity that he was never able to produce the work which would present in detailed analysis a "summa" of the best that the Greek and Christian traditions had to offer man. In this respect he stands in sharp contrast to his contemporaries who saw the proposition in terms of either-or. Clement desired to show that philosophy, when cleansed of its gnostic speculations, was not the enemy but rather the ally of the new faith which had lately entered the world in order to save mankind.[27]

NOTES

The text is in Migne, *Patrologia Graeca*, vols 8, 9; Wilson's translation is in *The Ante-Nicene Fathers*, vol. 2 (*see* Bibliography).

1. *Protreptikós* 9.

2. R. B. Tollinton, *Clement of Alexandria: A Study in Christian Liberalism,* vol. 2 (London: Williams and Norgate, 1914), p. 228 ff.
3. *Stromata* 7. 17.
4. *Christ the Educator* 1. 6.
5. *What Rich Man Will be Saved?* 42.2.
6. *Stromata* 2. 2.
7. Ibid., 5. 1.
8. *Christ the Educator* 3. 1.
9. *Protreptikós* 6. 68.
10. *Stromata* 5. 12.
11. Ibid., 6. 17.
12. Tollinton, *Clement of Alexandria,* vol. 1, p. 347.
13. *Protreptikós* 1. 7.
14. Ibid., 10. 110.
15. Ibid., 11. 111.
16. *Christ the Educator* 1. 6.
17. Tollinton, *Clement of Alexandria,* vol. 2, pp. 141-42.
18. *Christ the Educator* 1. 6.
19. Ibid., 2. 2.
20. *What Rich Man Will be Saved?* 42. 2.
21. *Christ the Educator* 3. 12.
22. *Stromata* 2. 23.
23. *What Rich Man Will be Saved?* 33.
24. *Adumbrationes in 1 Peter* 1. 3.
25. *Stromata* 7. 10.
26. *Christ the Educator* 2. 12.
27. Eugene de Faye, *Clément d'Alexandre: Étude sur les Rapports du Christianisme et de la philosophie Grecque* (Paris: Leroux, 1906).

Origen

Alexandria seems to have been the city in which Origen was born, probably about the year 185. His father Leonides gave him a splendid education and soon recognized that his son possessed more than ordinary ability. During the persecution under Septimius Severus in 202, Leonides was beheaded, and his wife succeeded in restraining her son from volunteering his own life, only by the drastic measure of hiding his clothes. The oldest of seven children, Origen supported his family by teaching grammar and literature while the bishop of Alexandria, Demetrius, secured him an appointment in the Catechetical School. Perhaps it was the later martyrdom of several of his students which pushed him to embrace an austere life and to take quite literally the injunction in Matt. 19:12 that "some have made themselves eunuchs for the Kingdom of Heaven's sake."

At Alexandria Origen came into contact with Clement, if not Pantaenus, and soon became famous himself as a teacher. Deeply interested in philosophy, he plunged into a thorough study of Neoplatonism as taught by Ammonius Saccas, and enrolled in the Philosophical School in order to broaden and deepen his own effectiveness as a Christian teacher. By the year 211 the Christians of Alexandria were no longer subject to persecution, and Origen had the opportunity to journey to Rome and to Arabia (Jordan). But he was driven into hiding when Emperor Caracalla, stung by some verses lampooning him in connection with the murder of his brother Geta, wreaked vengeance on the city by massacring a number of its citizens. Origen's exile in Caesarea in Cappadocia enabled him to visit Palestine, and he even preached in Jerusalem, although not yet ordained a priest. This action annoyed his own bishop, Demetrius (perhaps not altogether free of envy), who at once summoned Origen back to Alexandria. The year 230 finds him in Greece, adjudicating a dispute with some heretics, and since his route lay through Palestine, he stopped off and received ordination at the hands of friendly bishops there. This so infuriated Bishop Demetrius that he declared Origen's ordination illicit and convoked two synods to confirm his decision. In 231 Origen again left Alexandria to teach at Caesarea in Palestine—preferring the unity of the church to a possible schism resulting in his defiance of the bishop, and to his native city he never returned. His later life involved him in a number of activities, but teaching was always his first love, and he numbered among his illustrious pupils such greats as Gregory Thaumaturgus and Firmilian of Caesarea. In 250, the emperor Decius made a systematic attempt to root out Christianity from the empire, and thanks to his prominence Origen was a ready target. He was thrown into jail and savagely tortured, but subsequently released upon the death of the emperor. His health shattered, he lingered for a few years more, dying at the age of sixty-nine in the year 254. The cathedral of Tyre marked his resting place with a monument which existed until the thirteenth century.

A cradle-genius, Origen combined ascetic piety with monumental scholarship. He was no stranger to the slings and arrows of outrageous fortune, but managed always to rise above personal tragedy with a modesty and charm of great magnetism. On numerous occasions he was forced to be gracious to lesser men who suspected his orthodoxy as well as his personal motives. He exercised enormous influence over his students, was never lacking in benefactors and patrons, and admired by all, even those who could not altogether agree with him. Subsequently, the history of his ideas (Origenism) was to result in considerable ecclesiastical controversy and to force the church to a careful evaluation of the monumental contribution which he had made to her life and thought.

The *Hexapla,* or *Sixfold Bible,* is perhaps Origen's greatest work. It consists of six columns of Old Testament text: the Hebrew text in Hebrew characters, the same in Greek, plus the Greek translations of Aquila, Symmachus, the LXX and Theodotion. It is the first synoptic study of the Old Testament on a truly grand scale, and was consulted by no less a person than Saint Jerome himself years later in his work on the Latin Vulgate. Virtually the entire Bible was subject to Origen's exegesis; his commentaries, homilies, and scholia for a large part of his literary remains. A fairly early work is *On First Principles* a sort of catechetical manual not altogether free of erroneous doctrine in spite of Rufinus's later attempt to clean it up. It was written some time during the third decade of the third century; the first book deals with God and the angels, the second with creation and the fall of man and his redemption through Christ, as well as the last things. The third book deals with moral theology, and the fourth, Scripture.

The eight books *Against Celsus* are directed against the pagan philosopher who maintained that Christianity was pure fraud, and that its remarkable growth and diffusion rested on truths and presuppositions which amounted to a grand hoax. It is a late work in which Origen attempts to answer his critic line by line, and while Origen is not altogether convincing, his apologetic defense of Christianity is well-nigh exhaustive.

Then there are the shorter tracts *On Prayer* and the *Exhortation to Martyrdom* as well as two letters, one to Gregory Thaumaturgus and the other to Julius Africanus. A papyrus found in 1941 contains the *Disputation with Heraclides* and *On the Pascha*. Thanks to later writers, we have a considerable amount of biographical detail with regard to Origen, and while it must be used with caution, it enables us to draw a fairly extensive portrait of the great third-century Alexandrian, resulting in knowledge far more satisfactory than what we have regarding his predecessors.

Since Sacred Scripture looms so very large in the writings of Origen, we may well begin here to examine his doctrine of inspiration. That all Scripture is inspired by the Holy Spirit, Origen states explicitly in his commentary on the Psalms;[1] and in the homilies on Jeremiah, we are told that the prophets spoke from the fullness of the Holy Spirit, nor is there anything in prophecy, nor in the Law, nor in the Gospel or Saint Paul that has not come to us from the fullness of the Holy Spirit.[2] The aim of inspiration is to deal with those matters which touch primarily our salvation, yet covering all the Scripture and extending somehow even to the very words themselves. Eusebius tells us that Origen held as inspired only those accepted by Catholic tradition, and then proceeds to list the Old Testament canon, including the Books of the Maccabees. Four, only four, Gospels are recognized as authentic, and Origen doubts that the Letter to the Hebrews is actually by Paul, supposing it to be by Clement, Luke, or someone else.[3] But it is the same Holy Spirit who inspires the entire Scripture, whether it be in the Old or the New Testament, and the aim of the Spirit is to impart truth to the minds and hearts of men. Now it is necessary to read Scripture on various levels; the obvious sense of Scripture must be accepted first, but it may well be the least important part of Scripture, for there is a deeper spiritual truth which may even be clothed in allegorical language. Just as man may be described in Neoplatonic terms as body, soul, and spirit, Scripture may be taken in its literal, its ethical, or its spiritual sense. And to attain the spirit of Scripture is far more important than being bound by a slavish literalism, which Origen had once learned to his great regret. For example, the evangelists are not to be condemned if they sometimes deal freely with things which to the eye of history happened differently, and changed them to serve the mystical aims they had in view. They proposed to speak the truth (where it was possible) both materially and spiritually, and where this was not possible it was their intention to prefer the spiritual to the material. The spiritual truth was often preserved, Origen declares, in the "material falsehood."[4]

We may well be surprised that Origen not infrequently repudiated the literal sense of Scripture, but we must remember that he had constantly to guard against a too Jewish literalism and a too Gnostic allegorism.

Many feel that he went too far, and that he forced the Scriptures to yield through allegory what his restless mind demanded for answers to speculative questions.[5] In this respect he goes far beyond Philo, who for all his allegorizing had some regard for the literal and historical "Sitz-im-Leben" of the Old Testament text, but in his Homily on Leviticus, Origen says "Compared with the Gospel, the law is like those earthen vessels which the artist forms before casting the statue in bronze; they are necessary until the work itself is finished, but their utility ceases with the completion of the statue."[6]

What Origen lacked, and needed most of all, was a proper doctrine of the historical development of the Scriptures. The idea of progressive revelation would have undergirded his conviction that the Scriptures were always to be understood in a spiritual sense, and a few in Old Testament times had long realized this, but with the New Covenant what had formerly been realized by only the few, was now the common conviction of the many. It is Origen's great tribute that he brought to bear his full powers upon the interpretation of Holy Writ, but it is likewise sad that so much of his effort was dissipated in fruitless speculation.

The Alexandrian school was (on the whole) benign in its regard for pagan philosophy, and Origen reflects to a similar degree the toleration which Clement had had for the great Greek writers. However inadequate they both might view philosophy's knowledge of God, man, and immortality, they did consider it as a stepping stone to truth rather than a hostile impediment to it. Certain it was that the visible things of the world argued to a creator who must Himself be invisible, for from sense objects of the world man could reason to non-sensible invisible beings, and from these to a knowledge of the invisible God whose power is eternal. For God, in his love for men, has manifested his truth which is known not only to those who devote themselves to his service, but also to some who are far removed from the purity of worship and service which he requires.[7] The admirable order of the world is so plain to all that it compels us to worship the Maker of it as One Cause of one effect, and since it is wholly in harmony with itself, it cannot on that account have been the work of many makers.[8] And this is obvious to everybody, for it is written in the hearts and consciences of men. For that reason, says Origen, no one will have any excuse when God comes to judge him.[9]

The beauty of his creation and the loveliness of his creatures assures us that God himself is Supreme Beauty, existing not in a body but as an uncompounded intellectual nature. He is the mind and source from which all intellectual nature, or mind, takes its beginning. He admits of no addition of any kind, so that greater or less cannot be applied of him, but he is One and Unique.[10] In his treatise *On Prayer*

Origen reminds us that God is not in heaven in a local sense or in a physical place, for this would be tantamount to saying that God has a body, and hence divisible, material, and perishable. He is everywhere and fills all creation,[11] is incomprehensible and incapable of being measured and exceeds any knowledge we have of him either by perception or reflection.[12] And so, although no one is able to speak with certainty of God the Father, it is nevertheless possible for some knowledge of Him to be gained from visible creation and the natural feelings of the human mind.[13]

God knows all things present and future through one single intuitive act,[14] but this is not to say that things happen because God foreknew that they would. Origen always safeguards the element of human freedom; foreknowledge of an event does not thereby remove the possibility of its happening or not. The future event itself, which would have taken place even if it had not been predicted affords the occasion to the one gifted with foreknowledge of foretelling its occurrence. This problem will occur again in Saint Augustine; suffice it to say here that Origen has not yet produced a satisfactory synthesis of human freedom with God's omnipotence. The problem of predestination will require further and deeper plumbing.

By the time of Origen, the doctrine of the Trinity is common coin; the preface of the *De Principiis* states this clearly enough, and it is elsewhere, too, in the *Commentary on John,* for example.[15] The *Commentaries on Romans* distinguish the three members of the Holy Trinity while maintaining the unity of their nature.[16] Origen then goes on to discuss them individually. In the *Commentary on John,* he states that only the Father is unbegotten, while all things were made by the Logos, and that the Holy Spirit is the most excellent and the first in order of all that was made by the Father through the Word.[17] The son is coeternal with the Father, and consubstantial with him.[18] We worship the Father of truth, and the Son, who is the truth; and these, while they are two, considered as persons or subsistences, are one in unity of thought, in harmony and in identity of will. So entirely are they one, that he who has seen the Son has also seen the Father, for the Son is the image of God himself.[19] He is the Wisdom of God, his Splendor, his Logos.

The Holy Spirit is the result of the Father's generation through the Word, and is called the most excellent and first in order. Genesis 1:26 (Let us make man in our own image and likeness) is cited to show that the entire Trinity cooperated in the creation of the world and of man, a creation which embraces everything, and which came from nothing. Origen cannot understand how so many distinguished people can consider nature the result of mere chance, and thereby deny God's creative power or his providential administration of the world; they are impious who suppose that such a great work as the world could exist without an architect or overseer.[20] Nor does God have any other reason or desire to create apart from his own goodness, which is to say, himself.[21] The world was made, then, and took its beginning at a certain time, and will be destroyed on account of its wickedness. But this is not to say that something may have existed before the creation of the world, or that something may exist after it is destroyed; there is no clear statement on this in the church's teaching.[22]

God has created angels along with certain good influences which act as his servants in effecting the salvation of men; but it is unclear when they were created, of what nature they are, or how they exist.[23] Two angels are assigned to each one of us, a righteous and an evil angel who sponsor thoughts of one sort or another, but who are incapable of compelling our free will.[24] Why a human soul is acted on at one time by good spirits and at another time by bad is due, according to Origen, to certain causes of prior existence during which the soul contracted a certain amount of guilt in its sensitive nature, and so divine Providence has condemned them to this condition. The soul is always endowed with free will, whether in the body or outside of it; it was this doctrine of preexistence of souls which was to get Origen into trouble.[25] At any rate, man's free will is not subject to necessity, so that we are not forced to commit either good or evil, nor are we governed by the courses and movements of the stars. Whether the soul is derived from the seed by a process of traducianism—so that the reason or substance of it may be considered as placed in the seminal particles of the body—or whether the soul is bestowed on the body from outside is not distinguished with sufficient clearness in the teaching of the church.[26]

Origen cannot insist too strongly on man's free will, which has actually been exercised by preexistent spirits before their bodies were given to them. Therefore, a fall has occurred before the actual creation of the world, and God's purpose in creating the world was to help restore fallen spirits. And now Origen falls into line with Plato and adopts the threefold division of body, soul and spirit while at the same time rejecting any theory of the transmigration of souls. Yet somehow there is a hereditary contamination in all men as a result of the first man's sin. This is not to say that freedom has been totally destroyed and man utterly depraved and, in fact, there is even hope for the evil spirits and their ultimate repentance and salvation. Admitting therefore a hereditary taint, it is personal sin or virtue which determines whether a man will be damned or saved.

God the Word was sent as a physician to sinners, and this includes all men, contrary to what Celsus may think. So the healing power of Jesus Christ is requisite if man is to cease from evil, since there is no one who does not need the physician's care. God has revealed himself in four distinct stages. He has put the light of conscience into every man, although Origen clearly sees that this is insufficient for correct moral behavior. The Law and the prophets represent a further stage in the evolution of God's revealed mercy toward man. All of this has come to a fullness in the Christian Gospel where Christ stands as the fulfillment of the Law and the prophets. But even this is not the final word, for there is to be a Second Advent, Christ is to come again in all his glory and this will be the eternal Gospel which will supersede all other previous revelations.

But for all of this, grace is necessary. Human desire is not sufficient to attain the end, and spiritual athletes cannot gain the prize of the high calling of God in Christ Jesus without God's very own help. Just as we cannot piously assert that the production of full crops was the work of the farmer alone, so also our own perfection is brought about, not by us but by God who produces the greater part of it.[27] Yet, God's grace never destroys man's free will.

But beyond what is ordinarily understood by nature, there are certain things which go beyond nature's power which God can do at any time; this happens when God raises man above the level of human nature, causing him to pass into a better and more divine condition, and preserving him in the same as long as he who is the object of God's care shows by his actions that he desires the continuance of God's help. So man must dispose himself through faith and right action to the grace of God which effects his justification.[28]

In man's justification the Redeemer plays the all-important role. In the last days, as he had announced beforehand by his prophets, God sent into the world Our Lord Jesus Christ himself, who was a God next to the God and Father of all things. The soul and body of Jesus formed, after the οικονομια, one being with the Logos of God, who, when commanded, had obeyed the Father's will in creating the world. The Gospels, says Origen, do not consider him who in Jesus said, "I am the way and the truth and the life," to have been of so circumscribed a nature, as to have an existence nowhere out of the soul and body of Jesus.[29] And if it had been recorded that several individuals had appeared in human life as sons of God in the manner in which Jesus did, and each of them had gathered a party of adherents to his side, so that, a dispute would have arisen among the contending parties, each shouting, "Believe, if you want to be saved, or else begone!" then Celsus would have reason to be skeptical; but it has been proclaimed to the entire world that Jesus Christ is the *only* Son of God who has visited the human race.[30]

Christ is not only divine but also human, and for this reason throughout the whole of Scripture, not only is the divine nature spoken of in human words, but the human nature is adored by appellations of divine dignity. When we say that the Word became flesh we speak of a

union more intimate than that of a man with his wife. Christ also had a
human soul which elected to love righteousness, so that in proportion
to the immensity of its love it clung to it unchangeably and inseparably
with fixed purpose and immense affection. Christ's human and rational
soul which had no feeling for or possibility to sin was perpetually
placed in God so that it possessed immutability from its union with
the Word of God. Like an iron heated in the fire, Christ's soul radiated
a divine fire to other men. Was there a gradual glorification of Christ's
soul by the Logos, and the body by the soul? Origen suggests that
Christ's appearance varied according to the ability of different people
to receive him until finally he became pure spirit eternally united
to the heavenly Logos, and one with it.[31]

But Origen makes it clear that the nature of that deity which is
in Christ in respect to his being the only-begotten Son of God is one
thing, and that human nature which he assumed in the last times for
the purposes of the dispensation of grace is quite another.[32] Yet these
two natures are somehow united, as we have already seen. Origen is
perhaps the first to clearly enunciate the doctrine of the *communicatio
idiomatum*. If we consider Jesus in relation to the divinity that was in
him, the things which he did in this capacity present nothing to offend
our ideas of God, nothing but what is holy; and if we consider him as
man, unique because of his intimate communion with the Eternal Word,
with absolute Wisdom, he suffered as one who was wise and perfect
whatever it was fitting for him to suffer for the good of the human race.
His death was not merely an example of death endured for the sake
of piety, but also the first blow in the conflict which was to overthrow
the power of that evil spirit the devil, who had obtained dominion over
the whole world.[33]

The city of Alexandria had long harbored Gnostic sects which Clement
had combatted before the time of Origen. The desire to oppose these
Docetic tendencies compels Origen to insist on the real sufferings of
Christ, which were far from mere appearance. To say that Christ's
sufferings were unreal is to say that the resurrection is also unreal;
Christ really died and really arose from the dead, for to say that he only
appeared to die is likewise to make the resurrection an appearance.[34]
Yet for all his effort to combat the Gnostic tendencies toward Docetism,
Origen himself betrays upon occasion a kind of affinity for the very
position he desires to refute.[35]

The Incarnation was necessary because of man's sin, Origen tells
us when commenting on the Paschal lamb in the Book of Numbers
and in the *Commentaries on Matthew*.[36] We are saved from sin and
slavery to the devil. Christ effects our redemption in the manner of a
true sacrifice offering vicarious sacrifice in a superabundant measure.
Origen thus gives us a somewhat elaborate theory of the atonement.

Christ's death upon the cross and his resurrection dealt a crippling blow to the devil, who had hoped by possession of Christ's soul to dupe the entire human race.

In the third homily on Joshua, Origen states that no one may be saved apart from the church.[37] Christ himself teaches his church, which contrasts with other local assemblies as a beacon to the world. Even the inferior members of the church are more excellent than many who belong to the assemblies in the different districts. Could it have come to pass without divine assistance, Origen asks, that Jesus, desiring to spread his words and teaching, should have been so successful, that everywhere throughout the world not a few persons—Greeks as well as barbarians, learned as well as ignorant—adopted his doctrine, so that many struggled even to death in its defense rather than deny it? Jesus successfully accomplished works beyond the reach of human power. For although from the very beginning, all things opposed the spread of his doctrine in the world—the princes of the times, and their captains and generals, and all who had the slightest amount of influence—yet the spread of the Gospel proved victorious because by its very nature it could not be overcome.[38] The church is established upon solid rock and unshakeable foundation.[39] But beyond this, Origen does not elaborate, possibly because his experience with bishops and other clergy was not always a happy one.

In order that the sacraments may have efficacy, some faith is necessary on the part of the recipient. The sacrament of baptism was foreshadowed in the Old Testament by the cloud and the sea in Exodus, and the Eucharist by the heavenly manna which fell in the wilderness.[40] The Trinitarian formula must be used[41] and not merely the name of Jesus, and all must be baptized alike—adults and children—because all have been born in sin. Origen enumerates seven different types of baptism for the remission of sins: the first through water, the second through martyrdom, the third through almsgiving, the fourth when we forgive those who sin against us, the fifth when we convert a sinner from the error of his way, the sixth through an abundance of charity, and the seventh when we deplore and bewail our sins in a penitential manner.[42] The apostolic tradition was to baptize even children, he declares in the *Commentary on Romans.*[43]

Christ is really present in the Eucharist under the species of bread and wine, and the truth of his presence follows from the sacred words of institution.[44] But Origen also says that it is not the material of the bread but the word which is said over it which is of advantage to him who eats it not unworthily of the Lord; and these things indeed are said of the typical and symbolical body.[45] This is a good example of Origen's penchant for emphasizing the spiritual or mystical interpretation of the Gospel, perhaps in order to bridge the gap between himself and the position of the Gnostics. But it is sometimes not altogether clear whether the presence of Christ in the sacrament is or is not dependent upon the faith and dispositions of the recipient. He does say that that which is sanctified through the word of God and prayer does not, in its own nature, sanctify him who uses it, for, if this were so, it would sanctify even him who eats unworthily of the bread of the Lord. So, if there is to be any fruitful reception of the sacrament, the recipient must be in the "state of grace." Of the Eucharist or Mass as sacrifice, Origen says little.

The sacrament of penance receives considerable attention. Christians lament as dead those who have been vanquished by licentiousness or any other sin, because they are lost and dead to God; those who lapse and fall during time of persecution may be subsequently received back into the church, but they forfeit any office or post of rank.[46] Public penance is the implication here; for less serious sins, a private penance would suffice. And, of course, contrition through a perfect act of love would always justify the sinner. But, in general, some external act was required along with the confession made to God alone, and especially if a third party had been injured in any way by the actions of the sinner.[47] The sinner had to make a specific self-accusation of sin[48] but could confess privately to a priest.[49] Charity, prayer, and good works can help to wipe out venial sins.

There is no doubt that Origen suffered more than once from the hands of the hierarchical church as personified by his own bishop of Alexandria, Demetrius. The sacrament of orders is reflected more in Origen's life than in his writings. In the treatise on prayers there is reference to the consecrated deaconesses or widows in the early church, and we are painfully aware of all the difficulties attendant on Origen's own ordination. Perhaps the silences or absences of testimony here speak more loudly than any articulated discussion of the sacrament of holy orders would. Origen may well have felt that the clerical hierarchy was one of the less appealing aspects of the church.

It is God who has joined together two people in one so that they are no longer two "but one flesh" and so marriage according to the Word of God was a "gift" just as holy celibacy was likewise a gift. An indissoluble bond results which permits neither party to remarry as long as the other partner is still living. Origen complains that some rulers of the church have allowed this, contrary to the explicit teaching of the Gospel, and he then proceeds to preach a little moral theology. Both husband and wife should receive sexual satisfaction as well as being solicitous of the other, and failure to do so can result in sin on the part of each parner, which sin is really more attributable to him who withholds the marriage debt. So, careful discernment might declare that the real adulterer may be more the person who creates the situation than he who commits adultery.[50] Whatever is allowed in practice the Gospel is nonetheless clear on this point.

The *Homilies on Jeremiah* state that once we die, our destiny is clearly fixed for good or bad, and our formation in this life is at an end.[51] The apostolic teaching is, Origen assures us, that the soul, having a substance and life of its own, shall, after its departure from the world, be rewarded according to its desserts, being destined to obtain either an inheritance of eternal life and blessedness, if its actions shall have procured this for it, or to be delivered up to eternal fire and punishments, if the guilt of its crimes shall have brought it down to this; and also that there is a time of resurrection from the dead, when this body which now "is sown in corruption, shall rise in incorruption," and that which "is sown in dishonor will rise in glory" (1 Cor. 15:42).[52] But we do not maintain, Origen insists, that the body which has undergone corruption resumes its original nature, any more than the grain of wheat which has decayed returns to its former condition. But we do maintain, that as above the grain of wheat there arises a stalk, so a certain power is implanted in the body, which is not destroyed, and from which the body is raised up in incorruption.[53]

Origen now propounds his famous doctrine of the restitution of all things in a state of unity when God shall be all in all. And this result, he tells us, must be understood as being brought about, not suddenly, but slowly and gradually, seeing that the process of amendment and correction will take place imperceptibly in the individual instances during the lapse of countless and unmeasured ages, some outstripping others, and tending by a swifter course toward perfection, while others again follow close at hand, and some again a long way behind. Thus, through the numerous and unaccounted orders of progressive beings who are being reconciled to God from a state of enmity, the last enemy is finally reached, who is called death, so that he also may be destroyed, and no longer be an enemy.[54] Even the conversion of the devil is at least a possibility, for as long as there is free will, there is also the possibility of repentance, and who knows that ultimately all will not be converted to righteousness, given a sufficient amount of time? It's an open question which the reader may opt for or not, as he will.[55]

This process of restoration of all things in the unity of God might require worlds upon worlds, in short, a plurality of universes. In the meantime, Origen says, both in those temporal worlds which are seen, as well as in those eternal worlds which are invisible, all those beings are arranged, according to a regular plan, in the order and degree of their merits, so that some of them in the first, others in the second, some even in the last times, after having undergone heavier and severer punishments, endured for a lengthened period, and for many ages, so to speak, improved by this stern method of training, and restored at first by the instruction of the angels, and subsequently by the powers of a higher grade, and thus advancing through each stage to a better condition, reach even to that which is invisible and eternal, having traveled through, by a kind of training, every single office of the heavenly powers.[56]

There is no denying the magnificent sweep of Origen's thought with its vast speculative range and its heightened sense of imagination. He seems to reach across the centuries to Kant and his starry firmament and on to the cosmic majesty of science fiction as expressed in, say, *2001*. Nor is it correct to dismiss him as a dreamer sitting on cloud nine; he never loses sight of moral and practical considerations when he takes flight into the cosmic unknown. If his enemies thought him dangerous and heretical, they could hardly be accused of offering an orthodoxy which was equally as inspirational. Origen was led on by a consideration of the vast majesty of God, and the truly littleness of man's knowledge about him. He paints on a huge canvas and is a theological Titian or a Rubens. His system of thought did for the East, what Augustine was soon to do for the West, and his influence was enormous and incalculable. At least seven teachers followed him in the Catechetical School—Heraclas, Dionysius, Pierius—who had the reputation of being a second Origen—Theognostus, Peter the Martyr, Didymus, and Rhodon. But certainly the most eminent product of all was the great Athanasius, born at Alexandria at the end of the third century. However, the influence of Origen was not confined to the Catechetical School; it permeated Arabia, Palestine, and even Asia Minor, where it reached one of Origen's most famous pupils—Gregory Thaumaturgus. It was through such celebrated persons as Gregory that the ideas of Origen spread throughout the entire East. Even to his enemies and to those who most decidedly disagreed with him, his was a name and a system to be reckoned with.

Nor did everyone subscribe to the doctrines which were called Origenism. Despite the fact that certain passages can clearly be read in the orthodox sense, there are other passages in Origen which clearly suggest subordinationism, as illustrated in his doctrine of the soul of Jesus. The idea of the preexistence of souls and their fall in heaven resulting in their incarnation in bodies clearly lent itself to attack. The resurrection of the body which Origen seemed to take in a spiritual sense suggested that he denied this doctrine altogether. That all would ultimately be restored in God, evil spirits and possibly even the devil, seemed to contradict the clear New Testament teaching on the eternity of hell. And the continued creation of new worlds was really too large a thought for his opponents to grasp. So by the end of the third century Origen was already vulnerable. Methodius, Bishop of Tyre in Phoenicia, accused him of concocting fables about the eternity of the universe out of his head. But this is less serious than the failure to assert clearly the resurrection of the body, a doctrine which Origen seemed to spiritualize to too great a degree. The preexistence of souls is clearly taken from Plato, not from Christianity, and may show the great Alexandrian as too much influenced by current Neoplatonism. But then it is questionable that Methodius really understood the man whom he was attacking.

Eusebius, bishop of Caesarea and famous church historian, is without question very sympathetic to Origen. The impression is gained that those who attack the great Alexandrian do not really understand him. Meanwhile, translations into Latin were being made by no less than Hilary of Poitiers, Ambrose of Milan, and the young Jerome. The Cappadocian fathers, Basil and Gregory of Nyssa, as well as Gregory Nazianzus are obviously indebted to him for their theology. But the continuing controversy with the Arians in the fourth century seemed to many that Origen was more Arian than Nicene, and among some of the monks of the Egyptian desert he was particularly anathema. Finally, at a synod held in Alexandria in 399, Origen was condemned, whereupon the Egyptian monks who had upheld him, were forced to flee to Constantinople. Here they were befriended by John Chrysostom, who soon after was indiscreet enough to compare the empress to Herodias, and was seized and banished in 404. The controversy died down after that, but in 496, Pope Gelasius condemned Origen's writings with the exception of those which had been translated by Jerome. This was followed in 538 by a condemnation on the part of Emperor Justinian, who objected strongly to Origen's doctrine of preexistence. At that time the Christian world was agitated by monophysitism which resulted in the convening of the Fifth Ecumenical Council at Constantinople in 553. The Nestorian writings of Theodore of Mopsuestia, the polemical tracts of Theodoret of Cyrus against Cyril, and the letter of Ibas of Edessa were condemned (the "Three Chapters") along with Origen, who was listed as a more ancient heretic. And so, by the middle of the sixth century, the arguments which had swirled so long around the name of Origen, were brought to an end at least for the time being.

In our own day scholarly controversy has been renewed, thus raising the intriguing question: Is it possible to rehabilitate Origen? H. Crouzel, in his excellent article in the *New Catholic Encyclopedia* on Origen and Origenism (Vol. X, p. 772) says that "although statements that have given rise to Origenism are to be found in the works of Origen, all the arguments which serve for the refutation of Origenism can likewise be found there." The first step is to recover as far as possible the original text before it was colored by the translations of Rufinus (to make Origen more acceptable in the West), or the mystical emphasis of Evagrius Ponticus for ascetical purposes in the East. Thus, it can be shown, for example, that his doctrine of the ultimate restoration of all things was only a pious hope, and that his concept of a plurality of worlds was only a conjecture. As for the preexistence of souls, this can be viewed as merely a convenient way of refuting the Gnostic ideas of Valentinian. And one must always remember that "Origenism"— this collection of unacceptable ideas which were later integrated into a system quite repugnant to the orthodox—was drawn almost entirely from the *On First Principles,* an early work of Origen which he may well have repudiated in his more orthodox maturity.

Modern scholarship tends to view Origen in a much more favorable light. Space and time prevent a thorough examination of all the recent studies on Origen, but two especially must be mentioned. W. Völker *(Das Vollkommenheitsideal des Origenes,* Tübingen, 1931*)* rescued him from the nineteenth-century tendency to regard Origen more as a philosopher than a theologian and more a disciple of Plato than of Christ. After all, it is not for his philosophical speculations so much as his spiritual insights and theological profundity that Origen is to be remembered. Once he has been marked off from Origenism, he can be seen in a much more favorable light.

A second contribution, made by Henri de Lubac *(Histoire et esprit,* Paris, 1950*)* reminds us that Origen's exegesis of Scripture must be handled in a special way. This gives rise to the idea of the "Gospel in time" as opposed to the "eternal Gospel". The latter is only grasped completely by the soul in beatitude, whereas the "Gospel in time" can only be apprehended partially because of man's finite existence. All history revolves around Christ as its focal point, and Christ's mission was a prophetic announcement of the Kingdom of God foreshadowed by the characters and events of the Old Testament. Christ's coming abrogated the juridical and ceremonial precepts of the Law, and initiated a sacramental system of spiritual realities which now necessitates the understanding of Scripture in its spiritual rather than in its literal sense. One must always remember that the most traumatic experience of Origen's life came as a result of a too literal interpretation of Scripture, and for this reason he always emphasized in later life the mystical significance of Holy Writ. This is not to say that he abandoned the literal significance of Scripture altogether, but it is to remind us that Origen's exegesis of Scripture always proceeds along these definite lines. Whether or not a complete rehabilitation (along with his possible canonization) of Origen will be effected in the future remains at this date an open question. It would certainly do much to bring the churches of the East into closer communion with those of the West.

We may conclude this chapter by saying that actually it was the Augustinian synthesis which swallowed up Origenism in the West, which had always tended to shy away from an excessive mysticism, on the one hand, and intellectualism on the other. Moreover, the empirical evidence which supported a more somber anthropology seemed to belie the over-optimistic attitude of the East with regard to free will after man's fall from paradise. It is true that there are echoes of Origen in such men as John Scotus Eriugena and Erasmus and possibly even Teilhard de Chardin, but these have been the exception rather than the rule. Both because of intrinsic difficulties as well as historical reasons, the speculative system of the great Alexandrian failed to take hold in the Western church, and if it had more success in the East, it was ultimately to meet something of a dead end even there. To be sure, it survived "under false pretences" (as Prof. Chaim Wardi would say) in Syrian and Greek writers and even turns up in Evagrius Ponticus especially. But it was Augustinianism rather than Origenism which was to carry the day, nor does it seem likely that it will have any great renaissance in the future, but this too is only conjectural. Although they were wrong in their deplorable lack of charity toward him, his enemies, perhaps, were right in asserting that all was not well at the heart of this great synthesis of Alexandrian Christianity. Some centuries later Vincent of Lérins warned his readers that undue speculation which wandered from the deposit of faith was sure to end in disaster, as the unhappy case of Origen had so clearly illustrated. His warning was, on the whole, heeded in the West.

Yet for all of this, Origen stands very tall. Perhaps the best summary of him has been made by Saint Jerome in his letter to Pammachius and Oceanus, where he takes care to praise the commentator but not the theologian, the man of intellect but not the believer, the philosopher but not the apostle. He makes it quite clear that he himself was never an Origenist, and if people refuse to believe him, then he has ceased to be an Origenist. "So you want to extol Origen?" asks Jerome. "Praise him as I do. He was a great man from his infancy and son of martyrdom. He despised sensuality, and avarice he trampled under foot. He knew the Scriptures by heart and spent days and nights meditating on them. More than a thousand homilies come from him. He published innumerable commentaries. Who of us can read as much as he wrote? Who cannot but admire his burning love for Scripture? And if some Judas, jealous of his glory throws up to us his errors, we would say to him, 'Even the great Homer sometimes nods.' Powerless to follow his virtues, let us at least keep from imitating his faults."

NOTES

The text is in Migne, *Patrologia Graeca*, vols. 11-17 (*see* Bibliography).
1. *Commentary on Psalm* 1 No. 4.
2. *Homilies on Jeremiah* 21. 2.
3. Eusebius *Ecclesiastical History* 6. 25.
4. *Commentary on John* 10. 4.
5. Cf. William Fairweather, *Origen and Greek Patristic Theology* (New York: Scribner's 1901), p. 65 ff.

6. *Homilies on Leviticus* 10. 1.
7. *Against Celsus* 7. 37, 46.
8. Ibid., 1. 23.
9. Ibid., 1. 4.
10. *On First Principles* 1. 1.
11. *On Prayer,* chap. 23, n. 3.
12. *On First Principles* 1. 1.
13. Ibid., 1. 3.
14. *Commentary on Genesis* 3. 6.
15. *Commentary on John* 2. 10.
16. *Commentaries on Romans* 7. 13.
17. *Commentary on John* 2. 10.
18. *On First Principles* 4. 28; *Ex libris in epist. ad Hebraeos.*
19. *Against Celsus* 8. 12.
20. *On First Principles* 2. 1.
21. Ibid., 2. 9.
22. *On First Principles* 1. Praef.
23. Ibid., 1. Praef.
24. *Homilies on Luke* No. 12.
25. *On First Principles* 3.3.
26. Ibid., 1 Praef.
27. Ibid., 3. 1.
28. *Commentary on Romans* 7. 13.
29. *Against Celsus* 2. 9.
30. *Against Celsus* 6. 11.
31. Ibid., 2. 64.
32. *On First Principles* 1. 2.
33. *Against Celsus* 7. 17.
34. Ibid., 2. 16.
35. Cf. Fairweather, *Origen and Greek Patristic Theology,* p.183 ff.
36. *Homily on Numbers* 24. 1.
37. *Homilies on Joshua* 3. 5.
38. *Against Celsus* 1. 26.
39. *Homilies on Exodus* 5. 4.
40. *Homilies on Numbers* 7. 2; *Commentary on Romans* 3. 8.
41. *Commentary on Romans* 5. 8.
42. *Homilies on Leviticus* 2. 4.
43. *Commentary on Romans* 5. 9.
44. *Homilies on Exodus,* 13. 3; *Commentaries on Matthew,* series 85.
45. *Commentaries on Matthew* 11. 14.
46. *Against Celsus* 3. 51.
47. *Homilies on Luke* No. 17.
48. *Homilies on Leviticus* 3. 4.
49. Ibid., 2. 4.
50. *Commentary on Matthew* 14. 23, 24.
51. *Homilies on Jeremiah* 18. 1.
52. *On First Principles* 1. Praef.
53. *Against Celsus* 5. 22.
54. *On First Principles* 3. 6.
55. Ibid., 1. 6.
56. Ibid.

Saint Gregory Thaumaturgus

A declaration of faith attributed to Saint Gregory the Wonder-Worker by Saint Gregory of Nyssa is one of the few acknowledged writings which remain from one of the outstanding personalities of the third century. Saint Gregory clearly made an unforgettable impression on not only his own, but subsequent generations as well. An ardent disciple of Origen, his panegyric to that eminent Alexandrian stands as one of the first and finest attempts at Christian biography. After he and his brother had studied under Origen, Gregory later became bishop of Neo-Caesarea. The later stories of his working miracles show at least that here indeed was a charismatic personality whose brilliant mind and genuine piety deeply impressed his contemporaries. Little remains of his writing, and there is some doubt that the Declaration of Faith is actually genuine, but the weight of evidence favors its authenticity. It is not meant to be a complete creed, but only delineates the Trinitarian concept as Gregory understood it.

There is one God, the Father of the living Word, says Gregory, who is his subsistent Wisdom and Power and Eternal Image perfect Begetter of the perfect Begotten, Father of the only-begotten Son. There is one Lord, Only of the Only, God of God, Image and Likeness of Deity, Efficient Word, Wisdom comprehensive of the constitution of all things, and Power formative of the whole creation, true Son of true Father, Invisible of Invisible, and Incorruptible of Incorruptible, and Immortal of Immortal, and Eternal of Eternal. And there is One Holy Spirit, having his subsistence from God, and being made manifest by the Son to men δηλαδη τοις ανθρωποις.* Image of the Son, Perfect Image of the Perfect; Life, the Cause of the living; Holy Fount, Sanctity, the Supplier, or Leader of Sanctification, in whom is manifested God the Father, who is above all and in all, and God the Son, who is through all. There is a perfect Trinity, in glory and eternity and sovereignty, neither divided nor estranged. Wherefore there is nothing either created or in slavery in the Trinity; nor anything superinduced, as if at some former period it was non-existent, and at some later period it was introduced. And thus neither was the Son ever wanting to the Father, nor the Spirit to the Son; but without variation and without change, the same Trinity abides forever.

---

*Possibly a gloss.

VI

THE SCHOOL OF NORTH AFRICA

Tertullian, writing to Scapula in about 197, declares that many Christians were to be found at all levels of society in Carthage, so that Christianity must have been introduced into North Africa several years prior to that time. One characteristic of the church in this part of the empire was the large number of bishops, which seems to argue for quite small bishoprics. Sharp persecution broke out under Septimius Severus in 197, and again in 202, but it was brief, ceasing almost as suddenly as it had begun. The real time of testing would not occur until 250, when Decius would launch a systematic attack on Christianity throughout the entire Roman Empire.

Tertullian, Cyprian, and of course Augustine (who will be dealt with in a separate chapter) are the great names associated with the North African church. Their writings suggest a bent of mind less speculative and more practical than we find in the Alexandrian thinkers, and there is a prominent moral tone (in Tertullian's case a puritanical flavor) which one does not find in the East. The focus of interest is on man and his problems, with less emphasis on the speculative and the mystical.

The large number of works which survive testify to Tertullian's importance and the high regard in which he was held; he was a first-rate theologian and a trenchant stylist. Cyprian, with a better-bevelled personality, was clearly the heir of him whom he called "master," and the debt which the incomparable Augustine owed to both was by no means inconsiderable.

Minucius Felix

Minucius Felix is both a fascinating and an elusive figure. He may have lived any time from the early part of the second century to the latter part of the third. Saint Jerome says that he was a lawyer in Rome before he was converted;[1] he also had connections with North Africa. We do not know when the *Octavius* was written, although recent scholarship suggests that the date may be as early as 160.[2] Formerly thought to be a work of Arnobius, *Octavius* was restored to its rightful author in 1560 by Franciscus Balduinus. Ever since that time controversy has raged over the work because of certain parallel passages which are also to be found in Tertullian's *Apology*. Did Minucius borrow from Tertullian, or Tertullian from Minucius? Or did both borrow from a common source? The prose style of *Octavius* is polished Latin, reminiscent of Cicero and Seneca, whereas that of Tertullian is crabbed, terse, and brusque. Yet Tertullian has traditionally been credited with founding the North African Latin prose style of Christian writing in the latter part of the second century. But if *Octavius* was actually written as early as 160, then the palm must be ceded to Minucius Felix.

The *Octavius* is the report of a dialogue between three friends: Caecilius the pagan, Octavius the Christian lawyer, and Minucius (also supposedly a lawyer) who acts as a sort of referee. The disputation occurs on a trip to the marine baths of Ostia and begins when Caecilius makes a pious salute to a statue of Serapis, and is stung by a rebuke which Octavius addresses to Minucius. Thereupon, Caecilius offers a stout defense of paganism and challenges Octavius to refute him.

What follows is a careful statement of the case for paganism, something which has not occurred in any previous Christian writer. "The old-time religion was good enough for me," says Caecilius, and Christians ought not to meddle with it since it is clear enough that the world is governed by chance and that all things are doubtful and uncertain. Automatic forces operate without regard to any Providence; good men like Socrates suffer and wicked men prosper, and so the best way we can find happiness and wisdom is to follow the old maxim of "Know thyself." Christianity is a johnny-come-lately religion which is far inferior to time-honored paganism, proved by the fact Christians are ostracized by state and society, they practice unspeakable rites, and they talk nonsense. So people ought to remain faithful to the gods of Rome, since the new substitutions are far inferior to the traditional paganism. In fact, to neglect the gods is to invite disaster, for they it was who made Rome great.

Certainly Christianity has nothing to offer; Christians worship a crucified man and the head of an ass; they slaughter infants and drink their blood in initiation rites; they indulge in orgies in the dark; and whatever they do they try to conceal since they have no altars, temples, or images. Claiming that the entire universe is going to go up in smoke, they match this nonsense by saying we shall all rise with our bodies, the righteous to enjoy a blessed eternity and the wicked to burn in everlasting torture. If Christians have a hard lot in this life, it only serves them right for meddling in doubtful matters where the sanest approach is a healthy skepticism. Caecilius now challenges Octavius to refute if he can the charges against the Christians.

Octavius rejoins that the presence of Providence, law, and order prevailing in heaven and on earth argues to a Master and Author of the universe, one who is more beautiful than the stars themselves or anything on earth. God calls everything into being through his Word, arranges everything by means of his wisdom, and perfects it by his goodness. He is too bright for our sight—hence invisible, too fine for the touch of sense—hence intangible, and beyond our grasp, therefore, immeasurable. And the fact that there is but one God, Lord of all, is proven by the ordinary language of ordinary men and women when they say, "God is great," or "God is true," or "If God grant it." This is both the natural language of the common crowd as well as the prayerful profession of faith made by the Christian. The best poets and philosophers agree that God is really only One.[3]

Now follows the well-worn attack on the gods as being silly, irreligious, and immoral. Besides, many of the gods were originally men—great kings, statesmen, or benefactors; and other deities have had such absurd histories that people find them ridiculous and laugh about them. And some of the rites associated with various deities are downright disgusting.

It is significant that in the *Octavius* we have a rudimentary philosophy of history, for Caecilius had maintained that pagan piety had made the Romans great, but Octavius avers that the Romans were sacrilegious with impunity, started their territorial expansion as partners in crime, and simply were more ferocious than their enemies. Divine approval does not therefore guarantee political prosperity.

Why, then, are the Christians lied about, hated, and persecuted? This is the nefarious work of demons, the frequent answer of Christians to second-century ills and one that should be used more often by twentieth-century Christians. It is an obvious lie to say they worship a crucified criminal, for they believe that He was not only innocent, but He was God as well. Yet Octavius does not develop the Incarnation any further, although he has opened the door to a full discussion of the person and work of the God-man. The argument takes instead another tack: the very crimes that Christians are accused of are actually committed by their impious neighbors, and this leads to the oft-heard argument that Christian virtue is the very opposite of pagan vice. "We prove our modesty," says Octavius, "not by external appearance but by character; with a good heart we cling to the bond of one marriage; in our desire for offspring we have only one wife or none at all. The banquets we conduct are distinguished not only by their modesty, but also by their soberness. . . . Chaste in conversation and even more chaste in body, very many enjoy the perpetual virginity of a body undefiled rather than boast of it. In short, the desire of incest is so far from our thoughts that some blush even at the idea of a chaste union."[4]

The idea of a general conflagration at the end of the world was not a foreign one to Stoic thinking, and as we shall see, the *Octavius* is directed especially to a Stoic audience. But the idea of personal immortality would not be readily acceptable to the Stoic mind, and upon this belief Octavius dwells at length. It matters not what happens to the body on earth, nor the way in which it is buried since it still exists for God, the Preserver of the elements. And, indeed, we are consoled by the fact that all nature hints at a future resurrection. "The sun sets and rises again; the stars sink below the horizon and return; the flowers die and come to life again; the shrubs spend themselves and then put forth buds; seeds must decompose in order to sprout forth new life. Thus, the body in the grave is like the tree in the winter, which conceals its live sap under an apparent dryness. Why do you urge that in the depths of winter it should revive and return to life?"[5] And so, Christians have everything to hope for, since if they are righteous they will be rewarded with unending happiness, but evil men will have to endure eternal torment. And just as Etna and Vesuvius and other volcanoes all over the world burn without being exhausted, so hell is sustained by the bodies consigned to it.

Octavius's address is so admirable that Caecilius declares he has been vanquished by it, and all depart rejoicing—Caecilius that he has conquered his misgivings, Octavius that he has conquered Caecilius, and Minucius that each of the others has triumphed—a sort of Gilbert and Sullivan ending.

Now, the singular thing about the *Octavius* is that it actually contains very little theology which is distinctively Christian. In fact, it is the *omissions* in the tract which may be the most eloquent part of it. There is virtually nothing about Christ himself—that he had a miraculous birth, or is the Second Person of the Trinity, or that he is the Logos become flesh. Since Minucius does not describe man as under the dominion of

Satan, sin, and death, there is really no need for a Redeemer. When
Caecilius accuses the Christians of worshipping a crucified criminal, this
is denied, but no further explanation is offered about the Person of
Christ, indeed the discussion seems almost deliberately sidetracked.
Nothing else about him is mentioned—his preaching, his miracles, his
resurrection or his ascension. There is no mention of the Trinity, or the
work of the Holy Spirit, or of actual and sanctifying grace. Rather than
citing the Scriptures, Minucius shows a decided preference for the pagan
philosophers. There is no mention of the church or its hierarchical
structure, not a hint of Christian liturgy or worship, and we look for any
reference to any of the sacraments in vain. Previous writings are far
more informative than the *Octavius;* why is it that here the Christian
message seems to be reduced to a rigid monotheism, a strict ethic, and the
promise of future rewards and punishments?

Some scholars have maintained that Minucius was a modalist,
and that salvation for him consists in embracing the true Christian
sapientia or wisdom which is to know God as revealed by God. Thus,
Christianity is the rational religion, the true philosophy, and the *insita
sapientia,* the wisdom which has always dwelt within man, and only
needs to be revealed for what she truly is.[6]

Baylis suggests that Minucius deliberately adopts an approach which
by its very deficiencies would be the most effective method of bringing
a certain type of person into the church. Caecilius is not a skeptic, but a
religious young man who has had the wrong type of religious up-
bringing and merely parrots the popular prejudices against Christians
which he has picked up in the street. All that Minucius is trying to do
is to demolish the case for paganism, and this he does by showing that
Christianity is not new at all, but is implied already in the most
reverenced and ancient authorities. And this, for the present, is enough.
Minucius does not appeal to the divine inspiration of the Scriptures because Caecilius can claim that Homer is equally inspired. If the starting
point be taken with Christ as the Son of God, Caecilius may retort with
a reference to Jupiter's various "incarnations." If Minucius begins with
the crucifixion and resurrection, Caecilius may think that this merely
is a great man who has been raised to divinity. Far better, then, to be
silent on specific dogmas and simply to establish the Unity of God
and Providence, and this is precisely what Minucius does. At the end
of the dialogue, Caecilius has not actually accepted Christianity because
he has not heard enough of it, but the ground has been cleared of
previous prejudice and Caecilius has admitted enough to line himself up
with the Christian catechumens, and this is all that Minucius is trying to
do.[7] One of the great virtues of Cicero throughout the ages is that
people have read him, and being an admirer of Cicero, Minucius is
trying for the very same thing. He realizes that he will soon lose his

reading audience if he launches immediately into the distinctive features of Christianity. So he avoids this by attempting to clear the ground of prejudice, and establish some very simple propositions which will lead to the acceptance of Christianity as the only reasonable religion which is already implied in the best pagan tradition. And since his literary style (like that of the *Letter to Diognetus*) easily gets "A" on the report card, this is precisely the approach which will be the most effective with a sophisticated Roman reading public. Moreover, if the works of Tertullian should also happen to be available (adopting now a later date than 160 for Minucius) the interested can make further inquiry about the faith from him.

The *Octavius,* then, is a kind of "come-on" for young sophisticated Roman pagans, and Minucius Felix is a "front man." Its intention is by no means to present a complete exposition of the Christian faith, but it is a cleverly written propaganda piece intent on destroying the "old-time" pagan religion and thus clearing the way for an acceptance of the really "old-time" Christian religion. To expect more than this is altogether to miss Minucius Felix's objective.

NOTES

A translation of the text by R. E. Wallis is in *The Ante-Nicene Fathers,* vol. 4 (*see* Bibliography).
1. Jerome *De Viris Illustribus* chap. 58
2. Cf. Harry James Baylis *Minucius Felix and His Place Among the Early Fathers of the Latin Church* (London: S.P.C.K., 1928), p. 201 ff.
3. *Octavius,* chaps. 18, 19
4. Ibid., chap. 31.
5. Ibid., chap. 34.
6. Cf. Jakob Jan de Jong, *Apologetiek en Christendom in den Octavius van Minucius Felix,* (Maastricht: Boosten & Stols, 1935), p. 124 ff.
7. Baylis, *Minucius Felix,* p. 145 ff.

Tertullian

What little knowledge we have of the life of Tertullian (ca. 160-222(?)) comes principally from Saint Jerome[1] who says he was "a presbyter, the first Latin writer after Victor and Apollonius, a native of the province of Africa and city of Carthage, the son of a proconsular centurion: he was a man of a sharp and vehement temper, flourished under Severus and Antoninus Caracalla, and wrote numerous works, which, as they are generally known, I think it unnecessary to particularize. I saw at Concordia in Italy an old man named Paulus. He said that, when young, he had met at Rome with an aged amanuensis of the blessed Cyprian, who told him that Cyprian never passed a day without reading some portion of Tertullian's works, and used frequently to say, 'Give me my master,' meaning Tertullian. After remaining a presbyter of the church until he had attained the middle age of life, Tertullian was by the envy and contumelious treatment of the Roman clergy driven to embrace the opinions of Montanus, which he has mentioned in several of his works under the title of the New Prophecy; but he composed, expressly against the Church, the Treatises *de Pudicitia, de Persecutione, de Jejuniis, de Monogamia,* and six books *de Ecstasi,* to which he added a seventh against Apollonius. He is reported to have lived to a very advanced age, and to have composed many other works which are not extant."

Some have questioned whether he was actually a cleric since two treatises addressed to his wife have come down to us, but these are not irreconcilable facts and anyhow, celibacy of the clergy was not enforced until the eleventh century. Whether it was at Rome or at Carthage that he functioned as a presbyter is uncertain, but he certainly resided in each city at different times of his life. Obviously there was a "personality clash" between him and the Roman clergy, but whether this was the main reason for joining the party of Montanus is likewise a moot point. He seems to have been a convert, but this, too, is conjecture. The only certain date we have for the entire life of the great North African is the year 207, for in the fifteenth year of the reign of Septimius Severus he wrote the first book against Marcion. The remainder of his works offer rather scant internal evidence with regard to their possible date of composition; they fall into three main groups: the Catholic

168

writings, the Montanist writings, and those which cannot be labelled either Catholic or Montanist.

Probably too much has been made of the fact that Tertullian joined the party of Montanus, apparently around the year 200; his adherence to the party "of the strict observance" furnishes a puritanical flavor, less of a puritanical content to what he says. It is interesting to surmise what might have, or might not have happened to Tertullian in a more ecumenical age. It was the belief of Montanus and the people associated with him that the spirit of prophecy would remain in the church until the second coming of Christ; prophets, therefore, should occupy an important place in the church because they might be recipients of new or modified revelation. Montanus began to prophesy in the latter part of the second century in Phrygia in Asia Minor, along with two female associates, Maximilla and Priscilla (or Prisca). The Montanists acknowledged both the Old and New Testaments, the doctrine of the Trinity, the resurrection of the dead. They expected the heavenly Jerusalem to descend to a desolate spot in Phrygia where formerly the town of Pepuza lay located. The New Prophecy, as it was called (and it was generally accompanied with ecstatic transports), looked askance at marriage—if not positively forbidding it. It actually did forbid second marriages, and encouraged a life of celibacy, strict fasting, and general austerity. After all, this was the best preparation for the New Jerusalem where the saints would reign for a thousand years. In keeping with this austere stance the Montanists refused absolution to those guilty of sexual offenses and refused to grant that the church had the power to absolve the sins of adultery and fornication. They viewed martyrdom as a welcome finale to the Christian life, and rejected flight in the time of persecution as well as money-deals as a pledge for safety. Since the end of the world was soon to be expected, this would involve the collapse of the Roman Empire, the advent of Antichrist, followed by the Second Coming. All of this was not exactly calculated to win friends and influence people connected with the Establishment.

It is hard to say how much Tertullian was influenced by his Montanist friends. The influence may have been greater than appears in his writings since he may be speaking with prudence and caution without attempting to force upon others what he is actually convinced of himself. Yet scholars have found it necessary to try to classify his works according to whether or not the Montanist influence is prominent. Scholars generally agree that his Catholic writings include: *On Penance, On Prayer, On Baptism,* the two letters *To His Wife, To the Martyrs, On Patience, Against the Jews,* and *The Prescription Against Heretics.* The Montanist writings are represented by: *Against Marcion* (all five books), *On the Soul, On the Flesh of Christ, On the Resurrection of the*

Flesh, Against Praxeas, Scorpiace, On the Crown, On the Veiling of Virgins, An Exhortation to Chastity, On Flight in Persecution, On Monogamy, On Fasting, On Modesty, and probably *To Scapula, Against the Valentinians, On the Spectacles, On Idolatry,* and *On the Apparel of Women. The Apology (Apologeticus), To the Nations* (both books), *On the Testimony of the Soul, On the Pallium* and *Against Hermogenes* defy classification.[2] Twelve of his works have been lost.

Tertullian is one of those writers who "suffer most in translation." His style is notably terse, epigrammatic, suggestive more than explicit, and often witty and sarcastic. Sometimes a word or a phrase defies translation, and while his style is entertaining and indeed delightful, the course of his thought is occasionally difficult to follow and virtually impossible to summarize. Most of his works are in Latin, although he also knew Greek and occasionally used that language; it has been suggested that he was bilingual. His writings are often suggestive of legal pleadings and court procedure techniques, and he may have been a lawyer—in fact, there has been an attempt to identify him with a certain Tertullian who was a famous lawyer, but since the name is not an uncommon one, the evidence on this matter has been inconclusive. Tertullian is the first writer from whom we have received a considerable corpus which is probably only about three-quarters complete; this shows that antiquity took some care to preserve his thinking, and his personality loomed large on the scene despite his later Montanist aberrations. His influence on Saint Cyprian turned out to be enormous, and both were influential on Augustine, who acted both as a stimulus to medieval scholasticism as well as the Protestant Reformation. The Anglican church has always found in him a kindred soul because of his theological orthodoxy while at the same time being out of communion with Rome.

Tertullian's writings always deal with a specific problem or situation and are directed to commenting on the occasion which has evoked the difficulty. Some violence is done to his works when one attempts to make an overall survey of his thinking, because one is dealing with "legal briefs" where Tertullian's intention is far from presenting a summary of his thinking. I shall have occasion later to make more specific comments on some of his works, but for the modern reader it is perhaps of more interest to discover the main outlines of his thought since many of his occasional writings deal with problems and situations no longer relevant to our times. Tertullian was a polemicist whose crabbed style and barrister approach often outweigh his content and subject him to the accusation of being lopsided. For all these shortcomings, however, he stands as the great molder of Latin style in North Africa, and the first really great theologian in the West, to whom the Latin church has always been immensely indebted. Without Tertullian there would have been no Cyprian and no Augustine.

We may well begin a survey of Tertullian's thought with his famous expression: "O testimony of the soul, which is by natural instinct Christian."[3] This is not to say that every man is basically good; what is here affirmed is that natural religion lies in the heart of each of us, and this is born out by the common expressions of ordinary people when they say, "Good God!" or "God Almighty!" or "God grant it!" The soul knows the abode of the living God, and that is not at the Capitol but in heaven. If, then, the Christian Gospel is preached to the soul, then the soul recognizes naturally what is presented, and responds accordingly. Now, the Gospel has been interpreted by four different Gospel writers, all of whom bear the authentic stamp of antiquity. While only four are authentic, Tertullian has to show that there are indeed four writers, against Marcion who accepted only the decapitated Gospel of Luke. But who is to determine whether his, or Marcion's is the true Gospel? The principle of time, declares Tertullian, for time rules that the authority lies with that which shall be found to be more ancient, and assumes as an elemental truth that doctrinal corruption can be alleged against the latecomers. To amend the Gospel, then, is only to confirm both positions, that the traditional Gospel was the prior one, and the amended one the later.[4] For Tertullian, the Fourth Gospel is also genuine in spite of its very spiritual tone.

Now the Gospel(s) testifies that Jesus came into the world as a divine legate and preached a new law and a new promise of the Kingdom of Heaven. In *The Prescription of Heretics,* Tertullian offers us a short summary in credal form of the main points of the person and work of Christ.[5] The divine nature of the Gospel, Tertullian insists, is proved by its miraculous spread throughout the entire empire. He makes this point several times, but no more eloquently than in *Apologeticus,* where this famous passage occurs: "We are but of yesterday, yet we have filled every place among you—cities, islands, fortresses, towns, market-places, camp, tribes, town councils, the palace, the senate, the forum; we have left nothing to you but the temples of your gods.[6] In fact, it is the "Christians who are the cause of every public calamity and every misfortune of the people. If the Tiber rises as high as the city walls, if the Nile does not rise to the fields, if the weather will not change, if there is an earthquake, a famine, a plague—straightway the cry is heard—'Toss the Christians to the lion.'[7] And to Scapula he writes, "Though our numbers are so great—constituting all but the majority in every city—we conduct ourselves so quietly and modestly; I might perhaps say, known rather as individuals than as organized communities, and remarkable only for the reformation of our former vices."[8]

Reformation of character is the great miracle that Christianity produces, and Tertullian never tires of contrasting his stern morality with the general public depravity of his times. It is with men from this latter sort that the jail is always bulging, that the mines are always humming, that the wild beasts are always fattened, that the producers of gladiatorial shows feed the herds of criminals.[9] This contrast of Christian virtues with pagan vices is never more eloquent than in the *Apologeticus,* where the famous lines appear: "Crucify us—torture us— condemn us—destroy us! Your iniquity is the proof of our innocence. For this reason God permits us to suffer these things. In fact, by recently condemning a Christian maid to the pander rather than the panther *(ad lenonem quam ad leonem),* you confessed that among us a stain on our virtue is considered worse than any punishment or any form of death. Yet, your tortures accomplish nothing, though each is more refined than the last; rather, they are an enticement to our religion. We become more numerous every time we are hewn down by you: the blood of Christians is seed."[10]

So this change of morals argues for the divine nature of the Christian Gospel. Tertullian admits that it may all sound ridiculous upon first hearing: "These (Christian teachings) are points at which we, too, laughed in times past. We are from your own ranks: Christians are made, not born!"[11] It is the reformation of their former vices that Scapula is asked to note, not to judge Christian dogma in the abstract. And the proof of the Gospel's divine nature is the willingness of Christians to suffer martyrdom. Suppose, says Tertullian, that Christians had chosen rather to withdraw from society as malcontents; the loss of so many citizens would have caused marked embarrassment to the government. "You would have been exceedingly frightened at your loneliness, at the silence of your surroundings, and the stupor, as it were, of a dead world. You would have had to look around for people to rule; there would have been more enemies than citizens left to you."[12]

We turn now to his concept of the church. Like Irenaeus, Tertullian must do battle with the followers of Marcion, of Valentine, of Apelles, and his primary appeal is to the antiquity of the church and her Scriptures. Heretics have no right to be heard, for the Scriptures belong to the very church they reject. Heretics are not to be allowed to enter upon an appeal to the Scriptures, when the Scriptures are of no concern to them, for they are not Christians. The churches have the Scriptures from the apostles, the apostles have them from Christ, and Christ from God. Tertullian puts the matter in his peculiarly graphic style by asking: "By what right do you, Marcion, cut down my wood? By what licence do you, Valentine, turn the course of my waters? By what power do you, Apelles, remove my landmarks? This is my possession. I have held it of old; I held it first."[13] Heretics, therefore have no fellowship in the church, for their excommunication testifies that they are outsiders. Tertullian denies that they even have the same God, the same Christ, *and* even the same baptism!

No writer of ancient times testifies to the exclusiveness of Christianity with any greater vigor than does the "founder" of Latin Christianity. The Christian church represents a complete break with virtually every other institution in society. This is not the idea of a Justin Martyr or a Clement of Alexandria; the pagan world has nothing to offer the spirit of the new age, much less pagan philosophy to Christian thought. In *The Prescription Against Heretics (prescription* is a legal term meaning *formal objection)* occurs Tertullian's famous "What then has Athens to do with Jerusalem? What the Academy with the Church? What heretics with Christians? Our School is of the porch of Solomon, who himself also has delivered unto us, that we must in simplicity of heart seek the Lord. Away with those who have brought forward a Stoic, and a Platonic, and a Dialectic Christianity! To us there is no need of curious questioning now that we have Christ Jesus, nor enquiry now that we have the Gospel. In that we believe this, we desire to believe nothing besides. For this we believe first, that there is nothing which we ought to believe besides."[14]

Studies have been made (H. Richard Niebuhr's book *Christ and Culture* is a fine example of one such study) of Christianity in relationship to its environment, and the cultural coloration which may occur when the Gospel is presented to various ethnic societies. How much of the society's culture can be accepted without risking the essence of the Gospel? Is it possible for a fair degree of acculturization to take place, or does it become necessary for the Good News to make a clean sweep of all that has gone before it? The celebrated controversy over the Chinese rites in the seventeenth century evoked from Rome an uncompromising attitude which cost the church dear. In the United States, on the other hand, Christianity has sometimes become so identified with American culture that it is hard to separate the two. And in the history of Christian thought, there have been wide variations of opinion on this matter. Monasticism, as we shall see, tended to reject in its entirety the cultural milieu in which it found itself, whereas post-Reformation Protestantism often found a too comfortable equation between the Gospel and the protection of the state in the particular locale where the Lutheran or the Reformed church found itself. We cannot go into this question to any great extent here; Suffice it to say that Tertullian is clearly among those who cry "no compromise" with the world. This would include pre-Christian philosophical (and theological) thought as well. Far from preparing the ground for an acceptance of Christ, the Greek philosophical thinkers were a hindrance. For Tertullian, there were not tutors unto Christ, but rival institutions set up as a sign of contradiction.

The unity of all the churches, as well as their apostolicity and their primitive quality, is proved by the communication of peace, the title of brotherhood, and the token of hospitality, since all are one in the tradition of the same mystery. Now, heretical churches can be faulted on two counts: they are not in agreement even among themselves, much less the apostolical church, with regard to Christian doctrine; nor can they point to a succession of bishops or a distinguished apostle as founder of their particular church. Antiquity, agreement in doctrine, and apostolic succession are the touchtone to orthodoxy and authenticity. *The Prescription Against Heretics* returns again and again to the unity of faith and government of the churches. But while there is stress on apostolicity, we are at a loss to know what connection exists between the various churches and Rome.

Certainly Tertullian recognized that Peter held the primacy of jurisdiction among the apostles.[15] He even acknowledged this after he had joined the Montanists.[16] The church at Rome is the "happy church" on which the apostles had poured out all their doctrine with their blood and where Peter had imitated the passion of the Lord, and Paul and John had likewise undergone trials. Mention is also made of Clement's having been ordained at Rome by Peter, and in the tract *On Modesty,* Tertullian refers to the current bishop of Rome (Zephyrinus or Victor) as the sovereign pontiff, that is, the bishop of bishops. This is important, because the reference to the Roman bishop in this instance is by no means complimentary.[17] So there is clear testimony to the idea of apostolic succession in many of the churches, plus the fact that the bishop of Rome somehow enjoys a prestige which the others do not—even though he may sometimes issue an edict on which cannot be inscribed, "Good deed!" Bishops likewise are legitimate successors of the apostles and the authenticity of their teaching has been protected by the Holy Spirit. Is it probable, he asks, that so many churches, and such great ones should have gone astray in teaching the same faith?[18]

What place does Sacred Scripture occupy in Tertullian's thought? Catholic tradition, having its root in apostolic tradition, has been the lone criterion of canonicity, and to this appeal Tertullian turns in his attack on Marcion.[19] Scripture has been kept as a sacred deposit in the churches of the apostles, and preserved intact against the innovators. But the authenticity of the Scriptures rests on their antiquity and is thus bound up with the whole question of apostolic tradition. And so, tradition is likewise a source of revelation for Tertullian. Wherever both the true Christian rule and faith shall be shown to be, there will be the true Scriptures, and the true expositions, and all the true Christian traditions,[20] and this position scores off Praxeas in the treatise directed against him.[21] This is why Tertullian says that heretics are not to be allowed to enter upon an appeal to the Scriptures, since the Scriptures are of no concern to them. For it is part of apostolic tradition that the Scriptures belong truly only to those churches established by the apostles. This point is reiterated again and again, so that it takes on a kind of irony when Tertullian becomes identified with the Montanists. And yet it is a principal theme which we find in many of his works, even those which seem to be most unrelated to apostolic tradition as a rule of faith, such as *On the Veiling of Virgins,* for example.[22]

Turning now to his doctrine of God, we discover that Tertullian is at one with the common tradition that God can certainly be known through his creation by the natural light of reason. "Do you wish us to prove His existence," he asks, "from his numerous, mighty works by which we are supported, sustained, delighted, and even startled?"[23] And again, in *On the Spectacles,* "Nobody denies what nobody is ignorant of—for Nature herself is teacher of it—that God is the Maker of the universe, and that it is good, and that it is man's by free gift of its Maker."[24] God must first be known from nature, and afterward authenticated by instruction: from nature, by his works; by instruction, through his revealed announcements. God is one and the same—whether among the Egyptians, the Syrians, or the tribes of Pontus.[25]

When we say *God* we designate the substance of divinity itself, which always existed with himself and in himself, but when we say *Lord* we use a title which accrues to him after his act of creation. Although God is a spirit, he also has a body, for according to Tertullian, spirit has a bodily substance of its own kind, in its own form. Invisible things therefore have both substance and form even though they be visible to God alone. One may speak of God, then, as spiritual substance— a spiritual substance which is unchanging throughout eternity. Against Marcion, Tertullian insists that God is One and uniquely One. He is the great Supreme, existing in eternity, unbegotten, unmade, without beginning and without end.[26] This rules out any Demiurge as the creator of the world. Against Hermogenes, Tertullian's insistence on the unique oneness of the Deity is to exclude the idea of matter as an eternally coexistent principle. For apparently Hermogenes taught that God had created all things out of matter which was already preexistent. We shall return to this point in a minute. What Tertullian wishes to establish here is that preexistent matter would jeopardize the omnipotence of God, for God would be dependent upon matter since he would be too small, too weak and too unskillful to form what he wanted to out of nothing.[27] And so God is One—only because nothing else coexists with him. He is first, because all things are after him, and all things are after him because all things are by him, and all things are by him, because they are of nothing: so that reason coincides with the Scripture.[28]

The doctrine of the Trinity is enunciated clearly a good many times by Tertullian. In *On Baptism* he cites the traditional formula which is to be used in administering that sacrament. Against Praxeas he affirms that Father, Son, and Holy Spirit are three Persons, not in condition but in degree, not in substance, but in form, not in power but in aspect, yet of one substance, and of one condition, and of one power inasmuch as he is one God, from whom these degrees and forms and aspects are reckoned, under the name of the Father, and of the Son, and of the Holy Spirit.[29] This is specifically directed against Praxeas who taught a kind of modalism in which the Father had suffered as well as the Son. The principle of the divine economy in the Blessed Trinity introduces number in order that the Father may not be believed to have been born and to have suffered; there is only one God and Lord, and since Christ is also God, he is also called Lord. Thus the connection of the Father in the Son, and of the Son in the Paraclete produces three coherent Persons distinct from one another. These three are one essence, not one Person, for when Christ says, "I and my Father are One," this refers to unity of substance, not singularity of number.[30]

The Son of God is truly begotten of the Father, the perfect nativity of the Word proceeding forth from God, formed by God to devise and think out everything under the name of Wisdom, and afterwards to carry it all into effect. Thus, God the Father makes Christ equal to him, for by proceeding from himself, Christ became his first-begotten Son, because begotten before all things. The Psalmist describes this with the words: "My heart has emitted my most excellent Word" (Ps. 44:2). Christ comes forth from God just as a ray of light is shot forth from the sun; thus spirit proceeds from spirit and God from God just as light is kindled from light. Yet the source of the substance remains whole and unimpaired; Christ has not separated from the source of the substance, but proceeds from the proceeding cause.[31] So between the Father and the Son there is an identity of nature, but a distinction of Persons.

In some sense the Father may be said to be greater than the Son. For, says Tertullian, the Father is the entire substance, but the Son is a derivation and portion of the whole: "My Father is greater than I" (Jno. 14:28). In the Psalm his inferiority is described as being "a little lower than the angels." Thus the Father is distinct from the Son, being greater than the Son, inasmuch as he who begets is one, and he who is begotten is another; he who sends is one, and he who is sent is another; he who makes is one, and he through whom the thing is made is another.[32] The proper name of the Son is *Word,* and he was seen by the patriarchs in various ways and preached by the prophets. Thus Tertullian cites examples of theophanies in the Old Testament. And just as the tree is not severed from the root, nor the river from the fountain, nor the ray from the sun, neither is the Word separated from God.

Intellectual generation is the way by which the Son procedes from the Father; the Son devises and thinks out all things under the name of Wisdom, and afterwards carries everything into effect.

Inseparable from the Father and the Son is the Holy Spirit, who is also God; the Holy Spirit is third from God and the Son just as the fruit of the tree is third from the root, or as the stream out of the river is third from the fountain, and as the apex of the ray is third from the sun. Thus the connection of the Father in the Son, and of the Son in the Paraclete produces three coherent Persons who are yet distinct from each other; they are one essence but not one Person. Against Praxeas Tertullian says, "I believe the Spirit to proceed from no other source than from the Father through the Son."[33] And the various similes which he uses supports the contention that he accepted the idea of the Holy Spirit's procession from both Father and Son.

While the relationships and the appropriations of each member of the Trinity are not clearly worked out in Tertullian, other than to insist that creation takes place through the Word, the missions of the divine persons are explicitly stated. Christ himself employs the expression "sending" with regard to the Paraclete, in order to signify not a division or severance but a disposition of mutual relations in the Godhead; hence, he says, "I will pray the Father, and he shall send you another Comforter, the Spirit of truth," thus making the Paraclete distinct from himself.[34] In *The Prescription Against Heretics,* Christ sends the power of the Holy Spirit to work upon believers.[35]

The tract *Against Hermogenes* is designed to combat the notion that primordial matter existed coeternally with God, and the divine act of creation was to take existing matter and impose upon it form. Since God could not be the author of evil, Hermogenes sought for the origin of evil in matter and made it a co-principle with God. This old Docetic idea Tertullian disproves by tying Hermogenes up in contradictions, an old legal trick. Actually matter would be superior to God because he was dependent upon it in the creation of the world. It is more worthy of God, says Tertullian, that he produced even what seem to be evil things out of nothing, for the character of God is best described by liberty, not necessity. "In the beginning," then, is to be taken quite literally; prior to the beginning there was precisely nothing, therefore *principium* or beginning, is simply a term of inception, not the name of a substance.[36]

So God fashioned this enormous universe with its whole supply of elements, bodies, and spirits, by the Word with which he commanded it, the Reason whereby he ordered it, the Power by which he is powerful, simply for the glory of his majesty, and this is the one God who is the object of our worship. No one can remain in ignorance of such a Creator and those who are unwilling to recognize him commit grave sin. All three Persons of the Trinity cooperate in the act of creation; just how matter is produced out of nothing, Tertullian never bothers to say. He concurs with Hermogenes in assuring us that God is not the Author of evil, although not all things are evil which seem so, and then confesses that he would much rather that God should have even willed to create evil of himself, than that he should have lacked ability to hinder its creation.[37]

What is Tertullian's explanation of evil? It is the result of demons whose business it is to corrupt mankind, and in fact the spirit of evil was from the very start directed to this purpose. Demons are responsible for diseases and misfortunes and they work upon the souls of men sudden and extraordinary outbursts of violence. Tertullian says they have their own subtle, spiritual properties for assailing each part of human nature, and act as though they had wings. Hence, they can be everywhere in a moment and the whole world is for them only a single place; what happens and where it happened they can know and tell with the same ease. Their swiftness is considered a divine power because their nature is not understood.[38]

There are good angels as well as demons, and they are made of a spiritual substance which is at the same time corporeal in a special sense of the word. This makes it possible, Tertullian thinks, for them to assume to themselves bodily shape out of no material substance and communicate with men. Since an angel's essence and existence are two very different things, Tertullian is trying to say that everything which exists apart from God must have a bodily existence, although this is not to be understood in a corporeal sense; it is language which is groping and awkward, and must await the more sophisticated and precise nuancing of a later age.[39] We shall note later that the evil angels have been consigned to perdition without any hope of restoration to their former state. The work of Christ has reference to the salvation of men, not that of angels, which is proof also that Christ never bore an angelic nature.[40]

Just as angels bear a corporeal substance, so also the soul of man is corporeal, but corporeal in the sense that it is born of the breath of God, is immortal, is possessed of a definite form, is simple in substance and conscious of itself, developing in various ways, free in its choices, liable to accidental change, variable in disposition, rational, supreme, gifted with foresight, developed out of the one original soul.[41] Tertullian attributes corporeal extension to the soul in order not only to explain how the soul can be shaped by virtue and misshapen by vice, but also how it can be punished in the flames of hell. In *On the Soul* he takes issue with Plato's ideas of the soul, and insists that the human soul has both a definite shape and a corporeal extension.[42]

God constituted man free, master of his own will and power, indicating the presence of God's image and likeness in him by nothing so well as by this constitution of his nature; man's likeness to God is not in the shape of his body or his countenance, but in his freedom.

The fact that man is free is confirmed by the fact that God imposes a law upon him. For a law would not be imposed upon one, Tertullian notes, unless he had the power to render obedience to the law; nor again would the penalty of death be threatened against sin, if a contempt of the law were impossible to man in the liberty of his will.[43] Man was created directly by God himself, and in the creation of the first man, Tertullian asks us to imagine God wholly employed and absorbed in it—in his hand, his eye, his labor, his purpose, his wisdom, his providence, and above all, in his love. For whatever was the form and expression which was then given to the clay by the Creator, Christ was in his thoughts as one day to become man, because the Word, too, was to be both clay and flesh, even as the earth was then. And so God made man, that is to say, after the image of Christ.[44] But of our first parents, Tertullian adds little other than this.

We might, at this point, say a word about the three theological virtues of faith, hope, and love, as Tertullian conceives them. Faith for him must be universal and extend to every revealed truth. Faith is necessary for salvation for every adult; Christ has commanded that we seek until we find, and believe when we have found; there is nothing more except to hold on to what we have believed. And part of belief is to believe that there is nothing apart from Christ's teaching which we are required to believe in addition.[45] Tertullian says little of hope, but a good deal about love, although indirectly, never treating it as a specific virtue as such.

With regard to sin, Tertullian holds that this is impossible unless it has man's free consent; therefore the imposition of the Law postulates man's ability to keep God's Law. Yet, because of Satan's deception man was deceived from the beginning so that he transgressed the commandment of God and, therefore, was committed to death and made the whole human race, which was infected by Adam's seed, the transmitter of condemnation.[46] So death is the direct result of the first man's sin. Yet despite the loss of certain preternatural gifts, man's free will was not lost, even though Adam's sin was transmitted to all men.

Tertullian teaches that grace is necessary for any saving act. The evil tree will never bear good fruit unless the good branch be grafted onto it, and the good tree will not bear evil fruit unless it be cultivated. Stones will become sons to Abraham if they are formed in the faith of Abraham; a generation of vipers will bring forth fruits of repentance if they will but spit out the poison of their wickedness. The power of divine grace is so powerful that it can even make subject to itself the faculty of free will which is generally said to be master of itself.[47] So grace which can efficaciously move the will must be even more powerful than nature. Hence we are truly able to merit, for a good deed has God as its debtor, just as an evil has too; for, says Tertullian, a judge is a rewarder of every cause.[48] There is no great plumbing of the doctrine of grace here; we are not dealing with an Augustine or a Paul and we must again wait for a more profound scrutiny of this intricate subject.

Christ the Incarnate Word occupies a major position in the thinking of the great North African. The person and work of Christ were clearly announced to the Jews in the Old Testament; the holy voices which spoke all insisted always on the same points: that the day would come in the last cycles of time when God would select for himself worshipers from every race and people and place—worshipers much more faithful, to whom he would transfer his favor in fuller measure because they would be receptive of a fuller doctrine. In the *Apology,* Christ the Son of God is the Lord and Master of this grace and doctrine and therefore the Enlightener and Guide of the human race. There is no question that he is not divine, for he is sinless, and the only sinless man; yet God alone is without sin, and so Christ is God.[49] Marcion errs in thinking that the God of the New Testament is not that of the Old; Praxeas errs in supposing that God the Father and God the Son are the same person. In *The Prescription Against Heretics* there is a summary credal statement on the life of Christ,[50] and a similar one in the *Against Praxeas.*[51] All of this is designed to steer a middle course between the ditheism of the Marcionites and the modalism of Praxeas, Noetus, and their followers.

Having established the divinity of Christ, Tertullian is likewise insistent on his humanity. How could he be incarnate without taking on flesh, human without becoming a man, and a divine Christ without being God as Marcion presumes? If he was not human he could not have suffered, and if he only seemed to suffer, why should we imitate his patience? Nor would the Eucharist make any sense if it were only a phantom who pretended to be giving his body. But the Passion would make even less sense if Christ had not been truly human. "The Son of God was crucified; I am not ashamed because men need to be ashamed of it. And the Son of God died; it is by all means to be believed, because it is absurd. And he was buried, and rose again; the fact is certain, because it is impossible."[52]

Christ therefore has a true body formed from Mary, bearing her flesh and born with the name Jesus given to him. "Believe me," Tertullian says, "that Christ chose rather to be born, than in any part to pretend—and that indeed to His own detriment—that He was bearing about a flesh hardened without bones, solid without muscles, bloody without blood, clothed without the tunic [of skin], hungry without appetite, eating without teeth, speaking without a tongue, so that His word was a phantom to the ears through an imaginary voice."[53]

So Christ really clothed himself in the flesh, nor was there any transfiguration or change of substance; divinity and humanity are conjoined in one Person—Jesus, God, and Man. The property of each nature is so wholly preserved, that the Spirit on the one hand did all things in Jesus suitable to itself, such as miracles, and mighty deeds, and wonders; and the Flesh, on the other hand, exhibited the affections which belong to it. It was hungry under the devil's temptation, thirsty with the Samaritan woman, tearful over Lazarus, troubled even unto death, and at last actually died. We are not to understand that Christ was composed of some sort of *tertium quid*—a kind of mixture, like *electrum,* composed of gold and silver, for then there would be no distinct proofs apparent of either nature. For if such had been the case, by a transfer of functions, the Spirit would have done things to be done by the Flesh, and the Flesh such as are affected by the Spirit, or else such things as are suited neither to the Flesh nor to the Spirit, but confusedly of some third character. But this is to be rejected; the two substances acted distinctly, each in its own character, with their own specific operations and effects.[54] So Christ has not been somehow changed into humanity, nor into some sort of mixture, but has two distinct natures which are somehow united. And the result is a personal union.

What are some of the results of this union of natures? Tertullian maintains that what has been abolished in Christ is not *carnem peccati* (sinful flesh), but *peccatum carnis* (sin in the flesh)—not the material thing, but its condition. The flaw has been abolished rather than the substance. Christ was in the likeness of sinful flesh as the Apostle says (Rom. 8:3), because the flesh of Christ, which committed no sin itself resembled that which had sinned—resembled it in its nature, but not in the corruption it received from Adam; hence Christ had the same flesh as sinful man. So we can say that in the flesh sin has been abolished, because in Christ that same flesh is maintained without sin.[55] It follows that Christ was likewise free of personal sin since Tertullian has already established the fact that he is God. This is not to say that Christ is incapable of suffering; we put our faith in him because if he had not suffered, the whole work of God would have been subverted.[56]

The purpose of all this was to redeem man from sin and slavery to the devil. In *On Flight in Persecution* Tertullian expresses his indignation that a financial contribution should ransom men from persecution when God himself spared not his own Son. Christ was delivered up to death, the death of the cross, to redeem us from our sins. The Lord has ransomed us from the angelic powers which rule the world—from the spirits of wickedness, from the darkness of this life, from eternal judgment, from everlasting death.[57] And so Christ restores grace and immortality to men. The Resurrection implies resurrection of the flesh, and this is fitting since we die in Adam, and must therefore be made alive in Christ as a bodily substance, since we died in Adam as a bodily substance. For Tertullian, resurrection means quite literally a "rising again" and this is applicable to man because we are alive in Christ as a bodily substance, since he is truly human.

The details of Christ's sacrifice on Calvary are not elaborately worked out by Tertullian. Following his resurrection Christ went up to heaven, sat down at the right hand of the Father, and sent in his stead the power of the Holy Spirit. He will come with glory to take the saints to the enjoyment of eternal life and condemn the ungodly to everlasting fire, having caused the resurrection of both classes to take place, with the restoration of their bodies. Satisfaction, sacrifice, atonement, are not words which Tertullian employs to any great extent; he is content to state the facts without probing their meaning to any great depth.

Tertullian states several times that Christ was born of Mary who conceived as a virgin. In the *Apology,* Christ is spoken of as the ray of God, foretold in the past, descended into a certain virgin, and becoming flesh in her womb, was born as one who is man and God united. The flesh, provided with a soul, is nourished, matures, speaks, teaches, acts, and *is* Christ.[58] This is repeated in *On the Veiling of Virgins* with the addition of the angel Gabriel who hails Mary as blessed among women, and a reference to Paul's Letter to the Galatians.[59] In *On the Flesh of Christ,* a comparison is drawn between the virgin Eve and the virgin Mary. As Eve had believed the serpent, so Mary believed the angel; the delinquency which the one occasioned by believing, the other effaced by believing.[60] And there is a further reference in *On Monogamy,*[61] Tertullian refers to Mary as the mother who was both virgin and wife of one husband. He likes to draw the parallel between Mary and Eve, for it was while Eve was yet a virgin, that the ensnaring word had crept into her ear which was to build the edifice of death. And into a virgin's soul, in like manner, must be introduced that Word of God which was to raise the fabric of life; so that what had been reduced to ruin by this sex, might by the selfsame sex be recovered to salvation. One virgin cooperated in the ruin of mankind, the other in its salvation.

Regarding the sacraments, Tertullian adverts to both a material and spiritual element along with a laying on of hands which signifies in a special manner the conferring of grace. After the invocation of God the sacramental power of sanctification is effected by the Holy Spirit who immediately supervenes from the heavens. While Tertullian is referring principally to baptism, in *The Prescription Against Heretics* he shows that he is familiar with all the traditional sacraments and in the *Apology* makes reference to the arcane discipline of the early church.[62]

It goes without saying that Tertullian considers baptism a sacrament instituted by Christ. Noting that even the heretics baptize, he calls the baptismal water the happy sacrament, in that by washing away the sins of our early blindness, we are set free and admitted into eternal life; like little fishes, after the example of our IXTHUS Jesus Christ, we are born in water, and have no other safety in any other way than by permanently abiding in that water. The flesh is washed in order that the soul may be cleansed; therefore, the flesh is the very condition on which salvation hinges.[63] Christian baptism differs from that of John the Baptist which carried with it no celestial endowment of the Holy Spirit.[64] And it is the washing with water which makes up the matter of the sacrament; indeed, all the sacraments employ common things, or as Tertullian calls them, "the beggarly elements of the Creator."[65] In the tract *On Baptism,* the manner seems to be that of total immersion,[66] and this is confirmed in *On the Crown,* where he adds that those to be baptized first renounce the devil and his pomp and his angels. Then there is a triple immersion which avowedly is a somewhat ampler pledge than the Lord has appointed in the Gospel. After tasting a mixture of milk and honey, the newly baptized does not take another bath for an entire week![67] The law of baptizing has been imposed, and the formula has been prescribed: "Go," says Christ, "teach the nations, baptizing them into the name of the Father, and of the Son, and of the Holy Spirit."[68] The chief minister of solemn baptism is the bishop, and after him the presbyters and deacons, yet not without the bishop's authority, in that peace may be preserved and the honor of the church. Besides these, even laymen have the right to baptize; anyone can baptize, but reverence and modesty incumbent on laymen require them to defer to their superiors; but in case of necessity one is virtually required to administer baptism to avoid the loss of a human creature.[69] The same point is made again in *An Exhortation to Chastity,*[70] and Tertullian notes that even heretics may baptize, although he does not seem disposed to accept their baptism.[71]

Baptism is necessary for all, adults and children alike; without it salvation is attained by none. But there is also the second baptism of martyrdom, a baptism of blood which may take the place of the first baptism or restore its effects when they have been lost. Both baptisms the Lord sent out from the wound in his pierced side, in order that they who believed in his blood might be bathed with the water; they who had been bathed in the water might likewise drink the blood.[72]

A spiritual regeneration takes place with baptism, consisting in the wiping out of sin and its punishment and the infusion of grace. This is clearly set forth in *On Baptism,* and again in *On the Resurrection of the Flesh.* In connection with the baptismal rite, Tertullian also speaks of an anointing with oil. This "blessed unction" he declares to be a practice derived from an old discipline dating all the way back to the time when Aaron was anointed by Moses. The anointment is also reminiscent of the Father's anointing the Son with the Holy Spirit. The oil runs down the body for spiritual profit, although it does not seem to constitute a separate sacrament in *On Baptism*.[73] The evidence for confirmation is clearer in *On the Resurrection of the Flesh* where he speaks of the flesh being washed, anointed, signed with the sign of the cross, shadowed with the imposition of hands, and fed, while the soul is cleansed, consecrated, fortified, illuminated by the Holy Spirit and fattened on God—obviously a sort of rough list of the different sacraments.[74] And against Marcion we are told that Christ has not disdained the water which the Creator made wherewith he washes his people, nor the oil with which he anoints them, nor that union of honey by which he gives them nourishment, nor the bread by which he represents his own proper body, all of which he calls sacraments.[75] Oil is the proper matter for this confirming sacrament, and in *The Prescription Against Heretics* Tertullian notes that Mithra likewise seals his soldiers in their foreheads (although presumably not with the sign of the cross).[76] Since body and soul are united in the service of God, they cannot be separated in their reward, which in the case of confirmation is a more abundant outpouring of grace and the gifts of the Holy Spirit.

With regard to the sacrament of the Eucharist, Tertullian shows clearly that Christ is really present under the species of bread and wine. As we might expect, this is directed against Marcion and appears also in *On the Resurrection of the Flesh*,[77] where our flesh is said to feed on the body and blood of Christ. Daybreak is the customary time for participation in the Eucharist, which is received from none but the hand of the presidents,[78] and there is distress if any wine or bread should fall on the ground. All participate alike in the partaking of the Eucharist. The suggestion is made that Christ is entire under both species (at the least, under the species of bread), although it is dangerous to push any single passage too far for an interpretation of this sort.[79] At any rate the Eucharist is a permanent sacrament in that it is to be received again and again. In fact, according to *On Prayer,* it was customary to receive it daily.[80]

Tertullian says little of the sacrificial character of the Mass. He does designate participation in the Eucharist as "standing at the altar of God" and refers to the sacrificial prayers, but it is the communion of the Lord's body which occupies his major attention.[81] The idea of the Mass as sacrifice is more implicit than explicit. The major effect of the Eucharist is to bind the soul more closely to the service of God, and this is implemented in two ways—by participation in the sacrifice and by the discharge of one's duty.

A good deal of attention is devoted to the sacrament of penance. The tract *On Modesty* is an excellent mirror on the theory and practice of the forgiveness of sins in the early church. Whether Catholic or

Montanist, Tertullian always admitted that the church had the power to forgive sins; the sacrament of penance was often viewed as a plank floating on the waves of sin which a shipwrecked man could grasp and be carried into the port of divine clemency.[82] The power of the keys extended to all sins committed after baptism, but adultery, apostasy, and murder were grave sins which might indeed be forgiven by God, but could they be forgiven by the church? Tertullian thought not, and when he learned that the "bishop of bishops" had remitted the sins of both adultery and fornication, he railed at either Zephyrinus or Victor as both lax and inconsistent. But bad and peremptory as he thought the edict was, he does not challenge the validity of the edict. Or does he? The *On Modesty* seems to affirm later that the power of the keys was intended for Peter alone, personally. At any rate, the bars come down on adultery and fornication in about the year 220; later, on apostasy about the year 250, and still later, on homicide, some time during the reign of Constantine.[83] Certain it is that public penance was exacted for serious crimes; penitents sat in sack cloth and ashes, wept with groaning, made the rounds beseeching the prayers and intercession of the faithful, and bent their knees in supplication. Confession of sins was good for the soul and enhanced repentance; all of this says Tertullian, honors God and softens his indignation and by temporal mortification discharges eternal punishments. It abases man, but raises him up; it covers him with squalor but renders him more clean; it accuses but excuses; it condemns but it absolves. The less quarter we give ourselves, the more God gives us.[84]

Less serious sins, however, might obtain forgiveness from the bishop. Repeated sickness must have repeated medicine, and we show our gratitude to the Lord by not refusing what he offers; offense does not preclude reconciliation, and since the Lord is willing to accept the satisfaction, we should be willing to give it. This is the way man shows that he hates sin and the injury it does to God, with the intention of repairing it in whatever way he can. No one can gain forgiveness of sin without it, and thus *exomologesis* is a discipline for man's prostration and humiliation, calculated to evoke mercy—repentance invites clemency to itself.[85] Confession, then, cannot be made merely to God alone, but requires some external sign. Most men shun this work of penance, Tertullian complains, as being a public exposure of themselves, or they try to put it off. They are more modest than mindful of salvation and are like those who are ashamed to go to a physician after contracting a social disease. They all alike perish from bashfulness, and with a Tertullianesque flourish the great illiberal asks, "Is it better to be damned in secret than absolved in public?"[86]

If the wages of sin is death, then, the wages of repentance is life, even though after absolution the obligation still remained of making some sort of satisfaction to the justice of God. Repentance means salvation and it is necessary for everyone who sins after baptism. The bar of baptism on the gate of forgiveness, technically closed, is allowed to stand somewhat open but it is available only once, after serious sin. Once may be once too often; we get something we do not deserve, but in case anyone incurs the debt of a second repentance, his spirit should not be cut down and undermined by despair.[87] Tertullian seems to oscillate between a flexibility in his Catholic period and a rigidity gained from Montanism. As he grew older, he became more conservative, as he thought the church's penitential discipline had become more lax.

He seems to have nothing to say about extreme unction as one of the sacraments.

That the clergy constitute a distinct order in the church is clear from *The Prescription Against Heretics* and *An Exhortation to Chastity*. In the former treatise, Tertullian pours out his scorn on wanton, heretic women who dare to teach, to dispute, to enact exorcisms, to promise cures, and perhaps even to baptize! Heretic ordinations are careless, capricious, and inconsistent; novices, worldlings, and apostates are all apt to be in office at one time or another. One man may be bishop today, tomorrow a deacon or a reader or a presbyter or a layman, for even to laymen the priestly office may be committed. In the latter treatise there is a comparison of the "Order" to the lay state, with sharp distinctions drawn between the two. It is apparent, then, that minor orders existed at least by the end of the second century. If celibacy was not imposed upon the priest, he was certainly prohibited from marrying a second time, which even lay persons should be discouraged from doing. Saint Peter may have been married, but surely no more than once, and Tertullian understands the remaining apostles to have been either eunuchs or continent.[88]

Christian marriage is likewise a sacrament for Tertullian. How shall we ever be able adequately to describe the happiness of that marriage which the church arranges, he asks, the Sacrifice strengthens, upon which the blessing sets a seal, at which angels are present as witnesses, and to which the Father gives his consent?[89] Even if it is a "mixed" marriage it has at least the partial patronage of divine grace and should be successful in spite of difficulties, anxieties, obstacles, and defilements; whereas marriages not professed in the presence of the church run the risk of being adjudged akin to adultery and fornication.[90]

An Exhortation to Chastity fulminates against second marriages which automatically disbar any lay person from becoming a priest. Tertullian feels here that the rules which govern priests with regard to marriage should be the same for laymen also. Second marriages should be shunned lest a person expose himself to the necessity of administering a sacrament unlawfully. The position is a strict one, and characteristic of Tertullian as a Montanist.

We turn now to a consideration of Tertullian's teaching on the final end of man and the end of the world. Death results from the separation of man's body and soul, although properly speaking it is only the body which can be said to be dead. Without waiting for the restoration of the flesh, the soul is punished for the sins it committed without help from the body. Likewise it is rewarded before the flesh is restored for the pious and kindly thought elicited independently of the body. Besides, says Tertullian, even in actions which need the assistance of the body, it is the soul which first conceives, plans, orders, and carries out the acts in question. And although sometimes unwilling to act, the soul always deals first with the matter which the body is going to accomplish and it never happens that an act is performed without previous consciousness. So, on this basis it is fitting that that part of man should have its reward which has the prior right to its enjoyment.[91]

Hence, rewards and punishments are dealt to the soul prior to the general judgment; the prison house of which the Gospel speaks is Hell, and the "last farthing" is the smallest defect that has to be atoned for before the resurrection, at which time the body also will pay or be paid in full. But at least souls detained in purgatory may be helped by the remembrances of the living; in the tract *On Monogamy,* a woman prays for the soul of her husband and requests refreshments for him, meanwhile, and fellowship with him in the first resurrection, and she offers her sacrifice on the anniversaries of his falling asleep.[92]

For those who die in serious sin, hell is waiting, and what a hell it is! Tertullian waxes eloquent as he asks, "What do we esteem that treasure-house of eternal fire to be, when small vent-holes [*fumariola*] of it rouse such blasts of flames that neighboring cities either are already no more, or are in daily expectation of the same fate? The haughtiest mountains start asunder in the birth-throes of their inly-gendered fire; and—which proves to us the *perpetuity* of the judgment—though they start asunder, though they be devoured, yet come they never to an end. Who will not account these occasional punishments inflicted on the mountains as examples of the judgment which menaces sinners? Who will not agree that such sparks are but some few missiles and sportive darts of some inestimably vast centre of fire?"[93]

At the general judgment the entire human race will be restored to settle the account for the good or evil it has merited in this world, from then on to be requited for a limitless and unending eternity. No longer will there be death or resurrection again and again, but we will be the same as we now are—really worshipers of God and always with God, clad in the eternity of our own proper substance which we have put on. But the profane, and those who have not turned wholly to God will be in the punishment of perpetual fire, and they will have from the very nature of this fire a divine supply, as it were, of incorruptibility.[94]

If the loss of God is not stressed in the thinking of Tertullian, the pain of sense certainly is. The soul is said to suffer and be punished in the flames of hell, its tongue so parched that it begs from a more fortunate soul the comfort of a drop of cold water. And let no one imagine that the story of Lazarus and Dives is merely a parable, for bodily qualities would not be attributed to the soul unless it were really corporeal, nor would Scripture make up a statement about parts of the body if they did not exist in hell.[95]

This mysterious fire which serves the judgment of God is eternal; it does not consume what it burns and while it destroys it restores. Hell is rather like volcanoes which are always on fire, but always remain in existence. How will the guilty and the enemies of God fare? The *Apology, The Prescription Against Heretics,* and *On Penance* all warn that this punishment will last forever, as far as the damned are concerned.

The end of the world will occur when the dead rise again. Since God can produce material things out of nothing He will be able to call back the flesh from whatever abyss it may have fallen into. Surely He is most competent to recreate if he once already created, inasmuch as it is a far greater work to have produced than to have reproduced, to have imparted a beginning than to have maintained a continuance. On this principle the restoration of the flesh is easier than its first formation.[96] And so the flesh will rise again, wholly in every man, in its own identity, in its absolute integrity.

The general judgment of all mankind is both final and irrevocable, it is also righteous and consonant with God's great patience. The fullness and perfection of the judgment consists simply in representing the interests of the entire person. But every person consists of the union of two principles and must therefore appear in both, to be judged in his entirety, since that is the way he lived life. As therefore he lived, so also must he be judged, because he has to be judged concerning the manner of his life. For life is the cause of judgment, and it must undergo investigation in as many natures as it possessed when it discharged its vital functions.[97]

Tertullian appears as a millenarist in his five books against Marcion. The saints are promised a kingdom upon earth (after the resurrection) for a thousand years in the divinely-built city of Jerusalem, which will be let down from heaven. The prophet Ezekiel and the apostle John both testify to this, and to prove the prophecy there was recently suspended in the sky above Judea a city early every morning for forty days. As the day advanced, the entire figure of its walls would wane gradually, and sometimes it would vanish instantly. This city, Tertullian believes, has been provided by God for receiving the saints on their resurrection; after these thousand years are over there will ensue the destruction of the world and the conflagration of all things at the judgment.[98]

The saints will be changed in a moment into the substance of angels by the investiture of an incorruptible nature, and will enjoy a limitless and unending eternity; their bodies will be immortal and glorious and their happiness will last forever.

Since Tertullian's writings always have a specific object in view and are written for some designated occasion, it is somewhat necessary to piece together from here and there an overall synoptic view of his thought. While we have concentrated on his doctrinal works, this is not to say that the moral and ascetical writings are not without importance. Indeed, there is hardly a subject that Tertullian does not touch on somewhere or in some fashion. He was a prodigious writer, and yet he is not a profound thinker. Still, his legal cast of mind, his facility at words, his brilliant sarcasm, his clever turning of argument back on his opponents, all deliver a punch which few writers have been able to equal. The rigoristic attitude of the North African will adumbrate the later stance of both Saint Cyprian and Saint Augustine. He is an earnest writer, above all, and if he seems at times much too antirational, it is because he feared the turning of Christianity into a mere speculative system rather than a way of life. He did the church immense service, yet his very strengths proved his downfall. Possibly if he had been somewhat less clever, less of a theatrical drawing card, less of a "character," he might have been numbered for all time among the saints

NOTES

The text is in Migne, *Patrologia Latina,* vols. 1, 2; a translation by P. Holmes and S. Thelwall is in *The Ante-Nicene Fathers,* vols. 3, 4 (*see* Bibliography)

1. Saint Jerome, *Catalogus Scriptorum Ecclesiasticorum.*
2. Neander's list has been refined by Bishop John Kaye in *The Ante-Nicene Fathers,* vol. 3, p. 11.
3. *Apology* chap. 17
4. *Against Marcion* 4. 4.
5. *The Prescription Against Heretics* chap. 13.
6. *Apology* chap. 37
7. Ibid., chap. 40.
8. *To Scapula* chap. 2.
9. *Apology* chap. 44
10. Ibid., chap. 50
11. Ibid., chap. 18.
12. Ibid., chap. 37
13. *The Prescription Against Heretics* chap. 37.
14. Ibid., chap. 7

15. *On Monogamy* chap. 8.
16. *On Modesty* chap. 21.
17. Ibid., chap. 1.
18. *The Prescription Against Heretics* chap. 28.
19. *Against Marcion* 4. 5.
20. *The Prescription Against Heretics* chap. 19.
21. *Against Praxeas* chap. 2.
22. *On the Veiling of Virgins* chap. 2.
23. *Apology* chap. 17.
24. *On the Spectacles* chap. 2.
25. *Against Marcion* 1. 3.
26. Ibid.
27. *Against Hermogenes* chap. 8.
28. Ibid., chap. 17.
29. *Against Praxeas* chap. 2.
30. Ibid., chap. 25.
31. *Apology* chap. 21.
32. *Against Praxeas* chap. 9.
33. Ibid., chap. 4.
34. Ibid., chap. 9.
35. *The Prescription Against Heretics* chap. 13.
36. *Against Hermogenes* chaps. 8, 16, 17, 19.
37. Ibid., chap. 16.
38. *Apology* chap. 22.
39. Ibid., chap. 6.
40. *On the Flesh of Christ* chap. 14.
41. *On the Soul* chap. 22.
42. Ibid., chap. 9.
43. *Against Marcion* 2:5.
44. *On the Resurrection of the Flesh* chap. 6.
45. *The Prescription Against Heretics* chap. 9.
46. *The Testimony of the Soul* chap. 3.
47. *On the Soul* chap. 21.
48. *On Penance* chap. 2.
49. *On the Soul* chap. 41.
50. *The Prescription Against Heretics* chap. 13.
51. *Against Praxeas* chap. 2.
52. *On the Flesh of Christ,* chap. 5.
53. Ibid.
54. *Against Praxeas* chap. 27.
55. *On the Flesh of Christ* chap. 16.
56. *Against Praxeas* chap. 27.
57. *On Flight in Persecution* chap. 12.
58. *Apology* chap. 21.
59. *On the Veiling of Virgins* chap. 6.
60. *On the Flesh of Christ* chap. 17.
61. *On Monogamy* chap. 8.
62. *On Baptism* chaps. 1, 4, 7; *The Prescription Against Heretics* chap. 40; *Apology* chap. 7.
63. Ibid., chap. 1; *On the Resurrection of the Flesh* chap. 8.
64. Ibid., chap. 10.
65. *Against Marcion* 1. 14.

66. *On Baptism* chap. 7
67. *On the Crown* chap. 3.
68. *On Baptism* chap. 13.
69. Ibid., chap. 17.
70. Cf. *On Baptism* chap. 15.
71. Ibid.
72. Ibid., chap. 16.
73. Ibid., chap. 7.
74. *On the Resurrection of the Flesh* chap. 8.
75. *Against Marcion* 1. 14.
76. *The Prescription Against Heretics* chap. 40.
77. *On the Resurrection of the Flesh* chap. 8.
78. *On the Crown* chap. 3.
79. Cf. *To His Wife* 2. 5.
80. Cf. *On Prayer* chap. 19; also cf. *On Idolatry* chap. 7.
81. *On Prayer* chap. 19.
82. *On Penance* chap. 4.
83. *On Modesty* passim, esp. chaps. 1, 5, 21.
84. *On Penance* chap. 9.
85. *On Modesty* chap. 18.
86. *On Penance* chap. 10.
87. Ibid., chap. 7.
93. *On Penance* chap. 12.
88. *On Monogamy* chap. 8.
89. *To His Wife* 2:8.
90. *On Modesty* chap. 4.
91. *On the Soul* chap. 58.
92. *On Monogamy* chap. 10.
94. *Apology* chap. 48.
95. *On the Soul* chap. 7.
96. *On the Resurrection of the Flesh* chap. 11.
97. Ibid., chap. 14.
98. *Against Marcion* 3:24.

Saint Cyprian

One cannot think of Saint Cyprian without immediately associating with his name two problems which confronted the church in the middle of the third century—the readmission of the lapsed into the society of the faithful during the Decian persecution, and the rebaptism of heretics. Caecilius Cyprianus (who was also known to the pagans as Thascius) must have been born shortly after the year 200, probably in Carthage, and certainly of pagan parents who were affluent. He studied rhetoric and practiced law up until the time of his conversion in 246, which he describes in a letter to his friend Donatus. He adopted the name Caecilius in honor of the aged priest who baptized him, and then (says his biographer Pontius the Deacon) distributed his means for the relief of the poor by dispensing the purchase money of entire estates, in this way showing his contempt of the world's ambition and his thankfulness to God for his mercy, which is above all sacrifices.[1]

His conversion, while not so dramatic as that of the bishop of Hippo, nonetheless has an Augustinian flavor to it. "While I was still lying in darkness and gloomy night, wavering hither and thither, tossed about on the foam of this boastful age, uncertain of my wandering steps, knowing nothing of my real life, and remote from truth and light, I used to regard it as a difficult matter that a man should be born again, a truth which the Divine Mercy had announced for my salvation, and that a man quickened to a new life in the laver of saving water should be able to put off what he had formerly been, and, although retaining his bodily stature, should be himself changed in heart and soul."[2] What follows is a thorough exposé of the wickedness of the world, with all its cruelty, lust, and corruption, indicating that Cyprian had already been impressed by the lives of Christians living around him and that his own sins had gained such a mastery over him that any moral reform struck him as utterly impossible.

So thorough-going was his conversion, however, that he immediately became a priest, and not long after that was elected bishop to the see of Carthage, and this over the heads of older priests of greater experience and priority. But his gracious manner eventually subdued all opposition, because Cyprian was obviously destined to serve the church in a special way at a special time. The main sources of Cyprian's life

192

and work are his own letters, some eighty in number as well as various short treatises such as *On the Unity of the Church, On the Lapsed, On the Lord's Prayer, An Exhortation to Martyrdom,* along with observations regarding patience, works and alms, virgins' dress, and sundry other subjects.

Shortly after Cyprian had been made bishop, probably in the year 248, the Decian persecution broke out in all parts of the Roman Empire. Harassed by barbarian invasions of the borders, and torn by internal friction, the empire seemed to many pagans to have been abandoned by the old Roman deities. Clearly the Christian 'atheists' were responsible for this, belonging as they did to a kind of state-within-a-state organization which generally refused service to the army and avoided the duties of public office. Toleration of such a public cancer was surely an offense to the ancient deities, nor would they protect Rome again until this heinous evil were rooted out. The attack on the church was simultaneous in all parts of the empire, and its avowed objective was to destroy her organization. It was therefore directed primarily against the key men of the church, and especially the local bishops, and it soon claimed the bishop of Rome himself—Fabian. A host of martyrs and confessors suffered for the faith, and many more lapsed from fear of torture and death, by burning incense or by sacrificing or by securing certificates from friendly or corrupt officials stating that they had carried out the law in the prescribed way. An example of these *libelli* was unearthed in 1893 and another in 1894 near Cairo, and reads:

> To the commissioners of sacrifice of the village of Alexander's island from Aurelius Diogenes (son of Satabus) of the village of Alexander's Island. About 72. Scar on right eyebrow. I was both constant in ever sacrificing to the gods, and now in your presence, according to the precepts, I sacrificed and drank and tasted of the victims, and I beseech you to certify this. May you ever prosper. I, Aurelius Diogenes, have delivered this. . . .
> First year of the Emperor Caesar.
> Gaius Messius Quintus Trajanus Decius Pius Felix Augustus
> 2d day of Epiphi [June 26, 250]

Despite his many names, this emperor is known as Decius.[3]

The persecution was severe and was intended to be universal even though the imperial order may not have been carried out in some areas, and only seemingly in some others. It placed Cyprian in a cruel dilemma; if he were to remain in Carthage he would surely be apprehended and probably one of the first to be martyred, thus leaving the church without a head. If he were to take flight in persecution (and there was evangelical counsel to urge this) he could be accused of cowardice and he would certainly not be able to deal firsthand with the variety of critical situations sure to arise in his absence. At the time, the second course of action seemed the more logical one, although he may have rued this later. The treatise *On the Lapsed* finds him confessing that it is the first title to victory to confess the Lord under the violence of the hands of the Gentiles. It is the second step to glory to be withdrawn by a cautious retirement and to be reserved for the Lord—the first being a public, the second a private confession. But such a course of action must surely have undermined his position to some extent when he emerged from hiding in the spring of 251.

The fury of the Decian persecution produced several different categories of Carthaginian Christians. There were the martyrs who had died under torture and the confessors who had somehow survived it. There were those imprisoned for the faith, but whose final fate was still undetermined; there were those who had broken down in their agonies, and those who had rushed off to sacrifice all too quickly in an effort to save life, liberty, and property. There were those who did not actually sacrifice, but had secured a certificate stating that they had *(libellatici)*, and such persons did not always have to pay a large sum for this certificate; it is not inconceivable that they sometimes received these from pagan hands as a sign of friendship or sympathetic understanding. In some cases the pagans themselves had offered the sacrifices and in other cases a certificate might include a whole family, only one member of which had actually offered the sacrifice. To still others, the whole question was one of formality which was more a patriotic gesture than a religious affirmation.

To compound the problem, it was the custom of those imprisoned to distribute "letters of recommendation" to the bishop urging him to readmit the penitent into the fold. These letters would have had merely a suasive character except for the fact that Bishop Cyprian was in hiding; it became all the more natural, therefore, for a reconciliation to take place "on the spot" without awaiting the proper ecclesiastical endorsement. So the question rapidly became one of ecclesiastical authority, and this is the position that Cyprian is jealous to preserve again and again in his correspondence.

And so the bars come down on apostasy in the year 250. If a man make prayer with his whole heart, if he groan with true lamentations and tears of repentance, if he incline the Lord to pardon his sin by righteous and continual works, he will make the church, which he had lately saddened, glad, and will now deserve of the Lord not only pardon, but a crown.[4] Each individual case must be decided by the bishop, who is the final arbiter in such matters. And by moral authority and force of personality Cyprian succeeded in securing the support of most of his clergy, although there was always a fractious minority which resented what they felt was his highhanded manner of acting.

Since Cyprian was essentially a man of affairs, he does not present us with a well-rounded systematic theology but rather with a doctrine of the church, upon which his attention may be said to focus. The essence of the Catholic church is unity, and it is a unity which proceeds from Peter who received it from Christ. This is not to say that the other apostles were not endowed with an equal partnership of office and power, but it is upon Peter that the church is built and from which its unity proceeds.[5] Citing the *loci classici* in Matthew more than once, Cyprian describes how, through the changes of times and successions, the ordering of bishops and the plan of the church flow onwards, so that the church is founded upon the bishops, and every act of the church is controlled by these same rulers. Founded upon divine Law, the church is established in the bishop and the clergy and all who stand fast in the faith.[6] Another altar cannot be constituted nor a new priesthood be made, except the one altar and the one priesthood; whoever gathers elsewhere, scatters.[7] So the church is a monarchical institution ruled from the top down.

Much of this doctrine is directed, of course, against Novatian. Novatian had set up churches of his own but Cornelius had succeeded Bishop Fabian by lawful ordination and was the rightful ruler of the Christian church. Novatian, says Cyprian, is not even *in* the church, nor can he be reckoned as a bishop, who, succeeding to no one, and despising the evangelical and apostolic tradition, sprang from himself![8]

The church is the spouse of Christ and cannot be defiled; she is uncorrupted and chaste; she keeps us for God. To be separated from the church is to be separated from the promises of the church. Perhaps Cyprian is best known for his famous assertion that "one cannot have God as a father who does not have the church as a mother."[9] Just as no one outside the ark of Noah escaped the flood, no one outside the church will escape either. He who does not hold to the unity of the church does not hold the law of God, does not hold the faith of the Father and the Son, does not hold life and salvation.[10]

If the church is one, the episcopate is one also, held together by the individual bishops. The analogies of sunlight, trees, and streams, which by former writers had been applied to God and the Logos are applied by Cyprian to the church of Christ. Bathed in the light of the Lord, the church projects its rays over the whole world; she extends her branches over the whole earth in fruitful abundance, she extends her richly flowing streams far and wide. Yet she is the one mother copious in the results of her fruitfulness; by her womb we are born, by her milk we are nourished, and by her spirit we are animated.[11]

The center of this unity is at Rome; Bishop Fabian holds the place of Peter, and when Cornelius succeeded to the vacancy created by Fabian's martyrdom, Cyprian sees the judgment of God and his Christ expressed through the testimony of almost all the clergy and the suffrage of the people who were present; the unity of the church and the ordination of the church are inseparable—one cannot exist without the other. The African constituency writes to Cornelius to assure him that they are at one with him in unity and in charity.[12] Cornelius occupies the throne of Peter, and presides over the chief church from which priestly unity takes its source. So the entire church is constructed on hierarchical lines and looks to Rome for leadership and guidance.

While the church occupies the central point (and this is understandable) around which the thought of Cyprian pivots, this is not to say that he is exclusively occupied with ecclesiology. In the treatise *On Mortality,* he warns that reason must give its assent to that which is believed on faith. If an influential and reputable man were to promise us something, we would have confidence in his promise and would not believe that we would be deceived or cheated. It is God who promises us immortality and eternity to us on leaving this world—to doubt this is not to know God at all, to offend Christ, and not to have faith in the House of Faith.[13] Faith requires us to believe in one God, who is Creator, Christ, and Holy Spirit.[14] God made man in his image, but Adam, in violation of the heavenly command, was incapable of resisting the desire of the deadly food and fell into the death of sin; he did not preserve, under the guardianship of patience, the grace received from God. Hence, strength of body departed with immortality, and infirmity entered the body by death, and since strength cannot be regained except when immortality shall have been regained, it is necessary to keep struggling and contending in this state of bodily weakness and infirmity.[15] And so, all men have contracted the contagion of the ancient death at birth, and for this reason infants are baptized for the remission of sins and heavenly grace.[16] God's help and protection are mandatory for each of us, because no one is strong in his own strength, but is safe only by the indulgence and mercy of God.[17] "Buy for yourself a white garment," says Cyprian, "that you, who according to Adam had been naked and were before frightful and unseemly, may be clothed in the white raiment of Christ. And you who are a rich and wealthy matron, anoint your eyes not with the stibium of the devil but with the eye-salvo of Christ, that you can come to see God, when you merit God by character and good works."[18]

Testifying to the divine nature of Christ, Cyprian shows how Christ desired to be sent by the Father to preserve us, quicken, and restore us. The Son of Man desires to make us sons of God and underwent death that he might hold forth immortality to mortals. "For when the Lord had come and healed the wounds which Adam had borne and had cured the old poisons of the serpent, He gave him when made whole a law not to sin anymore lest something more serious happen to him in his sinning."[19] Christ's every action from the very beginning of the

Incarnation was characterized by patience; even though he was the Son of God, he did not disdain to put on man's flesh, and although not a sinner himself, he bore the sins of others.[20] God delivered him up for our sins; hence, only the Lord alone can have mercy and he must be implored, be placated by our own satisfaction. The merits of the martyrs and the works of the righteous may have very great power with the Judge, but it is he alone who ultimately grants pardon for sins committed against him.[21] And so, Cyprian presents us with a skeletal structure of theology, at the same time eschewing the elaborate detail or the speculation of an Origen.

Cyprian was after all a busy bishop of many affairs who had to find practical solutions to current problems. One such problem was whether or not to rebaptize those who had already received baptism from heretics out of communion with the church. The usual practice in North Africa had generally been to administer a second baptism; the practice in many other parts of the empire, and especially at Rome, was to readmit the penitent with a laying on of hands. Inspired by Tertullian, and possibly even Clement of Alexandria, Cyprian held firmly to the North African tradition, when he was asked, sometime around 255, his opinion in this important question. To Quintus he writes (256) that those who have been dipped by heretics have not been baptized at all, so it is not a case of re-baptism, but of an original baptism, pure and simple.[22] Of Jubianus (in the same year) he asks how heretics, who are established outside the church, arrogate to themselves a matter neither within their right nor their power. And he cites the recent ruling of seventy-one bishops from Africa and Numidia to the effect that there is one baptism which is appointed in the Catholic church. Here one is washed and sanctified by the truth of the saving water, having flown from the adulterous and unhallowed water of the heretics.[23] Baptism leads to the remission of sins, but the power of binding and loosing does not exist outside the church. "For if any one could be baptized among heretics, certainly he could also obtain remission of sins. If he attained remission of sins, he was also sanctified. If he was sanctified, he was also made the temple of God. I ask, of what God? If of the Creator, he could not be, because he has not believed in him. If of Christ, he could not become his temple, since he denies that Christ is God. If of the Holy Spirit, since the three are one, how can the Holy Spirit be at peace with him who is the enemy either of the Son or of the Father?"[24] What about catechumens who are martyred for the faith before they have received baptism? They, says Cyprian, are baptized with the most glorious and greatest baptism of blood, concerning which the Lord himself spoke in referring to "another baptism to be baptized with." Finally, at the Seventh Council of Carthage where eighty-seven bishops delivered their testimony, Cyprian clinches his position by referring to his letter to Jubianus and declaring emphatically that according to evangelical and apostolic testimony, heretics, who are called adversaries of Christ, and Antichrists, when they come to the church, must be baptized with the one baptism of the church, that they may be made of adversaries, friends, and of Antichrists, Christians.

Clearly Cyprian is holding for a doctrine of validity dependent on the one administering the "sacrament"—*ex opere operantis*, and does not hold that the sacrament when conferred by a heretic itself confers grace. At first sight, he seems logically to have the better case, but while his argument is more convincing, that of Rome is more profound, and it must have been a shock to Cyprian to learn that Pope Stephen took sharp issue with him. Whether this led to an actual excommunication is highly doubtful, but a break of some sort certainly occurred. For all his professed loyalty to the throne of Peter, Cyprian was now forced to disagree vehemently with the bishop of Rome. It is unfortunate that we have only scraps of information rather than correspondence from the Roman see, but from Cyprian's letters to others in his bishopric, we can piece together Stephen's position. The first appeal is to custom: *nihil innovetur nisi quod traditum est.* From ancient times, the custom had generally been not to rebaptize those who were entering the church, even though this custom may not have been observed on the whole in North Africa. Stephen's other argument (as reported by Cyprian writing to Pompey) is, that since those who are specifically heretics do not baptize those who come to them from one another, but only receive them to communion, neither should the church rebaptize them. The argument is somewhat curious, and so in order to understand what Stephen's real position very likely was, it may be convenient at this point to fall back on the anonymous treatise *On Re-Baptism.*[25]

We do not know who the author of *On Re-Baptism* was, but he does seem to have been a contemporary opponent of Cyprian, and quite possibly is articulating the position adopted in Rome by Pope Stephen. The basic rejoinder here is that baptism in the name of Jesus does not hinder the baptized from knowing the truth at some time or other, and correcting his error by coming to the church and to the bishop, sincerely confessing Jesus before men; so that, then, when hands were laid upon him by the bishop, he might also receive the Holy Spirit, and would not lose that former invocation of the name of Jesus.[26] Here we have an *ex opere operato* understanding of the sacrament; the implication seems to be that grace resides in the sacrament itself; otherwise, the baptism of orthodox but morally unworthy bishops might be just as open to question as that of heretics. At first sight, the position of the author of the treatise *On Re-Baptism* is less cogent, but it turns out to be more profound. The wave of the future was here, and not with Cyprian. "And thus," says the anonymous writer, "as our salvation is founded in the baptism of the Spirit, which for the most part is associated with the baptism of water, if indeed baptism shall be given by us, let it be conferred in its integrity and with solemnity, and with all those means which are written; and let it be administered without any disconnection of anything. Or if, by the necessity of the case, it should be administered by an inferior cleric, let us wait for the result, that it may either be supplied by us, or reserved to be supplied by the Lord."[27]

How strong was Stephen's directive coming from Rome and was the church of North Africa obedient to it? Was this an *ex cathedra* pronouncement that all were bound to follow? Could Cyprian continue to follow the North African custom without risking "contempt of court"? Here we must consult Saint Augustine, writing in the year 400 against the Donatists, who were citing Cyprian for their own position. Augustine insists that Cyprian always maintained the unity of the church, recognizing that Peter was its head, for if it had been Cyprian who had broken with Stephen, "how many there were who would have followed him! What a name he would have made for himself among men! How much more widespread would have been the name of Cyprianist than that of Donatist!"[28] Cyprian failed to see that the sacrament of baptism carries grace in and of itself without respect to the one conferring it; hence, he construed the entire argument largely in disciplinary terms. The tradition in Rome might be against the rebaptism of heretics; the tradition of North Africa was quite opposite, and Cyprian was determined to maintain his tradition in the face of the Roman tradition. Since the question was largely disciplinary in character, Cyprian could disagree with the bishop of Rome without himself becoming a schismatic or heretic. To maintain that Cyprian considered his authority on an equal basis with that of Stephen will not survive a close reading of the epistles; even though he considered Stephen clearly wrong in the controversy, he certainly deferred to the throne of Peter as at the least *primus inter pares*.

In the long run, the better case lay with Rome. Cyprian did not see that if baptism were dependent upon the character of the minister, there might be many orthodox ministers whose ethical conduct might leave much to be desired. It might be necessary, then, to rebaptize all those who had received the sacrament from hands less than worthy. But who is really worthy? Carried to its logical extreme, there would be grounds for declaring virtually every baptism invalid! Hence, Cyprian's position could be shown to be ultimately absurd.

But such clarity was not possible in the middle of the third century, and it may be that even Stephen himself did not see all the implications of his adherence to tradition à la Rome and the laying on of hands with the pronouncing of the Name. Virtually nothing has come down to us from Pope Stephen, so we are at a loss to know in any detail what his point of view really was.

Of this we are sure: the high veneration in which Cyprian was held by the church of his time and long after his time. He would soon seal with his blood a lifetime of service to the church, and if Bede is to be trusted, he may have even relented and acknowledged Stephen's position at the close of his life. In 258 he was beheaded in the presence of his clergy and people.

In the fifth book of his treatise *On Baptism, Against the Donatists,* a subsequent bishop of North Africa, Saint Augustine, summarizes the controversy in the following manner: "I am unwilling to treat again that which Cyprian angrily unloosed against Stephen. It is, moreover, quite unnecessary, for they are the same arguments that have already been discussed; and it is better to gloss over those things which involved the danger of a hateful dissension. Stephen thought that we should separate ourselves from men who tried to destroy early custom about the reception of heretics; but Cyprian, influenced by the difficulty of the question itself, and greatly endowed with the holy bowels of Christian charity, thought we ought to remain united with men who hold opinions different from our own. Therefore, though he was somewhat contentious in his anger, but in a fraternal way, yet the peace of Christ reigned in their hearts, so that no sinful schism should occur in such a controversy."[29]

The unity of the Catholic church was always uppermost in Saint Cyprian's mind.

NOTES

The text is in Migne, *Patrologia Latina,* vols. 3, 4; a translation by R. E. Wallis in *The Ante-Nicene Fathers,* vol. 5 (*see* Bibliography)

1. "The Life and Passion of Cyprian, Bishop and Martyr," by Pontius the Deacon, in *The Ante-Nicene Fathers,* vol. 5
2. *Letter to Donatus* 1. 3
3. John Alfred Faulkner, *Cyprian the Churchman* (Cincinnati: Jennings and Graham, 1906), p. 71
4. *On the Lapsed* chap. 36.
5. *On the Unity of the Catholic Church* chap. 4.
6. Epistle 26. 1, Oxford ed., 33
7. Epistle 39. 5, Oxford ed., 43.
8. Epistle 75. 3, Oxford ed., 69
9. *On the Unity of the Catholic Church* chap. 6.
10. Ibid.
11. Ibid., chap. 5.
12. Epistle 51. 8, Oxford ed., 55; Epistle 44. 3, Oxford ed., 48.
13. *On Mortality* chap. 6.
14. Epistle 72. 12, Oxford ed., 73.
15. *The Good of Patience* chaps. 17, 19.

16. *Epistle* 58. 5, Oxford ed., 64.
17. *The Lord's Prayer* chap. 14.
18. *Works and Almsgiving* chap. 14
19. Ibid., chap. 1.
20. *The Good of Patience* chap. 6.
21. *On the Lapsed* chap. 17.
22. *Epistle* 70. 1, Oxford ed., 71
23. *Epistle* 72. 1, Oxford ed., 73
24. *Epistle* 72. 12, Oxford ed., 73
25. *Epistle* 73. 1, Oxford ed., 74.
26. *On Re-Baptism* chap. 6.
27. Ibid., chap. 10.
28. Augustine *On Baptism, Against the Donatists* 1. 28.
29. Ibid., 5. 25.

Firmilian

Among the epistles of Saint Cyprian is one to him by the bishop of Caesarea in Cappadocia, Firmilian. A friend of Origen's and widely known in the East, Firmilian had already taken part in the synod of Iconium (ca. 230) which had pronounced against Montanist baptism. He had also played a part in condemning the schism of Novatus in 252 and sometime later had participated in the trial of Paul of Samosata. Firmilian died at Tarsus, in the year 268.

The communication to Cyprian is written with considerable heat and no little acrimony; mentioned in the same breath with Judas, Pope Stephen is excoriated with disrupting the peace of the church by his views on the rebaptism of heretics, although we may indirectly thank him for allowing Cyprian to come to the defense of the church with the true doctrine. There is an undercurrent of subservience and even flattery in Firmilian's letter to Cyprian. Nor does he add any light to the already overheated argument. A heretic may baptize, but he cannot communicate the Holy Spirit, much less effect the forgiveness of sins. Indeed, the symbol of the Trinity may even be lacking, to say nothing of the legitimate and ecclesiastical interrogatory which rightfully should accompany the baptismal ceremony. Quoting the celebrated passage in Matthew, Firmilian allows the power of remitting sins given to the apostles and to the churches which they, sent by Christ, established, and to the bishops who succeed to them by vicarious ordination.[1]

Firmilian concedes that Stephen does indeed hold the succession from Peter, and for that reason his folly is all the greater in declaring that remission of sins can be granted by them who are themselves in all kinds of sins. If there is one Lord, one faith, one baptism, one God, and if heretics can validly baptize, then the whole notion of heresy should be discarded, and the unity of the church maintained regardless of individual, private belief. It is essentially the same ground that has been traveled before, and Firmilian merely adds vehemence to the argument in his withering denunciation of Pope Stephen.

Having Firmilian on one's side may not have been altogether a blessing. But in his upholding of the tradition of Asia and the practice of many bishops in the East, he nonetheless testifies to the unity of the church which has Peter for its rock. It is the folly of Stephen, according to Firmilian, to have betrayed and even deserted this all-important unity.

NOTE

1. *Epistle* 75.16, Oxford ed.

Novatian

The thirtieth epistle in the collected letters of Cyprian was written by the Roman clergy in the year 250 after the death of the martyr Pope Fabian. A successor to the see of Rome had not yet been named, but very prominent among the candidates was the learned and articulate Novatian, who may well have been the leader of the rigorist party, and quite possibly the author of the letter sent from Rome to Cyprian. Novatian was about fifty years old at the time, and the first important writer to use Latin rather than Greek in the church at Rome. If Novatian had hoped to succeed the blessed Fabian, he must have been bitterly disappointed when the choice fell upon the more obscure and lenient Cornelius. When it became clear that official policy was to be more indulgent toward the unfortunate lapsed Christians who had faltered during the recent persecution, a number of clergy with Novatian at their head, withdrew and set up churches with bishops of their own. This schismatic movement with a distinct point of view more consonant with ancient standards maintained itself until the end of the seventh century.

Novatian was also the author of a number of works, of which two have come down to us, the *Treatise Concerning the Trinity,* and *On the Jewish Meats;* Saint Jerome mentions other writings, but they have been lost. The history of Novatian's schism is narrated by Cyprian to Antonianus (Ep. 51, Oxford ed., 55) and clearly shows Cyprian quite favorably disposed to Cornelius and hostile to Novatian. He who separates himself from the church of Christ by that very action ceases to be a Christian, and he who dares to create his own ecclesiastical body and populate it with false bishops is a pernicious schismatic, fervid perhaps at the beginning, but unable to increase that which was unlawfully begun. The irony here is that some years later, a decision at Rome by Pope Stephen would likewise put Cyprian in the position of a dissenter, but Cyprian never attempted the fatal mistake of Novatian, since the unity of the church was for him all-important.

Novatian's treatise on the Trinity was written after the heresy of Sabellius first appeared about the year 256, near the end of his life. It is an attempt to summarize Trinitarian teaching, and to expose certain current heresies, most especially the Sabellian heresy. God the

Father and Lord All-Powerful is the absolutely perfect Creator of everything, the Author of the varied loveliness which makes up the universe. But whatever one declares of God generally turns out to be some condition and power of his other than himself. We can only grasp mentally what God is if we consider that he is that which cannot be understood either in quality or quantity, nor, indeed, can come even into thinking itself.[1] At the head of his created world God placed man, made in his image and endowed with mind, reason, and foresight. He has even provided for the remedy of man's disobedience, as the Holy Scriptures tell us. Yet in reading the Scriptures, we must remember that they often speak of God in human language without intending to ascribe to him human limitations, sins or imperfections. This is the God, then, that the church knows and worships, and about whom all things visible and invisible testify.

The same rule of truth teaches us to believe in the Son of God, Jesus Christ, who was promised to mankind in the Old Testament and manifested in the New. This Jesus is truly man, not a mere appearance or phantasm who received nothing from Mary; nor did he choose an ethereal or starry flesh as some of the heretics have pretended, nor can we perceive any salvation of ours in him, if in him we do not even recognise the substance of our body.[2] But this is not to say as other heretics do that Jesus was only a man, but we maintain that by the association of the divinity of the Word in that very materiality that he was also God according to the Scriptures.[3]

The Son of God descended and took up into himself the Son of Man, thus making him the Son of God. Novatian holds that these two are not the same, a distinction must be made between them, so that while the Son of man cleaves in his nativity to the Son of God, by that very mingling he holds that as pledged and derived which of his own nature he could not possess. Christ the Son of man is received by the Son of God, so that Christ Jesus the Lord, connected on both sides, so to speak, is on both sides woven in and grown together, and associated in the same agreement of both substances, by the binding to one another of a mutual alliance.[4] This is novel language, to say the least, and if not heretical it certainly opens the door to thinking which will be anything but satisfactory to the church.

The Holy Spirit is the one who effects with water the second birth, as a certain seed of divine generation, and a consecration of a heavenly nativity, the pledge of a promised inheritance, and as it were a kind of handwriting of eternal salvation. The Holy Spirit makes us God's temple and fit for his house; he solicits the divine hearing for us with groanings that cannot be uttered, he is our defender and advocate, inhabits our bodies and effects our holiness.[5] Is the Holy Spirit divine? Clearly, yes. Is he a person? Here, Novatian is anything but clear.

The implication is that he is a person, but nowhere does Novatian specifically say so. It is one and the same Holy Spirit who distributes his offices according to the times, and the occasions and impulses of things. But the total burden of the tract on the Trinity is to demonstrate that both the Father and the Son are divine Persons who are both God, yet separate as Persons. Virtually the entire tract is centered at this point, and in reality Novatian has not a great deal to say about the Holy Spirit when measured against what is said about the Father and the Son.

The conclusion of the tract summarizes what Novatian wishes to say about God the Son. He was begotten of the Father, is always in the Father. No time can be assigned to him who is before all time, yet he had a beginning before time. He who was in the Father came forth from the Father, and is the divine substance whose name is the Word, whereby all things were made, and without whom nothing was made. So the Son is before all things, but after the Father, since all things were made by the Son, and the Son proceeded from the Father, of whose will all things were made. God proceeds from God, causing a Person second to the Father as being the Son, but not taking from the Father that characteristic that he is one God. For if the Son had not been born, he would make two unborn beings, and thus two Gods, and if he had not been begotten the same thing would likewise be true.[6]

The letter *On the Jewish Meats* is the third in a series, the first of which dealt with circumcision and the second the Sabbath. The Law of Moses is to be understood spiritually and its division of animals into clean and unclean is to be understood in a figurative sense. God originally pronounced all of the animals good, and all were taken into the ark so that they might later continue the species. In animals, the characters, actions, and inclinations of men are delineated; if an irrational animal is rejected for any reason, that means the irrational qualities he symbolizes for man must be likewise rejected. But God also forbade the Jews from eating certain meats in order to restrain them from intemperance. For Christians, these restrictions are no longer binding; to the pure all things are pure, and the true and holy food is a right faith and a clean conscience. But liberty is not a passport to luxury or license, and Christians must still fast and exercise continence. And, of course, meat which has been offered to idols is out of bounds for all Christians.

Possibly during Novatian's lifetime, about the year 255, an anonymous bishop fired off a tract against him for his hardhearted attitude toward the lapsed Christians. Although the author is probably not Cyprian, it represents his point of view and makes a plea that the hope of pardon should not be denied to the lapsed. The author excoriates

Novatian for forgetting the Gospel precepts of mercy, and reminds him that the church is like the Ark which contained beasts both clean and unclean. Just as the raven and the dove both issued out of the Ark, the church must embrace the unworthy as well as the worthy. The treatise concludes with a call to repentance and a demand for humility and confidence in the gracious Lord, who is able to forgive all our short-comings, provided we confess our wickedness to him. Novatian would have done well to have heeded it.

NOTES

1. *On the Trinity* chap. 2.
2. Ibid., chap. 10.
3. Ibid., chap. 11.
4. Ibid., chap. 24.
5. Ibid., chap. 29.
6. Ibid., chap. 31.

Saint Dionysius of Rome

The fragment of an epistle or treatise of Dionysius, bishop of Rome, preserved in a letter of Saint Athanasius is entitled, not altogether correctly, *Against the Sabellians*. Written in Greek, not Latin, it is perhaps the earliest doctrinal statement we have coming from that illustrious episcopal see, and was written about the year 260. Occupying the throne of Peter from 259 to 268 (and possibly even a shorter time), Dionysius was in communication with his illustrious namesake Dionysius of Alexandria, who in defending the Catholic faith against the Sabellians, had made statements which could be pushed into a tritheistic interpretation. The Sabellians, for their part, had been so jealous for the monarchy of God that they were asserting no difference whatever between the divine persons. Since God is one, then the Son must be in actuality the same as the Father, and the Father the same as the Son—a variation on the old heresy of modalism.

But Dionysius of Rome does more than refute these aberrations; his principal concern is with those who subordinate the Son to the Father. When the Scripture says, "The Lord created me the beginning of his ways" (Prov. 8:22), we are to understand *beget* and not *made* as the correct interpretation of the word create. For if the Son were made, there was a time when these were not in existence, but to say that, would be utterly absurd. And so, Dionysius quotes the formula which was to become so famous in the struggle with the Arians.

The admirable and divine unity of God, Dionysius tells us, must neither be separated into three divinities, nor must the dignity and eminent greatness of the Lord be diminished by having applied to it the name of creation, but we must believe in God the Father Omnipotent, and in Christ Jesus his Son, and in the Holy Spirit. Moreover, that the Word is united to the God of all—"I and the Father are one" (Jno. 10: 30), and "I am in the Father, and the Father is in me" (Jno. 14:10). And so the doctrine of the divine Trinity is maintained in its integrity, and the sacred announcement of its Unity.[1]

NOTE

1. *Against the Sabellians*, par. 3.

Saint Dionysius of Alexandria

Origen had had many illustrious disciples, but none was more outstanding than the great Dionysius of Alexandria and Gregory the Wonder-Worker. Next to Saint Cyprian, Dionysius the Great stands as the bishop par excellence of the third century, and although he equalled the North African in administrative ability, he lacks the originality and incisive quality of thought that marks the Carthaginian. Born at about the end of the second century, Dionysius in 231-32 succeeded Heraclas as head of the famed Catechetical School. Fifteen years later he also succeeded him as bishop of Alexandria, although it is not certain whether or not he surrendered or retained his former post. As bishop of Alexandria he played an important role in the readmission of the lapsed following the Decian persecution. He was also involved in the quarrel with Novatian and aided in the deposition of that factious cleric, Paul of Samosata. In the year 257 he was banished during the persecution of Valerian but returned in 260 when Gallienus adopted a policy of toleration. His correspondence with Saint Dionysius of Rome revolves about his repudiation of the Sabellian heresy and the accusation of tritheism which was levelled by some against him. He died about the year 264-65.

The epistle to Dionysius of Rome is divided into four books, only fragments of which remain, and it is thanks to Saint Athanasius that we have as much as we do. The question under discussion is the true nature of the Son of God, who is the brightness of the eternal Light and is himself also absolutely eternal. He is to the Father as brightness is to light, and always shines before him—hence the expression, Light of Light. Christ is also the breath of God's power. To those who accuse him of not believing in the consubstantiality of the Son with God, Dionysius replies that this word never appears in the Sacred Scriptures but is not inconsonant with what he himself personally holds. One must resort to human analogies in order to explain the relationship of the Son to the Father, but perhaps these are all inadequate in the long run.

And so, God is the spring of all that is good, but the Son is a river flowing from him. Likewise, a word of speech is an emanation of the mind and is emitted from the heart by the mouth. The mind uttered by the tongue is different from the word which exists in the heart, however. The mind remains the same after it has uttered the word, while the word flies out and is carried about in all directions. Yet each is in each, although one is from the other and they are one although they are two. And so it is that the Father and the Son are said to be one, and to be in one another.[1]

His enemies may have had some reason to accuse Dionysius of heresy, or at least of imprudence, but Saint Athanasius thinks it was mostly a matter of spite. At any rate, bishops may sometimes be excellent administrators without at the same time specializing in the necessary subtlety of thought which the doctrine of the Trinity was to demand.

NOTE

1. *Epistle to Dionysus, Bishop of Rome,* from the first book.

VII

POLEMICS FOR
THE FINAL STRUGGLE

The opening years of the fourth century saw a deliberate attempt on the part of the emperor Diocletian to root out the pernicious spread and malignant influence of Christianity from every part of the Roman Empire. The persecution, although brief, was intense and almost universal. It was followed, however, by the Edict of Milan in 313 which made the practice of the faith lawful, and this was followed by the subsequent triumph of the emperor Constantine, the first Christian to rule the Roman world. It was the singular good fortune of the writers in this chapter to have lived long enough not only to persevere during the time of testing, but also to see victory assured to the followers of the Nazarene and the ultimate triumph of his Cross.

Saint Methodius

Writing toward the end of the third century (probably some time between 270 and 290) one of the most fascinating but elusive figures is Saint Methodius, also known as Eubulius—Man of Good Advice. Tradition has it that he was both bishop and martyr, and it is certain that he was a Christian author of no little stature. Lycia, in Southern Asia Minor, was the general scene of his activity. *The Banquet of the Ten Virgins,* or a *Treatise on Chastity,* is the only work which has come down to us more or less intact. A dialogue between Orthodoxus and Valentinian enables Methodius to state his position on good and evil in *Free Will,* and a third treatise is entitled *On the Resurrection.*

Modeled on the style of Plato's *Symposium,* the *Banquet of the Ten Virgins* is actually a summary of dogmatic and moral theology, and is put together as a kind of enchiridion of the ascetic life. The key point is that no one may enter heaven unless he is chaste; therefore, we must understand what chastity entails for those Christians in all walks of life. This is not to say that Methodius overlooks such disparate topics as the allegorization of the Scriptures, how to pray and to fight against temptation, the snares of astrology and the ultimate meaning of the world's history, but his point of departure is the loss of chastity through the sin of the first man. For Adam was created without corruption in order that he might honor the King and Maker of all things, but when he transgressed God's command, he suffered a terrible and destructive fall which reduced him to a state of death. For this very reason the Lord left the ranks of angels and came from heaven into a human life, destroying the serpent and with it the condemnation of man's ruin; thus it was appropriate that the serpent should be overcome by a man, just as he had formerly overcome man.[1] Now when the Christian is baptized and enters the church, the church is said to give birth to a male, since the enlightened receive the features, the image, and the manliness of Christ. The church swells and travails in birth until Christ is formed in us, so that each of the saints, by partaking of Christ has been born a Christ; those who are baptized in Christ have been made Christ by communication of the Holy Spirit, and it is the church which here contributes a clear transformation into the image of the Word.[2]

God has freely created all things out of nothing, and this is eminently true of man himself whom God has created with free will. Hence, man's obedience or disobedience lies within himself alone and he works out his own salvation by the practice of chastity, or more precisely, continence. After Adam's sin, which upset the equilibrium between good and evil now being restored in Christ, no one was able to be chaste, but the New Testament dispensation now makes this possible. This is not to condemn marriage, but those in the marital state must practice continence and asceticism in their particular mode of life. And this they do by allowing the church to form the Logos, the divine teaching within them. All of this voluntarism, however, is perhaps more reminiscent of Aristotle than of Plato.[3]

The treatise *On the Resurrection* assures us that not merely the soul but also the body will become incorruptible, and therefore Our Lord went to considerable trouble to set the Sadducees straight on this point. In the resurrection people neither marry nor are given in marriage but are as the angels in heaven—not on account of having no flesh, but because they are incorruptible. Methodius does not oppose marriage as did the Encratites, but he is opposed to the ascetic practice and position which Origen occasionally took. It is therefore as an Asian-Alexandrian correction to Origen that Methodius sees himself, while at the same time adopting much of his allegorical interpretation.

The mystical asceticism of the *Banquet* suggests later medieval Eastern eschatological writings, and while the emphasis on chastity is pronounced, it must be remembered that the time is short and man must overcome the limitations of the flesh in the time that God has allotted him. The overview of the world from God's transcendent vantage point shows man to be created out of nothing; if he is not to lapse into nothingness, he must make right choices to show that his free will is ever fixed in Him who is from age to age the same.

NOTES

1. *Banquet of the Ten Virgins* 3. 6.
2. Ibid., 8. 8.
3. *On Free Will* (first speech of Orthodoxus); see also the brilliant introduction by H. Musurillo, "St. Methodius, The Symposium: A Treatise on Chastity," in *Ancient Christian Writers* (Westminster, Md.: The Newman Press, 1948), p. 7.

Arnobius

Our knowledge of Arnobius comes mainly from Saint Jerome, who tells us that he taught rhetoric at Sicca in Africa and had as his pupil Firmianus, better known as Lactantius. It is said that Arnobius embraced Christianity as a result of dreams, and in order to convince his bishop of his sincerity wrote the seven books *Adversus Nationes, (Adversus Gentes)* which is really more of an attack on paganism than a defense of Christianity. Writing around the year 300, this is the last apology that we have prior to the toleration of Christianity in the early fourth century. Written in Latin, *Against the Pagans* is clearly indebted to the North African School of Christianity, and especially that of Clement of Alexandria, Tertullian, and Cyprian. No one questions the vast learning of Arnobius, but some would question his appeal. The case against the pagans is presented convincingly enough, the case for Christianity less so—certainly we learn from it far more about paganism than the church. And in spite of his quite good literary style, Arnobius is frequently wordy, digressive, and hardly a profound scholar or thinker. For all that, possibly he has suffered unjust eclipse, while his more illustrious pupil Lactantius has fared more happily.

Arnobius's work falls into two parts: the first two books of *Against the Pagans* is a defense of Christianity—it cannot be held responsible for the calamities which have fallen on the world—while the last five books are a more direct attack on paganism itself. In this latter area Arnobius has a more secure grip, and it has been argued that as a neophyte, his understanding of the faith left something to be desired. Yet his writing also seems to show careful composition, and it may be that his principal concern was really not to present an exposition of Christianity so much as to clear the ground for its reception by discrediting paganism, much as the *Octavius* of Minucius Felix.

It is futile to say that the gods have withdrawn their protection from the empire because of the impiety of Christians. Calamities fall upon believers and non-believers alike, and have always done so; in fact, they have been less pronounced in recent times because there is more widespread peace. But Christians actually worship the Supreme Ruler of the Universe, not as Jupiter, but under the influence of Christ and his teaching. Nor let anyone retort that a mere man who died on the cross is being worshiped; this is God in reality and without any shadow of doubt, proved by his miracles and his resurrection, the power of his name and the spread of his church.[1] And let no one say that the Gospels should not be believed because they were written by unlearned and ignorant men; this only proves that they were put forth by men of simple mind, who knew not how to trick the public by deceitful polish or excessive prolixity.

But if Christ came as the Savior of men, why does he not free everyone without exception? Arnobius replies that Christ invites all— men of high rank, the meanest of slaves, women, boys, but if we spurn the proffered gift (thinking it, in our pseudo-wisdom, ridiculous and absurd), why should he keep inviting us, when it is up to our own free will to accept or reject him?[2] And so, Christ calls every man, but it is up to each one of us to work out our own salvation.

The first two books of *Against the Pagans* try to answer the objections raised against Christianity; there is no attempt to present anything like a systematic summary of Christian doctrine. The remaining five books represent a sustained attack against all the aspects of heathenism, with the single exception of emperor worship. We travel a well-worn path here as Arnobius rehearses the immorality of the gods, the confusion in heathenism, the doubt and ignorance which are everywhere rampant. But in his discussion of sacrifices (Book VII) he betrays an inadequate knowledge of the Old Testament, to say nothing of the sacrificial nature of Christ's death upon the cross. And in his discussion of the immortality of the soul we detect more of Plato than of Christianity when he argues that the soul is not by nature immortal, but immortality is conferred upon it by God's gift. Since the soul is polluted by sin we cannot say that it comes from God, but what its precise origin is must remain shrouded in mystery.[3]

As Plato is the greatest of the Greeks, the greatest Roman is Cicero, insofar as he was a popularizer of Lucretius. In his attack on the pagan deities Arnobius recapitulates all the ardor of the Epicurean in the latter's famous poem *On the Nature of Things*. And Tullius, the most eloquent of the Romans has stated boldly, firmly, and frankly what he thought about the carryings-on of the various deities, divided as they are into male and female; to attribute sex to the supreme Deity in this manner is patently gross and absurd.[4]

The origin of the soul, its true nature—corporal or non-material, its powers of memory and learning, its mortality or immortality, and its final destiny, are all questions which Arnobius poses, and tries to solve not too successfully. To these same questions Saint Augustine, the greatest North African, was himself to turn before another century had elapsed. If we find Arnobius a far better polemicist than a constructive theologian, more capable of sustaining an attack on the enemy than presenting a positive system of thought of his own, and speaking more eloquently to a past generation than to our own of today, we must remember that in his synthesis of decadent pagan thought he paved the way for the greatest of all theologians of the early church, who would finally give the coup de grace to heathenism in his *City of God,* the incomparable Saint Augustine.

NOTES

The text is in Migne, *Patrologia Latina,* vol. 5; a translation by Bryce and Campbell is in *The Ante-Nicene Fathers,* Vol. 6 (*see* Bibliography).
1. *Adversus Nationes* 1. 42, 43.
2. Ibid., 2. 64.
3. Ibid., 2. 47, 48.
4. Ibid., 3. 8.

Saint Hippolytus

Saint Hippolytus presents the historian of doctrine with difficulties which require some sort of arbitrary decision at the outset. While there may be two persons of the same name, I am assuming that the author of the *Refutation of All Heresies* is also the antipope who opposed Callistus and did not finally resign until both he and Pontianus were sentenced to the salt mines of Sardinia. I am also assuming that the statue found in 1551 near the Via Tiburtina containing a list of his works, but failing to mention the *Refutation,* refers to the same Hippolytus. And whether we are dealing with an abridgment of his major work, or actually have the original of which an abridgment has perished seems to me more a matter for the scholarly specialist. *The Refutation Against All Heresies* is sometimes referred to as the *Philosophumena;* actually it is a work of ten books, the first four summarizing Greek philosophy and religion (books two and three are still lost), while books five to nine deal with various forms of Gnosticism. Book ten is the one which concerns us primarily, for in addition to a summary of the previous books and a chronology of the history of the Jews, it contains Hippolytus' own understanding of the true faith.

Saint Hippolytus is more eclectic than original. In his exposition of the Gnostic heresies he is frankly indebted to Saint Irenaeus, while his summaries of Greek philosophy are poor. His writings are prolific and reminiscent of Origen, but he lacks the latter's originality, and in his austerity and rigorism he reminds us of Tertullian. Virtually all of his writings have been lost, although we have a good many fragments of some of them; his major work, the *Refutation* has survived best, but even of that we have only about eighty percent.

Saint Hippolytus writes in Greek, and it is generally thought that he grew up in the East and migrated to Rome where he eventually became bishop of Portus and one of the Roman clergy. He seems to have been of a rather uncompromising nature, and deplored with Tertullian the relaxing of standards of penitential discipline effected by Callistus whom he also accused of Sabellianism, or at least of being too friendly with heretics. In the ninth book of the *Refutation* he gives us an unsympathetic biography of Callistus, which suggests that what really irked Saint Hippolytus was not only the catering to the parties of laxity on the one hand and heresy on the other, but the fact that a "nobody" had become bishop of Rome by playing up to the previous pope Zephyrinus. As a result, Saint Hippolytus headed up a schism which lasted through the next pope Urban I (223-30) and Pontianus (230-35) until they both resigned in favor of Anteros (235-36), thus healing the schism, and both becoming martyrs to the faith in the Sardinian salt mines.

Saint Hippolytus is thus mainly interesting for the window that he opens for us on his own times, which reveals that ecclesiastical politicking went on even then. The fact that his voluminous writings have been largely lost suggests that the writings of an Irenaeus, an Origen, or a Tertullian were treasured more carefully because of their originality, style, or profundity.

Other works of Saint Hippolytus include a treatise *On Christ and Antichrist, Against the Heresy of Noetus, Against the Greeks* (Plato) and a number of fragments from the Biblical Commentaries. Eusebius (5:28) quotes from a lost work *Against Artemon,* who, according to Hippolytus, falsely maintained that the doctrine of the church had been corrupted in the time of Zephyrinus; these same followers of Artemon had decided to correct and to improve upon the Scriptures, failing to realize that the divine Scriptures were spoken by the Holy Spirit, or perhaps considered themselves to be wiser than He. Some had not even bothered to tamper with the Scriptures but simly rejected the Law and the prophets out of hand. One of the tests of orthodoxy, therefore, is to accept the Sacred Scriptures of the church in which no error can be found, since they are of divine authorship.[1]

God is Creator and Lord of all, and prior to creation there was nothing—not infinite chaos, nor measureless water, nor solid earth, nor dense air, nor warm fire, nor refined spirit, nor the azure canopy of the stupendous firmament. Through foreknowledge, God wills to create certain beings, some of them simple essences, others more complex. Simple essences are immortal for in their case dissolution does not follow, but the more complex substances are dissoluble and therefore mortal.[2]

The solitary and supreme Deity, by an exercise of reflection, brought forth the Logos first, not the word in the sense of being articulated by voice, Hippolytus tells us, but as a ratiocination of the universe, conceived and residing in the divine mind. The Word himself was the Cause of all created things. Being in the Father, the Logos bore the will of the Father, for simultaneously with his procession, he has the ideas conceived in the Father as a voice in himself. When the Father called all things into being, the Logos completed each object of creation, one by one. Earthly living things are either male or female, but inert objects are neither and angels are sexless and made of fire and spirit, as are the sun, moon, and stars.

God also fashioned man out of composite substances, not as a god or as an angel, but as a human capable of achieving divinity, as long as he obeys the Creator. For man is endued with a capacity of self-determination, yet not possessing a sovereign intellect, nor holding sway over all things by reflection, and authority, and power, but a slave to his passions and comprising all sorts of contradictions in himself. He is capable of both good and evil, and since he has free will, a law has been defined for his guidance by the Deity with a very specific purpose to it. He is commanded to perform the law, and there is a penalty for not carrying out what has been commanded. God did not and does not do evil; evil had no existence from the beginning, but came into being later, and that is why law was known even to primitive man and more recently reaffirmed by Moses, a devout man beloved of God.[3]

Everything is controlled by the Logos, who is the first-begotten Child of the Father, the voice of the Dawn antecedent to the Morning Star (Ps. 110:3). From time to time, friends of God have appeared called prophets, who recalled past happenings to the minds of the people, commented on current events, and foretold those in the future. Through the prophets the Logos promulgated the divine commandments, thus turning man from disobedience, not bringing him into servitude by force of necessity, but summoning him to liberty through a choice involving spontaneity.

Finally, the Father sent the Logos himself, so that the world might see him and reverence him, corporally present among men themselves, taking upon himself the holy flesh by the holy Virgin, and preparing a robe which he wove for himself, like a bridegroom in the sufferings of the cross, in order that by uniting his own power with our mortal body, and by mixing the incorruptible with the corruptible, and the strong with the weak, he might save perishing man.[4] The Logos was made out of our compounded humanity and has the same nature we do; if he were not, he would have no right to lay injunctions and commandments on weak sinful flesh and still call himself good and just. To prove he was human he worked and was willing to endure hunger and thirst, and even sank into the quietude of sleep. He did not protest against his Passion, but became obedient unto death, and manifested his resurrection. Now in all these actions he offered up his own manhood to keep us from becoming discouraged when we have to endure similar hardships.

Saint Hippolytus proclaims himself a disciple of the benevolent Logos, and urges his hearers to learn who the true God is. Away, then, with the fallacies of artificial discourses and the vain promises of plagiarizing heretics! The venerable simplicity of unassuming truth will enable us to escape the approaching threat of the fire of judgment, along with the rayless scenery of gloomy Tartarus, where the irradiating voice of the Word never shines. Instruction in the knowledge of the true God enables us to escape the boiling flood of hell's eternal lake of fire, and the eye ever fixed in menacing glare of fallen angels chained in Tartarus as punishment for their sins, as well as the worm that ceaselessly coils for food around the body whose scum has bred it.[5]

But believers will possess an immortal body far removed from the possibility of corruption, just like the soul. They will receive the Kingdom of Heaven, and become a companion of the Deity, a co-heir with Christ, no longer enslaved by lusts or passions nor wasted by disease. For, says Saint Hippolytus, "thou hast become God"; for whatever sufferings thou didst undergo while being a man, these He gave to thee, because thou wast of mortal mould, but whatever it is consistent with God to impart, these God has promised to bestow upon thee, because thou hast been deified, and begotten unto immortality."[6]

In *Against the Greeks,* the saint insists that the body is also raised at the command of God the Artificer; it buds and is raised, arrayed and glorious, but not until it has first died and been dissolved and been mingled with earth. It is dissolved on account of the primeval transgression, and is committed to the earth to be raised pure and no longer corruptible. To every body its own soul proper to itself will be given, and there will be great joy; but the unrighteous will receive their bodies unchanged, and unransomed from suffering and disease, and unglorified, and still with all the ills in which they died.[7]

When all are gathered together at the general judgment, men and angels and demons shall say with one voice, "Righteous is Thy judgment." To those who have done well shall be assigned righteously eternal bliss, and to the lovers of iniquity shall be given eternal punishment—unquenchable fire without end, an undying fiery worm which does not waste the body but continues bursting forth from the body with unending pain. No sleep will give them rest; no night will soothe them; no death will deliver them from punishment; no voice of interceding friends will profit them. For neither are the righteous seen by them any longer, nor are they worthy of remembrance.[8]

There is still time, then, for repentance and the washing away of sin from human beings to transform the old man into the new. God shows his love toward us by creating us in his likeness, and if we obey his solemn injunctions and become a faithful follower of him who is good, we shall resemble Him when He confers honor upon us. "For the Deity [by condescension] does not diminish aught of the dignity of His divine perfection; having made thee even God unto His glory."[9]

NOTES

The text is in Migne, *Patrologia Graeca,* vol. 10; a translation by Mac Mahon and Salmond is in *The Ante-Nicene Fathers,* vol. 5 (*see* Bibliography).

1. Eusebius *Ecclesiastical History* 5. 28
2. *Refutation of all Heresies* 10. 28 (MG 16, 3, 3446).
3. Ibid., 10. 29.
4. *On Christ and Antichrist* chap. 3.
5. *Refutation of all Heresies* 10. 30 (MG 16,3)
6. Ibid.
7. *Against the Greeks* chap. 2.
8. Ibid., chap. 3.
9. *Refutation of All Heresies* 10. 30.

Lactantius

Scholars of the Renaissance dubbed Lactantius the Christian Cicero because of his excellent Latinity, combining vast erudition with a fine writing style, yet we know very little about him personally. He was born in the middle of the third century and in all likelihood died at Trier about the year 325. He studied rhetoric under Arnobius at Sicca in North Africa, but whether he himself was a native of North Africa or came from Italy is open to conjecture. We are not even sure of his name—Lucius Caelius (sometimes Caecilius) Firmianus Lactantius—for the third name could refer to his birthplace Firmium on the Adriatic, while Lactantius could even refer to the milky suaveness of his style. Certain it is that the scholar outran the master; he became so famous as a teacher of rhetoric that Emperor Diocletian invited him to teach at Nicomedia. Here he did not fare well, and after embracing Christianity (possibly during the period of persecution in the early fourth century), he moved west and settled in Gaul. Around 315 he was tutoring Crispus, the young son of Emperor Constantine, dying approximately ten years later.

The Divine Institutes is Lactantius's major work, divided in seven books (possibly in imitation of Arnobius) and each dealing with a specific topic: the false worship of the gods, the origin of error, the false wisdom of the philosophers, true wisdom and religion, justice, true worship, and the happy life. Attached to the work is an epitome dedicated to Pentadius. *The Anger of God* is directed against the Epicureans and Stoics, who held that God or the gods were totally divorced from this world and could not be influenced by men's actions. This would undermine Lactantius's doctrine of future rewards and punishments. In *The Workmanship of God (The Formation of Man)* he analyzes the marvellous make-up of the human body and uses final causality to prove the wisdom and goodness of the Creator. There is also a discussion on the nature and origin of the soul. That the emperors who were most zealous in the persecution of Christians illustrated the vengeance of God by their untimely deaths is maintained in the treatise *On the Death of Persecutors;* there are also some fragments and minor works of doubtful authenticity.

Lactantius is the first writer (whom we have met) to discuss the notion of religion to any great extent. True religion is true wisdom, and neither can be separated from the other. But wisdom precedes religion because the knowledge of God comes first, and worship is the result of knowledge. Wisdom relates to sons, and this relation requires love while religion relates to servants and requires fear. Wisdom loves and honors the Father; religion respects and venerates the Lord. But since God is one only while sustaining the twofold character of both Father and Lord, we are bound to love him as sons but fear him as servants. And so, wisdom and religion cannot be separated from each other because it is the same God who is understood on the part of wisdom and honored on the part of religion.[1] For what is religion? It does not mean to gather up or collect carefully *(relegere)* as Cicero thought, but rather to tie up or tie fast *(religare)* since we are bound and tied to God with a chain of piety. For we are created on this condition, that we pay just and due obedience to God who created us.[2] Now it is true that philosophy not infrequently approaches the truth, but these precepts have no weight because they are human and lack divine authority; for that reason, no one believes them.[3] In the present order, then, a revealed religion is morally necessary for us.

Where philosophy is found wanting, prophecy succeeds, for being filled with the inspiration of the one God, prophets predicted things to come, which predictions have been fulfilled, and are in process of being fulfilled daily. Nor were the prophets frenzied speakers bordering on insanity, but they spoke as holy men quite indifferent to the consequences of their preaching, and with no eye to gaining riches, prestige or power as a result. Quite the opposite; they lived from day to day on what God provided, and some even endured torment and death.[4]

Now, one of the aims of religious worship is to imitate the divinity that is being accorded divine honors. But it is easy to show why the worshipers of the pagan gods cannot be just themselves. How can they, for instance, keep from shedding blood if they worship Mars and Bellona, or honor their parents if they worship Jupiter, who ejected his own father, or Saturn, who did not spare his own children? No one can uphold chastity and still worship a naked goddess, nor refrain from plunder and fraud when they worship the deceitful Mercury. So men who are naturally good are trained to injustice by the very gods they worship. It follows, then, that morality and worship are closely connected; immoral deities cannot produce moral behavior in their idolatrous clients.[5]

Contrast all this with the patience of the martyrs under torture, overpowering their tormentors by silence, and this through their own free will since they put their trust in God. Escape is possible even for women and boys, but instead they submit to the fire without so much as a groan. All of this is proof positive of the truth of the Christian religion.[6]

For the God of the Christians is not perceived directly through the senses, but by the eyes of the mind, since we see his illustrious, his wonderful works. Those who deny the existence of God do not deserve the name of philosopher; they are not even men, but more like dumb animals since they refer all things to the bodily senses, thinking that only what they can actually see must exist.[7] Surely no one is so uncivilized or uncultured as not to understand from the very magnitude of the objects, from their motion, arrangement, constancy, usefulness, beauty, and temperament, that there is some providence which has an even greater intelligence than the order which is everywhere around us. And so, God can be clearly known through the world which he has made.[8] He is perfect, he made all things, and there is no other god beside Him, all things are therefore in him. The world is made out of nothing, for God has the power not merely to make the world, but to make the materials from which the world is made.[9]

The great mystery of God is that he is Three Persons. The Father gives birth to the Son by a divine operation which cannot be known or declared by any one, but through the sacred writings we learn that the Son is the speech or the reason of God; the Son is the Word who was to be a teacher of the knowledge of God of the heavenly mystery to be revealed to men. Unlike a human voice, the voice of God both remains forever and is accompanied with perception and power, and if all of this seems a mystery, it is nonetheless clearly attested in the sacred utterances of the prophets.[10]

Born the first time of God without benefit of a mother, the Word is born the second time without a father, so that it was fitting that the Son should be twice born, "motherless" the first time, "fatherless" the second, a spiritual birth the first time, the second time "after the flesh." He became both the Son of God through the Holy Spirit, and the Son of man through the flesh—hence, both God and man.[11]

But when we speak of God the Father and God the Son, says Lactantius, we do not speak of them as different, nor do we separate each, because the Father cannot exist without the Son, nor can the Son be separated from the Father since the name of Father cannot be given without the Son, nor can the Son be begotten without the Father. So both have one mind, one spirit, one substance (and here Lactantius uses the traditional similes: the stream from the overflowing fountain, the light-ray from the sun); and since the mind and will of the one is in the other, or rather, since there is one in both, both are justly called one God; for whatever is in the Father flows on to the Son, and whatever is in the Son descends from the Father.[12]

Now, the power of God is so great that he even creates and manages incorporeal things, and because he can punish them in some unspeakable manner, even the angels fear him, and the devils dread him because they actually are tormented by him; all this, we shall see, applies likewise to the souls of men.[13] God creates man with a corporeal element and a non-corporeal element and endows him with the knowledge of good and evil. But knowledge of good and evil is not virtue; it lies in the doing; yet knowledge is so united with virtue that knowledge precedes virtue, and virtue follows knowledge, because knowledge is of no avail unless it is followed up by action.[14]

This makes it possible for everyone to have confidence in his own judgment and individual capacity for the investigation of the truth since God has given wisdom to all alike, that they might be able both to investigate things which they have not seen, and weigh the things which they have heard. The inquiry after truth is natural to all, so why accept slavishly the opinions of one's ancestors without looking into the matter on one's own? Not to do so is simply to be led by others like sheep.[15]

Unbiased inquiry such as this concludes that Christ must indeed have been God because he fulfilled the prophecies which had been spoken of him long ago. His suffering and death are even more convincing than his miracles because a magician like Apollonius or Apuleius may do miracles, but it was through the fulfillment of the Scriptures that Christ evoked man's belief in his divinity.[16] Belief in Christ does not rest on Christ's own testimony—although Lactantius never denies that—but rather extrinsic proof which must convince the inquiring and unprejudiced investigator.

There is no doubt that Christ's birth was miraculous. The Holy Spirit of God, descending from heaven, chose the holy Virgin, that he might enter into her womb; she was suddenly pregnant without any intercourse with a man, but by possession of the divine Spirit.[17] Christ appeared among men as a man, thus bearing a middle substance between God and man which enables him to take this frail and weak nature of ours by the hand and raise it to immortality.[18]

Scant notice is taken of the sacraments of the church, but this is understandable in view of our writer's aim. However, he does mention penance because the true Catholic church is that in which there is confession and repentance, for this treats in a wholesome manner the sins and wounds to which the weakness of the flesh is liable. Therefore it is the Catholic church alone which retains true worship; it is the fountain of truth, the abode of faith, the temple of God, and anyone who does not enter it, or leaves it, is estranged from the hope of life and eternal salvation. No salvation without confession and repentance, no salvation without the church, for it is the function of the church in this manner to heal mankind.[19]

With regard to the sacrament of marriage, Lactantius warns that he is an adulterer who marries a divorced spouse, and he who dismisses his wife commits adultery, for God is unwilling to dissociate the body.[20] He always insists on the body-mind dualism, sins of the flesh are punished in the body, those of the mind in the spirit.

And therefore souls, though they are immortal, are nevertheless capable of suffering at the hand of God. Lactantius implies a particular judgment as well as a general judgment. Because men have committed sins in their bodies, they will again be clothed with flesh that they may make atonement in their bodies; and yet it will not be that flesh with which God clothed man, like this our earthly body, but indestructible, abiding forever, that it may be able to hold out against tortures and everlasting fire, the nature of which is different from ordinary fire.[21] All of this suggests some sort of purgatorial state along with the eternal punishments of the damned. The pain of sense is administered by corporeal fire which differs from earthly fire, and the punishment of the wicked is amply witnessed by the Scriptures.

Lactantius is a millenarist. The Son of God will destroy unrighteousness and execute his great judgment, revivify the righteous and will rule among men for a thousand years. During this period an infinite multitude will be produced and their offspring shall be holy and beloved by God. About the same time the prince of the devils will be bound and imprisoned during the thousand years of the heavenly rule; the world will rejoice and all nature exult; beasts will not be nourished by blood, nor birds by prey, but all things shall be peaceful and tranquil. When the thousand years are over, God will renew the earth, and the heavens shall be folded together, the earth changed, and men transformed like angels—white as snow. They will always be employed in the sight of the Almighty, make offerings to him and serve him forever. At the same time, the second and public resurrection of everyone will take place, in which the unrighteous will be raised to everlasting punishments.[22] There is a vivid description of the divine fire which burns forever and consumes bodies only to restore them again, while those who have enough of God within them are capable of repelling the flame's violence. But this occurs after all have been detained in a common place of confinement until the arrival of the time in which the great Judge will make an investigation of each one's proper deserts. It would seem that everyone receives a period of waiting in purgatory if that is what Lactantius means.

Throughout the seven books of the *Institutes* it is Lactantius's express purpose to overthrow all false religion by refuting all possible arguments brought forward in its defense, and then to prove the system of philosophy likewise false. His aim is to show that true religion and true wisdom go together, and that both can be proved by arguments, examples, and witnesses.[23] But it is the Catholic church alone which retains true worship, and the contest is respecting life and salvation, which, unless it is carefully and diligently kept in view, will be lost and extinguished. Now it is only here (and not in the assembly of the heretics) that we learn that the world has been created for this purpose: that we may be born to acknowledge the Maker of the world and of ourselves—God. We acknowledge him for this end, that we may worship him to receive immortality as the reward of our labors, since the worship of God consists of the greatest labors; for this end we are rewarded with immortality; that being made like to the angels, we may serve the Supreme Father and Lord forever, and may be to all eternity a Kingdom to God. This is the sum of all things, this the secret of God, this the mystery of the world.[24]

But Lactantius is better at demolishing paganism and philosophy than he is at establishing Christianity as the one true religion. Charming and gracious as his style is, he is not so convincing as some of the other apologists, and in general the verdict of Jerome is correct. It was given to others to erect the imposing structure of Catholic Christianity in the fourth century; it was the office of Lactantius to clear the ground of the already demolished pagan rubble in order that this new structure could securely stand.

NOTES

The text is in Migne, *Patrologia Latina*, vol. 6; a translation by W. Fletcher is in *The Ante-Nicene Fathers*, vol. 7 (*see* Bibliography).

1. *The Divine Institutes* 4. 4.
2. Ibid., 4. 28.
3. Ibid., 3. 27.
4. Ibid., 1. 4.
5. Ibid., 5. 10.
6. Ibid., 5. 13.
7. Ibid., 7. 9.
8. Ibid., 1. 2.
9. Ibid., 1. 3; 2. 9
10. Ibid., 4. 8.
11. Ibid., 4. 13
12. Ibid., 4. 29.
13. Ibid., 7. 21.
14. Ibid., 6. 5.
15. Ibid., 2. 8.
16. Ibid., 5. 3.
17. Ibid., 4. 12.
18. Ibid., 4. 13.
19. Ibid., 4. 30.
20. Ibid., 6. 23.
21. Ibid., 7. 21.
22. Ibid., 7. 24.
23. Ibid., 3. 30.
24. Ibid., 7. 6.

Aphrahat

Aphrahat (Aphraates) was a Persian who wrote in Syriac during the fourth century a number of Demonstrations, or essays on various topics of the Christian faith. Originally twenty-two in number, to correspond to the letters of the Syriac alphabet, the first ten (as we learn from the text itself) were written in 337, and the last twelve in 344. A twenty-third Demonstration, entitled *On the Grape* was written a year later. The first ten deal with various aspects of the Christian life and are: *On Faith, Charity, Fasting, Prayer, Wars, Monks, Penitents, The Resurrection, Humility, Pastors.* In the last group the first three Demonstrations relate to Judaism: *On Circumcision, The Passover, The Sabbath;* these are followed by an address to the clergy and people of Seleucia and Ctesiphon which is entitled *Hortatory,* and then there are five more Jewish discourses: *On Various Meats, The Call of the Gentiles, Jesus the Messiah, Virginity, The Dispersion of Israel.* The last three discourses return to the generalized subject matter of the first group: *On Giving Alms, Persecution, Death and the Latter Times.* The final (twenty-third) essay *On the Grape* discusses the blessings which have come to us through Christ, and is a Demonstration of considerable stature.

It is difficult to determine whether these essays of Aphrahat come before or after those of Saint Ephraim; all that we can determine is that both writers are contemporaries, and if they are not the founders, they are at least the first important writers we know of who wrote in Syriac. While the Demonstrations of Aphrahat never achieved the popularity of the Hymns and Homilies of Saint Ephraim, they were nonetheless widely read. Certain it is that the Persian Sage, as he was called, was a priest and very likely a bishop as well, being possibly also a convert from paganism. His writings possess a certain detached quality; they do not reflect to any great extent the times in which he lived, much less the controversies raging in the West. But there is a warmth and geniality in the Demonstrations which show their author deeply immersed in the study of the Scriptures and a master of the Old Testament. His writings are forceful, persuasive, and often eloquent, and it is not hard to see why they were cherished by the various branches of the Eastern church.[1]

The ideas of revealed religion, of the church and its aspects, of Scripture and tradition, of God and his essence and attributes, and the salvific will, Aphrahat treats only indirectly and incidently. The faith of the church is to believe in God the Lord of all, who made the heavens and the earth and the seas and all that is in them; and he made Adam in his image; and he gave the Law to Moses; he sent of his Holy Spirit upon the prophets; he sent moreover his Christ into the world. Man must also believe in the resurrection of the dead, and should furthermore also believe in the sacrament of baptism.[2] And since the Trinitarian formula is used in baptism, God for Aphrahat is a three-personed Father, Son, and Holy Spirit.[3]

God created all things out of nothing, and molded Adam out of the dust of the earth, so that he is nothing also.[4] But Adam was also created with an immortal and incorporeal soul, and that is why it is possible for God to raise him up at the last.[5] Thanks to Adam's transgression, however, sin has reigned in all his descendants with the single exception of Christ, whose function it was to remove this curse from mankind.[6] But man is not so corrupted that he cannot be justified before God; he has the ability to implore the Almighty for graces both natural and supernatural.[7] Justification carries with it a spark of the divine, the Holy Spirit dwells in him at baptism.

It is a sure thing to say that Jesus our Lord is God, the Son of God, and the King, the King's Son, Light of light, Creator and Counselor, and Guide, and the Way, and the Redeemer, and Shepherd, Gatherer, and the Door, and the Pearl, and the Lamp, and a number of other names, says Aphrahat. But most important of all, he who came from God is the Son of God, and is God. Some have suggested a Nestorian tinge to the Persian Sage's theology, but it does not really seem warranted.[8] Yet the Son of God took his body from Mary and was truly made man, more glorious than Adam had been.[9] Christ received the Holy Spirit unstintingly: his Father loved him and delivered everything into his hands, and gave him authority over all that the Father had,[10] for the Son was free of both original and personal sin.[11] He was thus able to liberate us from sin by reconciling us with the Father, as Saint Paul says (2 Cor. 5:18, 19), and making of himself a vicarious sacrifice.

It is the sacramental theology of Aphrahat which is the most rewarding. The sacraments confer grace by virtue of the Holy Spirit who is present in the rite. This is especially true in baptism, for when the priests invoke the Spirit, the heavens open and it descends and moves upon the waters, carnal man thus becoming spiritual. Whereas the baptism of John was intended to incite penance among his followers, the baptism of Jesus, instituted during the Passover feast prior to his Passion, was for the remission of sins.[12] As already noted, the Trinitarian formula accompanies the rite, and mention is likewise made of an anointing with oil, which is the sacrament of life.[13]

The twelfth Demonstration, *On the Passover,* makes clear reference to the real Presence in the Eucharist by commenting specifically on the words of institution.[14] The words of Christ, then, are not to be taken in a figurative, but in a literal sense. But apart from this, Aphrahat does not have a fully worked-out doctrine of the Mass.

Penance has an external side as well as an internal forum; using the analogy from medicine Aphrahat likens the confessor to a surgeon who is to follow certain rules of prudence.[15] Private confession is made to a priest who is forbidden to publish the sins of the penitent.

The doctrines with regard to the last things occupy a prominent place in the thought of Aphrahat.[16] In death, the animal spirit of man is buried with the body, and sense is taken away from it, but the heavenly spirit goes according to its nature to Christ, to commend him or accuse him as the case may be. The Life-Giver will come, He who destroys death, and will nullify death's power over the just and the wicked. Then the dead will rise with a mighty shout, death being emptied and stripped of all its captivity. The children of Adam will all be gathered together for judgment and each shall go to the place prepared for him—the risen of the righteous unto life, while sinners are delivered unto death.[17]

Each man according to his work will receive his reward; he that toiled little shall receive according to his remissness, while he that made much speed will be rewarded in like fashion. Just as star excels star in brightness, as the Apostle says, rewards will differ—glory will excel glory and recompense will excel recompense. This is likewise true with regard to punishments, with various places assigned to the guilty— some going to outward darkness where there is weeping and gnashing of teeth (symbolic of remorse), while some are cast into fire and still others are gnawed by the worm which never dies, to become an astonishment to everyone. And so, rewards vary for both the good man and the evil.[18]

Aphrahat closes on a pleasant note of modesty. People are not to inquire who wrote these essays, but rather to pay attention to what has been written; for, after all, the author is only an insignificant son of Adam, fashioned by God, and a disciple of the Holy Scriptures. Moreover, since he is a sinner, he asks that prayers be diligently said for him, a brother of the Body, that through the petition of all the Church of God, his sins may be forgiven. And thus it will come about that the sower and reaper shall rejoice together (Jno. 4:36).[19]

NOTES

1. *See* John Gwynn, *Aphrahat the Persian Sage,* introductory dissertation in *Nicene and Post-Nicene Fathers,* second series, vol. 13, p. 152 ff; also Jacobus Forget, *De Vita et Scriptis Aphraatis* (Louvain: Valinthout Brothers, 1882)
2. Demonstrations 1. 19
3. Ibid., 23. 63
4. Ibid., 8. 6
5. Ibid., 6. 14
6. Ibid., 7. 1; 23. 3
7. Ibid., 23. 48,
8. Ibid., 17. 2,
9. Ibid., 23. 51
10. Ibid., 6. 12,
11. Ibid., 7. 1
12. Ibid., 12. 10
13. Ibid., 23. 3
14. Ibid., 12. 6
15. Ibid., 7. 3.
16. Ibid., 6. 14.
17. Ibid., 22. 15.
18. Ibid., 22. 22.
19. Ibid., 22. 26.

VIII

THE TRINITARIAN CONTROVERSY OF THE FOURTH CENTURY

There is abundant source material for the Trinitarian controversy of the fourth century as evidenced by such writers as Eusebius, Athanasius, Socrates, Sozomen, and Theodoret, to name only a few. Suddenly, at the beginning of the fourth century Christianity found itself no longer a persecuted minority, but in a favored religious position which was to perdure and improve as time went on. Despite a brief setback under Julian, church and state were to cooperate in the promotion of ecclesial and civil harmony for generations to come. But if Christianity was the cement which held the empire together, the emperor Constantine must have been astounded to discover the cement beginning to crack, due to a controversy over the precise relationship of the Son of God to the Blessed Trinity.

The correct or "orthodox" solution had been reached in fairly short order at Nicea in 325, when the First Ecumenical Council arrived at its far-reaching decision. The balance of the century was to be spent in a staunch defense of this *parti pris* against those who were determined to enforce Arian and modified Arian positions to the contrary. The quarrel was much more articulated in the East where it became inextricably mixed up in political chicanery. But through all the vicissitudes of the unhappy controversy, one man of exceptional ability and moral fiber stood firm until the very end where he triumphed magnificently, the redoubtable Athanasius.

Eusebius of Caesarea

Multifaceted is the word for Eusebius of Caesarea, or Eusebius Pamphili, as he preferred to be called, adopting for his own the name of his dear friend and benefactor Pamphilus, who was martyred for the faith in 310 when the persecution launched by Diocletian was raging at its height in Caesarea. Born about the year 260, his early life was spent in Palestine where he tells us that he once saw the young Constantine with the emperor Diocletian, and who even then furnished splendid proof of his coming greatness.[1] Baptized and ordained a presbyter at Caesarea, Eusebius came under the influence of the great Pamphilus, who was an enthusiastic disciple of Origen's. The library at Caesarea was excellent and enabled Eusebius to pursue his various scholarly interests to their fullest. But in March 303 Diocletian's edict was enforced against the Christians of Palestine, thus ending a hitherto unknown period of tranquility for the church. Unlike his colleague Pamphilus, Eusebius escaped martyrdom either by absenting himself from the scene of distress or temporizing in some manner, as his enemies were later to suggest. This last seems hardly likely since he was subsequently to become bishop of the city,[2] and indeed was even invited in 330 to the see of Antioch. Eusebius had the opportunity of witnessing the persecutions firsthand, and he has left us a vivid account of the years prior to 311, when the persecutions by order of the dying Galerius ceased. But Maximin revived the persecutions at the end of the same year, nor did they stop until he committed suicide in 313.

Constantine and Licinius now proclaimed peace, and before their falling-out in 314, eighteen months later, Eusebius was consecrated bishop of Caesarea. For the next ten years he was busy with the reconstruction of the devastated see, devoting his time to administrative work and the pastoral needs of his people. At the same time, the new era of good feeling had begun to be upset by the growth of Arianism, about the year 318. Eusebius was by no means sympathetic with Arius' attempt to subordinate the Son to the Father, declaring that there was a time before the Son existed, but neither did he endorse the orthodox party which he felt leaned heavily toward Sabellianism.

By the year 324 Constantine had at last succeeded in bringing Licinius to bay, thus reuniting the empire after many years of divisiveness.

But since Constantine was a Christian as well as emperor, he viewed himself as having a special relationship to the church, and determined to call an empire-wide council to meet at Nicaea and deal with a number of church matters, including the Arian problem. In the late spring of 325 the great council was opened by Emperor Constantine himself conducting the proceedings. In an attempt to mediate between the party of Arius and the orthodox party, Eusebius brought forth the creed of Caesarea as a compromise solution to the problem, and possibly as a vindication of his own position. This action had the effect of putting him back into the good graces of the emperor, but the creed itself was rejected by the council because it did not really solve the very point under dispute. And the newly formed Nicene creed seemed out of harmony with that of Caesarea!

The Arian dispute, far from ending with the Council of Nicaea in 325, had just begun. The latter years of Eusebius's life (he had returned to his former love of scholarship and writing) saw a good deal of political maneuvering and the attempt to oust Athanasius from Alexandria. In 335 Eusebius presided over a council meeting at Tyre to mediate between Athanasius and his enemies. Exasperated, Athanasius went to Constantinople to confer with the emperor himself; meanwhile, the council condemned him.[3] A new council met at Jerusalem to dedicate on September 14 the Church of the Holy Sepulchre, Arius was received into communion and now Athanasius was condemned. Eusebius wrote his oration *In Praise of Constantine* which he delivered in Constantinople and which (even he admits) is redolent with adulation.[4] The Arian controversy raged on, and in 337 the great emperor himself died. Eusebius was soon to follow him, having retired from the arena of dispute to the quieter life of the scholar; he died probably in the year 339 prior to Constantine II in 340.

Eusebius is such a prolific writer that only his most important works can be mentioned here. He is best known, of course, for his *Ecclesiastical History* which makes him the father of all church historians. It is divided into ten books, and deals with the history of the Christian church from its earliest beginnings up through the time of Licinius, if we consider Book X as included only in the second edition of 324.[5] The *Ecclesiastical History* contains a vast amount of information, but its value is offset by the author's inability to control his material. His discussion of Origen's life and work demonstrates enthusiasm and admiration for that great third-century figure. At the same time, Eusebius is less satisfactory when dealing with his own period, and he is not altogether to be trusted when dealing with Constantine. And it is a truism that the inflated style of the author often makes the reading dull. Still, the *Ecclesiastical History* is a great work, and will always be a landmark in the scholarship of church history. *The Martyrs of*

Palestine which usually appears at the end of Book VIII is a splendid firsthand account of the persecution in the early fourth century in the East.

The *Life of Constantine (Vita Constantini)* is comprised of four books and is clearly a paean of praise on behalf of the emperor; Eusebius deletes anything which does not redound to Constantine's praise, such as the death of his son Crispus, or his wife Fausta. But then this was no ordinary emperor in the eyes of Eusebius, it was the first Christian emperor who had finally brought universal harmony to mankind by a happy marriage between the great Roman Empire and the true religion of Christ which had been struggling for three centuries to convince the world that this was the one and only way in which God was rightly worshiped and salvation rightly attained. If the panegyrics often seem excessive it is because Eusebius idealized what he felt was a happy and final resolution of what had been a cosmic conflict of vast proportions.

The *Praeparatio* and *Demonstratio Evangelica* are actually two parts of a single book. The *Preparation* embraces fifteen books and is a mine of information on ancient philosophy. But the main target is Porphyry, the Neoplatonist, who was attempting to revive the ancient paganism by reinterpreting it in more spiritual, Neoplatonic terms. This had the advantage of appealing to antiquity, but pagan antiquity understood in modern, rationalistic terms. Eusebius rejects this attempt by countering, that while Christianity seems to be a new religion, actually it is the explicit fulfillment of very ancient religion. Thus we have an apologetic for Christianity which meets Porphyry on his own grounds, while at the same time showing that the Neoplatonistic revival of paganism is already foredoomed to failure. The *Preparation* is an apologetic of mountainous learning assembled together in a not very readable style.[6]

The *Demonstration* assumes that the previous section has been successful and is addressed to Christian converts. Of the fifteen original books, only ten have survived. The *Demonstration* is mainly devoted to combing through the Old Testament Scriptures to prove that they really prophesied the coming of Christ. The aim is to show that the religion of Abraham (and Christianity is its logical fulfillment) was really designed for the entire human race. That is why Christians have appropriated the Hebrew Scriptures while at the same time rejecting the ceremonial customs of the Old Testament. In this way Eusebius once again attempts to meet the charge of novelty leveled against Christianity by its enemies.

But suppose that the religion of Jesus was actually invented by the disciples, who pretended that he had risen from the dead and acclaimed him the greatest man who had ever lived, even though they might themselves have to endure incredible suffering and even death. What if the earliest Christians had deliberately set out to propagate a lie? Eusebius shows how absurd such actions would be, and thereby disposes of modern rationalism a good many centuries before its vogue in the eighteenth and nineteenth centuries.[7] His detailed commentary on the life of Christ involves him in a comparison of the Gospels, and makes him one of the first scholars to handle the so-called Synoptic problem.

The thorny question now arises: What is Eusebius's teaching regarding the relationship of the divine Son to the Father? Was he really an Arian, a Semi-Arian, or indeed quite orthodox?

First, it must be remembered that Eusebius's strength lies in the field of Biblical and historical criticism rather than in systematic theology. This is not to say that he lacked ability as a theologian, but rather that he lacked the subtle skill and precise nuance of some of his opponents. Further, while Eusebius's erudition was enormous, he still lacked the ability to synthesize it in such a manner that he could avoid Sabellianism on the one hand and tritheism or subordination- ism on the other. He was quite content to fall back on the creed of Caesarea, but this earlier creed simply did not deal with the problem at hand. When the emperor Constantine added the word $\delta\mu oo\nu\sigma\iota os$, Eusebius was forced to accept this with reluctance, for he thought it possessed unsavory connections with subordinationist heresies of the third century (Paul of Samosata) to say nothing of being unscriptural. It is quite likely that $\delta\mu oo\nu\sigma\iota os$ did not mean to him what it meant to the Nicene party. Eusebius was certainly no Arian; Christ was divine as well as human, the Word of God, the Power of God, the Wisdom of God, the Angel of Great Council and the Great Eternal High Priest,[8] but when speaking of his divinity he used the questionable expression "image of God" which may not imply a second God but at least implies some sort of subordination. Given his starting point, Biblical exegesis colored by Origenistic interpretation, Eusebius ended up (as Wallace-Hadrill has so ably shown) by postulating two Gods, a greater and a lesser, which he could never succeed in uniting. Intent on avoiding the Sabellian heresy, he fell into the opposite extreme and never could subscribe to the exact meaning of the Nicene position. In an attempt to mediate between it and the creed of Caesarea, he found himself defending an impossible position.[9]

But it is as historian that Eusebius is at his best. To assist him in the preparation of the famed *History* he tells us that he drew up chronological tables—a chronography outlining the history of the Assyrians, Hebrews, Egyptians, Greeks, and Romans, and supplemented by the *Canons,* a ready-reference table of comparative dates. The *Canons* have survived only in Jerome's Latin translation. Both the *Ecclesiastical History* and the *Canons* form the base of Eusebius's overall view of the meaning of history. Three great men punctuate the experience of the human race: Abraham, Christ, and Constantine. To Abraham came God's promise of being the father of many descendants, of possessing a land which was particularly blessed by the Deity, and of being a special vehicle of blessing to all the races of mankind. Abraham was a purveyor of the true religion, not yet enucleated in all its details, but present none the less in embryonic form. This primitive but true religion (for so Eusebius views it) embodied a pristine revelation which unfortunately was to be overlain later with the Mosaic cultus of laws and precepts. But in spite of this, a true and primitive revelation had been made to Abraham which could not be obliterated through the centuries. This, Christ came to restore, thus doing away with the Mosaic Law, and opening up the Gospel to Jew and Gentile alike. In a sense Christ becomes a second Abraham in whom all generations are to be blessed, and the church comes to mediate this blessing to a pagan world. But the demons who have long clouded men's minds and perverted their wills raise opposition to the New Dispensation, and the State, not realizing that the Church is actually its friend, persecutes unwittingly. But with the advent of Constantine the church and Christianity are recognized for what they really are—the cement which binds the empire together, and church and state are united in a harmonious embrace for the spiritual and temporal welfare of all men. As a philosophy of history this is perhaps a bit too neat, but from Eusebius's vantage point it did seem that gradually throughout the history of the ages men were coming together, that true religion had appeared with the ancient Hebrews, that the Pax Romana was a necessary and altogether appropriate vehicle for the birth of the Gospel and the spread of the Good News, and that now all had been finalized in his "Most Christian Majesty," Emperor Constantine, who for Eusebius not merely ruled the political destinies of his subjects, but also had some responsibility for their spiritual destinies as well. Eusebius was never so blind to the personal defects of Constantine as to make of him a kind of quasi-pope, but could see the very real advantages of a union of church and state, particularly when the emperor and his three sons exemplified the best of both possible worlds. It would not be too much to expect that a millennial reign of world harmony was about to be inaugurated which would make all men one in Rome and in the Lord simultaneously. That all the facts in the case cannot so easily be accounted for would not have troubled Eusebius; after all, Scripture itself is not detached history so much as history with a distinct religious bias.

In his last great work, *Theophany,* Eusebius sums up the principal concerns of his life. Once again, we are in the presence of a man of vast erudition, of a man who has played a prominent and significant role in the affairs of the empire, a man whose sole preoccupation has been with the person and work of Jesus Christ. He enjoyed enormous respect and prestige from the emperor on down, and there was no one who questioned his ability. Even his enemies respected him, and he was a big enough man to be a target of Athanasius himself. But Eusebius has never been canonized; the allegation is often made that he shed much light but little warmth.[10] While it may be unfair to claim that there is a total lack of spirituality in the immense volume of his writings, yet it is true that Eusebius represents a this-worldly rather than an other-worldly view of Christ's church on earth. At a time when the credibility gap between Everyman and the divine destiny of the Roman Empire was certainly widening, thanks to distress internal and external, and incipient monasticism was being started by such men as Paul of Thebes, Anthony, Pachomius, and others bent on fleeing the world, Eusebius reminded his age that the incarnate Christ had never been so mystical as to write the present age off altogether. But in a sense, his summing up came perhaps too late; already a new era was dawning for the church which would render Eusebius almost obsolete. His contribution would not be to the mystical speculation which was to make the fourth century redolent with theological precision; his contribution was the common-sense one of preserving for future generations an accurate record of the past, and as a church historian, to do monumental service for future generations in understanding the life and meaning of the church in its temporal aspect. In this respect he was too early for his time; he would not be appreciated fully until the revival of historical studies, which would not come into their own until modern times.

NOTES

The text is in Migne, *Patrologia Graeca*, vols. 19-24; a translation by Defarrari is in *The Fathers of the Church* (*see* Bibliography).

1. *Vita Constantini* 1. 19; cf. A. C. McGiffert's exhaustive introduction to Eusebius in *Nicene and Post-Nicene Fathers*, vol. 1.
2. Epiphanius *Against the Heresies of the Panarians* 48.8.
3. Socrates *Ecclesiastical History* 1. 32 (trans. A. C. Zenos); Sozomen *Ecclesiastical History* 2. 25 (trans. C. D. Hartranft), in *Nicene and Post Nicene Fathers*, vol. 2.
4. *Vita Constantini* 4. 46.
5. Cf. McGiffert, "Introduction," p. 45 ff.
6. Cf. Bishop Lightfoot's fine article on Eusebius in the *Dictionary of Christian Biography*
7. *Demonstratio Evangelica* 3. 5.
8. Ibid., 10. 1
9. D. S. Wallace-Hadrill, *Eusebius of Caesarea* (London: A. R. Bowbray & Co., 1960), p. 137 ff.
10. Wallace-Hadrill does a fine job of evaluating Eusebius in the conclusion of his penetrating study cited above.

Saint Athanasius

When the great emperor Diocletian abdicated the reins of power in 303 (actually persuading his colleague Maximian to do the same!) and retired to his villa in Salona to hoe cabbages,[1] he left the empire a prey to civil war which was not finally resolved until 323 when the great Constantine eliminated his last rival Licinius, and became sole ruler of an empire finally reunited. One of the ingredients in this long struggle for ascendancy was the position of the contenders vis-à-vis the Christian church, for the policy of persecution or toleration rested in no small part on political expediency. Nor would it be difficult for Christians themselves to throw their spiritual and temporal support behind the candidate who was most sympathetic to their cause and likewise offered a reasonable chance of ultimate success. After the famous vision of the cross in the noon day sky followed by the command of the Lord Jesus to "conquer in this sign," the success of the Battle of Milvian Bridge in 312 certainly seemed to have divine backing. The Edict of Milan followed the next year, granting equal rights for all religions and toleration for the long-persecuted church. It was not immediately evident at the time that the edict might not be overthrown at some future date by a contender less friendly to Christianity, but thanks to the continued success of Constantine, the edict was to hold firm.[2]

And so the fourth century opens a distinctly new chapter in the history of the church. Whatever Constantine's reasons for embracing the faith were, and there is no reason to doubt that he was fundamentally sincere and that his conversion was reasonably profound, certainly the effects were far-reaching, and not altogether salutary. From that time on, church and state were to be locked in an embrace which no doubt offered benefits to both sides, but which likewise brought serious handicaps. And this would continue until modern times when the doctrine of separation of church and state would likewise entail both bane and blessing. It was not long after the Edict of Milan that Constantine finally defeated his rival Licinius at Chrysopolis in 323 and executed him the following year. He then intervened in the Arian dispute and summoned the famed council of Nicaea in the following year in 325.

The actual proceedings of the First Ecumenical Council are no longer

241

extant; the emperor himself presided but we are not certain who really made the opening speech. There were a number of items on the agenda, but one of the most pressing was the dispute fomented by Arius over the nature of the Trinity. Arianism had broken out in Alexandria about the year 318 and had a good deal of popular appeal, thanks to the personality of Arius himself. Tall, gaunt, ascetic and handsome, Arius was a charismatic leader of no little influence, especially among ordinary folk, to say nothing of the opposite sex. There is no doubt that he excited some envy among the more staid clergy, and one thing which particularly outraged them was Arius' putting his doctrine into a kind of jingle form (Thalia) so that people could sing and remember it, in spite of the fact that the music was modeled on secular songs from the street. Today this might be called clever pedagogy, nor must we forget that almost all we know about Arius comes from people who are unsympathetic toward him.[3] Athanasius says his jingles were flippant and effeminate.

What did Arius teach? If we interpret him in the best possible light, Arius was trying to save the unicity of God by rejecting the Sabellian interpretations which seemed to him to compromise an essential monotheism. God alone is everlasting and unchanging so that one cannot speak of the Father as suffering, or of the Holy Spirit and the Son as coeternal with Him. Father, Son, and Holy Spirit may be God, but they cannot be God in the same sense that God is God. There must be some distinction made between the Eternal, and those who are not quite eternal. Hence it follows that God was not always a Father, for once he was alone and afterward became a Father. This must mean that the Son had an origin, certainly not in time or at the outset of creation, but like creation he was born out of nothing. It would not be quite accurate to say there was a time when he was not, but simply "there was when He was not." Arius was never so gross as to try to apply a time element to the internal economy of the Trinity. He was simply trying to exclude everything which to him seemed to compromise the aloneness of God without Word or Wisdom.

Then, wishing to form man, God produced a certain one and named him Word, Wisdom, and Son, that God might form us by means of him. It follows that there are actually two wisdoms: first, the attribute coexistent with God, and next, that in this wisdom the Son was originated, and was only named Wisdom and Word as partaking of it. Therefore, "Wisdom, by the will of the wise God, had its existence in Wisdom." So there is another Word in God besides the son who thus partakes of it, and is named Word and Son according to grace. Likewise, there are many powers, one of which is God's own by nature, and therefore eternal, but that Christ, on the other hand, is not the true power of God but merely one of many powers—hence the expression, The Lord of Hosts, or many powers. Now since these powers are alterable, the Word himself is also alterable; the Word remains good by his own free choice, and God, foreknowing that he would be good, bestowed on the Word this glory, which afterwards, as man, he attained from virtue. Thus, "in consequence of His works foreknown," says Arius, "did God bring it to pass that He, being such, should come to be."[4]

So the Word is not truly God, but by participation of grace, he is God in name only. Now everything is foreign and different from God in essence and this includes the Word which is alien and unlike in all things to the Father's essence and propriety but belongs to things which were created and hence had a beginning. It follows that even to the Son the Father is invisible, nor can the Word perfectly and exactly either see or know his own Father. What he does see and know is in proportion to his own measure. The Son fails to comprehend completely the essence of the Father, for the essences of the Father, Son, and Holy Spirit are separate in nature, estranged and disconnected, alien and without participation in each other and utterly unlike from each other in essence and glory unto infinity. Thus, as to likeness of glory and essence, the Word is entirely diverse from both the Father and the Holy Spirit.

This was new doctrine. It is incorrect to hold that Arius was simply making explicit what could already be found in earlier Christian thinkers, notably Origen. It is true that numerous passages in the writings of the Fathers might be interpreted in the Arian sense, but it is equally true that earlier ages had often been less precise in the expression of theological niceties. In making the Son unlike the Father, Arius was both rejecting the earlier tradition, and making the divine economy of salvation impossible for man.

And so the Council of Nicea met. The emperor attempted to bring all parties into a harmonious agreement in fraternal charity, but his military and gubernatorial skill far exceeded his ability in the realm of theology. Eusebius of Caesarea offered the creed of his hometown as a happy solution to the problem, but the Caesarean creed was simply inadequate to deal with it and had to be discarded, or at least modified out of recognition. The problem of the orthodox party was to find a word or phrase to which the Arians could not and would not subscribe, and this they ultimately found in the famous homoousion formula:

> We believe in one God, the Father Almighty, of all things visible and invisible, the Maker, and in one Lord Jesus Christ, the Son of God, begotten of the Father, only begotten, that is, of the substance of the Father. God of God, Light of Light, true God of true God, begotten not made, *being of one substance* with the Father.

The word *homoousios* was suspect to even some of the members of the orthodox party because nowhere does it appear in Scripture and is therefore not Biblical, plus the fact that it had until then been associated with the Sabellian heresy. But it was the only word which could not be taken in an Arian sense, and so it became the rallying point of the party of Athanasius. At the end of the Nicene Symbol were added certain anathemas designed to clinch the whole argument:

> Those who say that "there was when He was not, and that "He was not before He was begotten," and that "He was made of things that are not," or who confess that the Son of God was of a different hypostasis or substance, or that He was created, or changeable, the Catholic and Apostolic Church anathematizes.

Seventeen bishops at first refused to sign, but ultimately their number dwindled until only Eusebius of Nicomedia, Theognis, Secundus, and Theonas held out. Eusebius and Theognis were banished by Constantine, who now considered the matter once and for all settled, further discussion being impertinent. To his dismay, the emperor began to realize that the discussion was just beginning, for hardly was the ink dry when a reaction against the Nicene Creed set in at once. Before adjourning, the council also tried to resolve the Easter question successfully, and attempted to deal with the Meletian schism, which had begun in Egypt as an ecclesiastical protest against the bishop of Alexandria and soon became Arian in its sympathies to show that it owed nothing to Athanasius, who was soon to become the new Alexandrian bishop. The Meletian schism did not peter out until a century later.

The great spirit at Nicea had been the young Athanasius himself, who was not more than twenty-eight years old at the time. Whether or not as a child he actually baptized his playmates,[5] he was certainly precocious. After the martyrdom of Peter, Alexander of Alexandria succeeded as bishop and was not long in recognizing the brilliant talents of his young protégé. Athanasius's early treatises *Against the Gentiles* and *Concerning the Incarnation* are modeled on the style of the traditional apologies for Christianity in its struggle against paganism. The characteristic controversial note does not enter until later times. Among other writings, the major outline of his thought is developed in the *Four Discourses Against the Arians* (only the first three are accepted as genuine) written between 356 and 362.

There is little point in going into detail with regard to Athanasius's hectic career following the Council of Nicea. In 328 he was elected bishop of Alexandria by common consent, following the blessing and then death of Alexander. A period of relative tranquility lasted until 335, when Athanasius was summoned to the Council of Tyre to answer certain frivolous charges which had been blown up, mainly by his Egyptian enemies sympathetic to the Meletian schismatics, and the sympathizers with Arius. Despairing of justice from the Council of Tyre, Athanasius fled to Constantinople and intercepted the emperor who was out horseback riding, who heard his case and then sent him into seclusion at Treveri (Trier). After receiving baptism, Constantine died in 337, and Athanasius was back in Alexandria in November of that year, but his stay was short-lived. In 339 he was forced to take refuge at Rome until the spring of 342, at which time he returned to Milan and then Trier. In July of 343 the Council of Sardica reviewed the charges against Athanasius and exonerated him from all culpability, whereupon Emperor Constans decided to enforce the decisions of the council against the Arianizing sympathies of Constantius. It was not until 346 after an interview with Constantius, his persecutor, at Antioch that Athanasius returned to his see at Alexandria in October of that year. The next ten years were ones of relative tranquility. After the murder of Constans in 350, Constantius became sole emperor, but unpleasantness did not break out again until 356 with Athanasius exiled a third time until 362. The Arian party was now at its height, but decline had already set in. Councils met and creeds were formulated with such frequency that the entire situation was growing ridiculous.[6] The death of Constantius in 361 set the exiled bishops of the Nicene party free with the advent of Julian "the Apostate" to the throne. Athanasius reappeared in Alexandria in 362 amid wild popular rejoicing, but the new emperor's hostile intent with regard to Christianity directed itself against Athanasius as a personal target. A fourth flight was necessary but the exile was short, for in July 363 Julian died at Ctesiphon after campaigning against the Persians and the new emperor Jovian was known to favor Nicene Christianity. But Jovian himself died the following year, leaving the throne to the Arian emperor Valens, who proceeded to reinforce the edict of Constantius against Athanasius, resulting in his fifth flight, until an imperial order declared his reinstatement in February of 366. His last years were spent in Alexandria, his death occurring probably in the spring or summer of the year 373.

The entire life of Saint Athanasius was devoted to a defense of the Nicene definition, and his whole theology centers around this Trinitarian formulation. But like Arius, he is most insistent that God is one, a simple, blessed and incomprehensible essence, and although we do not understand what God is, we know that when we call him Father, and God, and Almighty, we are actually naming his very Being.[7] He is immense and everywhere present. But when we speak of God, we speak of him in a different sense than when we speak of creation, so that to make correct assertions about God, Athanasius must fall back on the doctrine of analogy. God does not create in the same way that man makes, and humans beget in an altogether dissimilar manner from the divine begetting. Thus it is possible for the everlasting Word to co-exist with the Father, and still be begotten, for to deny the eternal coexistence of the Word with the Father is to say that once Wisdom was not; the Word was not, Life was not. The formula of baptism itself declares the ineffable Trinity.[8] The Trinity is One, yet we must distinguish between Father, Son, and Holy Spirit. The fullness of the Father's Godhead is the Being of the Son, for the whole Being of the Son is proper to the Father's essence, as radiance from light, and stream from fountain, so that to see the Son is to see the Father.

Father and Son are one, not as one thing divided into two parts, nor as the same thing named twice so that at one time it is the Father and another time the Son—this is the mistake Sabellius made—but they are two distinct Persons with the same nature. However, the offspring of the Father is still the same God; they are one in propriety and peculiarity of nature, and in the identity of the one Godhead.

This is the major point which Athanasius makes in all his writings, and it is the fundamental truth which inspired his entire life. In order to understand why he insists on it so repeatedly in virtually all of his writings, we must remember that he is stoutly opposing those who hold a monarchical position on the one hand, and those subordinationists on the other who would with Arius make the Son less than the Father. The principal opponents of Athanasius were the Semi-Arians who held that the Son was like the Father in all things, but who rejected the homoousion formula and are therefore called Homoians. The likeness of the Son to the Father implied that the Son was somehow inferior to the Father, and so the doctrine came to be called subordinationism.

Why was the continued defense of the Nicene position so important to Saint Athanasius? Because the whole economy of man's salvation rests upon it. If we are not saved by God himself we cannot be saved by God at all. In the *Treatise on the Incarnation of the Word* the saint tells us that although man was made out of nothing, He gave us freely, by the Grace of the Word, a life in correspondence with God. But man, having rejected things eternal, and by counsel of the devil, turned to the things of corruption, became the cause of their own corruption in death, being by nature corruptible, but destined to escape their natural state if they had remained good. To undo this fallen state of man the Word took to himself a body capable of death, so that by partaking of the Word who is above all, he would be worthy to die in the place of all, and being incorruptible would make others incorruptible through the grace of the resurrection. So Christ offered his body as an offering and sacrifice free from any stain. Being over all, the Word of God, naturally, by offering his own temple and corporeal instrument for everyone else, satisfied the debt by his death. The incorruptible Son of God, therefore, being conjoined with all by a like nature, naturally clothed all with incorruption, by the promise of the Resurrection. All of this is summarized in the famous words: "He was made man that we might be made God," that is, divine, for by showing himself to us we obtain the idea of the unseen Father and thus inherit immortality.[9]

When we say that "In the beginning was the Word," and "the Lord has become man," we are talking about only one Person, the Word made flesh. But the expressions used about his Godhead, and his becoming man, are to be interpreted with discrimination and suitably to the particular context. To distinguish between the divine and the human attributes of the Word requires the discernment of a skilled and approved Moneychanger; when we talk about the Lord's weeping, or his hunger and thirst, his human character is exhibited, while the divine character appears in the feeding of five thousand persons or the raising of Lazarus. Similarly, a human body lay in the tomb, but it was raised as God's body by the Word himself.[10]

Therefore we must not think that the Word was somehow impaired when it received a body, for he deified what he put on and gave it graciously to the race of man. He is worshiped no less when he becomes man and is called Jesus, than he was Word existing in the form of God, because he has the whole creation under foot to the glory of God the Father. Both angels and archangels always worship the Lord and now worship him in the name of Jesus; this is our grace and high exaltation, that even when he became man, the Son of God is worshiped, and the heavenly powers will not be astonished at seeing all of us, who are of one body with him, introduced into their realms.[11]

The divine Mediator must be unalterable, loving righteousness and hating iniquity in order to overcome the serpent who tempted Adam, whose sin reached to all men. Even though the Lord took alterable flesh, he did so to condemn sin and to free flesh to fulfill the righteousness of the Law. Now if the Lord is himself a creature, begotten out of nothing, how can he save creatures? But the Son is not a creature, He is God's Word, and he would not have become man at all if the need of men had not required it. The Word became flesh that he might make man capable of Godhead.[12]

But why could not God just say the Word, and undo the curse? Why was the Incarnation necessary at all? Athanasius answers that God always does that which is fitting and proper for men. He could have led the people out of Egypt without Moses, but He does far more than what is merely possible. Nor did Jesus need to be delivered to Pilate, but events of the Passion are an example for us to profit by. The point remains that if the Son had been merely the first of all creatures, man would have remained under guilt since he could never be joined to God, the bite of the serpent would not have been stanched nor death, the companion of sin, abolished.[13]

Our unification to the Father through the Son is effected by the

Holy Spirit, who receives from the Word. Against the Macedonians, Athanasius insists on the unity of essence of the Holy Spirit with the Father and Son. Apart from the Spirit, we are estranged from God, but by the participation of the Spirit we are knit into the Godhead, so that our being in the Father is not ours, but is the Spirit's which is in us and abides in us, while by the true confession we preserve it in us. When a man falls from the Spirit because of any wickedness, but repents, grace remains irrevocably to those of good will; but if he remains unrepentant, the Paraclete deserts him.[14]

Athanasius insists on the divinity of all three persons in the Trinity, but his emphasis on consubstantiality of the Word does not cause him to neglect the human aspect of the Incarnation. Christ suffered for us in the flesh; He is said to hunger and thirst and to toil and not to know, and to sleep, to weep, to ask, to flee, to be born, to deprecate the cup, and in a word to undergo all that belongs to the flesh. The Godhead does not suffer, but Christ does all these things "in the flesh" and this proves that he has a true body. Athanasius does not probe the intricacies of the hypostatic union, but he certainly emphasizes the humanity of Christ even when this was not the point at issue with the Arians and Semi-Arians.

Of the sacraments Athanasius says virtually nothing, but it must be remembered that sacramental theology was not at issue, and the writings of the great Alexandrian are polemical in character. Hence, no argument from silence can be drawn since it is the doctrine of the Trinity as it bears on the Incarnation which is of primary concern for him; sacramental theology he took for granted.

The fourth century presents us with a variety of situations involving the church with the state. Prior to the time of Constantine official persecution had the result of separating both state and church into two opposing forces. When toleration came with the Edict of Milan and imperial patronage followed, large numbers of conversions occurred which brought considerable influence and prestige to the growing church. To become a Christian, in the eyes of many, was suddenly the fashionable thing to do. But the emperor now assumed the power of interfering in ecclesiastical affairs, so that religious questions became at the same time political. Moreover, differences within the church itself regarding theology, liturgy, and discipline became greatly exacerbated, and the complaint of the times was that one could not get a shave or a haircut without hearing the barber's opinion of the relation of the Father to the Son; theological niceties became the property of Everyman. What is more, imperial patronage might throw its weight on the side of heresy, as was the case during the reign of Constantius. So the new alliance of church and state had distinct disadvantages as well as assets.

Nowhere do we find a completely worked-out doctrine of church-state affairs in Athanasius; we have to infer his position through his conduct. When Constantius ordered Athanasius to reinstate Arius at Alexandria, he flatly refused to obey; five banishments at different times during his life must have caused him to look upon the emperor with mixed emotions. Still, the new freedom of the church (especially when backed by a Constantine or a Jovian) was obviously a tremendous advantage as well as a deathblow to paganism. And a Christian emperor could no longer be deified by the senate nor claim divine honors; as Constantine said on one occasion, he was just like everybody else when it came to Christian fraternity. Based on his life experience, therefore, Athanasius clearly declares for freedom of the church to handle its own affairs, but also looks to state protection which is both orthodox and benign. And so, the fourth century ushers in a long period of cooperation between state and church, a cooperation which was largely taken for granted throughout the Middle Ages, and was not to be seriously challenged until the time of the Reformation.[15]

The fourth century also saw a rash of synods, councils, and meetings, most of which Athanasius denominated as ridiculous. They properly belong to church history as well as ecclesiastical politics, and we cannot enter into them here. In general, the West—and therefore councils meeting in the West—favored the Nicene formula, while the East was more Semi-Arian in its sympathies. The situation in the East is complicated by parties like the Eusebians and colorful figures like Theonas and Maris, Ursacius and Valens. The West is characterized by less prominent leadership, but more administrative know-how. In fact, the papacy gained considerable prestige when Pope Julius and Hosius of Cordova succeeded in having ecclesiastical decisions reviewed by Rome. This bolstering of position was unwittingly aided by Athanasius himself when he appealed to the Roman church during one of his exiles. But the continuing religious friction produced an estrangement between East and West which would eventually result in permanent rupture. Furthermore, the shift of the empire's capital from Rome to Constantinople was to leave the bishop of Rome and the West more freedom to develop its own destiny. Saint Ambrose of Milan was free to call Emperor Theodosius to account; Saint John Chrysostom in the East was far less successful.

Saint Athanasius was more important as a church leader than as a creative thinker, and hence it is difficult to do him justice in a book which concentrates on Christian thought. As a thinker he is not original, his entire writings may be considered as an explication and defense of the Nicene Symbol. But what he lacks in comparison to an Origen or an Augustine, he makes up by a clear perception of the essential point in the Arian controversy: man can only be saved by God himself, and not by anyone less than God. A correct understanding of the awful mystery of the Trinity and a right knowledge of who it is who takes upon himself flesh in the Incarnation, is imperative to man's salvation. When the proper distinctions between ousia (being or essence) and hypostasis (substance) became more common, it became increasingly clear to larger numbers of churchmen that the Nicene formula as expounded by the saint was the correct one. And it was for this that Athanasius had spent his entire life and expended every energy. He is magnificent for dogged determinism no less than clear insight, and it is significant that the great Gibbon (hardly sympathetic to the church in any period) singles him out alone for unstinting praise. Though the whole church might wake up some morning with a groan and find itself Arian, the bishop of Alexandria was never known to waver from the truth, and the highest tribute which can be paid to him requires only three words: *Athanasius contra mundum.*

NOTES

The text is in Migne, *Patrologia Graeca,* vols. 25-28; a translation by Archibald Robertson is in *Nicene and Post-Nicene Fathers,* vol. 4 (*see* Bibliography).

1. E. Gibbon, *The Decline and Fall of the Roman Empire* (New York: Modern Library), chap. 13.
2. The conversion of Constantine is narrated in Socrates *Ecclesiastical History* 1. 2; in Sozomen *Ecclesiastical History,* 1. 3; see also "The Conversion of Constantine" in *European Problem Studies* (New York: Holt, Rinehart & Winston, Inc., 1971)
3. Athanasius *First Discourse Against the Arians* chap. 5.
4. Ibid.
5. Socrates 1. 15; Sozomen 2. 17
6. Athanasius *De Synodis* 3. 35
7. *Defense of the NiceneDefinition* No. 27.
8. *Letter to Serapion* 3. 6.
9. *Treatise on the Incarnation of the Word* pars. 5, 9
10. *On the Opinion of Dionysius* No. 9.
11. *Four Discourses Against the Arians,* 1. 42.
12. Ibid., 2. 59
13. Ibid., 2. 68.
14. Ibid., 3. 24.
15. Cf. Karl Friedrich Hagel's stimulating study *Kirche und Kaisertum in Lehre und Leben des Athanasius,* a doctorial dissertation (Giessen, 1933).

Saint Cyril of Jerusalem

Saint Cyril of Jerusalem was a contemporary of Athanasius who is famous as the author of the *Catecheses,* delivered at Jerusalem in the year 348 or 349 to those who were candidates for baptism and were to be received into the church at Eastertime. Cyril seems to have been born of affluent Christian parents about the year 313; he was ordained deacon, later priest, and still later became bishop of Jerusalem, dying in that city in 386 or 387. We know little of his life there, even though Jerusalem could not have been unaffected by the storm of theological controversy which had broken out in the fourth century. Cyril was long suspect to the orthodox party because of his refusal to use the homoousion formula as such, declaring that the word *homoousios* was not Scriptural and therefore unacceptable to faith. But this did not make him an Arian sympathizer, for upon close examination his doctrine was discovered to be thoroughly orthodox.

The *Catechetical Lectures* are twenty-three in number, the first eighteen of which are certainly from his hand, and the remaining five (called *Mystagogica*) are either his or his successor's, John of Jerusalem. They are a fairly complete manual of instruction for baptismal candidates, and they are the only one of its kind from this period. The neophytes are not to disclose the teaching to those who are not Christians, nor even to catechumens, and before making their decision are to weigh their motives carefully, for the seal of salvation is given only to those who have a good conscience. God grants his grace freely, but each candidate must guard it and cleanse himself to receive more, for though the remission of sins is given equally to all, the communion of the Holy Ghost is bestowed in proportion to each man's faith.[1]

Baptism is necessary for salvation, the lone exception being martyrs who may receive the Kingdom without it.[2] One enters the water dead in sins, but emerges quickened in righteousness as the Holy Spirit comes upon us with the words, "This has now been made my son," since we do not have the sonship by nature, but receive it by adoption.[3] Baptism, then, washes away all previous sin, and, providing sincere piety is present, bestows the gift of the Holy Spirit.

The *Catecheses* now follows the Creed of Jerusalem and elaborates the various beliefs which it summarizes. There is One Only God who foreknows things that will happen and is not subject to any necessary sequence of events, or chance or fate. He is perfect in everything, and equally possessing every form of virtue, neither diminishing nor increasing, but in mode and conditions ever the same. He has prepared punishment for sinners, and a crown for the righteous.[4]

In speaking of the Son of God, Cyril nowhere calls him consubstantial with the Father, either because he felt that it smacked of Sabellianism, or was non-Scriptural, or imprudent to use it when there were so many Arian sympathizers around. But his position is perfectly clear. Jesus is God of God, begotten Life of Life, begotten Light of Light, who is in everything like to Him that begat, who received not his being in time, but was before all ages eternally and incomprehensibly begotten of the Father: the Wisdom and the Power of God, and his Righteousness personally subsisting; he sits at the right hand of the Father before all ages.[5] Now, it is true that all this can be understood in an Arian sense, but I do not think that Cyril means them in any other way than in the Nicene construction. However his failure to use the word consubstantial annoyed Jerome and Rufinus, and placed him for years under a cloud which he did not justly deserve.[6]

Because of our sins, the only-begotten Son of God came from heaven to earth, took upon himself our human nature with all its passions, being made man of the Holy Virgin and the Holy Spirit. Nor did he pass through the Virgin as through a channel, but was made truly flesh, and he truly ate and drank. For, says Cyril, if the Incarnation was a phantom, salvation is a phantom also. The Christ was of two natures, man in what was seen, but God in what was not seen; as man truly eating like us, for he had the like feeling of the flesh with us, but as God feeding the five thousand with five loaves.[7]

Christ also went down into the regions beneath the earth in order to redeem the righteous, and here we have one of the earliest statements of Christ's descent into the netherworld. "For, tell me," asks the saint, "could you wish the living only to enjoy His grace, and that, though most of them were unholy, and not wish those who from Adam had for a long while been imprisoned to have now gained their liberty? Isaiah the prophet proclaimed with loud voice so many things concerning Him; would you not wish that the King should go down and redeem His herald?"

In the fifth Catechesis Cyril distinguishes between two meanings of faith. Dogmatic faith involves an assent of the soul to some particular point, and it is profitable to the soul because it hears and accepts the word of the Lord. But there is a second kind of faith, which is bestowed by Christ as a gift of grace. For to one is given through the Holy Spirit the word of wisdom, and to another the word of knowledge, and to another faith, and to another the gifts of healing. This type of faith is not merely doctrinal, but also works things above man's power, even to moving mountains. So there is a faith which has the assent of the intellect as its referrent, and there is a trust in the word of the Lord which actually goes beyond this and is also imparted by the Holy Spirit.[8]

Contrary to the Macedonians and others, Cyril insists that the Holy Spirit shares with the Father and Son. The Holy Spirit is He who glorifies the Son and receives from him in order to inspire men. The Father through the Son, with the Holy Spirit, is the giver of all grace; the gifts of the Father are none other than those of the Son and those of the Holy Spirit, for there is one Salvation; one Power; one Faith; one God, the Father; one Lord, his only-begotten Son; one Holy Spirit, the Comforter. But being of a practical turn of mind, Cyril finds it useless to speculate on the nature or substance of the Holy Spirit; it is sufficient for our salvation to know that there is Father, Son, and Holy Spirit, and that these three are One.[9]

The work of the Holy Spirit is to inspire good thoughts and resolutions. "While you have been sitting here," asks Cyril, "has a thought of chastity or virginity come into your mind? It is the work of the Holy Spirit's teaching. Has not often a maiden, already at the bridal threshold, fled away, He teaching her the doctrine of virginity? Has not often a man distinguished at court, scorned wealth and rank, under the teaching of the Holy Spirit? Has not often a young man, at the sight of beauty, closed his eyes, and fled from the sight and escaped the defilement?" In spite, even, of the many opportunities for greed presented by the world, yet Christians refuse possessions because of the teaching of the Holy Spirit.[10]

The Catecheses lays strong emphasis on the work of Christ, who is both God and man, or King and Physician, as Cyril likes to say. Adam's sin had power to bring death to the world, so the righteousness of Jesus restores life. If because of the tree of food our first parents were thrown out of paradise, shall not believers now more easily enter into paradise because of the tree of Jesus? If the first man formed out of the earth brought in universal death, shall not Jesus who gave himself up for a ransom, put away the wrath which is against mankind?[11] Nor was Christ compelled to give up his life, or put to death by murderous violence. He came of his own set purpose to his Passion, rejoicing in his noble deed, smiling at the crown, cheered by the salvation of mankind, not ashamed of the Cross, for it was to save the world. It was no ordinary man who suffered, the saint reminds us, but God in man's nature, striving for the prize of his patience.[12]

The death of Christ made peace for things in heaven and things in earth through the Blood of his Cross. For being enemies of God through sin, God had appointed the sinner to die. Two things then had to happen: either God would have to destroy all men, or that in his loving kindness he should cancel the sentence. But the wisdom of

God preserved both the truth of his sentence, and the exercise of his loving kindness. Christ took our sins in his body on the tree, that we by his death might die to sin, and live unto righteousness. Great though the transgression of sinners might be, it was not so great as the righteousness of Christ who died for them, who laid down his life for us when he pleased, and took it up again when he pleased.[13]

The true Christ is to come a second time, but not before Antichrist appears first. Cyril gives us certain specific details about the Antichrist and how to recognize him—he will be a magician, expert in sorceries, and will seize for himself the power of the Roman empire, deceiving the Jews by calling himself Christ, and then attacking the Christians. His crimes of inhumanity and lawlessness will outdo anybody who has preceded him, and this will continue for three years and six months; afterwards he will be destroyed by the glorious second advent from heaven of the Lord and Saviour Jesus, who will kill the Antichrist with the breath of his mouth and deliver him over to the fires of hell.[14]

Turning now to the sacraments, Cyril amplifies what he has already said about baptism, reminding the neophytes that the Holy Spirit baptizes the inward soul as the water flows about the exterior body. Just as fire can make a whole lump of iron glow, so also does the Holy Spirit enter the inmost recesses of the soul. This is likewise symbolized by the anointing which takes place after baptism, which is no ordinary anointing with plain ointment, but is Christ's gift of grace, and by the advent of the Holy Spirit it is made fit to impart his divine nature. The body is anointed with a visible ointment, the soul is sanctified by the Holy Spirit. Is Cyril actually describing the sacrament of confirmation? If so, then confirmation was originally attached to baptism and was only separated from it later. Or does Cyril consider it merely as a part of the baptismal ceremony?

Next follows a description of the Eucharist. Before the invocation of the Holy and Adorable Trinity, there is only simple bread and wine, but afterwards the bread becomes the Body, the wine, the Blood of Christ. By partaking of the Body and Blood of the Lord we are made into the same body and blood with him since we now bear Christ in us and become partakers of the divine nature. Since the Lord once turned water into wine in Cana of Galilee, it can hardly be incredible that he should turn wine into blood. Taste may be deceptive, but from faith we are assured that the Body and Blood of Christ have been given to us as a gift. Saint Cyril insists on the real Presence in such a way as to foreshadow the later famous *Tantum Ergo*.[15]

Following the Eucharist proper, Cyril goes on to describe spiritual hymns, and prayers to God for the common peace of the churches, for the welfare of the world, for kings, soldiers and allies, for the sick, the afflicted, and in a word, for all who stand in need of help. A commemoration is then made of those who have fallen asleep—first patriarchs, prophets, apostles, martyrs—asking for their intercessions. Then the holy fathers and bishops as well as others are mentioned, for these commemorations are of great value to souls when offered at the time of the Eucharist. But someone will ask how this can possibly be of any profit to a departed soul. Cyril borrows a homely illustration: If a king were to banish certain people who had given him offense, and then their friends should weave a crown and offer it to him on behalf of those under punishment, would not the king grant a remission of their penalties? In the same way we, when we offer to Him our supplications for those who have fallen asleep, though they be sinners, weave no crown, but offer up Christ sacrificed for our sins, propitiating our merciful God for them as well as for ourselves.[16]

All of this is directed toward the hope of the Resurrection and it is this hope that nerves the soul to do good works. It is only when men tire for no good reason that their hearts sink as well as their bodies. But he who believes that his body will remain to rise again, is careful of his robe, and defiles it not with fornication; but he who does not believe in the Resurrection gives himself to fornication and the misuse of his own body. Faith therefore in the resurrection of the dead, says Cyril, is a great commandment and doctrine of the Holy Catholic church —great and most necessary, though contradicted by man, yet surely warranted by the truth.[17] What is raised is not a weak body, but the very same body fashioned anew by incorruption. Our bodies will all be eternal, but they will not all be alike, for the righteous will receive bodies which enable them to converse with the angels, but if a man is a sinner, he will receive an eternal body fitted to endure the penalties of sins, that he may burn eternally in fire without ever being consumed. Since we never do anything without the body, it will share with us in the future the fruits of the past.[18]

All of these things does the Catholic church teach, and she is called *Catholic* because she extends over all the world and teaches universally and completely one and all the doctrines which ought to come to man's knowledge—things visible and invisible, heavenly and earthly. The Catholic church addresses itself to the whole race of mankind, governors as well as governed, the learned with the unlearned. The Catholic church universally treats and heals the whole class of sins committed by soul or body, and possesses in itself every form of virtue which is named, both in deeds and words, and in every kind of spiritual gifts. So whenever we go on a trip, we are not to inquire simply where the Lord's house is (for the other sects of the profane also attempt to call their own dens houses of the Lord), nor merely where the church is, but where the Catholic church is. For this is the peculiar name of this Holy church, the mother of us all.[19]

Saint Cyril of Jerusalem forms an important link between the early church and subsequent ages. He was born at the time of the Edict of Milan and the rise of Arianism and he lived to see that important heresy finally crushed in 381 at the Council of Constantinople in the time of Theodosius the Great. Whatever his outward life may have been, his inward life was marked by serenity and unwavering faithfulness to the substance if not the word of the Nicene Confession. What he could not accept or did not believe to be rooted in Scripture—the homoousion formula—he refused to give his name to, in spite of Westerners like Jerome or Rufinus. Yet his *Catecheses* is a gem of Christian instruction, balanced as few other writings had been up to that time. His tone is deliberately pastoral in character nor does he pretend to enter deeply into speculative theology. He is by no means glamorous; rather in an age of extremes he held firmly to the truth as he saw it and as it had been transmitted in the tradition of the Catholic church. If his writing was to receive centuries of neglect as a result of this, it was only in order that at a future time, his discovery would excite all the more the admiration of the Renaissance scholars. Today, Cyril is coming into his own as one of the more readable of the church fathers, who has as much to say to the now-generation as he did to his contemporaries in the fourth century.

NOTES

The text is that of W. K. Reischl and J. Rupp, in *Patrologia Graeca;* a translation by Fr. Leo P. McCauley, S.J., is in *The Fathers of the Church* (*see* Bibliography).

1. *Catecheses* 1. 5.
2. Ibid., 3. 10.
3. Ibid., 3. 14.
4. Ibid., 4. 5.
5. Ibid., 4. 7.
6. Cf. A. A. Stephenson's introduction to Saint Cyril of Jerusalem in *The Fathers of the Church*. I concur however in Fr. Leo McCauley's opinion.
7. Ibid., 4. 9.
8. Ibid., 5. 10.
9. Ibid., 16. 24.
10. Ibid., 16. 19.
11. Ibid., 13. 2.
12. Ibid., 13. 6.
13. Ibid., 13. 33.
14. Ibid., 15. 11.
15. Ibid., 22.
16. Ibid., 23. 10.
17. Ibid., 18. 1.
18. Ibid., 18. 19.
19. Ibid., 18. 26.

Saint Ephrem

Theologian, exegete, Doctor of the Church, deacon, *the* Syrian par excellence, saint—all are terms appropriate to Saint Ephrem, who was born at Nisibis in Mesopotamia in or around 306 and died at Edessa in 373. With Aphrahat, he is the cofounder of Syriac literature in the fourth century, and was known not merely locally but throughout the entire Christian world—famous especially for his celebrated hymns. Thanks to his renown, however, later generations enlarged fancifully upon his life, so that it is often well nigh impossible to separate truth from legend.

Ephrem's mother may have been a Christian, but his father was very likely a pagan, and even a pagan priest. After his baptism as a young man he was possibly disowned by his father but adopted by the saintly Bishop James of Nisibis who stamped his own personality and ideas very forcefully on the young convert. In Ephrem we encounter the blend of cultural training and asceticism, for he was later to become famous as both a voluminous writer and the father (or at least leading spirit) behind anchorite monasticism. Up until the year 364 he was teaching at Nisibis, but after the defeat of the emperor Julian the Apostate, the successor, Jovian, was forced to cede on unfavorable terms the city of Nisibis to Persia. This resulted in a general emigration of Christians, Ephrem making his way to Edessa. According to Sozomen, the fifth-century historian, Ephrem received the diaconate but not the priesthood because of his great reserve or humility, nor is it likely that he later became a bishop. He died in 373 at Edessa.[1]

Sorting out the manuscript difficulties in connection with Saint Ephrem is a scholarly problem of the first magnitude and cannot detain us here. In general, the various hymns of faith, hymns against heresies, in praise of virginity, on the church, on the Passion of the Lord, the sermons, the *Carmina Nisibena,* and the *Commentaries on the Old Testament,* are in Syriac. In Greek, there are some more or less literal translations of many items in the above group; there are likewise very ancient Latin translations, while the commentaries on the New Testament are in Armenian. Additional material discovered in recent years has been throwing more light on the Ephrem corpus which is still somewhat in a state of flux. His influence on the liturgy of the church in the fourth

century is unparalleled, as is also his leadership in the anchoritic typ
of monasticism which was becoming popular after the cessation of th
early persecutions and the greater infrequency of martyrdom. In hi
articulation of various principles of mortification and self-denial he i
also one of the co-founders of ascetic theology as it developed in th
Middle Ages.

Emphasizing as he does special points of doctrine, Saint Ephrem'
thought is nonetheless quite well-rounded. The miracles wrought b
Christ prove him to be a divine legate sent by God, for while h
lived on earth he never once abdicated his celestial throne, and whe
he dwelt with Mary he did not abandon heaven. When he rebuked th
sea and the waves, when he changed water into wine, he proved tha
he was truly God.[2]

Among his disciples Christ clearly separated out Peter to hold th
primacy of jurisdiction in his church. Peter is the fountain, the sourc
from which Christ is to draw his doctrine, through whom he will satisf
the thirst of all peoples. Peter is the firstborn of the church, the heir t
Christ's riches, the chief dispenser of Christ's treasure. Peter wil
sustain the entire foundation of the church, for Christ has made hir
its chief cornerstone.[3]

The existence of God is proved by the way in which the worl
is governed. Just as a flock is held together by the shepherd, a shi
steered by a pilot, so all things prosper because of God's providentia
care for the world.[4] In fact, his very essence is his Being, and h
clearly revealed his name to Moses when He said, "I am." His nam
is glorious because it is his essence, and this is what sets him apar
from all other things. He is so great that creatures strive to know hir
in vain, since nothing in him is similar to any creature whatsoever.
God is one and unique; two Gods would be impossible, for if God i
not one he is no longer God. He cannot be supreme over all thing:
and at the same time have something equal to himself. His essence ha
no beginning, his substance is prior to everything else.[6] And God is
hidden God; no matter how hard man tries he cannot find out ho
and in what manner God has his being.[7] For, says Ephrem, Go
hears without ears; He speaks without mouth; he works without hands
and he sees without eyes. He is ineffable and incomprehensible.[8]

Through the created world we can reach some understanding of God
provided we employ the threefold path of negation, causality, an
preeminence. It is idle to inquire who God is and what he is like
how can we picture to ourselves a spiritual being? We can only say wha
God is not, at the same time declaring him the cause of all things an
having an essence more excellent than that of any created being.[9]

God is a Trinity of Persons, the Father begets, and the Son i
begotten from his bosom while the Holy Spirit procedes from Fathe

nd Son; the Father makes the world out of nothing; the Son cooperates with his Father, and through the Holy Spirit all things are perfected which were and are to come. The Father is mind, the Son is the Word, the Spirit is voice—three names, one will, one power.[10] For their will is one in consent, there is no confusion in conjunction, nor is there a division in the Godhead even though the Persons are distinct. They are conjoined, not confused; distinct, not divided; their conjunction is not confused, nor their distinction a division. It is a profound mystery and our minds must take refuge in silence.[11] Saint Ephrem very clearly, then, teaches that the procession of the Holy Spirit is from both Father and Son, and that all things have been created through the Word. Creation is out of nothing, and it is the Trinity who creates.

Although man's body is corruptible, his soul does not undergo corruption; the earth may indeed be the custodian of the body of the dead, but their soul is preserved in paradise by the Creator. For this reason we can say that in a sense the dead are still with us, since their souls are imperishable.[12] And while one body may generate another body, one soul does not generate another, so that Adam and Eve may indeed have been one flesh or one body, but never one soul. The case against traducianism is clear enough.[13] Man is made in the image of God, woman is made from man, and everyone has his ultimate origin in Adam and Eve.

But Adam, we learn in the tenth hymn for the Feast of the Epiphany, sinned and earned all sorrows, and likewise the world after his example, incurred guilt.[14] The transgression in the garden written in Adam's hand, in a manner of speaking, was operative on the entire human race, thus necessitating a Savior who would obliterate the handwriting.[15] Now the goodness of God toward man is shown by the fact that he does not constrain man's freedom, nor does he allow him to abuse it; for if God forces us, he takes away our free will, but if he abandons us we are destroyed. To constrain us is to deprive us of freedom; to cast us off is to destroy us.[16] But his goodness is shown in doing neither; rather he has taught, chastened and won us. Grace, from Ephrem, operates both with regard to the intellect and the will.

Christ is both divine and human, but Saint Ephrem lays stress on his humanity. Human nature was truly assumed by the Lord, and so Christ has a real body taken from Mary. The Firstborn of the Father enters the Virgin as God, and is born as man. The greatness of God is communicated to us at the same time Jesus acquires our weakness, and he is made mortal in order that, infused with his life we may never die.[17] This is not to say that the Word was converted into human nature or mingled with it, but that the Lord assumed it in such a manner that he has two distinct natures which are somehow united in a personal union. For, says Ephrem, Our Lord's nature is not merely humble human nature, nor an exalted nature alone, but there are two natures that are mingled, the one with the other, the exalted and the humble. Therefore these two natures show forth their qualities, so that by the quality of each of the two, men may distinguish between them; Christ was two with respect to this commingling or blending of natures, though he was one in respect of his Being.[18]

And so, Christ is honored in his human nature and afflicted in it, but his divinity is incapable of suffering and dying. In assuming a human body the Word of God underwent birth and growth, his visible form required nourishment. His natures were hypostatically united in humanity and divinity, yet the Son of God made man is one without division, his domination showing his divinity, his subjection his humanity. He suffers as man, but not as God; yet it is not merely his body which hung on the cross, it is the complete God-man himself. It was the hidden God who cried out with a loud voice, who died, whose side was pierced with the lance. Yet he is one without division in divinity and humanity; those who divide him in two will not rejoice with him in Eden, and those who confuse the Father with the Son separate themselves from the church. Saint Ephrem thus clearly teaches a true communication of idioms.[19]

The purpose of the Incarnation has already been indicated—to restore man to the former state lost by Adam and to confer grace and immortality upon him. He who hung on the cross cancelled the debt of sin, destroyed the victory of death and confounded the devil. But in this economy of salvation we must remember that his mother played an important part. He who from all eternity is equal to the Father resided in the womb of the Virgin, who became his mother without losing her virginity. Nor did he lose his divinity while taking from her his humanity, nor did she, the pure virgin, suffer when he was born. Saint Ephrem frequently breaks forth in praise of Our Lady; she is most glorious, most beneficent, most sublime, more pure than the sun's rays, the budding rod of Aaron, virgin before and after Christ's birth, and in a sense reconciler between him and us.[20] She is completely beautiful, with no stain or spot of any kind, and her sanctity is unique. Thus we have a rounded-out theology of the Blessed Virgin, and while there is no testimony to Our Lady's Assumption, there is no testimony to the contrary, so that Saint Ephrem is unique not so much for his praise of Mary, but by his full articulation of the major ingredients of a Marian theology. We have had many of these in earlier writers, but nowhere do we find them in synthesis as we do here. It is precisely this quality which makes his own theology distinctive, if not unique.

The new life in Christ begins with baptism; the Purifier of all things was baptized with all and sanctified the water of our baptism.

The command is to be baptized in the name of the Father, Son, and Holy Spirit.[21] A spiritual and indelible stamp is conferred by baptism and must not be repeated,[22] and Ephrem also adds an anointing with olive oil which is symbolic of the suave operation of the Holy Spirit.[23] The sacrament of baptism is mentioned several times although not greatly elaborated upon beyond the traditional purification with water and the invocation of the Trinitarian formula.

With regard to the Eucharist, the *Sermons on Holy Week* emphasize this as a memorial service in which the body and blood of Christ are consumed under the species of bread and wine. Christ is truly present, we are not to hesitate in the least to believe this on faith through Christ's own words. One crumb, one drop, is enough to sanctify thousands of thousands and to confer eternal life upon all who partake. The pure will be maintained in purity, but sinners will be condemned; and he who spurns the sacrament or treats it with contumely will receive comparable treatment from the Lord himself.[24] The Eucharist is then a kind of material food which serves for the spiritual refreshment of the soul. He who eats partakes of spirit and of fire as well as eternal life. But beyond this Ephrem does not go; of the sacrifice of the Mass he has little if anything to say.

In the *Sermons Against Heresies* Ephrem observes that the power of binding and loosing has been granted to the church; those who seek pardon are granted it, but he who sins knowingly and willingly must be excluded.[25] Nonetheless, true compunction of heart can secure the answering of prayer in a twinkling of an eye, and the force of tears can be well-nigh irresistible before the Almighty. Saint Ephrem is said to have had the gift of tears in profusion, and if perhaps this type of spirituality is unpopular and suspect today, the fundamental necessity of humility still remains. Lack of cheerfulness and laughter may be forgiven one whose natural habitat was the desert.[26] A sermon on penance indicates that confession to God must also be accompanied by external action as well.

With regard to the last things, Saint Ephrem's teaching is somewhat fuller. The souls of the just are in heaven awaiting the general resurrection while the dead are aided by the oblation made by the living. If the sons of Mathathias expiated the crimes of the dead who had fallen in battle by their sacrifices (2 Macch. 12:43), how much more can priests of the eternal High Priest expiate the sins of the dead by their sacrifices and prayers.[27] And so, some sort of place of detention for the dead appears clearly in Ephrem's *Testament*.

Gehenna awaits the wicked who will eat fire while fire eats them, and this will be a never-ending process. Some, however, will avoid fire but enter shadows of darkness, others will be thrust into the abyss. Those who depart for a holy place will sit, some in the second rank, some in the third, the fifth, the tenth, the thirtieth, and some will sit in the highest spots.[28] If the saint were writing today he would no doubt refer to box seats for some on the fifty-yard line. At any rate, in the divine economy, each one will receive the due reward of his labors. Of a tremendous judgment in the future, most severe in its condemnation of sinners, Ephrem warns his hearers. The torments of the wicked will be eternal, nor will there ever be a time when they abate in the least; there will be an awful judgment of vengeance when the wicked will receive their just deserts.[29] This judgment will affect all men, and all the angels as well. But the righteous will gain eternal felicity which can never be lost, as they take their several places allotted to them by the divine goodness.

The main outlines of Saint Ephrem's eschatology are fairly complete. Perhaps this was the sort of meditation which was most conducive to solitary life in the desert. There is a warmth, an intensity, a sincerity which runs through the various writings of the Syrian doctor and saint.

Stories which grew up around the name of Saint Ephrem later became legion, most of them doubtful to say the least, but one is true in its larger sense. As a youth, he dreamed one night (or perhaps had a vision) that a vine sprang from his mouth and proceeded to grow so high that it embraced everything under heaven and produced clusters of grapes so profusely that the birds fed on them. This only resulted in the production of more grapes in a kind of biological regeneration. The *Testament* tells us that these clusters were his sermons while the leaves of the vine were his hymns. Whether or not the story is true, it shows how highly later generations regarded the Syrian saint of the desert.

NOTES

1. See John Gwynn in *Nicene and Post-Nicene Fathers,* second series, vol. 13, p. 113 ff; Arthur Vööbus, *Literary, Critical and Historical Studies in Ephrem the Syrian* (Stockholm: Etse, 1958); L'Abbé C. Ferry, *Saint Ephrem* (Paris, 1877).
2. *Various Hymns* 15. 1.
3. *Sermons on Holy Week* 4. 1.
4. *Reprehensio sui ipsius*
5. *Sermons Against Heresies* 53. *Sermons Against Investigators (Skeptics)* 4.
6. *Sermons Against Heresies* 3.
7. *Sermons Against Investigators* 47.
8. *Nisibene Hymns* 3.
9. *Sermons Against Investigators* 45, 47.
10. *Hymn on the Dead and the Trinity.*
11. *Sermons Against Investigators* 2.
12. *Necrosima, seu funebres canones* 1.

13. *Commentary on Genesis* 2. 22.
14. *Hymns for the Feast of the Epiphany* 10. 1.
15. *Hymns on the Renewal of the Church* 4. 1; *Various Hymns* 22. 8.
16. *Hymns for the Feast of the Epiphany* 10. 14.
17. *Hymns on the Blessed Virgin Mary* 18. 2.
18. *Homily on Our Lord*, 33.
19. *Sermons on Holy Week*, 6:9.
20. *Prayer to the Most Holy Mother of God*, J. S. Assemani, AG 3. 545.
21. *Sermons Against Investigators* 51.
22. *Hymns on Oil and the Olive* 4; *Sermons Against Heresies* 2.
23. *Commentary on Joel* 2. 24.
24. *Sermons on Holy Week* 4. 4.
25. *Sermons Against Heresies* 2.
26. *Cf. On Compunction.*
27. *Testamentum* 72.
28. *Sermo de magis, incantatoribus, et divinis, et de fine et consummatione* 11.
29. *Sermo de fine et admonitione* 8.

Saint Hilary of Poitiers

Saint Hilary of Poiters (315-367) was to the West what Saint Athanasius was to the East in the fourth-century struggle between the Arians and the defenders of the Nicene formula. But in addition to this latitude in space he also has a longitude in time, for the Eastern point of view was transmitted through Hilary to Augustine, and on to the Latin thinkers of the Middle Ages. So he is an important link between the Greek Fathers, Ambrose and the bishop of Hippo, and (if we except Irenaeus) the first really European writer in Latin. He seems to have been converted from paganism and in 353 became bishop of Poitiers before reaching his fortieth year. The fourth century was peppered by church councils and in 356 one met at Béziers to condemn Athanasius, whom Emperor Constantius II considered a troublemaker. Hilary refused to concur, and for his defiance was exiled to Phrygia. But in the East Hilary propagated his point of view with such effectiveness that in 361 he was returned home. He died in his hometown of Poitiers a few years after in 367.

The celebrated work *On the Trinity (De Trinitate)* is Hilary's masterpiece, and the writing for which he is best known. Its twelve books are a thorough exposition of Trinitarian doctrine, three of which were written prior to 356, and the remaining nine composed while in exile in the East.

The *On Synods (De Synodis)* comes from the same period, and is an attempt to explicate the Eastern point of view to the West; Hilary's exile did not prevent him from contacting the folks back home. A tract or commentary on Matthew as well as one on the Psalms has been preserved, and there are fragments of a *Book of Mysteries (Liber Mysteriorum)* which have come down to us. Taking his cue from Arius, Hilary seems to have fostered hymn singing in the West (so Jerome says) as a vehicle for imparting Christian doctrine to his congregation. Ambrose was to have even more success with this teaching technique, if we may so call it. In 1851 Pius IX declared him a Doctor of the Universal Church.

To accept the apostolic faith, one must accept the promises of the Gospels as put forth by the church. The church, instituted by the Lord and strengthened by the apostles is the one church of all men, which is to be understood not only through her own teachings, but through those of her adversaries as well. Separation from the faith comes about as the result of a defective and perverted understanding, which adapts the Gospel to one's own views rather than submitting one's views to that of the Gospels. So while all the heresies are directed against the church alone, she refutes the most godless error of all of them by the very fact that she is alone and is one. Heresy is actually self-destructive because the heretics contradict each other, and the church conquers heresy by simply letting her opponents exhaust each other. So in Hilary's view, heretical thinking serves a kind of purpose by allowing the truth taught by the church to appear. The teachings of church and Scripture are therefore the base from which Hilary make his defense of the Nicene teaching.[1]

In his exposition of correct Trinitarian doctrine, the saint is not unmindful of his awesome task. Book I concludes with the moving prayer that God will grant his Spirit so that the proper meaning of the words which the saint uses will accord with the realities they signify, for human vocabulary is inadequate to deal with the ineffable mystery of the Trinity and requires at the least the correct meaning of words, the light of understanding, nobility of diction, and the faith of the true nature. An outline plan is submitted for the remainder of the book and the reader is to ascend step-by-step to the more esoteric doctrine, but the author repeats himself so frequently that the resulting impression is one of traveling in a circle. Still, both Saint Augustine and Saint Thomas Aquinas paid high tribute to Hilary, whose exhaustive work on the Trinity was to be a landmark in the West.

We begin with the unity and simplicity of God, whose essence is existence itself. Nothing is more characteristic of God than to be, because that which truly is can never end, so that God's everlasting eternity is combined with unending happiness. Infinite, invisible, ineffable, even speech is silent in speaking of him, while the mind becomes weary in trying to fathom him, and the understanding is limited in comprehending him. No matter what kind of language is used, it will be unable to speak of God as he is and what he is. The perfection of learning is to know God in such a manner that, although you realize he is not unknown, you perceive that he cannot be described. We must believe in him, says Hilary, understand him, adore him, and by such actions we shall make him known.[2] Yet the nature of this subject exhausts the meaning of words, an impenetrable light darkens the vision of the mind, and whatever is without limits is beyond the capacity of our power of reasoning.

The Word of God, together with the very power of its own truth, commands through the Evangelist that all believers be baptized in the name of the Father, Son, and Holy Spirit; that is, in the confession of the Origin, the Only-begotten, and the Gift. It is from the Father, then, from whom everything that exists has been formed. The Father's being is in himself and he does not derive what he is from anywhere else, but possesses what he is from himself and in himself. He is infinite because he himself is not in anything and all things are in him. He is always outside of space and unrestricted, always before time since time comes from him. But God is also present everywhere and is present in his entirety wherever he is. He even transcends the realm of understanding, and nothing exists outside of him since he is eternal being, the true nature of the mystery of God, the name of the impenetrable nature in the Father.[3]

To say "Father" is to say "Son," or only-begotten Offspring of the unbegotten God, who has received everything from him who possesses everything. He is God from God, Spirit from Spirit, Light from Light, and from the whole Father the whole Son is born; he is not from anywhere else, because nothing was before the Son. The Son is not a God in part only, because the fullness of the Godhead is in the Son; whatever is in the Father is also in the Son and both are one substance but not one person, but one is in the other because there is nothing different in either of them. Hilary makes it quite clear, then, that the Arian position is simply unacceptable and at no time was the Father not a Father, nor the Son not a Son. The real difficulty, as we have seen before, lies in the word "begetting" and "begotten" which seem to imply a time factor. But no time factor can be applied to the internal operation of God without denying his simplicity and immutability.[4]

It goes without saying that Hilary rejects an Adoptionist interpretation. Many of us are the sons of God, but not such as this Son. He is the true and the proper Son, by origin, not by adoption; in truth, not in name; by birth, not by creation.[5]

Without using the term *circumincession,* Saint Hilary repeatedly emphasizes the fact that the Son is in the Father and the Father in the Son. The expression *perichoresis* was first used by Gregory Nazianzus to refer to the two natures in Christ, and through the translation of the works of Saint John of Damascus by Burgundia of Pisa (ca. 1150) the expression *circumincessio* became current in the West. Later, *Circumincessio* became *circuminsessio,* the former expressing more the idea of the active penetration while the latter expresses more the idea of passive coinherence and is the more Latin way of looking at the problem.[6] The Son is in the Father and the Father is in the Son, and if this seems to contradict the law of physics, we must understand that the Scriptures teach this clearly to show that the only difference between Father and Son is the opposition of relationship.

The apostolic faith, Hilary continues, does not have two gods because it does not have two fathers and two sons. To acknowledge the

Father is to acknowledge the Son, to believe in the Son is to believe in the Father, because the name of the Father likewise contains the name of the Son in itself. There is no father except through a son; the designation of a son reveals the Father to us because there is no son except from a father. There is not one person but two, but they have the same nature.[7]

Saint Hilary has both the Arian and the Sabellian heresies in mind as he continually insists on the Son as the living image of the Father, and although born from the Father does not have a different nature. When the Arians speak of the Son's being born of the Father, what they really mean is that the Father has created the Son. The idea of birth is to stress the identity of the natures, not to suggest a creation in the Son of God. So the Arians really end up with two Gods, an obvious absurdity.[8]

The Holy Spirit plays a far less prominent role in the *De Trinitate;* was Hilary less secure of himself here? Not at all; the *De Trinitate* is a polemic work, and the focus of interest is not on the Holy Spirit. Yet clearly the Son sends the Advocate from the Father, Who is the Spirit of truth proceeding from the Father; he who sends manifests his power in that which he sends, and to receive from the Son is the same as to receive from the Father. We are all spiritual if the Spirit of God is in us, but this Spirit of God is also the Spirit of Christ. And, since the Spirit of Christ is in us, the Spirit of him who raised Christ from the dead is in us, and he who raised Christ from the dead will also give life to our mortal bodies because of the Spirit of him who dwells in us. We are vivified, however, because of the Spirit of Christ that dwells in us through him who raised Christ from the dead.[9]

A correct understanding of the Trinity is necessary to a correct understanding of Christ's Incarnation whose purpose is to redeem men. Hilary now turns to this consideration. Christ Jesus is true man without ceasing to be true God. Christ himself has been appointed as the mediator in his own person for the salvation of the church. By reason of the two natures that are united in him, Jesus is the same person in both natures, but in such a way that he is not lacking in anything that belongs to either, so that he does not cease to be God by his birth as man, and again, he is man even while he remains God. Hence the true faith of human blessedness is to acknowledge him as God and man, to proclaim him as the Word and as the flesh, to know of God that he is man, and to know of the flesh that it is the Word.[10]

But Christ, who emptied himself, is not another or a distinct person from him who receives the form of a slave. The emptying of the form is not the destruction of the nature, because he who empties himself is not wanting in his own nature and he who receives remains. When Christ empties himself and receives himself no destruction takes place; the emptying brings it about that the form of a slave appears, but not that the Christ who was in the form of God does not continue to be Christ, since it is only Christ who has received the form of a slave. Since he who emptied himself that the abiding Spirit-Christ might be the same Man-Christ, the change of the outer appearance in the body and the assumption of a nature did not remove the nature of the Godhead that remains, because it is one and the same Christ who changes and assumes the outward appearance. But it's all a mystery, says Hilary, and we shouldn't pretend that we really understand it.[11]

Assuming a soul by himself, Christ takes flesh from the Virgin, who conceived by the power of God. Thus the Word becomes flesh, but this is not to say that two persons result; the Son of Man himself is at the same time the Son of God, because the entire Son of Man is the entire Son of God. Hilary is forestalling the Christological controversies that were already beginning to tear the East apart.[12]

Without sacrificing his divinity, Christ assumes a true manhood. This means that he truly suffers, is crucified, and dies. The suffering which rushes upon the body of the Lord was a suffering, but, says Hilary, it does not manifest the nature of suffering. On the one hand suffering rages with the function of pain, but on the other hand the divinity of the body receives the force of the pain rushing against it, but without feeling pain. Christ possesses a body to suffer, and suffer he did, but he does not possess a nature that could feel pain. His body has a nature peculiar and proper to it, for it was transfigured on the mountain, drives away fevers by its touch, and restores eyes by its spittle. What Hilary is saying is that Christ's human nature, since it was not conceived according to the ordinary laws of human generation, did not possess human defects since it was closely united to his divine nature. But this is not to say that he did not have the capacity of suffering and dying, even though his human nature was "peculiar and proper" to him.[13]

This raises the question so often put by the Arians with regard to Christ's knowledge. If Christ is coeternal with the Father, how does it happen that he says he does not know certain information— indeed, that the Father is greater than he is? Saint Hilary feels he must meet these particular objections. When Christ denies knowing something, it is in order that this knowledge may be hidden; his lack of knowledge does not come from his nature, since he knows all things, and, conseqeuntly, he is only ignorant for the sake of keeping it hidden. This then, becomes a sort of noncommunicable knowledge which Christ has but is not bound to reveal since it is not related to the economy of salvation. It might be correct also to say that Christ did not have this knowledge from his human nature, although of course he possessed it as a divine person. Saint Hilary, therefore, does not admit that any real ignorance actually existed in Christ.[14]

The doctrine of the person and two natures of Christ is not so meticulously worked out in the latter books of the *De Trinitate* as the Trinitarian doctrine, which occupies the main part of his work and is, after all, his primary interest. This, along with elaborate digressions, unusual use of words, the coining of new meanings for traditional terminology, and a sometimes too-brief treatment of a subject where a more elaborate one is called for, makes the *De Trinitate* an uneven work, and one which is not easy reading. But it must always be remembered that Hilary is blazing a new trail, and while he has rich precedent in the writings of Eastern theologians before him, he is pretty much confined to Irenaeus and Tertullian as far as the West is concerned. Later writers were to improve on Hilary, but if they did their work well, it was because he had so very ably prepared the way for them.

NOTES

The text is in Migne, *Patrologia Latina,* vols. 9, 10; a translation by Stephen McKenna is in *The Fathers of the Church* (*see* Bibliography).

1. *De Trinitate* 7.4; see also Stephen McKenna's introduction to Saint Hilary of Poitiers in *The Fathers of the Church* series; Paul Galtier, *Saint Hilaire de Poitiers* (Paris: Beauchesne, 1960); Gabriele Giamberadini, *S. Ilario di Poitiers* (Cairo: Franciscan Oriental Seminary, 1956); R. P. Largent, *Saint Hilaire* (Paris: Librairie Victor Lecoffre, 1924).
2. *De Trinitate* 2. 7.
3. Ibid., 2. 6.
4. Ibid., 3. 4.
5. Ibid., 3. 11.
6. Cf. Ludwig Ott, *Fundamentals of Catholic Dogma,* third printing, (St. Louis: B. Herder, 1958), p. 71.
7. *De Trinitate* 7. 31.
8. Ibid., 7. 14
9. Ibid., 8. 19, 21.
10. Ibid., 9. 3.
11. Ibid., 9. 14.
12. Ibid., 10. 22.
13. Ibid., 10. 23.
14. Ibid., 9. 69.

IX

THE
CAPPADOCIAN FATHERS

The Cappadocian fathers, Basil of Caesarea, Gregory Nazianzus, and Gregory of Nyssa, have much more in common than mere geography. Their family background was aristocratic, which meant they enjoyed, at least, some political influence, as well as cultural interests. All three writers possessed administrative ability, although (with the possible exception of Basil) they chafed under its responsibilities. They threw their support squarely behind the growing monastic movement, and safeguarded its orthodoxy while simultaneously enlisting its support in the service of the church. One important task was to underwrite the enormous influence of Origen, while pruning away his heterodoxy and toning down an occasional infelicitous use of language. And they also brought a mystical influence to bear on the life of the church which was to have far-reaching effects in later times. Although there are marked differences in personal temperament and emphases in each of the Cappadocian fathers, their personal friendship for each other is clearly evident in the common goals which they pursued in the strengthening of the Nicene church during a difficult time. Nor was their influence limited merely to Asia Minor, but was felt in the West as well as in the East.

Saint Basil of Caesarea

Cappadocia is a high plateau lying in the central east section of Asia Minor, hardly a prosperous region, with only one city of any importance, Caesarea. Gregory of Nazianzus, in one of his orations, calls the city "illustrious, . . . the metropolis of letters, no less than of the cities which she excels and reigns over," for Caesarea had long been a center of Christian influence even before the time of the Cappadocian fathers, Basil of Caesarea, Gregory Nazianzus, and Gregory of Nyssa. Bishop Firmilian, who had corresponded with Cyprian, as well as Gregory Thaumaturgus, had already made the archepiscopal see distinguished even before Basil was born, in about the year 329. His family was strongly Christian, and suffered exile during the severe persecution of Maximinus in spite of their community status, achieved over the years by having a number of the family in civic administration. Trained in piety and given a liberal education by his father, Basil finished school in Caesarea and continued his education in Byzantium and then Athens, where he arrived in 351. It was here that his friendship with Gregory Nazianzus ripened into David-Jonathan proportions; they studied together, they played together, they pursued virtue together, became proficient in philosophy, and possessed but one soul occupying two bodies, says Gregory, in his *Panegyric on Saint Basil*.[1] Separation came at last when Basil returned to Caesarea in 355-56 where a deputation waited on him to become a teacher of rhetoric in that city. But the ascetic ideal of monasticism had already determined him to make a visit to Egypt, where he could study for himself the monastic idea already set in motion by Pachomius, Antony, and Athanasius.

Egypt offered the most attractive refuge for the solitary life because of its dry, hot weather and the numerous opportunities for dwelling in caves and other simple habitations. The Decian persecution in the middle of the third century, as well as economic distress, set in motion a desire to escape the world and live a life of contemplation. Heroic asceticism allegedly brought with it a keen discernment of spirits and the ability to work miracles; in the fourth century it became a substitute for martyrdom. Originally the monks were anchorites, but gradually a cenobitic type of organization became more frequent after the founding of Tabennisi by Pachomius about the year 318. He developed a rule for communal living for the benefit of the weaker brethren; the stronger were supposed not to need a rule, and for the very strong, the ideal was still the anchorite life of the solitary. Basil had an opportunity to tour Palestine, Syria, and Mesopotamia to see for himself the type of monasticism practiced there, and quite possibly decided that the Egyptian style was much more to his liking. In the summer of 358 he was back once again in Caesarea.

Having returned to Asia Minor, he determined to become a monk and urged his friend Gregory to join him. Basil had nothing but high praise for the monastic life which he had recently witnessed; "I admired their continence in living, and their endurance in toil; I was amazed at their persistence in prayer and at their triumphing over sleep; subdued by no natural necessity, ever keeping their soul's purpose high and free, in hunger, in thirst, in cold, in nakedness, they never yielded to the body; they were never willing to waste attention on it; always, as though living in a flesh that was not theirs, they showed in very deed what it is to sojourn for a while in this life, and what it is to have one's citizenship and home in heaven. All this moved my admiration. I called these men's lives blessed, in that they did indeed show that they 'bear about in their body the dying of Jesus.' And I prayed that I, too, as far as in me lay, might imitate them."[2]

But what kind of asceticism should Basil adopt? He could retire completely from the world as a solitary, or he could live a celibate life in the world and combine prayer with an active apostolate. Gregory of Nazianzus says he did both. Making his headquarters on the banks of the Iris river opposite Annesi, where his mother and sister were living, Basil attracted a number of like-minded followers. But from the very start in 358, Basil set up a system which included prayer, work and study for members of the cenobium. In writing later of a visit to Basil, Gregory alludes to prayers, psalmodies, wood-gathering, stone-cutting and other activities all in the same breath.[3]

Using the cenobium as a base for his activities, he visited Constantinople in 360, returning to Caesarea. In 361 he visited with Gregory in Nazianzus. In 362 he was in Caesarea to help elect the new bishop, Eusebius, and probably to be ordained. Shortly after he fled Caesarea and did not return until 365—the emperor Valens now reigning in the East. The next five years find him establishing a hospital in Caesarea, after which time Basil become the city's bishop.

The last nine years of his life were spent in episcopal administration, and in 379 he died on the first of January at the age of fifty, acknowledged by all as a great man and a saint.

Basil's *Rules* and ascetical writings belong more properly to a history of asceticism than to a history of Christian thought. Those generally regarded as genuine are *On the Judgment of God (De Judicio Dei),*

On Faith (De Fide), Moralia, Regulae Fusius Tractate, Regulae Brevius Tractatae, Praevia Institutio Ascetica, Sermo Asceticus, De Renuntiatione Saeculi, and Sermo de Ascetica Disciplina. The Rules as a whole deal with the important steps of joining the monastery, withdrawal from the world, and the renunciation of possessions, each of which Basil treats with considerable detail. Life in the monastery requires the practice of common life, prayer, eating, clothing, and work. It also requires order and discipline and obedience to superiors. Other points of discussion include earthly relationships, trips, charitable and educational work. There is also a discussion of relationships with the outside world, the official church, as well as neighboring monasteries and convents of women. In spite of the fact that Basil wrote no formal rule as such, the East has always considered him the founder of monasticism, and both East and West were indebted to him for the organization of already existing ascetical practices and modifying them to form a practical and enduring type of Christian commitment; he also introduced the basic principles of common life and enlisted monasticism in the active service of the church. While Western monasticism was to owe more to Saint Benedict of Nursia, both West and East had a common father in Basil of Caesarea.

The doctrinal struggle between the Nicene and the Arian parties had concentrated on the relationship of the Son to the Father, without throwing the light equally on the Holy Spirit. If, as the Arians maintained, the Son was only of similar substance to the Father then what was the relation of the Spirit to both? And if the Son were subordinate to the Father, would the Holy Spirit not be likewise subordinate to the Son? In fact, might not the Holy Spirit be merely the first of all creatures, but not divine himself? In 360, Macedonius was ejected from the see of Constantinople, thus highlighting the new doctrine of Macedonianism as distinct from Arianism. In order to contradict those who denied the divinity of the Holy Spirit (Pneumatomachoi), a disciple of Basil's, Amphilochius, urged the saint to write a treatise on the subject. The result was the De Spiritu Sancto composed in the year 375.

Through the Holy Spirit, says Basil, comes our restoration to paradise, our ascension into the Kingdom of heaven, our return to the adoption of sons, our liberty to call God our Father, our being made partakers of the grace of Christ, our being called children of light, our sharing in eternal glory, and, in a word, our being brought into a state of all "fullness of blessing," both in this world and in the world to come, of all the good gifts that are in store for us, by promise whereof, through faith, beholding the reflection of their grace as though they were already present, we await the full enjoyment.[4]

Now the Spirit is spoken of together with the Lord in precisely the same manner in which the Son is spoken of with the Father. The name of the Father and of the Son and of the Holy Spirit is delivered in the same way, and according to the coordination of words delivered in baptism, the relation of the Spirit to the Son is the same as that of the Son to the Father. And if the Spirit is coordinate with the Son, and the Son with the Father, it is obvious that the Spirit is also coordinate with the Father. When, then, the names are ranked in one and the same coordinate series, what room is there for speaking of either *con*-numeration or *sub*-numeration?[5]

In our worship of God, we both confess the distinction of the Persons, while insisting upon the oneness of God. There is no such thing as a divided plurality, because one Form, so to speak, united in the invariableness of the Godhead, is beheld in God the Father, and in God the Only-begotten. For the Son is in the Father and the Father is in the Son; the one is like the other, who is as the first, and herein lies the Unity. So that according to the distinction of Persons, both are one and one, and according to the community of nature, one. How, then, of one and one, are there not two Gods? Because when we speak of a king, and of the king's image, there are not two kings, nor is the majesty of God split in two or his glory divided. The sovereignty and authority over us is one, and so the doxology ascribed by us is not plural but one; because the honor paid to the image passes on to the prototype. What in the one case the image is by reason of imitation, that in the other case the Son is by nature.[6] Thus the way of the knowledge of God lies from One Spirit through the One Son to the One Father, and conversely the natural goodness and the inherent Holiness and the royal Dignity extend from the Father through the Only-begotten to the Spirit. Thus there is both acknowledgement of the hypostases and the true dogma of the Monarchy as well.[7]

And so Basil preserves the unity of God by insisting that the Father is the sole Beginning, *Arche,* Well-of-Being, who communicates the divine Godhead to the Son co-eternal and consubstantial, as well as to the Spirit. To say that the Spirit proceeds from both the Father and the Son seems at first sight to imply the existence of two principles of being in the Godhead *(Archai)*, and in fact, two Gods, and this is the objection raised by the Eastern church to the *filioque* clause, but such is not really the case since the procession of the Spirit from both the Father and the Son presupposes at the same time the eternal generation of the Son from the Father.

Those who would claim that the Holy Spirit is actually an angel, Basil would remind that the powers of heaven are not by nature holy; their sanctification is external to their substance and is attained only through the communion of the Spirit. Their relative excellence in heaven is in proportion to the holiness which they receive from the Spirit. They are like branding irons heated by the fire, but distinct from the fire nonetheless. They exist in space and may even become visible and appear in their proper bodily form to those who are worthy, but they retain their rank by abiding in the true and the good, and while they always have freedom of will, they never fall away from their patient attendance on Him who is truly good.[8]

In the creation of angels, therefore, the Father is the original cause, the Son is the creative cause, and the Spirit, the perfecting cause; the ministering spirits subsist by the will of the Father, are brought into being by the operation of the Son, and perfected by the presence of the Spirit. This is not to say that there are three original hypostases, or that the operation of the Son is imperfect; the first principle of existing things is One, creating through the Son and perfecting through the Spirit. The operation of the Father who works all in all is not imperfect, neither is the creating work of the Son incomplete if not perfected by the Spirit. The Father, who creates by his sole will, could not stand in any need of the Son, but nevertheless wills through the Son; nor could the Son, who works according to the likeness of the Father, need cooperation, but the Son too wills to make perfect through the Spirit.[9]

Nor is it permissible to speak of the Holy Spirit as begotten; the Spirit of truth proceeds from the Father, and he, too, is God uncreated. To speak of the Spirit as ministerial is likewise to make him a creature, but this above all is important: that we keep unaltered and inviolable that order which we have received from the Lord, "Go and teach all nations, baptizing them in the name of the Father and of the Son, and of the Holy Spirit."[10] In order correctly to profess the Christian Faith, Basil insists, we must add the particular to the common. The Godhead is common; the fatherhood is particular; we must therefore combine the two and say, "I believe in God the Father." The like course must be pursued in the confession of the Son; we must combine the particular with the common and say "I believe in God the Son," so in the case of the Holy Spirit we must make our utterance conform to the appellation and say "in God the Holy Spirit." Hence a satisfactory preservation of the unity results by the confession of the one Godhead, while in the distinction of the individual properties regarded in each there is the confession of the peculiar properties of the Persons. The distinction between ousia and hypostasis is the same as that between the general and the particular, so the church confesses one general substance but three particular hypostases.[11] Basil is now in firm command of language which will be normative in describing the Trinitarian relationships.

Saint Basil's letters reveal a variety of theological interests too vast to deal with here. He writes at length on the person and work of Christ, the relationships of faith to knowledge, the union of the Holy

Spirit with the church, and the correct understanding of the different sacraments. The focus has been placed on the Holy Spirit because of Basil's felicitous use of hypostasis with respect to ousia. Thanks to Basil's opposition, the Macedonian heresy did not long flourish, and what length of life it did have may have been due more to vested financial interests than to theological conviction. But the saint's work was not confined to this doctrinal aberration; he saved the work of Origen from oblivion by making it the source of his inspiration without endorsing its excesses. And what Basil does best of all is to combine three quite disparate elements—the spirit and practice of asceticism, which he had learned from the monks of Egypt, with a competent ecclesiology that kept their asceticism within the church and not separated as a foreign movement outside it, making this synthesis meaningful in Christian service to the poor. And so, Basil is the ascetical ecclesiastic who is at once world denying and world affirming, for he devotes his strength to the repairing of social ills by a genuine Christian service, which is all the more effective because so deeply rooted in one who is both a profound mystic and a concerned churchman.

NOTES

The text is in Migne, *Patrologia Graeca*, vols. 29-32; a translation by Blomfield Jackson is in *Nicene and Post-Nicene Fathers*, vol. 8 (*see* Bibliography).

1. Saint Gregory of Nazianzus *Panegyric on Saint Basil* No. 14.
2. Saint Basil *Epistle* 223.
3. Saint Gregory of Nazianzus *Epistle* 6.
4. *On the Holy Spirit* 15. 36.
5. Ibid., 17. 43.
6. Ibid., 18. 45.
7. Ibid., 18. 47.
8. Ibid., 16. 38.
9. Ibid.
10. Saint Basil *Epistle* 125. 3.
11. Saint Basil *Epistle* 236.

Saint Gregory Nazianzus

Saint Basil's close friend (for at least part of his life), Gregory, was born in 329 or 330 at Arianzus in southwestern Cappadocia. His early education he received at Nazianzus and Caesarea, where he met Basil for the first time, but their paths separated when Gregory continued his studies in Palestine and then Alexandria, finally ending up at Athens, having braved a November storm and shipwreck before reaching the celebrated capital of philosophy. Here he was soon joined by his boyhood friend, and the two of them made the pious resolve to eschew the frivolities of university life, and to beat a path only to the lecture halls and the church. At this time the young Julian, soon to be dubbed "the Apostate" was also studying at Athens, and Gregory claims to have foreseen even at this early date the evil which the Roman state was nourishing.[1] The stay in Athens seems to have lasted around twelve years, for he did not conclude his philosophical studies and lecturing in rhetoric until 358-59, after Basil had left, and his brother Caesarius had finished his medical studies in Constantinople. Returning to Cappadocia, he was baptized and then urged by Basil to take up the contemplative life which he himself had adopted at Pontus. Gregory made the visit for friendship's sake, stayed a while, but finally begged off from a permanent commitment because of family responsibilities and an uncertainty regarding his own vocation. It was then that his father moved in on him by consecrating him priest in the year 361, quite against Gregory's will. Furious, Gregory fled back to Pontus to make up his mind in solitude, not finally making a decision for active pastoral duties until Easter 362. His second *Oration* is a defense of his flight to Pontus and an explanation of the contemplative life compared with the active life, and was to serve Saint John Chrysostom as a model for his exposition of the priesthood. By the year 370, Gregory had become virtual bishop of Nazianzus, as his father's health had seriously declined. Suddenly he learned of the death of Bishop Eusebius of Caesarea through Basil's plea for help in securing the episcopal succession for himself. Gregory Nazianzus supported Basil, but his aversion to ecclesiastical politicking was accentuated the following year when his friend Basil, to prevent the dismemberment of his diocese (resulting from the emperor's new creation of Cappadocia

279

Secunda with its capital at Tyana), forced Gregory to become bishop of Sasima, and Basil's own brother Gregory, bishop of Nyssa. Sasima was hardly more than a crossroads, and so beneath his dignity that Gregory refused to occupy the episcopal chair. He wrote a bitter protest to Basil in which he made it clear that he thought his old friend had sold out to worldly ambition; "I have gained one thing from our friendship," he declared, "I have learned never to trust friends, or to prefer anything to God."[2]

Gregory obviously felt that Basil had betrayed their youthful ideal of detachment and noninvolvement in the world; Basil felt that his actions were necessary to preserve certain areas for the orthodox faith, and it is apparent that Gregory's father sided with Basil in their appraisal of the situation. But the elder Gregory died soon after, leaving the son free to resign his duties at Nazianzus, despite the protest of the church. Solitude had been achieved at last, or least for a time, when his retirement in Seleucia was rudely interrupted by a summons to Constantinople to defend orthodox doctrine and lead the orthodox party in its contest with the Arians. In the following year (380) the emperor Theodosius decided to attempt the reconciliation of all parties to the Nicene faith, and in the spring of 381 the celebrated Council of Constantinople met with one hundred and fifty bishops in attendance. Gregory presided at the ecumenical council, but his role of peacemaker was frustrated by schismatics who proceeded to contest his own episcopal election which he himself had never wanted. Quite disgusted by all this, he forced the emperor finally to agree to his resignation, and returned to Nazianzus. In a letter to Procopius, he wrote later: "My attitude toward all gatherings of bishops is to avoid them."[3]

By now the Apollinarians had entered upon the scene, and the closing years of Gregory's life were stormy. He attempted to administer the church at Nazianzus, but his health began to fail until he was forced to spend the last five years of his life at Arianzus where he had first grown up. Here he devoted himself to letter-writing, and the composition of poetry, but his days of oratory were over. He died in 389-90.

Bishop of Constantinople, father, and Doctor of the Church, Saint Gregory's major writings include his correspondence of some two hundred and fifty letters, forty-four orations, and over five hundred poems—some on his life. The orations are the most important of these, and of the orations, five stand out for their theological character—those numbered twenty-seven to thirty-one. Extant manuscripts are very numerous; he may be the best preserved of all the writers designated as Church Fathers. He is famous as a rhetor and philosopher, a man of wide catholic interests and deep human sympathies, but our interest will be confined to his theological position represented by the *Orations*.

A theologian who is bent on philosophizing about theological questions, Gregory tells us, must be, as far as he can, pure, in order that light may be apprehended by light; he ought to consort with serious men, so his words do not fall on barren soil; he must choose a suitable season when he enjoys inward calm, and be inwardly molded by the Sacred Scriptures. Only in this way can he enter into a discussion of the one God, who is One in diversity and diverse in Unity. Now our eyes themselves and the Law of Nature, as well, teach us that God exists and that he is the Efficient and Maintaining Cause of all things—our eyes, because they fall on visible objects and see them in beautiful stability and progress; and natural law, because through these visible things and their order, it reasons back to their Author.[4]

But since we are not pure spirits and inhabit bodies, it is impossible for us to be conversant with objects of pure thought apart from bodily objects, for we are prisoners of earth and covered with the denseness of carnal nature. And so our reason must lead us up to God by means of visible things—our reason, which itself comes from God and is implanted in all of us from the beginning and is the first law in us. What God is in his nature and essence, no man has ever yet discovered or can discover; for in our present life all that comes to us is very little indeed, a small effulgence from a great Light. Only when that which is within us becomes godlike and divine, our mind and reason shall have mingled with its Like, and the image ascended to the Archetype, shall we know "even as we are known."[5]

As far then as we can reach, He Who Is and God are the special names of God's essence, and of these, especially He Who Is; not only because when God spoke to Moses on the mountain top, and Moses asked what his name was, this was what God called himself, but because the name "I AM" was quite strictly appropriate to his nature. Being is in its proper sense peculiar to God, and belongs to him entirely, and is not limited or cut short by any *before* or *after,* for indeed in him there is no past or future. We may indeed speak of God as Unbegotten, or Unoriginate, or Unchanging, or Incorruptible, or Incorporeal, but Being is that which describes his essence most accurately. But when we call God "Father" we are not referring either to his essence or any of his actions. "Father" is the name of the relation in which the Father stands to the Son, and the Son to the Father. These names make known a genuine and intimate relation and they denote as well an identity of nature between him that is begotten and him that begets.[6]

The Second Person of the Trinity is called Son because he is identical with the Father in essence, and not only for this reason, but also because he is of the Father. And he is called Only-begotten, not because he is the only Son and of the Father alone, and only a Son;

but also because the manner of his sonship is peculiar to himself and not shared by created things. He is called the Word, because he is related to the Father as Word to Mind; nor only on account of his passionless generation, but also because of the Union, and of his declaratory function.[7]

The Holy Spirit proceeds from the Father, but since he proceeds from that Source, he cannot be a Creature, nor is he a Son because he is not Begotten, yet inasmuch as he is between the Unbegotten and Begotten, he is also God. But what do we mean by Procession? If you tell me what the unbegottenness of the Father is, I will tell you the physiology of the generation of the Son and the procession of the Spirit, and we will both be locked up in a madhouse. To say however that the Spirit is not a Son does not imply that anything is lacking in God, for God has no deficiency. But the difference of manifestation, or rather of their mutual relations one to another, has caused the difference of their names. There is not some deficiency in the Son which prevents his being Father since sonship is not a deficiency, nor is there a deficiency in the Father because he is not the Son. One is not the other, and yet this is not due to either deficiency or subjection of essence, but the very fact of being Unbegotten, or Begotten, or Proceeding, has given the name of Father to the First; Son to the Second; and of the Third, him of who we are speaking, of the Holy Spirit, that the distinction of the three Persons may be preserved in the one nature and dignity of the Godhead. For neither is the Son Father, for the Father is One, but he is what the Father is; nor is the Spirit Son because he is of God, for the Only-begotten is One, but he is what the Son is. The Three are One in Godhead, and the One, Three in properties (ἰδιότητες); so that neither is the Unity a Sabellian one, nor does the Trinity countenance the present evil distinction. So what? Is the Spirit God? Most certainly. Then is he Consubstantial? Yes, if he is God.[8]

And so, there is one God, for the Godhead is One, and all that proceeds from him is referred to One, though we believe in three Persons. For One is not more, and another less, God; nor is One before and another after; nor are they divided in will or parted in power, nor can you find here any of the qualities of divisible things; but the Godhead is undivided in separate Persons, and there is one mingling of Light, as it were of three suns joined to each other.[9] Or rather, God is one Nature in three Personalities—intellectual, perfect, self-existent—numerically distinct, but not separate in the Godhead.

God the Son assumed human flesh and became Man in Jesus Christ, in order to sanctify humanity and to act as a leaven for the whole lump; by uniting to himself what was condemned, he releases it from all condemnation, becoming for all men body, soul, and mind but not taking on their sin. This God in visible form is Son of man, both on account of Adam, and of the Virgin from whom he came. He is Christ because he is of the Godhead; he is the Anointed One who sanctifies by his fullness; he is the Way, because he leads us through himself. What is the cause of this Manhood, which for our sake God assumed? It was surely our salvation, says Gregory, what else could it be?[10]

If anyone should say that the Son must be subordinate to the Father because he does not know the last day and hour, Gregory asks: "How can Wisdom be ignorant of anything? How can you say that all things before that hour he knows accurately, and all things that are to happen about the time of the end, but of the hour itself he is ignorant? For such a thing would be like a riddle; as if one were to say that he knew accurately all that was in front of the wall, but did not know the wall itself; or that, knowing the end of the day, he did not know the beginning of the night—where knowledge of the one necessarily brings in the other. Thus everyone must see that he knows as God, and does not know as Man—if one may separate the visible from that which is discerned by thought alone."[11]

The Word of God took on flesh for the sake of our flesh, and an intelligent soul for the sake of our own souls, and was conceived by the Virgin, who was first purified by the Holy Spirit (for it was needful, Gregory insists, that childbearing should be honored, and that virginity should receive a higher honor). Christ came forth then as God with that which he had assumed, One Person in two natures, Flesh and Spirit, of which the latter deified the former. "O new commingling; O strange conjunction!" exclaims Gregory.[12] What Christ had been he laid aside; what he was not he assumed; not that he became two, but he deigned to be One made out of the two. For both are God, that which assumed, and that which was assumed; two natures meeting in One, not two Sons.[13]

Against Apollinaris, Gregory insists that Christ had a human mind, and rejected the Apollinarian notion that the mind of Christ had been supplanted by the Logos. Anyone who puts his trust in a God-Man who has no mind, has no mind himself and is quite unworthy of salvation. For that which Christ has not assumed he has not healed; but that which is united to his Godhead is also saved. If only half Adam fell, then that which Christ assumes and saves may be half also; but if the whole of Adam's nature fell, it must be united to the whole nature of him that was begotten, and so be saved as a whole.[14]

To Cleodonius the priest, Gregory writes that if anyone does not believe that Holy Mary is the Mother of God, he is severed from the Godhead. If anyone should assert that Christ passed through the Virgin as through a channel, and was not at once divinely and humanly formed in her (divinely, because without the intervention of man; humanly, because in accordance with the laws of gestation), he is in like manner godless. If anybody says that the Manhood was formed and afterwards was clothed with the Godhead, he too is to be condemned. Nor is Christ two Persons, God forbid! Both his natures are one by the combination, the Deity being made Man, and the Manhood deified. Unlike the Trinity, where we have different Persons but only one element, we have here one Person with two elements.[15]

Christ nailed our sins to the cross. He offered his Blood, which was shed for us because we were detained in bondage by the Evil One, sold under sin, and receiving pleasure in exchange for wickedness. Now, since a ransom belongs only to him who holds in bondage, to whom was the ransom offered and why? Certainly not to the Evil One, but how can it have been offered to the Father since we were not oppressed by Him? Gregory believes that the Father accepts Christ on account of the Incarnation, and because Humanity must be sanctified by the Humanity of God, that God might deliver us himself, and overcome the tyrant, and draw us to himself by the mediation of his son.[16] All of this results in newness of life, for just as God gave existence to that which did not exist, so He gave new creation to that which did exist, a diviner creation and a loftier than the first, which is to those who are beginning life a Seal, and to those who are more mature in age both a gift and a restoration of the image which had fallen through sin.[17]

This Gift of Baptism, this Seal, causes different reactions in different people. Some fail to receive it because they are altogether animal or bestial, according as they are either foolish or wicked. Others know and honor the gift, but put it off. Still others are not in a position to receive it for various reasons. The first class, says Gregory, will have to suffer punishment; as for all their sins, so for their contempt of baptism. The second will also have to suffer, but less, because it was not so much through wickedness as through folly that they wrought their failure. The third will neither be glorified nor punished by the righteous Judge, as unsealed and yet not wicked, but persons who have suffered rather than done wrong.[18] In addition to the baptisms of Moses (circumcision), John the Baptist, and Jesus, there is also a fourth baptism—that by martyrdom and blood, which Christ himself underwent, and this one is far more august than all the others, the saint assures us, inasmuch as it cannot be deified by after-stains.[19]

Gregory warns of two fires, a cleansing fire which Christ came to send upon the earth, for he himself is analogically called Fire. There is also the avenging fire—that fire of Sodom which God pours down on all sinners, mingled with brimstone and storms, or that which is prepared for the Devil and his angels, or that which proceeds from the face of the Lord, and shall burn up his enemies round about. There is a fire even more fearful still—the unquenchable fire which is ranged with the worm that does not die but is eternal for the wicked.[20]

Rosemary Ruether has shown that there are tensions in Gregory between Christianity and culture, philosophy and rhetoric, literature and piety,[21] and that these tensions were solved not *in abstracto* so much as on the personal level. If Gregory loved solitude, it was in no small part due to the fact that it afforded him time and leisure for cultural development. Character develops best, perhaps, in conflict, and if this be true, Gregory had plenty of opportunity for that in his busy days of episcopal administration in Constantinople, when through his *Orations* he was spokesman for the orthodox party. Despite his love for monasticism and literature, if the defense or restoration of the faith demanded of him the active life, he was ready for that. What was most important was that there be harmony in the church, a reconciliation of all parties in the true faith and in Christian charity. Clearly, he possessed an irenic character which shunned the hurly-burly of ecclesiastical or temporal politics. That he was often overly sensitive, there is no doubt. Perhaps his greatest insight was somehow to come to terms with his own temperament, and to pursue a sanctity which was at once universally appealing, and yet peculiarly his very own.

NOTES

The text is in Migne, *Patrologia Graeca*, vols. 35-38; a translation by Charles Gordon Browne and James Edward Swallow is in *Nicene and Post-Nicene Fathers*, vol. 7 (*see* Bibliography).

1. *Oration* 5. 23, 24.
2. *Epistle* 48.
3. *Epistle* 130.
4. *Oration* 28. 5.
5. *Oration* 28. 17.
6. *Oration* 29. 16.
7. *Oration* 30. 20.
8. *Oration* 31. 8.
9. *Oration* 31. 14.
10. *Oration* 30. 2.
11. *Oration* 30. 15.
12. *Oration* 38. 13.
13. *Oration* 37. 2.
14. *Epistle* 101.
15. Ibid.
16. *Oration* 45. 22.
17. *Oration* 40. 7.
18. *Oration* 40. 23.
19. *Oration* 39. 17.
20. *Oration* 40. 36.
21. Rosemary R. Ruether, *Gregory of Nazianzus, Rhetor and Philosopher* (Oxford: Clarendon Press, 1969), p. 174.

Saint Gregory of Nyssa

Grandmother, mother, and sister all played important parts in the early education of Saint Gregory of Nyssa, the third of the great Cappadocian fathers, brother of Basil and close friend of Gregory Nazianzus. Born about the year 335, he began his early education at home under the aegis of his brother Basil, who had been to Athens. There is some doubt as to whether he married, but if he did his matrimonial life was short. His intention had been to become a rhetorician like his father, but a conversion experience and the urging of his sister Macrina resulted in his retirement for several years to his brother's monastery at Pontus. The tract *On Virginity* reflects this period in his life.

The election of Basil to the see of Caesarea in 370 created a storm of opposition from the Arian party which made it necessary for the new bishop to strengthen his position by installing his adherents in nearby ecclesiastical posts. Sasima was assigned to Gregory of Nazianzus, Nyssa to brother Gregory, in spite of the obvious distaste each had for these out-of-the-way posts. But with the disaster at Adrianpole and the death of the emperor Valens in 378, the Arian cause collapsed and Gregory returned to Nyssa (from which he had been temporarily banished) when the new emperor Gratian restored the orthodox bishops. But his brother Basil died not long after and in 381 Gregory was called to take his place in Caesarea. By now he had become so eminent for learning, ascetical life, and defense of the Nicene faith that the new emperor Theodosius named him one of the hundred and fifty bishops to attend the Second Ecumenical Council at Constantinople. The Imperial Court honored him by choosing him to deliver the funeral oration on infant Princess Pulcheria, and some time later on the empress herself. We hear little of him during the latter part of his life. He was certainly at a Synod of Constantinople, in 394, and in all likelihood he died in that year or the year following, fulfilling the prediction of his brother Basil that in spite of its obscurity, Gregory would render Nyssa famous.

The thirteen books against Eunomius (actually a series of writings) set out to refute the Arian heresy. Eunomius's position is that there is the Supreme and Absolute Being, and another Being existing by reason of the First, but after it—yet before all others; and a third Being not ranking with either of these, but inferior to the one, as to its cause, to the other, as to the energy which produced it. It follows that the energies accompanying these Beings vary with respect to the Beings.[1] Thus Eunomius taught that the Son is somehow inferior to the Father, and the Holy Spirit was likewise inferior.

Because Gregory was very faithful to the teaching of his older brother, it is not always easy to determine which thought is his and which is Basil's; this is particularly true when we come to their clarification of the doctrine of the Trinity. In the West, the Greek word υποστασις corresponded to the Latin *substantia,* to refer to the unity of God, while προσωπον was generally rendered by the Latin *persona.* In the East, the doctrine was the same, but ουσια referred to the unity of God, while υποστασις denoted the three Persons. It was therefore necessary either to define the latter term or to avoid using it at all, for if one said μια υποστασις this savored of Sabellianism, while the term τρεις υποστασεις seemed to imply three Gods. In order to avoid confusion, and at the same time to rally those who were in essential agreement while using different language, Basil and Gregory set out to explicate the relationship between ουσια and υποστασις. Whatever the nature of the Father is, we do not understand it, but we know that the Son and the Holy Spirit possess this same nature. Just as the properties of man can be predicted of Paul and Barnabas and Timothy, so whatever is predicated of any one of the three divine Persons can be predicated of the other two. And as there are three men who participate in an undivided manhood, there are three divine Persons participating in one divine substance. Gregory falls back on a monetary illustration: there may be many gold coins, but gold itself is one, while those who are exhibited to us severally in the nature of man, as Peter, James, and John, are many, yet the man in them is one,[2] although by "man" Gregory really means manhood. To avoid the accusation that τρεις υποστασεις actually sounds like three Gods, it would perhaps be better not to use the concept of three at all, although the inadequacy of human language seems to require it. But the Persons of the Holy Trinity are not differentiated in any other way than by the mode of their being. So it is incorrect to say with Eunomius that *unbegottenness* is the essence of the Father, and begottenness the essence of the Son, these refer to the mode of their existence, by which one Person is distinguished from another. Gregory thinks of all divine operation as a single, inseparable unity—originating in the Father while advancing through the Son to culminate in the Holy Spirit. Yet there is only one divine will, which makes it impossible to speak of these names in the plural. Ultimately, the illustration used with regard to the three men, Peter, James and John, breaks down when applied to the Trinitarian economy. The use of number is permitted when speaking of the υποστασεις because there is a basis for the analogy, but in speaking of the ουσια of God one must insist on undivided unity.

Yet while we may have a moderate apprehension of the doctrine of God's nature, we are still unable to explain clearly in words the ineffable depth of this mystery. How can the same thing be capable of being numbered and yet reject numeration? How is it observed with distinctions, yet is apprehended as a monad? How is it separate as to personality and yet is not divided as to subject matter?[3]

The traditional doctrine on the creation of man was to regard Adam and Eve as representative of the entire human race, endowed with certain gifts subsequently lost through their disobedience. But Gregory holds that God first created an ideal humanity, of which Adam and Eve were the first representatives. When the Scripture speaks of man's being made in the image of God, this refers to an archetypal humanity not yet divided into sexes, but participating in the prototype of humanity—Jesus Christ—in whom there is neither male nor female. Thus the creation of our nature is in a sense twofold: one made like to God (created in his image) and one with a distinction of the sexes. The rational and intelligent element of human nature is divine and does not admit the distinction of male and female; the irrational element which follows the rational comprises our bodily form and structure, and is divided into male and female.[4] It is this second element which draws us toward matter by means of our passions, all of which have been created by God. Gregory never says that God actually willed man's disobedience, but it certainly seems that man's nature carries with it a propensity toward evil, and that the dice are loaded against him. Because of the mixed quality of man's human nature, this would almost seem like a necessary consequence. Yet Gregory is not so stupid as to fall into the Manichaean heresy. However, the redemption of man was planned by God prior to man's fall, which God could foresee almost as a direct consequence of man's created human nature.

This requires a more careful look at the relationship between body and soul, spirit and matter. Prior to his creation of the material world, God created angels and the souls of men, a fixed number of each. The human soul is non-material, but it is unlike God by being created, finite, and mutable. When soul is embodied in flesh, both soul and body have a common bond of fellowship in their participation of affections—be they good or sinful. But we have no way of knowing how this union of two such unlike elements is effected, this is a mystery just as the participation of Divinity in humanity is a mystery. Soul and body are both subject to death, however, and the soul is likewise subject to purgation after death. Just as the scalpel, incisions, and cautery often precede the restoration of health, in similar manner, when after long periods of time, the evil of our nature, which now is mixed up with it and has grown with its growth, has been expelled, (and when there has been a restoration of those who are now lying in sin to their primal state), a harmony of thanksgiving will arise from all creation—from those who in the process of the purgation have suffered chastisement, as well as from those who needed not any purgation at all.[5]

But there is an unquenchable fire reserved to torment sinners, of which earthly fire is a very inadequate illustration indeed. For earthly fires can be added to and extinguished, but supernatural fire is qualitatively different and cannot be put out. To escape this judgment, our body must become immortal by participating in incorruption through fellowship with the immortal body of Christ.

Unmistakable traces of Origen not infrequently bob up in the thinking of Gregory. He considers evil as an absence of good or a lack of a perfection, rather than a positive quality. Nor is evil to be equated with matter, although it is true that matter can act as an occasion for evil, since it contains within it a proclivity away from mind, spirit, God, toward nothingness. All created spirits, however, are subject to evil because of their changeable quality, and this mutation is due to the fact that they are created beings. Only the Uncreated, God, is free from this proclivity toward sin, evil, and death.

Redemption takes place through the death and resurrection of the divine and human Christ, who has promised that in the sacrament of baptism that the Deity, when invoked, will be present in a special way. It is a matter of faith that grace is present because He who promised to give it is divine, while the testimony to his divinity comes through the miracles; that the Deity is present in all the baptismal process therefore admits of no question.[6] The descent into the water, and the threefold immersion of the person in it, involves another mystery— the three-day delayed grace of the Resurrection. Likewise, he who is baptized is in a measure freed from his congenital tendency to evil, by his penitence he advances to a hatred of and an aversion to sin, and by his death he works out the suppression of the evil. So to be baptized with water is to rise again from the dead. Now, both water and fire have a cleansing value; they who by the mystic water have washed away the defilement of their sin have no further need of the other form of purification, while they who have not been admitted to that form of purgation must be purified by fire.[7] Baptism is thus the gateway to a new life, and when He is invoked in a special way, God has promised to be present in this sacrament.

The body now comes into fellowship and blending with the Author of our salvation in another way—by partaking of that very Body which has been shown to be superior to death, and has been the First-fruits of our life. But how is it possible, Gregory asks, that that one Body, being for ever portioned to so many myriads of the faithful throughout the whole world, enters, through that portion, whole into each individual, and yet remains whole in itself—at the same time being transmuted by the indwelling of God the Word to the dignity of Godhead itself? It is nonetheless true that the bread which is consecrated by the

Word of God is changed into the Body of God the Word. What was formerly bread is now consecrated by the inhabitation of the Word that tabernacled in the flesh. Therefore, from the same cause as that by which the bread that was transformed in that Body was changed into a divine potency, a similar result takes place now. Just as the grace of the Word made holy the Body, the bread is now sanctified by the Word of God and prayer. This is not to say that it advances by the process of eating to the stage of passing into the body of the Word, but it is at once changed into the Body by means of the Word, as the Word itself said: "This is my Body." By dispensation of his grace, Christ disseminates himself in every believer through that flesh, whose substance comes from bread and wine, blending himself with the bodies of believers, to secure that, by this union with the immortal, man, too, may be a sharer in incorruption. Christ gives these gifts by virtue of the benediction through which he transelements the natural quality of these visible things to that immortal thing.[8]

Saint Gregory is an attractive writer, if not always a consistent one. If he seems uncertain on some issues—human generation is a case in point—it is because he approaches the same problem, now from the philosophical, now from the theological, now from the mystic angle. He is more concerned with being persuasive than being consistent, nor does his late fourth-century Greek always contribute to clarity of thought. Yet for all this, he stands forever as one of the three great Cappadocian fathers. In rejecting the tripartite description of man as body, soul, and spirit, he departed from Origen and at once discredited the view of Apollinaris, who was teaching that the rational soul in Christ had been supplanted by the Logos. In thus insisting on a simple body-spirit dualism in man, he simplified Christian anthropology and safeguarded the divine and human nature of Christ. In this way he rendered an incalculable service to Christian thought, and strengthened the orthodox party in its subsequent struggles with regard to the nature and will of the God-man.

NOTES

The text is in *Patrologia Graeca,* vols. 44-46; translations are in *Nicene and Post-Nicene Fathers,* vol. 5 (*see* Bibliography).
1. *Against Eunomius* bk. 1, chap. 13.
2. *On Not Three Gods*
3. *The Great Catechism* chap. 3.
4. *On the Making of Man* chap. 16.
5. *The Great Catechism* chap. 26.
6. Ibid., chap. 34.
7. Ibid., chap. 35, passim.
8. Ibid., chap. 37.

X

CHURCH AND STATE IN THE FOURTH CENTURY: SAINTS AMBROSE, JEROME, AND CHRYSOSTOM

To unite Ambrose, Jerome, and Chrysostom in a chapter with special reference to church and state may seem at first sight to be somewhat temerarious. Jerome's "conflict" with the establishment was purely personal, and he solved it by withdrawing to an area where the stress no longer prevailed; but the reaction of Ambrose later came to symbolize Western independence and the successful resistance of state encroachment, whereas that of John Chrysostom was foredoomed to failure in the face of Eastern complacency and a strongly entrenched despotism. Obviously, all three were engaged in other areas of action, nor did they have clashes with the authorities every day. Each had his special temperament and forte—Ambrose the administrator and public leader, Chrysostom the popular public preacher, and Jerome the encyclopedic scholar. None holds first rank as a profound theologian, but each made special contributions to the church, and these contributions would soon be integrated in the bishop of Hippo, the greatest of all the church fathers, Saint Augustine.

Saint Ambrose

The transfer of the capital from Rome to Constantinople in the fourth century was to allow the church in the West more freedom from state interference in its affairs, but the church's course of action could not have been secured if it had not been for such courageous and independent spirits as Saint Ambrose of Milan. Thanks to his leadership, the encroachment of civil authority was resisted, and resisted successfully, more than once, whereas in the East, a John Chrysostom would attempt much the same thing with far less success. Of course, the continued threat of barbarian invasions in the West plus the fragile texture of civil government, helped in no small measure to strengthen the policy of an Ambrose, but by the beginning of the fifth century the relationships between church and state were to take on a much more different shape in the Latin church, than they would be able to in the East. The popes of Rome could breathe more easily and act more independently than they otherwise could have, once the chief seat of government had been shifted to the banks of the Bosphorus.

Interest in Saint Ambrose centers principally around these encounters he had with the secular rulers, and while he offers very little in the way of originality—his forte was more in moral or pastoral theology—his courageous behaviour and administrative success as bishop of Milan were enormous, as no less a person than Saint Augustine himself testifies. Here was a busy man of affairs who had little time for study and speculative thought, and yet in the press of everyday matters was working out a viable theory of church-state relationships which was to carry far into the Middle Ages.

Born undoubtedly at Trier about 339, Ambrose represented the best of the old Roman aristocracy; his family had already served in administrative capacities of one kind or another, and at least some of them were Christians. Ambrose was to see his own sister Marcellina receive the veil from Pope Liberius when he himself was scarcely fourteen. Rome was the obvious place for an education in the legal profession and the liberal arts, and here it was also that Ambrose learned Greek and deepened his understanding of Christian doctrine. In 365 both he and his brother Satyrus took posts in the civil service and five years later both received promotions as governors of provinces, Ambrose's assignment requiring him to take up residence in Milan.

In 374 the Arian bishop Auxentius died, leaving the see of Milan vacant. Paulinus, the earliest biographer of Ambrose, relates that during the discussion which occurred in the congregation, a child cried out, "Ambrose for Bishop" to which the entire assembly immediately responded, "Ambrose for Bishop"! Although he was only a catechumen, he was soon baptized by a Catholic priest, and consecrated eight days later as bishop on December 7. His secular interests he left in charge of his brother Satyrus, who lived only four years longer.

At the request of young Emperor Gratian, Ambrose wrote two, then five, books *On the Christian Faith,* a defense of the Nicene position against the Arians. The truth of the doctrine of the Trinity in Unity is based firmly on Scripture, and to deny that Christ is truly the Son of God is Arian blasphemy. Other unacceptable points of view (Sabellianism, Patripassianism, Macedonianism) Ambrose rejects in a close analysis of the Nicene faith. Despite its lucid style, there is little that is really new here. And unfortunately for Ambrose, his imperial admirer was murdered in 383, thus bringing more Arian influences into play in the person of Justina, the queen mother.

The three books *On the Holy Spirit* establish that the Third Person of the Trinity is also God, of the same substance and nature, and was written at the request of Gratian, who in the same year (381) published a second edict against paganism. But disaster had struck in the East when Emperor Valens was defeated and killed at Adrianople in 378, opening the way to the proclamation of Theodosius as emperor in the following year, a year of famine in Rome.

Doctrinal distress was one of the reasons for the summoning of the Second Ecumenical Council at Constantinople in 381, which promptly reaffirmed the Nicene Symbol and anathematized the Anomaeans, Arians, Eudoxians, Semi-Arians, Pneumatists, Sabellians, and the followers of Marcellinus, Photinus, and Apollinaris.[1] At about the same time a Synod meeting at Rome under Pope Damasus was concerned with similar problems.

The assassination of Gratian at Lyons placed the young Valentinian and his mother in grave jeopardy from the usurper Maximus, which resulted in a legation sent by Ambrose on behalf of mother and son. A second intercession occurred in 387, but Maximus took arms against Valentinian II, and was then defeated by Theodosius, who executed him at Aquileia in 388. Since Ambrose considered Maximus the murderer of Gratian, the political intrigue during these years proved tricky to the bishop of Milan.

Paganism, though on the defensive, was by no means dead. In 382, the prefect of Rome, Symmachus, spearheaded a delegation to Gratian to ask the re-erection of the Altar of Victory in the Senate House, as well as a restoration of the endowment of the Vestal Virgins. But a counter-legation headed by Pope Damasus blocked this plan successfully. It is interesting to see how Ambrose views this affair. The state has indeed the right to interfere in religious matters only on behalf of the true faith—Nicene Christianity. To support paganism is not to defend religion, but superstition, and will surely incur the censure of the church. The impiety is not merely religious, but insulting to the memory of the emperor's predecessors. No need, either, to argue that the recent economic distress in Rome has angered the pagan deities. Ambrose argues that the gods were inoperative long before that. Hannibal worshiped the same gods as the Romans, but paganism handed out quite different deserts in the days of the Republic.[2] The request was repeated to Theodosius after the defeat of Maximus, and to Valentinian II in 392, and finally was successful in 393 when the request was made to Eugenius but removed by Theodosius on the defeat of Eugenius and Arbogastes. A final fruitless attempt may have been made in 403-4.[3] Ambrose's position throughout this affair is not that the state shouldn't interfere in religious affairs, but that it cannot lawfully back a false religion. The question is not one of separation of church and state, but illegal support of a false "church."

A more serious encounter occurred with Empress Justina in 385, when she demanded that the Portian Basilica, outside the walls of Milan, be surrendered to the Arians. When this request was frustrated, she demanded the very cathedral church were Ambrose presided, and she chose Holy Week in which to press her demand. Some counsellors of state urged Ambrose to give up his basilica, and to prevent the people from making a disturbance. "The temple of God cannot be surrendered by a Bishop," was his fearless reply. But soldiers occupied the Basilica anyhow, and the emperor commanded: "Surrender the Basilica," only to hear

It is not lawful for me to surrender it, nor advantageous for you, O Emperor, to receive it. By no right can you violate the house of a private person, and do you think that the House of God may be taken away? It is asserted that everything is lawful for the Emperor, that all things are his. My answer is: Do not, O Emperor, lay on yourself the burden of such a thought as that you have any imperial power over those things which belong to God. Exalt not yourself, but if you desire to reign long, submit yourself to God. It is written: "The things which are God's to God, those which are Caesar's to Caesar." The palaces belong to the Emperor, the churches to the Bishop. Authority is committed to you over public, not over sacred buildings.

When the emperor stated that he ought also to have one basilica, Ambrose answered: It is not lawful for you to have it. What have you to do with an adulteress? For she is an adulteress who is not joined to Christ in lawful wedlock.[4]

Here the question is very clearly one of jurisdiction. Ambrose does not deny civil jurisdiction in its proper place, but he warns against the idea that even the things of God fall under the state. The imperial party clearly felt that Ambrose represented a real threat to their authority, and in fact, Emperor Valentinian later complained that if Ambrose had ordered them, his soldiers would have delivered him in chains to the bishop! But, aside from the vivid personalities involved, very clear guidelines are being laid down for medieval practice, and it will be many centuries before they are finally disrupted. Not merely did his courage save the church, but his clear thinking formulated a policy which was to inspire subsequent generations. Nicholas I and Gregory VII are only two examples of popes who profited later by his example.

An even more celebrated incident occurred at Thessalonica in 390, when one of the principal charioteers was imprisoned during the racing season on charges of immoral conduct.[5] In the assault to free the popular athlete, the general of the city guard was murdered along with several officers. When news of this reached Theodosius, he was furious. He commanded the races to be held, but at a given signal, the doors of the amphitheater were closed, and the imperial soldiers began to slaughter the citizenry indiscriminately. No fewer than seven thousand persons perished, and possibly more. When news of this event reached Ambrose, he was appalled. He retired to the country to avoid the emperor's visit, but soon after wrote him to warn that the holy sacrifice could not be publicly offered in his presence, until public penance satisfied the scandal which the emperor had caused. The appeal here is to follow the penitential example of King David, the ancestor of Christ, when reproved by the prophet Nathan. Ambrose is saying that the church has a right to demand external satisfaction for crimes outraging the moral conscience, and not even the emperor himself is free from complying with this divine law. Theodosius may indeed be emperor, but he is also a man before God whose sin requires public satisfaction. The Old Testament illustrates this idea in several places, but nowhere so pointedly as in the case of David, who was, after all, Israel's ideal king. So the prophet Nathan lives again in Ambrose.

But a parallel situation evokes from Ambrose a somewhat different response. The monks and populace of Callinicum, an unimportant town on the Persian frontier, led on by their bishop, had burnt a Jewish synagogue. The magistrate of the provinces ordered the bishop either to rebuild the synagogue or to repay the damage, which sentence was confirmed by the emperor. But it was not confirmed by Ambrose, who somehow seems to have known all the secret decisions which were reached in the emperor's consistory, or so Theodosius complained. It is difficult to sympathize with Ambrose at this point, but he is declaring that to build a synagogue from the money of the church is a sacrilege. To reimburse the Jews is to deny the true faith, and while it may seem good to put on a show of discipline, it is better to serve the cause of true religion. When Emperor Julian attempted to rebuild the temple in Jerusalem, fire broke out and the work of restoration had to be abandoned. And how many worthy people in Rome have had their houses destroyed by fire, but received from the state no compensation! To rebuild a synagogue—a home of unbelief, a house of impiety, a receptacle of folly—is to restore what God Himself has condemned.[6] Clearly Ambrose is at his worst here; zeal for the true faith seems to have driven out charity altogether.

The twentieth letter of Saint Ambrose (to his sister) gives us the first instance of the expression "to celebrate Mass." Since Ambrose is noted for his use of liturgy and the composition of hymns and spiritual songs, and since his accent is heavily on moral and pastoral theology, this is perhaps not inappropriate. About the year 391, he composed his *On the Duties of the Clergy,* modeling it somewhat on the lines of Cicero's *De Officiis.* The aim of the treatise is to lay down not merely guidelines for his own clergy, but to show how much higher Christian morality is than that of pagans. Both what is decorous and what is useful are to be combined to prepare us primarily for the next life. The saint discusses the commandments, and then the counsel of perfection, and these lead to a discussion of appetites and reason, and finally the four cardinal virtues of prudence, justice, fortitude, and temperance. The third book treats of the duties of perfection, drawing numerous examples from the lives of holy men.

But it is on the subject of virginity and advice to widows that Ambrose was most articulate. Augustine says that celibacy seemed to carry austerity a little too far, but Ambrose was so effective in preaching the celibate life that the women of Milan allegedly forbade their daughters to attend the bishop's sermons. He himself complained that his effectiveness was felt everywhere except in Milan, and that perhaps he would have more success in his own city if he went and preached somewhere else. Three tracts of his—*On Virginity, On the Training of a Virgin,* and *Advice to Widows*—assert that while marriage is a sacrament, virginity is to be preferred. He is one of the first writers to present virginity in a positive light and to urge it on a widespread scale.

Ambrose surprises us by attacking the right of private property. God has ordained that all things be held in common, and nature provides that all shall have food, but human greed has resulted in the institution of private property. This leads to an attack on wealth, which Ambrose holds to be not merely unprofitable, but demoralizing as well. He could see clearly the social injustices of the fourth century which had resulted from economic inequalities, but he could not see that wealth had very much positive use. If he preaches a kind of socialistic community, it is one in which Christian influences will make the poor content with their lot, and where there will be no rich. He hardly would countenance a social revolution which would result in a forced redistribution of the world's goods. Ambrose always places the religious motive foremost; wealth and private property must serve the interests of Christ's Kingdom exemplified by the church.[7]

As a theologian Ambrose offers little that is new. His forte lay in the active life of administration, not as a speculative thinker. He was indebted to the Cappadocian fathers for much of his inspiration, but also for the traditional teaching of the church as it had come down to him via such men as Athanasius. As we have already seen, his distinctive contribution was made in the area of church and state relations. This is all the more remarkable when we remember that his early life had been devoted to civil administration. Separation of church and state were the farthest from his mind; both must cooperate closely in carrying out their separate functions. It is the duty of the state to protect the church against all who do not profess the orthodox religion; and if there is indeed a doubt about what the orthodox religion is, the state has the obligation to summon a church council. But the state must not interfere in the affairs of the church, for they belong to God and not to Caesar. As trustees of the church, and administrators of the patrimony of the poor, bishops enjoy a special exemption from state jurisdiction, although he did not exempt the rest of the clergy from it. For him, the state is actually a result of sin, and monarchy is the end result of a lust of power among men. Yet both church and state have real functions to fulfill in society, and they must cooperate with each other in carrying out their separate roles. But it is noteworthy that the saint grants rather more freedom to the church than he does to the state; that is, the state must not encroach upon the church in her divine mission. For all his old Roman blood, Ambrose staunchly defends the independence of the church.

Ambrose is an appealing figure; even the surviving mosaic of him in Milan projects much of his personality. Approximately ninety of his letters remain, several of which narrate contemporary events and others which disclose details of the saint's personal life. There are also a number of addresses and sermons. The funeral sermons, on the emperors Valentinian and Theodosius show the intimate relationship which existed between him and the Establishment, and the sermon for his brother Satyrus is a masterpiece of fraternal tenderness. In all of this we see the active and effective bishop and teacher, the orthodox pastor championing the faith, the tireless administrator, the courageous spokesman for truth and morals in a violent and decadent age.[8]

NOTES

The text is in Migne, *Patrologia Latina*, vols. 14-17; a translation by H. de Romestin is in *Nicene and Post-Nicene Fathers*, vol. 10 (*see* Bibliography).

1. C. J. Héfélé, *Histoire des Conciles*, vol. 2. (Paris: Letouzey et Ané, 1907) p. 20.
2. *Letter* 18.
3. Cf. *Nicene and Post Nicene Fathers*, vol. 10, Saint Ambrose, p. 411.
4. *Letter* 20.
5. E. Gibbon, *Decline and Fall*, chap. 27.
6. *Letter* 40.
7. *De Officiis* 1. 32.
8. F. Homes Dudden, *The Life and Times of St. Ambrose*, 2 vols. (Oxford at the Clarendon Press, 1935). See also Claudio Morino's stimulating study, *Church and State in the Teaching of Saint Ambrose*, trans. by M. Joseph Costelloe, S.J. (Washington, D.C.: Catholic University of America Press, 1969).

Saint Jerome

The enormous influence of Saint Jerome on the Middle Ages was due to his translation of the Bible into Latin—the so-called Vulgate translation, as well as his introduction of the ascetic life into Western Europe. Among his copious and varied writings, the most readable are his letters, around one hundred and fifty in number, for along with much personal information, they give us wonderful glimpses into the life of the later fourth and early fifth centuries.

Jerome was born in the city of Strido on the border of Dalmatia and Pannonia, of Christian parents sometime in the 340s.[1] The family was prosperous and enjoyed good connections.[2] Jerome had a sister and at least one brother named Paulinian. Despite a certain laziness he received a good education, and then went to Rome to study rhetoric, where he was also baptized, possibly by Pope Liberius, about the year 366. The next four years find him in Gaul with his friend Bonosus, where he traveled, copied some manuscripts, and made Trèves his headquarters. About 370 he returned to Aquileia in Italy where with a group of companions he adopted the ascetic life and began the study of Scripture. Although he and his friends were monks, there was no set rule, nor specific community; each person lived a single life either as a solitary or in small groups, and more or less on his own terms. Eventually the group of friends broke up and Jerome determined in 373 to travel to the East.

Arriving in Antioch in 374, Jerome fell ill and the other members of his party went in different directions. It was during this rather prolonged sickness that he underwent his famous dream. "Suddenly," he writes, "I was caught up in the spirit and dragged before the judgment seat of the Judge; and here the light was so bright, and those who stood around were so radiant, that I cast myself upon the ground and did not dare to look up. Asked who and what I was I replied: 'I am a Christian.' But He who presided said: 'Thou liest, thou art a follower of Cicero and not of Christ.' For 'where thy treasure is, there will thy heart be also.' Instantly I became dumb, and amid the strokes of the lash—I was tortured more severely still by the fire of conscience."[3] Finally recovering from this fever, he renounced secular studies, and determined to spend the next five years in the Desert of Chalcis, east of Antioch.

300

The years 374 to 379 were spent in rigorous asceticism, and although he lived as a solitary, he was in touch with other monks in the desert, and their leader Theodosius. At first he practiced only contemplation as he earned his keep, clothed in sackcloth, but he came to realize that some regular mental discipline was necessary to avoid the hazardous excesses of mere contemplation. "How often, when I was living in the desert," he wrote later in his famous twenty-second letter to Eustochium, "in the vast solitude which gives to hermits a savage dwelling-place, parched by a burning sun, how often did I fancy myself among the pleasures of Rome! Now, although in my fear of hell I had consigned myself to this prison, where I had no companions but scorpions and wild beasts, I often found myself amid bevies of girls."

And so it was he began the study of Hebrew from a converted Jew and translated the Gospel according to the Hebrews.[4] Toward the end of this period he allowed himself to get involved in a three-way struggle for the bishopric of Antioch between the Arian and Orthodox parties. Jerome joined Paulinus's party and was ordained priest in 379, accompanying his orthodox bishop to Constantinople the following year to attend the Second Ecumenical Council in 381. It was here that his former teacher, Apollinaris, was condemned, but by this time Jerome had linked up with the Cappadocian fathers, the two Gregories. Following the Council, he accompanied his bishop Paulinus to Rome, where Pope Damasus urged him to make a new translation of the Psalms, plus a revised version of the New Testament.

Jerome counted many friends in Rome who were interested in living the ascetical life, but upon the death of Pope Damasus, the new pope Siricius (384) opposed Jerome's "hard-line" policies and his trenchant satires. The funeral of Blesilla, an ardent and ascetic disciple roused the populace against the monastic party with the cry, "The Monks to the Tiber." Jerome resolved to retire to the Holy Land, and set sail at once for Antioch. In 386 he and some friends arrived in Palestine and he settled at Bethlehem for the remainder of his life.

A monastery was erected at Bethlehem through the generosity of his wealthy patroness Paula, and a convent for women over which she presided, plus a hospice for pilgrims to the Holy Land. The saint's entire life was devoted to reading, writing, and the expounding of Scripture; he did not engage in an active apostolate. His correspondence was enormous, and he was frequently compelled to entertain distinguished guests, take care of administrative detail, and battle frequent illness as well as harassment from his enemies, to say nothing of the barbarians who in 417 burned his monasteries.

The Vulgate version of the Scriptures was completed in the period 391-403. The problem here was to take all the various readings of the Septuagint, and to collate them in an effort to discover the correct reading. All of this took time, suffered frequent delays and interruptions, required money, copyists, and publishers, and was subject to frequent revisions. Finally, by the year 404 the entire work was finished, and gradually took precedence over other Latin translations already in existence. "The New Testament I have restored according to the Greek original; the Old, I have translated in accordance with the Hebrew," he says at the close of his *Lives of Illustrious Men.*

The period from 393-404 is Jerome's great period of controversies, and there are at least six of them. The controversy with Jovinianus, a Roman monk, held that in the sight of God marriage was just as pleasing as virginity. Nor could any higher value be placed on abstinence than on the ordinary partaking of food. He held that those baptized with water and the Spirit, could not sin, and that all sins were equal in the sight of God. In the future glory, all would enjoy the same reward, just as all would endure the same punishment in hell. He also denied that Our Lord had undergone a real birth, and approached Docetism in his view of the Nativity. His aim seems to have been to avoid putting too high a premium on the ascetic life which Jerome and his friends were making popular in Rome. Pope Siricius condemned Jovinianus particularly with regard to marriage and virginity, and Jerome answered him at considerable length in two books *Against Jovinianus*, in dyspeptic fashion. "These are the hissings of the old serpent; by these the dragon expelled man from Paradise," Jerome hisses himself, and in writing later against Vigilantius, he remarks, "This man, after being condemned by the authority of the Roman Church, amidst his feasts of pheasants and swine's flesh, I will not say gave up, but belched out, his life."

The years 393-403 saw a sharp controversy over the orthodoxy of the great Origen, who had flourished in the third century at Alexandria, and whose system of thought we have already had occasion to meet. If Jerome was at first enthusiastic about Origen, it was no doubt more from his great command of Scripture and his literary use of allegory rather than to endorse Origen's peculiar theological point of view. But when leading monks began to take sides and divisions began to polarize, Jerome was instrumental in having Origenism condemned in the West, supporting the condemnation which had already occurred in the East. What Jerome did was to make a clear distinction between the literary and allegorical writings of Origen which he could understand, and the theological position of Origen with which he could have little sympathy.

The tract *Against John of Jerusalem* forms a kind of subplot to the foregoing. Bishop John was sympathetic to the pro-Origenists, and when Epiphanius arrived in Jerusalem to preach in the church, he made John look as though he were virtually a heretic, while the bishop refused to take him seriously and called him "that old dotard." But the monks of Bethlehem took the part of Epiphanius, and proceeded to upstage John of

Jerusalem by forcibly ordaining Jerome's brother Paulinian as an orthodox counterweight to "heretical" John, who then promptly placed some of the monasteries under interdict. His appeal to Rome, to Alexandria, and to certain clerical dignitaries evoked some support at first, but gradually he lost ground, and ultimately he and Jerome reached a rapprochement as the entire affair petered out.

A rapprochement was never reached, however, between Jerome and his old friend Rufinus. On the surface of it, Jerome resented a too neat equation between himself and Origen, while Rufinus, by lauding Jerome's scholarly ability, may have seemed to be fastening heretical Origenism on Jerome. We must also remember that the mail service was not always reliable in those days, and important letters often went astray, or what is worse, were simply not delivered into the proper hands until years later. But there is a personal note in the quarrel between these two eminent teachers, with the result that the whole affair was disedifying to the entire church. Even after Rufinus's death, Jerome spoke bitterly of him, betraying a personal rancor which goes beyond the facts. W. H. Fremantle says that all of this has only one redeeming feature to the historian, namely, that it brings to our knowledge many instructive facts which would otherwise have lain hid.[5]

The quarrel with Vigilantius is a mixture of the one with Jovinianus and Rufinus. Vigilantius accused Jerome of favoring Origen, and that brought a sharp reply from Jerome, but a reply more heated than illuminating. Vigilantius complained that undue veneration was being given to relics, and the vigils at the tombs of martyrs were leading to public scandal. He felt that the virtue of virginity was being exaggerated, and that money collected as alms was better spent at home rather than being sent to the East. He questioned prayers for the dead, and felt that superstition rather than piety had taken over some of the practices of the church. And he had the sympathy of his bishop, Exsuperius of Toulouse. The short tract *Against Vigilantius* treats him as an idiot, but while he may not have been exceptionally bright, he made some telling points with which Jerome never really came sufficiently to terms.

A final word needs to be said on the relationships between Saint Jerome and Saint Augustine. Their mutual friend Alypius helped to explain each to the other and brought news from Hippo to Bethlehem. But Augustine felt the need to question some of the interpretations of the Psalms, as well as the interpretation of Galatians 2, where Paul and Peter had their famous encounter. To make matters worse, the correspondence gets crossed up, and others publish the letters before the original recipients have had a chance to read them. Jerome accuses Augustine of acting behind his back, Augustine questions some of Jerome's scholarly interpretations, and Jerome loses patience. Augustine sends an olive branch, consults Jerome on Pelagianism and the origin of souls, and Jerome—the lesser theologian—gives a sort of blanket endorsement to all that Augustine teaches. Mutual friends act as go-betweens, and the story finally has a happy ending when each saint recognizes and acknowledges the greatness of the other.

Everyone agrees that Saint Jerome is the High Priest of Scripture Scholars, and on his feast day, September 30, the church calls him *Doctor Maximus in exponendis Sacris Scripturis.* Louis Hartmann has correctly shown that this means much more than merely translating the Scriptures; it includes all forms of Biblical science, such as philology, textual criticism, history, and archaeology as well as exegesis and interpretation (or translation).[6] Nor is the saint's particular expertise limited to the Vulgate; this is only his outstanding contribution among many others. Where Jerome shines is not in the speculative theology of an Augustine nor in the brilliant writing of a John Chrysostom, but in his fantastic erudition which was not to be equaled until the time of the Renaissance. He had mastered Hebrew and Aramaic, and he was the only ancient writer to tackle successfully the major and minor prophets. It was the importance of the Old Testament that he insisted upon, the New could not be understood without it, and yet the Old required accurate and competent explanation.

It is doubtful whether Jerome knew the entire Scriptures by heart, but he unquestionably knew a great portion of them intimately because of his ability to associate one passage with another. He says that he worked with considerable speed—a day for the translation of Tobias, a night for Judith. This is not to be taken too seriously because his translations show very careful polishing. It is very true that he was as much engrossed in learning as well as translating or commenting, and the judicious choice of Bethlehem for the last years of his life afforded him the splendid opportunity of getting to know the Holy Land very intimately. He had read anything that had been written on the church up to his time, and his knowledge of the various allegorical interpretations of Scripture which had been offered by Clement or Origen was encyclopedic. It is often not clear just which of the allegorical interpretations he himself preferred; this may well be because he wished to leave the option open to the reader.

All of this vast scholarship Jerome carried on in the context of church teaching, nor did he have to seek official approval for what he wrote since he knew the mind of the church almost as well as the church herself. To Minervius and Alexander he writes: "I made it my resolve to read all the men of old, to test their individual statements, to retain what was good in them, and never depart from the faith of the Catholic Church." But Church, Christ, and Scripture were somehow all equated in the mind of the saint, who sums up his entire attitude in a letter to his beloved Paula: "What honey is sweeter than to know

God's plan? Others, if they wish, may have wealth and drink from jeweled cups, enjoy the plaudits of the multitude, and try to use up all their money in the widest assortment of pleasures. Our wealth is to meditate on the Law of the Lord day and night, to knock when His door is closed, to receive the three loaves of bread of the Trinity, and while the Lord goes before us, to hike upon the billows of the world."[7]

Coupled with his study of Sacred Scripture, Saint Jerome preached and practiced a rigorous asceticism. In fact, this was uppermost in his scale of values, for Jerome builds his entire life around the theme of renunciation. Money and possessions must be surrendered for the sake of the Kingdom, family ties and personal reputation are likewise expendable. The true Christian must be indifferent to the insults and ridicule of the world. This particular stance got Jerome into considerable trouble when he was in Rome directing his group of noble women in the higher counsels of the Gospel; Pope Damasus might approve, but Pope Siricius did not, and when Blesilla died as a result of too great austerities, Jerome found it wise to quit Rome for the East.

The Catholic church has always held that marriage is one of the sacraments, but that virginity is a preferable state to marriage. This Jerome preached, but laid stress on virginity. At various times of the church's history the whole notion of virginity, clerical celibacy, and sexual abstinence comes under attack. It is better to marry than to burn, it is said; virginity is a wasted life; the clergy would know more about marriage if they were not compelled to remain single, etc., etc. In his works against Helvidius, Jovinian, and Vigilantius—the hermit of Bethlehem had to meet the well-worn arguments. Helvidius erred in claiming that Mary had had other children than the Savior, thus attacking her perpetual virginity. Jovinian held that the whole ascetic concept of Christianity was unhealthy, while Vigilantius thought that the entire concept of celibacy, particularly clerical celibacy, was heretical.

Jerome emphasizes the idea that virginity is a counsel of perfection. Its great purpose is to create singleness of mind and undivided service to the Lord, and no one has articulated this point better than Saint Paul. Marriage is never condemned, it is simply that in Jerome the state of virginity is extolled. Marriage is to virginity as silver is to gold, and the apple tree to the apples which it bears. Marriage is indeed honorable, but it must always be subordinated to virginity. It is not the *what* so much as the *how* in Jerome's teaching which seemed objectionable to many; the saint seemed to commend virginity so warmly as almost to suggest Manichaeism.

Self-denial, prayer, and the study of the Scriptures, in particular, round out Jerome's program for the ascetic life, which is the perfect following of Christ. Such a program is not designed to make us harsh and unapproachable, however, but to make us saints in Christ's image.

If any think Jerome austere, then all of his warmth, his compassion, his kindness and tenderness have been missed. His letters reveal the great personal charm and affection he had for Paula, Marcella, and Nepotian. Asceticism for Jerome was never an end in itself, but only the means by which the soul could draw closer to Christ.

To what extent can Jerome be called the Father of Christian Humanism? Certainly he set in motion during the Middle Ages and also the Renaissance the love of learning—both sacred and secular—which was to culminate in Erasmus of Rotterdam. That Jerome himself was an enormous encyclopedia of classical learning is evident from his letters alone. For Laeta's little daughter Paula, he outlined a whole educational course which omitted virtually nothing. But what was his precise attitude toward pagan, or classical, learning? Had he renounced it forever in favor of the Scriptures after the traumatic experience of the angel's accusing him of being a Ciceronian? Jerome seems to shift back and forth. At one time, he is completely engrossed in Scripture studies to the exclusion of all else. At another time he is instructing Christian youth in the very pagan humanism that he had supposedly renounced. Perhaps these polarities can be reconciled if we remember that Jerome's primary allegiance was to Scripture, but the road for educated pagans and Christians of his day had to be along the way of classical culture. Tertullian might reject this, but Clement of Alexandria had already shown that an appeal to the ancient mind had to be made by underscoring all that was of value in Vergil, in Cicero, in the ancient Greek philosophers, and giving it a Christian baptism. And when we remember that Jerome is neither a bold nor an original thinker, but an enormously synthetic mind, then we can see that his natural gifts would make it virtually impossible for him really to renounce classical culture. It was too closely associated with the glory of Rome, indeed, Christian Rome, and when Alaric's barbarians destroyed this, Jerome wept. His avowed intention may have been far from a desire to father Christian humanism, any more than to choose a lion for a companion, but because he was Jerome, it was inevitable that his saintly scholarship should force upon him for all posterity this particular role.[8]

A final word about Saint Jerome as a person.[9] He was certainly dyspeptic and at times irascible. That he seems vindictive against his old friend Rufinus may only indicate how very deeply he had been hurt by their mutual falling out. And it is true that Jerome is sometimes given to exaggeration of his own problems and difficulties. But these shortcomings are eclipsed by his tremendous magnanimity of spirit. He was above all "catholic" and "monkish." If his earlier commentaries show too great an influence from Origen, he recoiled from this later on by insisting on his orthodoxy. He was foremost a "man of the church" but not being a speculative thinker in either philosophy or theology, he would not be tempted to entertain temerarious ecclesiastical opinions. His monastic life in Bethlehem had also to take into account the necessary time for Scripture study, plus his enormous correspondence, and the granting of interviews to the many who flocked to visit him. What is more remarkable, his natural powers never flagged but sustained themselves to the very end. He seems to have been highly imaginative and quite emotional. One finds tenderness and warmth in Jerome with perhaps a touch of loneliness; he needed desperately to be loved. And yet there is sometimes a harshness. But for all this, he was eminently a man of single purpose, who early in life set himself a personal lifestyle and then a task to perform which he pursued until the day of his death. Though Rome should fall, though friends should die and strangers take their place, Jerome labored on, becoming a legend in his own time, and along with Augustine, destined to shape the religious thinking of not only the Middle Ages, but the Renaissance as well.

NOTES

The text is in Migne, *Patrologia Latina,* vol. 22-30; a translation by Charles Christopher Mierow is in *Nicene and Post-Nicene Fathers,* vol. 6 (*see* Bibliography).

1. *Lives of Illustrious Men* chap. 135; Preface to the Book of Job.
2. *Apology* 1. 30.
3. *Letter* 22.
4. *Illustrious Men* 2, 3.
5. *Nicene and Post-Nicene Fathers,* vol. 6, Prolegomena to Saint Jerome, p. xxii.
6. See Louis Hartman, "Saint Jerome as Exegete" in *A Monument to Saint Jerome,* ed. Francis X. Murphy, C.S.S.R. (New York: Sheed & Ward, 1952).
7. Ibid., p. 76.
8. Ibid., p. 203 ff. (See the stimulating article by Edwin A. Quain, S.J., "Saint Jerome as a Humanist" in *A Monument to Saint Jerome.*)
9. Ibid., p. 15 ff. (See "The Personality of Saint Jerome" by F. Cavallera in *A Monument to Saint Jerome;* also his *S. Jérome, Sa Vie et Son Oeuvre,* (Louvain and Paris, 1922).

Saint John Chrysostom

As in the case of Saint Ambrose, it is the life of Saint John Chrysostom, Father and Doctor of the Universal Church, which commands our interest more than any specific contributions which he made to the growth of Christian thought. In his less successful contests with imperial authority he resembles the more adroit bishop of Milan, Ambrose; in his championing of Sacred Scripture from the pulpit, he resembles the hermit of Bethlehem, Jerome. It is his preaching and his moral courage which make John eminent, and whom the next century was to dub "Chrysostom" Gold-mouth. There are a good many contemporary references to him along with the biography of Palladius, written a year or two after his death. In spite of a plethora of material, it is impossible to fix his birth—sometime between 344 and 349, possibly as late as 354, but certainly at Antioch. Her husband Secundus, a top-drawer military official, left Anthusa a widow at the age of twenty, and a widow she chose to remain in spite of the difficulty of bringing up two children, John being the youngest.

Antioch was the eastern fortress-city of the empire; beyond it lay the desert and the great Parthian empire. The Semi-Arians had been strong there in the fourth century, and now two Catholic bishops, Paulinus and Meletius, divided the orthodox forces; it was Meletius who baptized John in 368, and then made him lector in 371. Having finished his studies in philosophy and rhetoric, he then retired to the desert for approximately six years to practice the ascetic life (somewhat indiscreetly) and to study Sacred Scripture. The eremitic life proved too much; it ruined his stomach, and he returned to civilization to be ordained deacon by Meletius in 381 and to help him out in the administration of the church's affairs. Meletius was succeeded by Flavian, who ordained John a priest in 386, and it is probably from this period that his best-known work, *On the Priesthood,* was written.

The spring of 387 witnessed a revolt in Antioch as a result of the emperor's increase in taxes; radicals tore down the statues of the family of Theodosius, and toppled that of the emperor himself. Order was finally restored and the threat of imperial vengeance imminent, as the city plunged from defiance to remorse. Fearful of the worst, Bishop Flavian made the arduous trip to Constantinople at no little personal cost in the hope of softening Theodosius's wrath and gaining clemency. Meanwhile, back at the cathedral, John poured forth his eloquence in an effort to calm and then console the people. The effort was a success resulting in a joyous Easter celebration of thanksgiving, and increasing the prestige of both Flavian and John. These were happy years for Chrysostom as he distinguished himself in Christian polemics and apologetics while advancing the teachings of the Catholic church. It seemed obvious that he would soon step into the shoes of the aging Flavian to become bishop of Antioch himself.

But in 397, Bishop Nectarius of Constantinople died, leaving a number of contenders for his ecclesiastical throne, foremost of whom was Palladius of Alexandria. Arcadius, now emperor in the East, on the death of his father Theodosius, agreed with his eunuch-minister, Eutropius, that an outsider would prevent the palm from being awarded to any of the local aspirants, and by a ruse "kidnapped" John and spirited him off to the capital. Here he was consecrated bishop by Alexandria's Palladius, the very man who coveted the same post! The resulting position was difficult because his backing at court came from not-too-savory elements. In fact, his chief backer, Eutropius, lasted only until the following year, when he was forced to plead for sanctuary at the altar, a church-sanctuary which he had repeatedly violated during his ministry. This gave John the dubious honor of having to preach against his benefactor while attempting to spare his life. In 400, the rival of Eutropius, Gainas, attempted a revolt which should have, but failed to unhorse the indolent Arcadius.

The real power at court was now Empress Eudoxia. She at first had favored the saint, but his repeated sermons against the vanities of women, and his defense of a widow who had been wronged by the empress, as well as the machinations of enemies such as Severian and Acacius, resulted in a loss of imperial favor. Meanwhile, complications had occurred with the patriarch of Alexandria, Theophilus. Accused by Egyptian monks of greedy, unscrupulous and high-handed behavior, he was finally summoned by John to Constantinople to answer serious charges of malfeasance. He countered by summoning a Synod of his own to prefer charges of heresy and malpractice against the patriarch of Constantinople (the Synod of the Oak). John refused to recognize this counter-synod composed entirely of his enemies, and he was declared deposed, a move which the empress ratified. John now had to leave the city, but no sooner had he left when a palace disaster occurred; in all probability the empress suffered a miscarriage. Viewing this as a possible judgment of God, Eudoxia issued a recall of the bishop of Constantinople. Hesitant at first, John finally returned to his see amid general rejoicing.

Late in 403 another clash of temperaments occurred when John

complained of the noise outside the cathedral caused by the erection of a
statue in honor of the empress. "Again Herodias rages, . . . again she
demands the head of John on a platter," were the alleged words of a
sermon seized or fabricated by the bishop's enemies to further estrange
him from imperial favor; events came to a climax during Lent of the year
404. The cathedral was closed to him, and on Easter, soldiers forcibly
prevented the baptism of catechumens, mixing holy water with their blood.
The pliant Arcadius issued a second order for John's banishment, and
on June 24 he was exiled again. No sooner had he stepped on board
ship than this time the cathedral and the Senate House went up in
flames. Arsacius, his old enemy, was installed as bishop in his place,
and Atticus soon followed him; but both were subsequently exiled
shortly afterwards.

The emperor of the West, Honorius, and Pope Innocent I now attempted to intervene in the dispute, but their legates were dishonorably
treated and sent packing. Exiled in Cucusus for three years, John seems
to have been able still to exercise considerable influence on ecclesiastical
politics in the capital. Many letters of his survive from this period
(404-7) and his numerous contacts with sympathizers from all parts
of the empire suggested to the court that he be transported to a more
inaccessible spot. He was therefore re-exiled to Pityus and forced to
march there in spite of sickness and near exhaustion. On the last
day of his travels he collapsed after a few hours and was transported
back to Camana in the Pontus, where he received the Eucharist, made the
sign of the cross, and expired with the words: "Glory to God in all things.
Amen." In 438 his relics were brought back to Constantinople by
Theodosius II, and laid to rest in the Church of the Apostles. But in
1204 when the Fourth Crusade assaulted the city, the saint's remains
were again removed and sent to Rome, to the choir chapel of Saint
Peter's. As Dom Chysostomus Baur says so well, Rome was the saint's
last resort in life, and his final resting place in death.[1]

It was principally through his preaching that the enormous influence
of Saint John Chrysostom was felt; indeed, he is the best preserved
(manuscript-wise) of all the church fathers. When he ascended into the
pulpit, he hardly looked like a man who would impress his audience,
but when he spoke, all sorts and conditions of men heard him gladly.
He generally presented a commentary on the Scripture of the day, and
brought all of his powers of spiritual interpretation and moral insight to
bear on it. He was not of necessity "organized"; he not infrequently
digressed, was overly long in his introductions, and even repetitive. But
genius was nonetheless there. He moved easily from his text to modern
applications of the Gospel message. Sometimes he appeared ill-prepared
and rambling, but this was often a rhetorical device, for he brought all of
his natural powers to bear when expounding the Word of God to his

listeners. It is indeed unfortunate that we do not know exactly *how* he preached; the sermons or homilies we have, but the intonation of voice, the gestures, the subtle nuances that go to make up any great preaching have been lost. However, more important than the way in which he preached was what he preached. He clearly had something to say, and it was the content of his message that ultimately held people. This content was almost invariably based on Scripture, which he made relevant to the problems of everyday life. He was certainly fearless; one of the reasons for his downfall was his open and undisguised criticism of court life, and particularly of Eudoxia. Was he anti-feminist in his preaching? He certainly lacked prudence on occasion, and yet it was his very boldness, the simple way in which he stated the truth of things, which so endeared him to his hearers. He had failings, to be sure, but his oratorical failings were actually part of his very genius, and his impact is all the more forceful in spite of inadequacies which would have been fatal to a lesser man.[2]

Ascetical and pastoral theology were the forte of Saint John, as dogmatic theology was not. This is due partly to his particular temperament, and partly due to the fact that the Arian controversy had more or less burnt itself out, while the Nestorian had not yet come to full flower. Besides, John did not speak to theology-orientated audiences; he had to furnish more "practical" fare. But this is not to say that he does not have a theology; he does, and it is an accurate mirror of Catholic thinking in his own time.

He is clearly not an Arian. Not even an angel or an archangel can do anything with regard to what is given from God: the Father, Son, and Holy Spirit dispense everything. But anyone who has seen Christ has seen the Father, which proves that they must be of the same essence. To use a crude illustration, says Chrysostom, no one who does not know what gold is can tell when gold is mixed in silver. In all of his homilies he is in clear possession of the Nicene terminology,[3] but he does not elaborate it, nor does he discuss the matter of processions in God.

The thorny question of Nestorianism he anticipates and disposes of in a single passage later cited by the Council of Chalcedon; the Word truly assumed flesh, so that by a Union and Conjoining, God the Word and the Flesh are One, not by any confusion or obliteration of substances, but by a certain union ineffable, which is past understanding.[4] Being Son of the unoriginate God, and his true Son, Christ allowed himself to be called also ·Son of David, that he might make you and me sons of God. Christ was born after the flesh, that we might be born after the Spirit; he was born of a woman, that we might cease to be the son of a woman.[5] So there is an insistence on the real Incarnation of the Son of God, and his two natures—one divine, one human.

Baur observes that "the recognition of the perpetual virginity and of the miraculous conception and birth of Christ is found in Chrysostom, but never the designation *Theotókos,* although the expression had been under discussion at least since the year 380, and in Antioch itself, had been made the subject of disagreeable discussions in public. But neither had he protested against the expression."[6] Because of a possible inclination in John to anti-feminism, his Mariology is not clearly worked out, and some aspects of it are clearly not acceptable; in another generation, language suitable to Mary would be explicated more precisely, but not under the leadership of Chrysostom.

Free will and grace operate jointly in every man, but no one really knows how they operate. Chrysostom insists on individual free will, but the calling of God is of grace, and not of free will—a free will which is indeed weak and needs every assistance. His position is pretty much summed up in the idea that if we do our part, God will not fail to do his. This is not to say that he is a Pelagian, it is rather that Chrysostom never probes this problem to anything like its Augustinian depths. God gives his gift of grace first, but it is up to man to cooperate with God and work out his own salvation.

Turning to his sacramental theology, we find Chrysostom a strong witness for the Real Presence in the Eucharist, and the Mass as a Holy Sacrifice. In his celebrated work *On the Priesthood,* the saint asks: "When you see the Lord sacrificed, and laid upon the altar, and the priest standing and praying over the victim, and all the worshipers empurpled with that precious blood, can you then think that you are still among men, and standing upon the earth?"[7] The Word of God commands us to believe what may seem to be contrary to our senses. For it is through sensible objects that the mind perceives the hidden reality. Thus the gift of renewal comes to us via the water of baptism, as food for the soul comes to us through the Eucharist. Many foolishly say how wonderful it would be to see Christ and to touch his clothes or his shoes. But you *do* touch him, you *do* eat him, you *do* see him, and you receive him within yourself.[8] In the twenty-fourth homily on First Corinthians he eulogizes the cup of blessing spoken of by Paul in 10:13 because by holding it in our hands, we exalt him in wonder and astonishment at his unspeakable gift. "Tell me," asks Chrysostom, "what can be more tremendous than this? What more tenderly kind?"[9] Those who partake of this awful mystery become the one body of Christ. Just as a loaf of bread is composed of many undistinguishable grains of wheat, so are we conjoined both with each other and with Christ: there is not one body for you and another for your neighbor, but the very same for everyone.[10] These are just a very few of many references to the Eucharist and the Holy Sacrifice.

Chrysostom takes a stringent position on baptism. Those who do not receive this sacrament are simply outside the palace; they are with the culprits and the condemned. Weep for them! They deserve our wailing and our groans. Part of this attitude may be attributed to the frequent practice of delaying baptism as long as possible in order to enter the next life as unsullied as possible. But the saint allows for no exceptions here; without baptism one lands in hell.[11]

In not quite so dire straits are those who died in wealth, but did not supply any solace for their soul. They can be assisted in a small way if we pray for them and entreat others to aid the poor on their behalf. The apostles have rightly ordered that remembrance for the dead should be made in the awe-inspiring Mysteries. Great gain results to the departed, for when the whole people stand with uplifted hands, a priestly assembly, and that awful Sacrifice lies displayed, how can we not prevail over God in our entreaties for those who have departed in the Faith?[12]

In his *Letter to the Fallen Theodore,* Chrysostom takes the traditional position that virginity is preferable to marriage, even though the married state itself is honorable. In Theodore's case marriage was adultery because he had already been betrothed to a heavenly bridegroom. This particular saint rejects "temporary vocations." Marriage is indissoluble since man is not to sever what God has joined together. He also insisted that marriage should be celebrated before a priest.[13]

Reference has already been made to *On the Priesthood* which is a classic on holy orders. The priest has received authority (among other things) to deal, not with bodily leprosy as did the Jewish priests, but with spiritual uncleanness; they do not pronounce it removed after examination, but actually and absolutely take it away. This means that God has bestowed a power on priests greater than that of our natural parents, who merely introduce us to the natural life, whereas priests induct us into the supernatural life of the world to come. They can save a sick soul, or one on the point of perishing; they can procure for some a milder punishment and prevent others from falling away altogether. And they have authority to forgive sins.[14]

Therefore, it is better to repent now than on the day when we repent of necessity and to no avail. Either we repent and are forgiven now, or the Judge will hear us publicly in the presence of the world, and we shall no longer have any hope of pardon. The punishment of hell is eternal, nor is there any final release from its torments. This parallels the eternal beatitude of the blessed. If Peter, when he beheld some dim image of the things to come, immediately cast away all other things out of his soul, on account of the pleasure produced in it by the vision, what would anyone say when the actual reality of the things is presented, when the palace is thrown open and it is permitted to gaze upon the King himself, no longer darkly, or by means of a mirror, but face to face—

no longer by means of faith, but by sight?[15] And here we may conclude a general survey of Saint John Chrysostom's general dogmatic position, admirable in its comprehension and an accurate inventory of the thinking of the church in his times, but hardly foreward-thinking, much less revolutionary in any of its aspects.

A man may believe in the Father, Son, and Holy Spirit, but if he does not lead a good life, his faith will avail nothing. Faith is indeed God's gift, but good works must follow. The moral Christian life is possible only because God's grace has made us fit to be loved. It is as though, Chrysostom says, one were to take a leper, wasted by distemper, disease, by age, poverty, and famine, and turn him all at once into a graceful youth, surpassing all mankind in beauty, shedding a bright luster from his cheeks, and eclipsing the sunbeams with the glances of his eyes, and then set him in the very flower of his age, and clothe him in the royal purple. So God arrays this soul of ours and makes it an object of his delight and love.[16]

In his preaching, Chrysostom touched on the manifold duties of the Christian life, but no theme was more frequent than the necessity of social justice toward the poor. In both Antioch and in Constantinople there existed considerable disparity of wealth, and one of the reasons Chrysostom made enemies was his frequent criticism of luxurious displays on the part of the wealthy. He was masterful in portraying the needs and the wretchedness of the poor, and while he could not, of course, abolish slavery, he could do much to alleviate the condition of slaves and protect them against unscrupulous owners. His criticism of the wealthy touched the court and the empress on more than one occasion. While by no means a Marxist, he saw clearly the Christian demand for justice and love toward the needy. It was this fearless attack on wealth and entrenched power which so often delighted his congregation, but at the same time aroused a storm of opposition against him. One of the charges against him was the selling of church treasure to build hospitals for the poor.

Slaves are to be treated with kindness and love. "Remember," he says, "that if the slave is a Christian, she is also your sister! But she drinks! Then take care that she does not get any wine. But she is unchaste! Then have her married. But she steals! Then take better care of your possessions. But she is a gossip and a slanderer! But how many free-born women are just the same! Against their slaves they will fall into such absurd passions of anger that they will tear the veils from their heads and pull them around by the hair! . . . Practice patience with your slaves, then you will also be more patient with your husband."[17]

"And again, and why do you need such a swarm of slaves? Give them their freedom! But in any case, know that it is inhuman to strike a slave or to put him in chains."[18] "In general, slavery is simply the result of sin. Only avarice, envy and insatiability have produced it."[19]

The contests of Saint John Chrysostom with the court have been compared with those of Saint Ambrose of Milan, who was more successful in carrying off the palm of victory than hapless John. In Constantinople, where church and state were so closely united in a remarkable cultural unity, it was almost inevitable that the church should be subordinated to the state. The success of Ambrose was due in no small part to the collapse of local government in the West. The church was soon to have in that part of the empire the opportunity she never enjoyed in the East—of fashioning society along Christian lines where the church would be not only independent of the state, but where the state would often be dependent on the church. In the East this was never to happen; not even the moral prestige of a Chrysostom could ever free the church from state domination. This truth is unwittingly expressed in a delightful mosaic in the Church of San Vitale in Ravenna. The emperor Justinian (sixth century) is shown with a number of dignitaries—civil and ecclesial—but because the artist has not solved the problem of perspective, the emperor has his foot on the toe of the man next to him, who may well be the patriarch. It is beautiful symbolism of the exact church-state relationship in the East for centuries to come.

Rome would be more successful in its fight against Caesaro-papism in the West. And John looked to Rome for leadership and unity among all the churches of the empire. But already East and West were drifting apart, and before long serious differences would sunder the churches completely. It was the great genius of John to be recognized in the West as one of the great saints intent on the unity of the church. A prophet is not without honor except in his own country; if his successors had had half the sanctity and ability of him they called "Gold-mouth" the church might have survived the impending crisis, to remain united throughout the entire world.

NOTES

The text is in Migne, *Patrologia Graeca,* vols. 47-64; translations appear in *Nicene and Post-Nicene Fathers,* vol. 10 (*see* Bibliography).

1. See also Chrysostom Baur, O.S.B., *John Chrysostom and His Times,* 2 vols., trans. Sr. M. Gonzaga, R.S.M. (London: Sands & Co., 1959): The best modern work on Saint John Chrysostom. Neander's *The Life of Saint John Chrysostom,* trans. J. C. Stapleton, 1st ed. (Berlin, 1820) is old but good.
2. Baur, *John Chrysostom,* vol. 1, p. 206 ff.
3. *Homilies on John* 74. 1; 86. 4.
4. Ibid., 11. 2.

5. *Homilies on Matthew* 2. 2.
6. Baur, *John Chrysostom*, vol. 1, p. 359.
7. *On the Priesthood* 3. 4.
8. *Homilies on Matthew* 82. 4.
9. *Homilies on First Corinthians* 24. 1.
10. Ibid.
11. *Homilies on Philippians* 3.4; cf. Neander, *Life*, vol. 1, p. 78 ff.
12. Ibid.
13. *Homilies on Genesis* 48. 6.
14. *On the Priesthood* 3. 6.
15. *Letter to the Fallen Theodore* 1. 11.
16. *Homilies on Ephesians* 1. 3.
17. Ibid., 15. 1, quoted from Baur, *John Chrysostom*, vol. 1, p. 383.
18. *Homilies on First Corinthians* 40.5; cf. Baur supra.
19. *Homilies on Ephesians* 22. 2; cf. Baur supra.

XI
SAINT AUGUSTINE

The enormous influence of Saint Augustine makes him a convenient figure with which to conclude this survey. His autobiography proves that his wide grasp of theology arose from life situations, and almost always has a real, practical dimension. He recapitulates the achievement of the classical age and transmits it to the medieval and modern world with the firm stamp of fifth-century Christianity upon it. The Catholic church as well as the early Protestant reformers view him as a towering figure. Eminently a man of the church as well as a master of philosophy and theology, he brought to bear a very strong personal dimension to the life of the church, especially in the West. Above all, he stands in the North African tradition of Tertullian and Cyprian, whom he far surpasses, but to whom he is nonetheless indebted. His greatness can be measured by the fact that when Saint Thomas Aquinas finds it necessary to depart from the Augustinian tradition, he always does so with what seems like a deferential apology.

This chapter does not pretend to offer any new insights into Augustine's genius, but attempts merely to summarize from the saint's own writings, the barest outlines of his monumental intellectual achievement.

Saint Augustine: I

LIFE

The celebrated *Confessions,* written about the year 400 by Augustine himself, furnishes us the principal information about his early life. Tagaste, his birthplace, was a small town in Numidia, now eastern Algeria and his father was a minor government official. His mother, Monica, the Christian of the family, zealously enrolled him as a catechumen. When he was about twelve, he was sent off to Madaura, about twenty miles south of Tagaste, to study what today would be called the liberal arts, but was then denominated grammar and literature. His success earmarked him for legal studies in Carthage, but he had to sit around for a year while his father raised the necessary funds. On arriving in Carthage in 370, he contracted a liaison and bore a son Adeodatus.

Augustine tells us he was somewhat wild as a youth. His willfulness dates, he says, all the way from the crib, and his infant psychology holds that long before they are able to talk, babies can make demands which adults find impossible to resist. The incident of the pear orchard, when he joined a group of "Eversores" who wantonly destroyed green pears merely to fling them to the hogs, demonstrates the inner tendency of human beings to want to smash and destroy things with no apparent reason, as well as the low moral level to which crowds may sink when they are acting in consort. As a depth psychologist, Augustine has few equals.

The reading of Cicero swung the saint away from law to the study of literature, and after a year's teaching in his hometown he returned to Carthage to hang out his shingle as a rhetorician. At about the same time, he fell in with the Manichaeans, and took instruction in their sect, which attempted to create an overall synthesis of philosophy and religion. But on discovering that their leader Faustus was more ignorant than knowledgeable, Augustine drifted off from Carthage and the Manichees in order to try his luck at Rome, and then at Milan, where he encountered the great Ambrose. Meanwhile he had written his first book, *On the Beautiful and the Fit,* won a poetry contest, and had been badly shaken by a friend who had been baptized in a coma, and who chided Augustine for his impiety, dying soon after.

319

Part of the reason for coming to Milan was to study the forensic habits of Bishop Ambrose, but Augustine soon found here more than mere speaking ability; he found moral force, conviction, and indefatigable energy as well. By 385 he had disentangled himself from the Manichaean belief in the evil nature of matter, and had embraced the philosophy of the Neoplatonists. Here he found much that was Christian in character, but the idea "that the Word became flesh and dwelt among us" he did not find. Having formerly neglected the study of Scripture because of its poor style, he began a study of the New Testament, and especially the Pauline epistles.

Intellectually convinced of Christianity's truth by the time he was thirty-two, Augustine still lacked the moral courage and force to break with his old habits; a number of stories of conversions inspired him to surrender himself to God, not the least of which was that of Saint Anthony, who gave up all that he had to the poor when he heard that particular Gospel passage read in church. Augustine retired to a villa and heard the voice of a child in a neighboring yard, sing-songing: "Take. Read. Take. Read." Opening the Scripture to Romans 13:13, 14, he took the injunction literally to put on the Lord Jesus Christ, and to make no provision for the lusts of the flesh. He was baptized with his son Adeodatus and his friend Alypius, by Ambrose in Milan, deciding next to return to Africa, but the death of his mother at Ostia delayed him at Rome. His first major doctrinal work, *On the Morals of the Catholic Church,* now appeared as a great Polemic against the Manichees. By the year 388 he was back in Tagaste, where he retired with a few friends to lead the monastic life. His son Adeodatus died the following year.

This contemplative life came to an abrupt end in 391, when the aged bishop of Hippo began casting about for a successor. Augustine, quite contrary to his inclinations, was ordained priest and began a very active assistance to the ailing bishop, succeeding him in 395-96. For the next thirty-five years until his death in 430 he poured his entire energy into the cause of the church in North Africa.

Augustine's writings are voluminous, and during this period they deal in large part with controversies against the Manichees, the Donatists, and the Pelagians. To refute the false notions of the evil of the flesh and cosmic dualism is the purpose of the writings against the Manichees; the Donatists pose the problem of "easy repentance" and the unity of the Catholic church, and the Pelagians adopted a too-flattering notion of man's free will. But in addition to his many writings, Augustine was a busy parish priest and bishop who preached and taught constantly, presided over civil and ecclesiastical courts, and was involved in endless administrative detail. His celebrated book *On Christian Doctrine* began to appear in 397, his *Confessions* a few years later, followed by his classic *On the Trinity.*

Meanwhile, the political situation was beginning to deteriorate. The sack of Rome by Alaric in 410 sent shivers up the spine of the ancient classical world, touching off a controversy between pagans and Christians on the desertion of the Old Roman deities. It was not long before Augustine began his most famous *City of God* to refute heathen calumnies, and to outline a philosophy of world history which was to dominate the Middle Ages. Thirteen years in the writing (413-426), the *City of God* was to become a "great book" with an enormous influence.

During the latter part of his life, Augustine was involved in writing a number of *Retractions,* or modifications of his theology and point of view. Meanwhile the Vandals had landed in North Africa, and had proceeded to defeat the imperial forces, which holed up in Hippo, Augustine's bishopric, for a last stand. Here, during the third month of the siege in 430, the saint died on August 28.

One of the greatest minds ever to appear, Augustine is also a summary figure for the classical world. He brings together in a synthesis the best thinking of the Greco-Roman world, and is one of the prime architects of the Middle Ages. But his influence did not stop there, for the Protestant reformers in their rejection of the medieval synthesis, returned to Augustine for many of their ideas. Today he is still a force not only in philosophy and theology, but in psychology and political theory as well. Along with Plato, Aristotle, and Aquinas, he is a towering figure whose influence will last until the very end of time.

RELIGION AND REVELATION

"God," says Saint Augustine, "is the fountain of our happiness; He is the end of all our desires. Being attached to Him, we tend toward Him by love, that we may rest in Him, and find our blessedness by attaining that end. For our good, about which philosophers have so keenly contended, is nothing else than to be united to God."[1] Now, this name of God is somehow known by the whole of creation, and thus to all mankind, because the energy of the true Godhead is such that it cannot be hidden completely from any rational creature which still makes use of its reason. The entire race of men acknowledged God as the maker of this world, long before they ever heard of Christianity. Except for the most utterly depraved, therefore, there is a natural religion existing in every man.[2]

But the natural capacity of man's mind is so disabled by besetting and inveterate vices, that it first had to be impregnated with faith and purified before it could even tolerate, much less abide in, God's unchanging light. To make it possible to advance confidently toward the truth, God founded and established this faith through the God-man, that there might be a Way for man to man's God.[3]

The government of the whole world and the administration of the universal creation are so familiar through their never-failing constancy that no one even bothers to see the miracles wrapped up in a single grain of wheat; God has, agreeably to his mercy, reserved to himself certain works beyond the usual course and order of nature which would excite wonder precisely because they are uncommon. The government of the whole world is a greater miracle than the feeding of five thousand with five loaves of bread, but the latter incident excites more wonder because it is more rare.[4] But this is not to say that miracles happen contrary to nature because they happen through the will of God which has determined the nature of things in the first place. So miracles only happen contrary to what we know as nature, and they offer supporting evidence (rather than proof) that God is acting in a special way to confirm his revelation to man.[5]

Prophecy is another external criterion of revelation.[6] Prophets and heralds have proclaimed the great mystery of godliness, in this way verifying the preaching of the apostles. Thus miracles and prophecies are external signs of the testimony of the soul—the internal criterion of revelation. In the *Confessions* the saint says of God: "You cried to me from afar, 'I am Who am,' and I heard this, as things are heard in the heart, nor was there room for doubt; and I should more readily doubt that I live than that Truth is not, which is clearly seen, being understood by the things that are made."[7] Commenting on the Gospel of John, he says a man is drawn to Christ when he delights in the truth, when he delights in blessedness, delights in righteousness, delights in everlasting life—all of which Christ is. "Give me a man that loves, and he feels what I say. Give me one that longs, one that hungers, one that is travelling in this wilderness, and thirsting and panting after the fountain of his eternal home; give me such, and he knows what I say."[8]

God is the Author of the Old Law as well as the New. The things in the Law and the prophets which Christians do not observe are only the types of what they do observe. These types were figures of things to come, and are necessarily removed when the things themselves are fully revealed by Christ, that in this very removal the Law and the prophets may be fulfilled. Even animal sacrifices were types of Christ, by whose blood we are purified and redeemed. Thus, it was the work of Christ to fulfill the Law, and thus do away with it. Now, other sacraments are instituted, greater in efficacy, more beneficial in their use, easier in performance, and fewer in number.[9]

There are indeed four Gospels, although we may better say four books of the one Gospel. Only four are genuine, containing genuine history.

In *Reply to Faustus the Manichaean,* Augustine acknowledges his books to be genuine; he likewise testifies to the genuinity of the Gospel of Matthew. In this case, Matthew could just as well be any of the other Gospels. Where will you find any authority, he asks, if not in the Gospel and apostolic writings? How can we be sure of the authorship of any book, if we doubt the apostolic origin of those books which are attributed to the apostles by the church, which the apostles themselves founded?

Jesus Christ truly came into the world as a divine legate. Christ performed miracles, but many did not believe him because he was a man, in spite of the fact that he was doing divine works. They erroneously concentrated on his manhood, blind to the implication of his divine works which argued that he must also be God.[10] Christ also fulfilled the prophecies foretold about him, but lest anyone say that Christians have not only forged the Gospel, but the prophets as well, he should be convinced that the very writings in which Christ was prophesied are in the hands of the Jews, the opponents of the Christians. We produce documents from enemies to confound other enemies. A Christian believes because a Jew carries his document, so that Jews have become the librarians of the Christians.[11]

Of course, the greatest miracle of all was Christ's resurrection, and this even his enemies would admit, if they had not been bribed to tell lies. But "sleeping witness" is a contradiction in terms, and it is the enormous success of the Gospel preached in the world which confirms the greatest of Christ's miracles. It is incredible, says Augustine, that Jesus Christ should have risen in the flesh and ascended with the flesh into heaven; it is incredible that the world should have believed so incredible a thing; it is incredible that a very few men, of mean birth and the lowest rank and no education, should have been able so effectually to persuade the world, and even its learned men, of so incredible a thing. This one grand miracle suffices for us, that the whole world has believed without any miracles.[12]

THE CHURCH

The church is the body of Christ, who is its head, and it extends not merely throughout the entire world, but also through the centuries, from Abel down to those who will believe in Christ at the very end of the world. This whole assembly of the saints belongs to one city, a city not entirely of this world, but with which we have contact, and from which we have received letters exhorting us to live well.[13] This same assembly is the holy Church, the one Church, the true Church, the catholic Church, fighting against all heresies. Fight, it can; be fought down, it cannot.[14] The church is both body and soul, and

therefore visible and invisible. On earth she embraces both the good
and the bad, but she does not embrace either heretics or schismatics.
Echoing Cyprian, the bishop of Hippo tells us to love the church as
a mother, just as we love God as a Father. Let no man say, "I go
indeed to the idols, I consult possessed ones and fortune-tellers: yet
I abandon not God's Church; I am a Catholic." You offend the
Father while holding to the Mother. Nor should one say, "I consult
no sorcerer, I seek out no possessed one, I never ask advice by
sacrilegious divination, I do not worship idols nor bow before stones,
though I am in the party of Donatus." That is to offend the Mother
and likewise the Father if He should choose to avenge her. So one
must hold with one mind to both Father and Mother.[15] Heretics and
schismatics do indeed style their congregations churches, but heretics, in holding false opinions regarding God, do injury to the faith
itself; while schismatics, on the other hand, in wicked separations
break off from brotherly charity, although they may believe just
what Catholics believe. So heretics offend God; schismatics, fraternal
charity.[16]

Salvation can be found only in the Catholic church. Outside the
church, you may have anything else. One can have honor, sacraments,
one can sing Alleluia and respond with an Amen, one can have
the Gospel, one can pray in the name of the Father, Son, and Holy
Spirit and preach in this Name, but only in the Church Catholic is
salvation an exclusive property.[17] How can the Catholic church be recognized? The consent of peoples and nations testify to her, and so
does her authority, inaugurated by miracles, nourished by hope, enlarged by love, established by age. The priestly succession so testifies,
beginning with Apostle Peter down to the present episcopate. And so,
lastly, does the name itself of Catholic, which, not without reason,
amid so many heresies, the church has thus retained; so that though
all heretics wish to be called Catholics, yet when a stranger asks where
the Catholic church meets, no heretic will venture to point to his own
chapel or house.[18]

The church is called catholic because it embraces all truth, and
there are even some fragments of this truth to be found in different
heresies. The church is indeed worldwide, but its catholicity rests more
on the promise of God rather than observance of all the divine commands
and sacraments.[19] It is called apostolic, as we have seen, because it
stretches back to Peter, as Augustine has already indicated in his *Against
the Epistle of Manichaeus Called Fundamental*.[20]

Peter received from Christ the primacy of jurisdiction, says
Augustine in one of his sermons[21] and cites the *locus classicus* in
Matthew; in a letter to Generosus he ticks off all the bishops of Rome
by name with this interesting variation—he places Anacletus after

Clement instead of before.[22] He calls Rome the apostolic see, and approves of the fact that two councils regarding the Pelagians (that of Carthage and Milevis) have already received rescripts from Pope Innocent I. In 420, after the death of Innocent, mention is made of his successor's approval of Innocent's actions in a pamphlet called catholic because it applied to the entire church.[23] Of bishops he says less, but since he was one himself there is no reason to believe that he did not hold the traditional view that they were legitimate successors of the apostles, although the transmission of jurisdiction to them in early times may have taken place in different ways.

In a famous passage in *Against the Epistle of Manichaeus Called Fundamental,* the saint says, "For my part, I should not believe the Gospel except as moved by the authority of the Catholic Church." This implies that church authority takes precedence over the Gospel, and that the church is infallible in its transmission.[24] This infallibility would seem to extend to the Roman pontiff,[25] for it certainly extends to the bishops convened in ecumenical council. Regarding those observances which do not derive from Scripture but from tradition, we are given to understand that they have been ordained or recommended to be kept by the apostles themselves, or by plenary councils, whose authority is well founded in the church.[26]

SACRED SCRIPTURE

Certain sacred books written under the inspiration of the Holy Spirit have God as their author. As has been said, they are letters from the heavenly city exhorting us to live well. There are those who say that Christ wrote nothing himself, but the truth is that his members (the evangelists) accomplished only what they became acquainted with by the repeated statements of the Head. For all that he was minded to give for our perusal on the subject of his own doings and sayings, he commanded to be written by those disciples whom he used as if they were his own hands.[27] God thus speaks through a man, and as a man, and in this sense he seeks us.[28] This is what we mean by inspiration, it involves the action of God moving the mind and will of the sacred writer to His purpose.

In the *Harmony of the Gospels,* Augustine asks: "What difference does it make whether the Evangelist inserts the matter in its proper order, or brings in at a particular point what was previously omitted, or mentions at an earlier stage what really happened at a later, provided only that he contradicts neither himself nor a second writer in the narrative of the same facts or of others? For as it is not in one's own power . . . to determine the order in which he will recall them to memory, . . . it is reasonable enough to suppose that each of the evangelists believed it to have been his duty to relate what he had to relate in that order in which it had pleased God to suggest to his recollection the matters he was engaged in recording. . . . The question of order detracted nothing from evangelical authority and truth."[29]

When we come to the Old Testament, the problem is more tricky, for the canonical Scriptures sometimes refer us to other books written by other prophets, which books are not part of the Scriptures. But even though the Holy Spirit has revealed certain things which ought to be held on religious authority, some things are written only by "historical diligence" rather than "divine inspiration" which gives the Scriptures a kind of human-divine quality; but in either case it is God who speaks through the writer, and in that authority the canon is safeguarded.[30]

It follows that no error is to be found in the Sacred Books. To Jerome in 395 he wrote that it was extremely dangerous to admit that anything in Scripture should be a lie. (Jerome had maintained that the scene in Galatians 2, in which Saint Paul rebukes Saint Peter for inconsistent compliances with Judaism, was a merely pretended argument, cooked up between the two apostles in order to clarify the truth to members of the church.) And even to admit a polite lie is impossible since there will be nothing left of those books, because whenever anyone finds something difficult to practice or hard to believe, he will follow this most dangerous precedent and explain it as the idea or practice of a lying author.[31] Ten years later in another famous letter he thanks Jerome that he has learned to pay such honor and respect to the Scriptures, that not one of their authors has erred in writing anything at all. "If I do find anything," he says, "in those books which seems contrary to truth, I decide that either the text is corrupt, or the translator did not follow what was really said, or that I failed to understand it.[32]

To Faustus the Manichaean he reasserts this position practically verbatim. In consequence of the distinctive peculiarity of the sacred writings, we are bound to receive as true whatever the canon shows to have been said by even one prophet, or apostle, or evangelist. Otherwise, not a single page will be left for the guidance of human fallibility, if contempt for the wholesome authority of the canonical books either puts an end to that authority altogether, or involves it in hopeless confusion.[33] It is therefore a useful principle to suppose that there is no divergence from truth when the evangelists introduce some saying different from what was actually uttered by the person concerning whom the narrative is given, provided that they set forth as his mind precisely what is also so conveyed by that one among them who reproduces the words as they were literally spoken. Our aim should only be to ascertain what is the mind and intention of the person who speaks.[34] So every assertion of the sacred writer is true, consonant with the sense that he wished to express and actually did.[35] And in this way, says the saint in the *Commentary on Genesis,* what seem to be errors in Scripture with regard to science or history are easily ironed out.[36]

Where can one find any authority if not in the Gospel and apostolic writings? But how can we be sure of the authorship of any book, if we doubt the apostolic origin of those books which are attributed to the apostles by the church, which the apostles themselves founded, and which occupies so conspicuous a place in all lands? And if at the same time we acknowledge as the undoubted production of the apostles what is brought forward by heretics in opposition to the church, whose authors, from whom they derive their name, lived long after the apostles? Augustine asks.[37] In regard to the canonical Scriptures, he must follow the judgment of the greater number of Catholic churches; and among these, first place must be given to churches where an apostle was, or received letters. To judge therefore, of canonicity means to prefer those that are received by all the Catholic churches to those which some do not receive. And of course, the Scriptures which are received by nearly all the churches will take precedence over those received by only a few.[38] *On Christian Doctrine* contains Augustine's own list, which is the same as the Tridentine canon.[39]

But suppose that not one, but two or more interpretations are put upon the same words of Scripture, even though the meaning the writer intended remains undiscovered? No danger arises if one can show from other passages of Scripture that any of the interpretations put on the words is in harmony with the truth. Even if the reader when searching the Scriptures draws a different meaning from the intention of the author through whom the Holy Spirit spoke, he is still free from blame so long as he is supported by the testimony of some other passage of Scripture, and as long as it is not opposed to sound doctrine.[40] So there is a multiple sense to Scripture.

TRADITION

It is clear from the foregoing that Augustine had a high regard for church tradition. He refers specifically to it in his letter to Januarius; he cites it against Julian of Eclanum when he cites a long list of writers opposing Julian on original sin; what Irenaeus, Cyprian, Hilary, Ambrose, and others found in the church, they held too; they taught only what they had learned from her, and handed down to her sons what they had received from the fathers.[41]

But should you meet up with a person who disbelieves the Gospel, how could you convince him of its truth? Only through the miracle of the church itself. As we have already seen, in a very famous passage in the *Against the Epistle of Manichaeus Called Fundamental,* Augustine declares: "For my part, I should not believe the gospel except as moved by the authority of the Catholic Church."[42] She it is who gives an authentic interpretation of her own sacred writings.

While apostolic tradition has always acted as a norm for the rule of faith, this is not to say that there is no such thing as progress or development in Christian thought. While the deposit of revelation can neither be increased or diminished, the necessity of defending it forces us both to investigate the articles of the Catholic faith more accurately, to understand them more clearly, and to proclaim them more earnestly.[43] It is the consensus of the fathers, and after them the bishops, which defends the truth against garrulous vanities. They were learned, serious, holy, zealous defenders of doctrine, and it was thanks to such planters, waterers, builders, shepherds, that the holy church grew in post-apostolic times.[44] This is not to claim that each was infallible in his private judgment; the holy Cyprian erred on the matter of baptism, but he held to the unity of the church. And so, tradition like Scripture, is a true source of revelation since both stem from the living church.

THE UNITY OF GOD

"Ask the world, the beauty of the heaven, the brilliancy and ordering of the stars—ask all things (says Augustine in one of his sermons[45]) and see if they do not, by language of their own, answer 'God made us.' " Thus God can be known from reason through the things which he has made, and by his work of art, we can come to know the Artificer. Paul's famous text (Rom. 1:20) is cited again in the *Confessions*[46] and *On Genesis*[47] to remind us that God is actually nearer to us than the things which he has made. Thus the name of God must be known in some way to the whole of creation because the energy of the Godhead is such that it cannot be completely hidden from any rational creature as long as it makes use of its reason. For, with the exception of a few in whom nature has become outrageously depraved, the whole race of man acknowledges God as the maker of this world. And so, all nations know God as the maker of heaven and earth whether they have heard of Christ or not.[48] Every good conscience must acknowledge the orderly governance of the world, and so no positive revelation is necessary for this knowledge which is actually innate. But what is innate is not the idea of God as such, but rather the ability easily and to a certain extent to know spontaneously from created things that God is their Maker.[49] All things proclaim that they were made, for they are changed and are varied; they are beautiful because God is beautiful; they are good because he is good; they exist because he exists; and while their beauty, goodness, and is-ness are derived from him, in comparison to their Creator they are neither beautiful, good, nor exist at all![50]

The essence of God is his own existence, and in a sense God alone should be called essence because He is the only unchangeable Alone, as Moses discovered in the incident of the burning bush (Ex. 3:14).[51] Since all things depend on God, he himself is independent of them inasmuch as their being is derived from him. His attributes are the same as his essence, or substance; in God, to be is the same as to be strong, or to be just, or to be wise. God is truly called in manifold ways, great, good, wise, blessed, true, and whatever else is not unworthy of him, but his greatness is the same as his wisdom, his goodness is the same as both, and his truth the same as all those things. Yet he is most simple, allowing for no composition whatever. This does not exclude the fact that he is a Trinity of Persons, as we shall see, for although Father is different from Son, yet their substance is not different, because they are so called, not according to substance but according to relation, which relation, however, is not accident, because it is not changeable.[52] He is unlimited in all perfection, and cannot be called measured, but if we say that he is the highest measure, perhaps we say something, if in speaking of the highest measure we mean the highest good.[53] He is unchangeable, eternal, unique, and omnipotent. But to say that he is omnipotent is not to say that he can die or fall into error. Omnipotent means he can do what he wills, not because he suffers what he does not will, for that would not make him omnipotent. Therefore, God cannot do some things for the very reason that he *is* omnipotent.[54]

No creature in the state of nature is able to see God. But what about the various theophanies in the Old Testament to various patriarchs and holy men? They were made through creatures, angels, and were suitable to the situation, although no one can say precisely how they were effected. In this life, any knowledge of God is like looking in a cloudy mirror, but in the light of glory we shall be able to see God through our physical faculties. Either the eyes, says Augustine, will possess some quality similar to that of the mind, by which they may be able to discern spiritual things, and among these God, or God will be so known by us (and this seems much more likely) and shall be so much before us, that we shall see him by the spirit in ourselves, in one another, in himself, in the new heavens and the new earth, in every created thing which will then exist.[55] This vision is reserved as a reward of our faith. We shall in the body see God, but whether we shall see him by means of the body, as now we see the sun, moon, stars, sea, earth, and all that is in it, that is a difficult question indeed. To reach to God in any measure by the mind is a great blessedness which should result in a pious confession of ignorance rather than a rash profession of knowledge. To comprehend God is altogether impossible; if we comprehended Him, He would cease to be God.[56]

Although we can never find out all the ways by which God exists, we must think nothing of him that he is not. What we do not find in our own *best,* we ought not to seek in God who is far better than that best of ours, so we may understand God as good without quality, great without quantity, a creator though he lacks nothing, ruling but from no position, sustaining all things without "having" them, in his wholeness everywhere, yet without place, eternal without time, making things that are changeable without change of himself, and without passion.[57] The perfections of God can be drawn from creatures, so long as we negate their imperfections *(via negationis).* And since creatures do not produce their own beauty, goodness, or even existence, we must see that it is God who is the source of these attributes *(via causalitatis).* This thing is good and that good, but take away this and that, says Augustine, and regard good itself if you can and you will see God as good of all good. For in all these good things, we cannot say that one is better than another unless a conception of the good itself has been impressed upon us. This allows us to judge things as good or not, and to prefer one good to another. So God is to be loved, not this and that good, but the good itself. *(via eminentiae).*[58]

Nor is anyone to look for an efficient cause of evil in God, for evil is a defect from that which supremely is to that which has less being. To seek to discover the causes of these defections—causes not efficient but rather deficient—is equivalent to trying to see darkness, or to hear silence.[59]

How is the foreknowledge of God related to man's free will? Certainly he knows all future things, and that means He knows what is in the power of man's will, which is indeed limited, but which also has a real existence of its own. Therefore, we are by no means compelled, either retaining the foreknowledge of God, to take away the freedom of the will, or to deny that he is prescient of future things. We embrace both, Augustine affirms. A man does not therefore sin because God foreknew that he would sin. It cannot be doubted that it is the man himself who sins when doing sinful acts, because God, whose prescience is infallible, foreknew not that fate, or fortune, or something else would sin, but that the man himself would sin, who also would *not* have sinned, if he had willed not to.[60]

Conditioned free futures plunge us into the heart of the problem. Some stupid people say that the dead are still responsible for sins they would have committed if they had not departed this life. It is indeed true that God can prevent any man from sinning, simply by not tempting him beyond his strength. He is also able to remove people from life before they make a fatal fall. But in that case, they would never merit the gift of perseverance, which is a free gift of God dependent on man's cooperation. And all of this leads us now into a discussion of God's salvific will, predestination, and reprobation.

God certainly wishes all men to be saved and to come into the knowledge of the truth, but yet not so as to take away from them free will, for the good or the evil use of which they may be most righteously judged (cf. 1 Tim. 2:4). This being so, unbelievers act contrary to the will of God when they do not believe his Gospel; nevertheless they do not therefore overcome his will, but rob their own selves of the great, indeed, the very greatest good, and implicate themselves in penalties, and are destined to experience the power of God in punishments whose mercy in his gifts they despised.[61] Therefore, all are saved and come to the knowledge of the truth at his willing it. Infants who do not as yet have the use of free will are regenerated by the will of God through whose creative power they are generated, and those who have the actual use of free will cannot exercise it except through the will and assistance of God by whom the will is prepared.[62] Accordingly, says Augustine, when Scripture tells us that God will have all men to be saved, although we know that all men are not saved, we are not on that account to restrict the omnipotence of God, but are rather to understand this as meaning that no man is saved unless God wills his salvation: not that there is no man whose salvation He does not will. Otherwise, how could you explain the fact that Jesus was unwilling to work miracles in the presence of some who, he said, would have repented if he had worked them? We are to understand by "all men" the human race in all its varieties of rank and circumstances—kings, subjects, nobles, plebes, the highborn, lowborn, the learned and unlearned, the sound in body, the feeble, the clever, the dull, the foolish, the rich, the poor, and those in middling circumstances. And we should pray God to will our salvation, because if he wills it, it must of necessity be accomplished.[63]

All those who are predestined for salvation are included in God's will that all men shall be saved. Just as one speaks correctly of any teacher of literature who is alone in a city that he teaches literature here to everybody—not that all men learn, but that there is none who learns literature there who does not learn from him—so we may justly say that God teaches all men to come to Christ, not because all come, but because none comes in any other way. And so God teaches all such men to come to Christ, for He wills all such to be saved, and to come to the knowledge of the truth.[64]

What does Augustine mean by "the predestination of the saints"? It includes those who escape the original condemnation by such a bounty of divine grace that when they hear the Gospel they believe it, and in the faith which works by love they persevere to the end; and if, by chance they deviate from the Way, they return to it when rebuked;

and some return to the path even when they have not been rebuked, while some who have received grace in any age whatever are withdrawn from the perils of this life by swiftness of death.[65] But in all this, the church should avoid laborious disputations, but rather look to its own daily prayers. The church prays that the unbelieving may believe, and so God converts them to the Faith; the church prays that believers may persevere, therefore God gives perseverance to the end. God foreknew that He would act in such a manner, and this is the very predestination of the saints "whom He has chosen in Christ before the foundation of the world" (Eph. 1:4).[66]

So "the predestination of the saints" implies the foreknowledge and the preparation of God's kindnesses by which the saints are most certainly delivered, whoever they are. But the righteous divine judgment leaves all others in the mass of ruin with those of Tyre and Sidon, who might have believed if they had seen Christ's wonderful miracles, but were denied the means of believing since it was not given to them to believe.[67] Both the beginning of faith and perseverance to the end are gifts of God, and since he foreknew that he would give them, he certainly must have predestined them.[68]

Augustine seems to think that few will be saved in comparison to those who are not, but that these few are actually many because their deliverance is effected freely by grace. Since all have passed under condemnation through the sin of Adam, no one could justly blame the judgment of God even if nobody should be delivered, because deliverance is the free gift of God so that he who glories must glory in the Lord.[69] We cannot deny that perseverance even to the end of this life is the gift of God, since he himself puts an end to this life when he wills, and if he puts an end before a fall that is threatening, he makes the man to persevere even unto the end. But more marvelous and more manifest to believers is the largess of God's goodness, that this grace is given even to infants, although there is no obedience at that age to which it may be given.[70]

But why should God create men whom he knows will belong to destruction and not to grace? This would indeed be unjust if the whole lump of clay had not been condemned in Adam; the fact that men become vessels of wrath at birth is due to the penalty deserved, but that they become vessels of mercy at their second birth is due to an undeserved grace. The grace of God is completely gratuitous; he certainly does not choose us on the grounds that he foreknew we would be good, for grace would no more be grace if we maintained the priority of merit.[71] Consequently, in the long run, there is no difference among those who have never heard the Gospel, those who have heard it but refused to believe it, those who believed it for a while but did not receive the gift of perseverance, and infants who died without receiving baptism—

all go into condemnation because they belong to the same "lump" which quite plainly has been condemned.[72] Yet, it is equally true that salvation has never been lacking to him who was worthy of it, and that he to whom it was lacking was not worthy—but this is not in reference to human will but by divine grace or predestination. Between grace and predestination there is only this difference, that predestination is the preparation for grace, while grace is the donation itself.[73]

It hardly needs to be said that predestination is an occult work of God! "I simply hold what I see the apostle has most plainly taught us," says Augustine in *On the Soul and Its Origin,* "that owing to one man all pass into condemnation who are born of Adam unless they are born again in Christ, even as He has appointed them to be regenerated, before they die in the body, whom He predestinated to everlasting life, as the most merciful bestower of grace; while to those whom He has predestinated to eternal death, He is also the most righteous awarder of punishment, not only on account of the sins which they add in the indulgence of their own will, but also because of their original sin, even if, as in the case of infants, they add nothing to it. Now this is my definite view on that question, so that the hidden things of God may keep their secret, without impairing my own faith."[74] Why, of two infants, one should be chosen for justice and the other for mercy, is an insoluble problem. And why miracles were not wrought in the presence of men who would have repented at the working of the miracles, while they were wrought in the presence of others who, it was known, would not repent, is likewise an insoluble mystery.[75] Nor will we know in this life why certain angels through their own free will became outcasts from the Lord God, while others through the same free will stood fast in the truth and merited the knowledge that they would never fall—is likewise a tremendous mystery.[76] The judgments of God are truly unsearchable, the saint concludes.

A distinction must be made between those who are "called" and those who are "predestined"; those who are predestined are also called, but those who are called are not necessarily predestined. In both instances God does the calling and predestining, but why are there many of the former and few of the latter? Certainly we are not called because of our faith nor are we chosen because we believed; these follow upon the action of God but do not precede it. The grace of God both begins a man's faith and enables him to persevere to the end, nor is it given according to our merits, but is given according to God's own most secret, just, wise, and beneficent will since those whom he predestinated he also called with that calling of which it is said, "The gifts and calling of God are without repentance (Rom. 11:29). And there is no man living who can be said to belong to the elect with any certainty, so that we indeed use our own wills, but it is God who works in us according to his good pleasure; this is part of the great mystery, and it contributes to our humility.[77] Moreover, the number predestined for the Kingdom of God is so fixed, so certain, that it is impossible to either add or subtract one person from it; those who do not belong to this fixed number of the elect are judged justly, for although their will was free it was never freed from the inherited debt. They may have received the grace of God for a while, but in the end they foresook him and were foresaken by him.[78]

Is it proper, then, to speak of the predestination of the wicked to eternal death; is Augustine a Calvinist? In his writing *On the Merits and Remission of Sins, and on the Baptism of Infants,* he asks:

> Since by divine grace assisting the human will, man may possibly exist in this life without sin, why doesn't he? To this question I might very easily and truthfully answer: Because men are unwilling. But if I am asked why they are unwilling, we are drawn into a lengthy statement. And yet, without prejudice to a more careful examination, I may briefly say this much: Men are unwilling to do what is right, either because what is right is unknown to them, or because it is unpleasant. . . . But that what was hidden may come to light, and what was unpleasant may be made agreeable, is of the grace of God which helps the wills of men; and that they are not helped by it, has its cause likewise in themselves, not in God, whether they be predestined to condemnation on account of the iniquity of their pride, or whether they are to be judged and disciplined contrary to their very pride, if they are children of mercy.[79]

Yet, those who are ultimately lost are clearly lost through their own fault.[80] God is good, God is just. He can deliver some men not meriting good, because God is good, Augustine reminds Julian of Eclanum; he cannot condemn any man not deserving evil, because he is just.[81] But grace is never given to anyone according to his merits, while no one is punished except for his own misdeeds.[82] And with that, we may leave the matter for the time being, and turn to Augustine's doctrine of the Trinity.

THE TRINITY OF GOD

In the first book of *On the Trinity,* Augustine cites the tradition of the first three centuries to remind us that the church has always taught that three Persons coequally exist with the same indivisible substance. Traces of Trinitarian teaching may be found even in the Old Testament, especially in Genesis 1:26 where God says "Let us make man in our own image . . . so God created man in the image of God." The doctrine of the Trinity is expressed in the traditional form of baptism conferred in the name (sing.) of the Father, Son and Holy Spirit. In ancient times, God is said to have made some appearances to various men, but all those appearances to the fathers, when God was present to them according to his own dispensation, suitable to the times, were wrought through a creature—angels, probably—but no one can say how, while the unchangeable essence of the Trinity is never visible in its proper self.[83]

A certain faith is in some way the starting-point of knowledge, but a certain knowledge will not be made perfect, except after this life, when we shall see face to face. And so, while Father, Son and Spirit are one God, the Father is not the Son, and the Son is not the Holy Spirit, nor the Holy Spirit the Father or the Son, but a Trinity of Persons mutually interrelated, and a unity of an equal essence. No matter if the Greeks use the expression three substances, one essence; that is the same as the Latin three persons, one substance. Yet, all language actually fails here, for the Most Holy Trinity is really an ineffable mystery.[84]

God the Father is from no one since he has no one from whom to be, or from whom to proceed, therefore he alone is called Unbegotten. But the Father begets from all eternity and the Son is born from all eternity, because his Son is his wisdom, which is the brightness of eternal light. One has in his heart the Word which he speaks in time, but God begets the Son outside of time, by whom he created all times.[85] This does not hinder either of them from being consubstantial, and hence co-eternal, nor is one greater and the other less because one is begetter and the other begotten. Accordingly, as though uttering himself, the Father begat the Word equal to himself in all things; for he would not have uttered himself wholly and perfectly, if there were in his Word anything more or less than in himself.[86] The Son (and none other) is called the Word of God and also the Wisdom of God, and hence the Son is said to proceed from the Father through intellectual generation.

With respect to the Holy Spirit, Augustine thinks that there has not yet been in his time a discussion on the part of learned theologians to determine what constitutes his special individuality *(proprium)*. We cannot call him either the Son or the Father, but only the Holy Spirit, and he is the gift of God, nor does God give a gift which is inferior to himself.[87] He is consubstantial with the Father and the Son, and therefore the Spirit from both of them. But these names refer not to the substance of the Persons so much as their mutual relationships.[88] The Father and the Son are the Beginning of the Holy Spirit, but not two Beginnings, for as the Father and the Son are one God, and one Creator, and one Lord relatively to the creature, so are they one Beginning in reference to the Holy Spirit.[89] Therefore, the Holy Spirit proceeds from the Son as well as the Father[90] but principally from the Father, the Father giving the procession without any interval of time, yet in common from both Father and Son. Now if Both had *begotten* him, he would be called the Son of the Father and of the Son—a thing abhorrent to all sound minds, Augustine says. Therefore, the Spirit of both is not begotten of both, but proceeds from both.[91] These points are emphasized several times, both in *On the Trinity* and *On the Gospel of Saint John*. It remains to be observed that the Holy Spirit is eminently called Holy, as if he were the substantial holiness consubstantial with the other two. He is also eminently called Gift.

To the Father, Son, and Holy Spirit belong the same eternity, the same unchangeableness, the same majesty, the same power. In the Father is unity, in the Son equality, in the Holy Spirit the harmony of unity and equality; and these three attributes are all one because of the Father, all equal because of the Son, and all harmonious because of the Holy Spirit.[92] The Holy Spirit consists in the same unity of substance, and in the same equality with the Father and the Son. For whether he is the unity of both, or the holiness, or the love, or the unity because of the love, and therefore the love because of the holiness, it is obvious that he is not one of the two, through whom the two are joined, through whom the Begotten is loved by the Begetter, and loves him that begat him.[93]

Each individual Person, whichever it be of the three, is no less than the Trinity itself. The divine Persons are distinguished among themselves only by their relationships, and hence they are coequal with regard to their perfections. The Trinity operates as a single unity outside of itself, all actions being common to the three Persons, and yet creation occurs through the Word, while sanctification is effected through the Holy Spirit. In speaking of the mission of the divine Persons, the Son is sent by the Father, without implying any diminution of equality or consubstantiality between Father and Son, and the same would be true in speaking of the sending of the Holy Spirit. And so it is that Augustine summarizes and integrates the traditional teaching on the Trinity which he had received from earlier times, and was to transmit to the medieval thinkers and to normative Catholic thinking for centuries to come.

Saint Augustine: II

CREATION

All inconstant things have been created by the one immutable Lord, out of nothing. Only God can create, and this he does freely, for by the words, "God saw that it was good," it is sufficiently intimated that God made what was made not from any necessity, nor for the sake of supplying any want, but solely from his own goodness.[94] He creates through the divine ideas in the mind of the Creator, and this means that it is the Trinity that creates, since all actions outside the Trinity must be attributed to the three divine Persons in common. And if the sacred and infallible Scriptures say that in the beginning God created the heavens and the earth, says Augustine, in order that it may be understood that he had made nothing previously, then assuredly the world was made, not in time, but simultaneously with time.[95] "I own that I do not know what ages passed before the human race was created, yet I have no doubt that no created thing is coeternal with the Creator," he adds.[96]

Among all created things, nothing was better than those spirits whom He endowed with intelligence, and made capable of contemplating and enjoying Him. It was He who gave to this intellectual nature free will of such a kind, that if the angel wished to forsake God—his blessedness—misery should immediately result.[97] That these created intelligences possessed a lofty sublimity can be inferred from the fact that the Creator of all good imparted no grace for the reparation of angelic evils, so that their fault was judged all the more damnable because of their previous excellence.[98] Angels are really spirits, and only become angels when they are sent, for angel is the name of its office, not of its nature. Its essence is to be a spirit; from the fact that it acts, it is an angel. The angels were created free, and all had good wills from him who created them with a good will. Certain angels became by their own free will outcasts from the Lord God. Yet although they fled from his goodness in which they had been blessed, they could not flee from his judgment, by which they were made most wretched.[99] The angels are marked off into separate ranks, and were elevated to the supernatural order. Those whose wills were found to be good were confirmed in their goodness, by receiving the due reward of their continuance—such a fullness of blessing that by it they might have the fullest certainty of always abiding in it.[100] The true cause of the blessedness of the good angels is found to be this, that they cleave to him who supremely is. And if we ask the cause of the misery of the bad, it occurs to us that they are miserable because they have forsaken him who supremely is, and have turned to themselves who have no such essence.[101]

The good angels are ministers of God and aid men in the business of salvation, while the evil angels have it within their capacity to injure men; but whether they be good or evil, they are such by their own free will, which has fixed their condition irretrievably for all time.

According to Saint Augustine, God created all things simultaneously, endowing creatures with seminal reason. In his *Commentary on Genesis,* he warns us, however, against understanding the creation story in too literal terms, reminding us, for example, that "day" is not to be understood in the same way as an ordinary day of our own experience. The biblical account is to be taken literally, true; but it is also to be understood in a much larger sense and according to the spirit of the writer and the times in which he wrote.[102]

Turning now to his doctrine of man, Augustine begins with the threefold division of man into body, soul and spirit, and then adds that actually there is only a twofold division because the soul is "named along with the spirit" which is the rational portion of the soul, and of which animals are devoid.[103] That the soul is immaterial is a fact which men of slow understanding are hard to be convinced of, for it pervades the whole body which it animates, not by a local distribution of parts, but by a certain vital influence which enables it to be present in its entirety in all parts of the body, and not less in smaller parts and greater in larger parts—but here with more energy, and there with less energy; it is in its entirety present both in the whole body and in every part of it.[104] There are those who stupidly claim that souls are begotten from one which God gave to the first man, and who say that they are derived from their parents (following Tertullian), but to say this is to hold that souls are not spirits but bodies and are produced from corporeal seed. What folly! The soul is made by God and it is immortal because it can never lose its own life. Nor does man have more than one soul, and each soul is created new for each individual at his birth. Of all that God has created, the principal place is given to the soul, which was made from nothing and breathed into him by God.[105]

Souls do not exist in some previous life, and therefore have no previous merits of any kind, but at the time of carnal birth they share along with Adam in the contagion of the primal death.[106] So neither preexistence nor traducianism are acceptable to Augustine. Eve was made from Adam, and all men derive their origin from these first two parents. Every man is created in the image of God, and this by nature, not by grace or by faith. It is man's intellect which gives him preeminence over cattle, so that is the only thing he can glory in. The wild beasts out do him in strength, flies can take off faster than he can, peacocks surpass him in beauty. His sole excellence lies in the fact that he is created in the image of God, and the image of God is in the mind, in the intellect.[107]

Original justice, freedom from concupiscence, and from the necessity of dying were gratuitous gifts of nature bestowed on Adam and Eve before their fall. In paradise man lived as he desired so long as he desired what God had commanded. He lived in the enjoyment of God, and was good by God's goodness, living without any want and having it in his power to live that way forever. He had food that he might not hunger, drink that he might not thirst, the tree of life that old age might not waste him. There was in his body no corruption, nor seed of corruption, which could produce in him any unpleasant sensation. He feared no inward disease, no outward accident. Soundest health blessed his body, absolute tranquility his soul. As in paradise there was no excessive heat or cold, so its inhabitants were exempt from the vicissitudes of fear and desire.[108] Adam did indeed possess the grace of God, but he had a different kind of it. He did not need the death of Christ to absolve him from guilt, for in this state of blessedness he enjoyed perfect peace with himself. Nor was he deserving of these benefits in which he suffered absolutely no evil, but was placed in the midst of them simply through the goodness of his own Creator.[109] He was even free from death, since death is not according to nature, but is God's righteous infliction on account of sin. Therefore God would have been willing to preserve even the first man in that state of salvation in which he was created, and would subsequently have removed him to a better place, where he should have been not only free from sin, but free even from the desire of sinning, if God had foreseen that man would have the steadfast will to persist in the state of innocence in which he was created.[110] It is important to be able to distinguish between being able not to sin and not being able to sin, being able not to die, and not being able to die, being able not to forsake good, and being able to forsake good. The first man was able not to sin, was able not to die, was able not to forsake good. Therefore the first liberty of the will was *to be able not to sin,* but the last will be much greater, *not to be able to sin;* the first immortality was to be able not to die, the last will be much greater, not to be able to die; the first was the power of perseverance, to be able not to forsake good—the last will be the felicity of perseverance, not to be able to forsake good.[111]

THE VIRTUES

Virtues must be distinguished from vices, not by their functions but by their ends. The function of a virtue is *that* which is to be done, the end is that *for* which it is to be done. When a man does something in which he does not seem to sin, yet does not do it because of that for which he ought to do it, he is guilty of sinning. A true virtue can never be separated from its end; whatever good is done by man, yet is not done for the purpose for which true wisdom commands it to be done, may seem good from its function, but because the end is not right, it is sin.[112] The infused virtues of faith, hope, and love are given by God, and no one will lose the faith except him that shall have despised it. The enemy of souls may deprive a man of his money or of his house against his will, but he can never deprive a man of his faith unless than man consents to it. The sacrament of baptism is also called the sacrament of faith because it enables a child to partake of the faith which resides in the will of the believers. Of the three infused virtues of faith, hope, and love, there is no gift of God more excellent than the love of God shed abroad in our hearts by the Holy Spirit. Love alone distinguishes the sons of the eternal kingdom and the sons of eternal perdition. Other gifts, too, are given by the Holy Spirit, but without love they profit nothing; faith without love can indeed exist, but it cannot profit.[113] Man is made perfect in righteousness when that which is perfect is come (1 Cor. 13:10), for to faith and hope shall succeed at once the very substance itself, no longer to be believed in and hoped for, but to be seen and grasped. Love, however, which is the greatest among the three, is not to be superseded but increased and fulfilled—contemplating in full vision what it used to see by faith, and acquiring in actual fruition what it once only embraced in hope.[114]

Other virtues (classical writers list four) are given to us by God in the valley of weeping, and from these virtues we mount to the supreme virtue which is the contemplation of God alone. Works of mercy, affections of charity, sanctity of piety, incorruptness of chastity, modesty of sobriety—these things are always to be practiced, because all of these virtues dwell within the man. But who can name them all? They are like an emperor's army seated within the mind. For just as an emperor by his army does what he wants, so the Lord Jesus Christ, once beginning to dwell in our inner man (in the mind through faith) uses these virtues as his ministers.[115]

God himself is the primary object of faith. There are indeed those who think that the Christian religion is something to smile at rather than to hold fast to, because men are commanded to have faith in the things which are not seen. They say it is imprudent to believe what you cannot see, but if the unseen truths of Christianity could be seen there would no longer be any room for faith. And so the object of faith embraces mysteries which exceed the bounds of reason. The faculty by which God made us superior to all other living things is the mind; therefore, we must refuse so to believe as not to receive or seek a reason for our belief, since we could not believe at all if we did not have rational souls. So, then, in some points that bear on the doctrine of salvation, which we are not yet able to grasp by reason—but shall be able to sometime—let faith precede reason, and let the heart be cleansed by faith so as to receive and bear the great light of reason. This alone would be reasonable. "If you will not believe, you will not understand," says Isaiah (7:9), undoubtedly making a distinction between these two things and advising us to believe first so as to be able to understand whatever we believe. It therefore follows that faith precedes reason.[116]

But no one believes who is unwilling to believe because believing is consenting to the truth of what is said, and this consent is certainly voluntary; faith is therefore in our own power. Since, however, all power comes from God, and no one has anything which he has not at first received, it is God who makes it possible even for us to believe. And yet, believing also requires our free consent even though no man comes to Christ unless the Father draws him (Jno. 6:44). A man can come to a church unwillingly, can approach the altar unwillingly, partake of the sacrament unwillingly, but he cannot believe unless he *is* willing.[117] Faith eventuates in a supernatural act made willingly, freely, because God makes it possible. But we believe in order that we may know; we do not know in order that we may believe, because faith is believing what we do not see. The motive for faith is not rational evidence so compelling that there is no room for doubting the object proposed, it is rather (considered from the intrinsic point of view) the authority of God himself as Revealer.

Faith is of hearing and hearing by the word of Christ. For although unless he understands something, no one can believe in God; nevertheless by that faith itself by which he believes he is healed, in order that he may understand more. For there are some things, says Augustine, which unless we understand we do not believe, and there are others which unless we believe we will not understand. Christ, who has called us to believe, never abandons us but enjoins us to believe what we do not see, nor are we required to believe on the basis of nothing, but on certain evidence presented by Christ Himself.[118]

Augustine describes his own condition in a beautiful passage from the *Confessions*:

I found myself to be far off from Thee, in the region of dissimilarity, as if I heard this voice of Thine from on high: "I am the food of strong men;

grow, and thou shalt feed upon me; nor shalt thou convert me, like the food of thy flesh, into thee, but thou shalt be converted into me." And I learned that Thou for iniquity dost correct man, and Thou dost make my soul to consume away like a spider. And I said, "Is Truth, therefore, nothing because it is neither diffused through space, finite, nor infinite?" And Thou didst cry to me from afar, "Yea, verily, 'I am that I am.'" And I heard this, as things are heard in the heart, nor was there room for doubt; and I should more readily doubt that I live than that Truth is not, which is "clearly seen, being understood by the things that are made."[119]

Faith, which is more certain than any natural knowledge on the human plane, does not contradict human reason. We must have reasons for our belief, since our rational souls make belief possible; while faith must precede reason in some matters of our personal salvation, it does not conflict with human reason man's rational faculty, which is also God-given. Faith and reason interact on each other, faith raising the intellect to a more perfect mode of cognition. While the mind is naturally capable of reason and intelligence, it is often disabled by besotting and inveterate vices and cannot tolerate, much less abide and delight in, God's unchangeable light. Reason must be gradually healed, and renewed, and made capable of felicity, and so faith is necessary to purify it. And that reason might advance in this faith more confidently toward the truth, the truth itself, God, God's Son, assuming humanity without destroying his divinity, established and founded this faith, that there might be a way for man to man's God through a God-man.[120]

Reason is able to demonstrate the foundation of faith. If believing is to think with assent, there must be some thinking before assent can be given. For a certain faith is in some way the starting point of knowledge, but a certain knowledge will not be made perfect, except after this life, when we shall see face to face. It is in this way that reason, illumined by faith, is able to cultivate a knowledge of divine things. Faith must be universal and extend to all revealed truth; to believe what one pleases, and not to believe what one pleases, is to believe one's self, and not the Gospel.[121] Always there is a certain obscurity involved in faith because it is unseen truths which are involved; they are blessed who have not seen and have yet believed, and to believe on the truth is to know the truth, which leads to true freedom. So, while faith's assent is firm, we see in a darkened mirror, and will not be able to see face to face until the next life, when faith and hope will be done away with.

Salvation is totally impossible without faith, which merits the grace of doing good works. Faith enables us to obtain love, which alone truly performs good works and is so much the gift of God that it is called God. Nor is faith to be attributed to the human free will nor to any antecedent merits, since any good merits—such as they are—come from faith, but we must confess it as a free gift of God, if we are thinking of true grace without merit.[122] Faith comes through hearing the word of God, which must be preached, for no one is delivered from the condemnation which was incurred through Adam except through faith in Jesus Christ. He is the one Mediator between God and men, and it is precisely in the Resurrection of Christ (and this includes his Incarnation and death) by which God has given assurance to all men that they can be saved by believing in him. It is by faith in this Mediator that hearts are cleansed and the love of God is shed abroad in our hearts through the Holy Spirit, who blows where he wills, not following men's merits, but even producing these very merits himself. For the grace of God, says Augustine, will in no wise exist unless it be wholly free.[123] Even the saints in the Old Testament were freed from their sins by the blood of the Redeemer himself; it is improper to say that they possessed perfect righteousness; they required the incarnation, passion and resurrection of Christ just like anybody else.[124]

It is the possession of God himself which is the object of our hope and our future beatitude. The reward which God gives as the end of supernatural hope is God himself. But until that reward is given, we must cling to him through hope; to seek any other reward than himself is folly, our only portion is God-everlasting.[125] Hope is founded in faith and is most certain. Faith believes, but hope and love pray, for without faith these cannot exist. What is hoped for must also be an object of faith. Now it is true that a thing which is not an object of hope may be believed—for instance, we may believe in the punishment of the wicked, and yet no one actually hopes for that. But in the whole process of our justification and our salvation, hope is absolutely necessary for adults.

Charity is the most excellent of all the virtues; it alone distinguishes the sons of the eternal kingdom and the sons of eternal perdition. Other gifts, too, are given by the Holy Spirit, but without love they profit nothing. Love, unlike faith and hope, is never superseded, but increased and fulfilled, contemplating in full vision what it used to see by faith, and acquiring in actual fruition what it once only embraced in hope.[126]

The greater the measure in which love dwells in a man, the better is the man in whom it dwells, for when there is a question as to whether a man is good, one does not ask what he believes, or what he hopes, but what he loves. For the man who loves correctly, no doubt believes and hopes correctly, whereas the man who has not love believes in vain, even though his beliefs are true, and hopes in vain, even though the objects of his hope are a real part of true happiness, unless he believes and hopes that he may obtain by prayer the blessing of love. Unless love is shed abroad in our hearts by the Holy Spirit, the Law can command, but it cannot aid, and moreover it makes a man sinner because he can no longer excuse himself on the plea of ignorance.[127]

In *On the Morals of the Catholic Church,* Augustine places charity at the very foundation of the Christian faith with these words:

> To live well is nothing else but to love God with all the heart, with all the soul, with all the mind; and, as arising from this, that this love must be preserved entire and incorrupt, which is the part of temperance; that it give way before no troubles, which is the part of fortitude; that it serve no other, which is the part of justice; that it be watchful in its inspection of things lest craft or fraud steal in, which is the part of prudence.[128]

Inchoate love is inchoate holiness; advanced love is advanced holiness; great love is great holiness; "perfect love is perfect holiness." Perfect love is to love God above all created things. Charity is that affection of the mind which aims at the enjoyment of God for his own sake, and the enjoyment of one's self and one's neighbor in subordination to God. Lust is just the opposite—it is that affection of the mind which aims at enjoying one's self and one's neighbor, and other corporeal things, without reference to God.[129] God is to be loved, not this and that good, but the good itself, and this is the characteristic of those in the heavenly city: their love of God and their contempt of self.

Love of God must carry with it love of neighbor, but all of this presupposes the context of faith, for no one can truly love unless he first has faith. After all, it is God who has first shown his love to us and did not spare his only Son, so we are really asked to make a return of love since the Lord Jesus Christ, as God-man, is both a manifestation of divine love towards us, and an example of human humility with us, to the end that our great swelling might be cured by a greater counteracting remedy. For here is great misery, proud man! says Augustine, but there is greater mercy—a humble God![130] And like faith and hope, love is absolutely necessary for salvation.

A word may be inserted here on the communion of the saints, who are honored but not with the divine honor *(latreia)* which is due to God alone. The purpose of such honor is to share in their divine merits by following their example, and by gaining the assistance of their prayers. For the souls of the pious dead are not separated from the church, which even now is the Kingdom of Christ, otherwise there would be no remembrance made of them at the altar of God in the partaking of the body of Christ. It may be also, the saint adds tentatively, that the spirits of the dead do learn some things which are occurring here, what things it is necessary that they should know, and what persons it is necessary should know the same, not only things past or present, but even future, by the Spirit of God revealing it to them.[131] There is a possible reference to relics in the first book of the *City of God* (chap. 13) and *On the Gospel of Saint John,* there are at least two references to the sign of the Lord's cross when used in connection with the various sacraments.[132]

SIN

Sin is a turning away from God and a turning toward creatures. Three things enter its makeup: the suggestion of, the taking pleasure in, and the consenting to. Suggestion takes place either by means of memory, or by means of the bodily senses, when we see, or hear, or smell, or taste, or touch anything. And if it gives us pleasure to enjoy this, this pleasure, if illicit, must be restrained. But if consent shall take place, the sin will be complete, known to God in our heart, although it may not become known to men by deed.[133]

Sin, then, is any transgression in deed, or word, or desire, of the eternal law. And the eternal law is the divine order or will of God, which requires the preservation of natural order, and forbids its being broken. Man is made upright in order that he may not live to himself but to God. For when he lives to himself, he turns from the One who is, to what is not, and for this reason all sin is said to be a lie, because it pretends to be something which it is not. Even good acts which are done from an incorrect purpose can be sinful, because not done for the purpose for which true wisdom commands them to be done. Sin, therefore, has no positive but rather a negative character. It is a defection from that which supremely is, to that which has less of being. It is like darkness in relation to light, or silence in relation to sound.

A sin does not require a visible effect in the external order, an evil will by itself is already a sin, even if the effect is lacking. Nor are all sins equally serious; there are certain venial sins which do not hinder the righteous man from the attainment of eternal life, and which are unavoidable in this life; likewise there are some good works which are of no avail to an ungodly man towards the attainment of everlasting life, even though the lives of the worst of men contain some good actions. A man, so long as he is in the flesh, cannot but have some light sins. But those which we call light, do not make light of! The accumulation may be serious, requiring at all times confession and charity, for charity covers a multitude of sins. Every crime is a sin, but every sin is not a crime; many holy men may be free from crime, but no one is free from sin, as the apostle John says, "If we say that we have no sin, we deceive ourselves, and the truth is not in us" (1 Jno. 1:8). So there is a distinction between grave sins such as homicide or adultery, and lighter sins which may always threaten to coalesce into greater sins. At any rate, sharp exception is taken to the Stoic doctrine, that all sins are equally grave.[134]

But there is no sin without the free consent of the will, and ignorance in those who refuse to know is likewise a sin. Sin is the will to retain and follow after what justice forbids, and from which it is free to abstain—the law divinely written in every mind. But no one sins if contrary nature compels us to commit a specific act, for he who is compelled by nature to do anything, does not sin. But he who sins, sins by free will.[135]

God is never the author of sin, although he may permit it; even though all power comes from God, our wills are still free. No one is forced by God's power unwillingly either into evil or good, but when God forsakes a man, he deservedly goes to evil, and when God assists a man, without deserving, he is converted to good. Always we have these two imponderables to reconcile: that all power comes from God, and that man's will nevertheless remains free.

In *On the Gospel of Saint John,* Augustine remarks that every one who sins dies. But every man is afraid of the death of the flesh; few, of the death of the soul. In regard to the death of the flesh, which must certainly come some time, all are on their guard against its approach: this is the source of all their labor. Man, destined to die, labors to avert his dying; and yet man, destined to live forever, labors not to cease from sinning.[136] And even when sins pass away once they are committed, the guilt yet is permanent, and (if not remitted) will remain forever; so, when the concupiscence is remitted, the guilt of it also is taken away. For not to have sin means this, not to be deemed guilty of sin. If a man has, for example, committed adultery, though he does not repeat the sin, he is held to be guilty of adultery until the indulgence in guilt be itself remitted. He has the sin, therefore, remaining, although the particular act of his sin no longer exists, since it has passed away along with the time when it was committed.[137] All of this has special reference to personal sin, but in order to probe this mystery we must now consider what is meant by original sin.

It was through the serious sins of our first parents that original righteousness was forfeited. One result was that all are subject to bodily death, which originally had not been by the law of nature but is now the righteous infliction on account of sin. Even after their subsequent return to righteous living, by which they are supposed to have been released from the worst penalty of their sentence through the blood of the Lord, our first parents were still not deemed worthy to be recalled to paradise during their life on earth. And no matter how righteous our life has been, we are still not worthy to gain exemption from death.[138] But Adam did not lose his free will, nor did his descendants. Through sin freedom indeed perished, says Augustine, but it was that freedom which was in paradise, to have a full righteousness with immortality, and it is on this account that human nature needs divine grace.[139] "For all have sinned"—whether in Adam or in themselves— "and come short of the glory of God" (Rom. 3:23).

Concupiscence undoubtedly, by means of natural birth, passes on the bond of sin to a man's posterity, but in the case of the regenerate, concupiscence is not itself a sin any longer, whenever it is not consented to for illicit works, and when the members are not applied by the presiding mind to perpetrate such deeds. By a certain manner of speech, however, it is called sin, since it arises from sin, and when it has the upper hand, produces sin; its guilt prevails in the natural man, but not in the man regenerated through the grace of Christ, as long as he does not yield to its temptations.[140]

Against Julian of Eclanum who asks how sin is to be found in an infant—through the will, or through marriage, or through its parents— Augustine replies that it is not through the infant's will which is not yet matured in him for sinning, nor marriage, which was instituted and blessed by God, nor through parents united properly together and lawfully for the procreation of children. Sin entered into the world by one man, and death by sin, and so death passed upon all men, for in him all have sinned, as Paul says (Rom. 5:12).[141] Since Adam forsook God of his own free will, he experienced the just judgment of God, that with his whole race, which sinned with him, he should be condemned. Now, as many of this race as are delivered by God's grace are certainly delivered from the condemnation in which they are already held bound. But even if none should be delivered, no one could justly blame the judgment of God.[142]

Is sin to be equated with concupiscence? No, it is the result of sin, just as a writing is said to be someone's "hand" because the hand has written it. Carnal concupiscence is the daughter of sin, and whenever it yields assent to the commission of shameful deeds, it becomes also the mother of many sins. Now, from this concupiscence, whatever comes into being by natural birth is bound by original sin. And so, concupiscence passes on the bond of sin to a man's posterity.[143]

What happens to infants dying without baptism? Holy Scripture and Holy Church both testify that they are doomed to perdition. Unless they are born again in Christ through grace, they carry the contagion of the primal death contracted in Adam. And let no one, says Augustine, promise for the case of unbaptized infants, between damnation and the Kingdom of Heaven, some middle place of rest and happiness, such as he pleases and where he pleases; for this is what the heresy of Pelagius promised them.[144] It may be nice to say that infants which are forestalled by death before they are baptized may yet attain to forgiveness of their original sins, but this is not the Catholic faith.[145]

ACTUAL GRACE

Nothing can be done without the grace of God, whether to convert the soul from evil to good, or to persevere and advance in good, or to attain eternal good, where there is no more fear of falling away. For the commission of sin we get no help from God, but we are not able to do justly, and to fulfill the law of righteousness in every one of its parts unless we are helped by God. Light never helps the eye if one shuts it or turns away from the source of illumination, and neither does God, who is the light of the inner man, help our mental sight, in order that we may do some good, not according to our own, but according to his righteousness.[146]

This grace of Christ, without which neither infants nor adults can be saved, is not rendered for any merits, but is even *gratis,* and that is why it is called *grace.* "Without me you can do nothing," says the Lord (Jno. 15:5) and this must be understood literally at face value. Likewise, "No man can come to me, except the Father who has sent me draw him" (Jno. 6:44), means that God first gives us the grace to will to believe. But there are those who will say that many good men abound in virtue without the aid of grace and without faith. Such men, by the mere powers of their inborn liberty, are often merciful, and modest, and chaste, and sober. But the truth of the matter is, says Augustine, that these are gifts of God given to them, they are not manufactured as their own, and they are powerless to salvation if the man himself be unwilling.[147] True virtues do not exist in anyone unless he is just, but the just man shall live by faith. How can an unbeliever be just? How can the ungodly be just?

The whole work of salvation belongs to God, who both makes the will of man righteous and thus prepares it for assistance, and assists it when it is prepared. For the man's righteousness of will precedes many of God's gifts, but not all; and it must itself be included among those which it does not precede. We read in Holy Scripture, says Augustine, both that God's mercy "shall meet me," and that his mercy "shall follow me." It goes before the unwilling to make him willing; it follows the willing to make his will effectual.[148]

All of this is summed up in the tract *On Grace and Free Will* where the statements of Saint Paul on grace are closely analyzed. It was not Paul alone, nor the grace of God alone, but the two in combination which enabled Paul to say that he had fought the good fight and could look forward to a crown of righteousness. Yet all of this was possible only because grace had preceded his actions to justify the ungodly.[149]

The first man, Adam, did not have the grace to will never to be evil; but he had the grace in which (if he willed to abide) he would never be evil; without grace he could not by free will be good, yet he did have free will to forsake it. God, therefore, did not will even Adam to be without grace, which he left in his free will; because free will is sufficient for evil, but is too little for good, unless it is aided by Omnipotent Good. And if Adam had not forsaken that assistance of his free will, he would always have been good; but he forsook it, and was forsaken himself. Such was the nature of the aid, that he could forsake it if he wanted, and he could continue in it if he wanted, but it was not such that it could be brought about that he would continue.[150]

When such great Doctors of the Church as Cyprian, Ambrose, Gregory Nazianzus, and others says that there is nothing of which we may boast as if of our own which God has not given us, and that our very heart and our thoughts are not in our own power; and when they give the whole to God, and confess that from him we receive conversion from him in such wise as to continue—so that what is good appears good also to us and we desire it—so that we honor God and receive Christ— so that from having been undevout people we are made devout and religious—so that we believe in the Trinity itself, and also confess with our voice what we believe: these great saints certainly attribute all these things to God's grace, acknowledge them as God's gifts, and testify that they come to us from God, and are not from ourselves.[151]

Without grace man can still perform acts which are good in the natural order; men do by nature the things contained in the Law, and such are rightly praised. God's image has not been so completely erased in the soul of man by the stain of earthly affections that there are not still some linaments of it, so that even ungodly men at least appreciate and even do some things contained in the Law.[152] The Law is written on the hearts of everyone to the extent that they do not do to others what they do not want done to themselves, but men without faith sin in that they do not refer their works to the end to which they should be referred—God himself.

God does not command impossibilities, but in his command he counsels us both to do what we can for ourselves, and to ask his aid in what we cannot do. But we should see whence comes the possibility and whence the impossibility. What one cannot accomplish in his own weakness he will be able to accomplish by remedial aid. For those alone are to be called good works which are done through love of God. But faith must precede these, since no one can work for the love of God who does not first believe in God. And so, without the help of God man cannot observe the Law for very long, in fact without his assisting grace the Law is "the letter which killeth" but when the life-giving spirit is present, the Law causes that to be loved as written within, which it once caused to be feared as written without.[153] For without the Holy Spirit, the Law can command but it cannot assist, and moreover, it makes a man a transgressor, for he can no longer excuse himself on the plea of ignorance. For carnal lust reigns where there is not the love of God, Augustine concludes.[154]

Most especially is grace necessary for the initial act of faith and a man's conversion. It is a true grace without merit, and therefore a free gift of God. It is God who both works in man the will to believe, and in all things goes before us with his mercy. To yield our consent to God's summons, or to withhold it is the function of our own will. For if faith is simply of free will, and is not given by God, why do we pray for those who will not believe, that they may believe? This it would be absolutely useless to do, unless we believe, with perfect propriety, that Almighty God is able to turn to belief wills that are perverse and opposed to faith.[155]

The tract *On the Predestination of the Saints* (along with several others) makes this point most emphatically. Augustine sums up his view this way in chapter five:

> The capacity to have faith, as the capacity to have love, belongs to man's nature; but to have faith, even as to have love, belongs to the grace of believers. [This] capacity for having faith does not distinguish man from man, but faith itself makes the believer to differ from the unbeliever. . . . If anyone dare to say, "I have faith of myself, I did not, therefore, receive it," he directly contradicts this most manifest truth—not because it is not in the choice of man's will to believe or not to believe, but because in the elect the will is prepared by the Lord.[156]

Without grace no man is able for long to resist concupiscence and serious temptations. To God's grace must also be attributed whatever evil we have not committed, for who dares to ascribe his chastity and innocence to his own strength when he reflects upon his own weakness? But we love God more when we realize how we owe to him everything that has been good in our lives.[157] The Pelagians imagine they are clever when they say that if we have not the will, we commit no sin; nor would God command man to do what was impossible for human volition. But they do not see that in order to overcome certain things, which are the objects either of an evil desire or an ill-conceived fear, men need the strenuous efforts, and sometimes even all the energies of the will, and that we should only imperfectly employ these in every instance.[158]

Nor can anyone be completely free from concupiscence and light sins without a special privilege of grace. For this reason we are to forgive our debtors since the Lord must also forgive us our debts. Light sins are blotted out by daily prayer, and especially the Lord's Prayer. In three ways, then, are sins remitted in the church: by baptism, by prayer, by the greater humility of penance.[159] If I were asked, says Augustine, whether it be possible for a man in this life to be without sin, I should allow the possibility, through the grace of God and the man's own free will, not doubting that the free will itself is ascribable to God's grace, in other words, to the gifts of God—not only as to its existence, but also as to its being good, that is, to its conversion to doing the commandments of God. Thus it is that God's grace not only shows what ought to be done, but also helps to the possibility of doing what it shows. I cannot doubt, he continues, that God has laid no impossible command on man, and that, by God's aid and help, nothing is impossible, by which what he commands takes place. In this way may a man, if he pleases, be without sin by the assistance of God. But as to whether there actually is a sinless man, or not—Augustine says he thinks there is not.[160] The reason for this is man's pride, which makes the will of God either unknown to him, or unpleasant. Now, if it should so happen that none of the conditions pertaining to righteousness were hidden from us, and at the same time these so delighted our mind, that whatever hindrance of pleasure or pain might otherwise occur, this delight in holiness would prevail over every rival affection, then it would not be intrinsically impossible for a man to be sinless. But the fact that this is never realized in actuality is due to God's judicial act.[161]

The single exception would be the holy Virgin Mary, who had abundance of grace for overcoming every sin, and this privilege was granted to her by the Lord Himself. But suppose, asks Augustine, that you assembled all the holiest men and women of history, and asked each one of them whether they were free from sin; would they answer in the words of Pelagius, or rather in the words of the apostle John: "If we say we have no sin, we deceive ourselves, and the truth is not in us."[162] But if any man says that we ought not to use the prayer, "Lead us not into temptation" (and he says as much who maintains that God's help is unnecessary to a person for the avoidance of sin, and that human will, after accepting only the Law, is sufficient for the purpose), then such a person should be anathematized by everybody.[163]

And so the Pelagians are wrong. Because we are weak human beings sins are committed daily, and daily they are remitted for those who pray in faith and work in mercy. In such wise does the believer make satisfaction for daily sins of a momentary and trivial kind, which are the necessary incidents of this life. But if this were not so, the Lord's Prayer would become meaningless. So, just as the eye of the body, even when completely sound, is unable to see unless aided by the brightness of light, so also man, even when most fully justified, is unable to lead a holy life, if he is not divinely assisted by the eternal light of righteousness.[164]

Every just person may obtain the grace of perseverance if he really wishes it, but he also requires this particular grace. It is indeed a great gift of God, who wills that his saints should not glory in their own strength, but in himself alone. And so, aid is brought to the infirm will in order that it might be unchangeably and invincibly influenced by divine grace, and thus, although weak, it still might not fail, nor be overcome by any adversity.[165] It is uncertain whether any one has received this gift so long as he is still alive. It is equally certain that no one can lose it. This gift of God may be obtained by prayer, but when it has been given, it cannot be lost by contumacy. But all of this ends up in mystery. Of two infants, equally bound by original sin, why the one is taken and other left, or of two wicked men why one is called to repent and follow the Lord, and the other not, is indeed a mystery. But of two pious men, why to one should be given perseverance unto the end, and to the other it should not be given, makes God's judgments even more unsearchable.[166] To summarize then: the grace of God which both begins a man's faith and enables him to persevere to the end, is not given according to his merits, but is given according to God's own most secret and, at the same time, most righteous, wise, and beneficent will; since those whom he predestinated, them he also called, with that calling of which it is said, "The gifts and calling of God are without repentance." To this calling there is no man that can be said with any certainty of affirmation to belong, until he has departed from this world. We therefore will, but God works in us to will also. We therefore work, but God works in us to work also for his good pleasure. This is profitable for us both to believe and to say—this is pious, this is true, that our confession be lowly and submissive, and that all should be given to God.[167]

There is a larger sense in which the word *grace* can be applied. It can be identified with the favor of our creation by which we escape nothingness and by which we are something more than a corpse which is not alive, a tree which has no consciousness, or a sheep which has no understanding. With being, life, consciousness, and understanding, we are able to give thanks for this great benefit from our Creator, and in this sense creation is a grace because it is not granted through the merits of any previous actions, but by the unsolicited goodness of God. Evangelical exhortations and even the commands of the Law are another such external grace, whereas internally a man's own free will is a special grace which allows him to consent or dissent to the actions of God on the reasonable soul. So the Holy Spirit works within a man in order that the medicine externally applied may have some good result. Preaching of the Gospel is therefore another external grace which permits God to sway and act upon the mind.

Protection from sin may also be said to be a kind of grace, as Augustine says so eloquently in the *Confessions*.[168] And in one of the sermons, God speaks to the soul which has not committed sins, thus:

> I was guiding thee for Myself, I was keeping thee for Myself. That thou mightest not commit adultery, no enticers were near thee; that no enticers were near thee, was my doing. Place and time were wanting; that they

were wanting again, was my doing. Or, enticers were near thee, and neither place nor time was wanting; that thou mightest not consent, it was I who alarmed thee.[169]

On all sides God calls to amendment, says the saint; on all sides he calls to repentance, he calls by the blessings of creation, he calls by giving time for life, he calls through the reader, he calls through the preacher, he calls through the innermost thought by the rod of correction, he calls by the mercy of consolation.[170]

Actual grace breaks down into two large categories: illumination of the mind and an inspiration of the will. God's grace not only shows what ought to be done, but also helps to the possibility of doing it. When we pray to God to give us his help to do and accomplish righteousness, what else do we pray for than that he would open what was hidden, and impart sweetness to that which gave no pleasure?[171] Thus we discover not only what ought to be done, but also that we do it— not only that we believe what ought to be loved, but also that we love what we have believed.

Augustine always insists that the will of man is forestalled by the grace of God and that it is prepared by grace rather than rewarded in receiving it. His mercy anticipates us that we may be healed, but then he also follows us, that being healed we may grow healthy and strong. He anticipates us that we may be called; he will follow us that we may be glorified. He anticipates us that we may lead godly lives; he will follow us that we may always live with him, because without him we can do nothing. Thus the whole work belongs to God, who both makes the will of man righteous and thus prepares it for assistance, and assists it when it is prepared. This grace which precedes salutary acts is called prevenient, because it summons or calls the will into action. Once operating in conjunction with a man's free will, it is designated *aiding, cooperating,* or a *subsequent* grace. Thus we read in Scripture that God's mercy "shall meet me," and that his mercy "shall follow me"; it goes before the unwilling to make him willing; it follows the willing to make his will effectual.[172] Commenting on an incident at the Last Supper, the saint says: "However small and imperfect Peter's love was, it was not wholly wanting when he said to the Lord, 'I will lay down my life for Thy sake'; for he supposed himself able to effect what he felt himself willing to do. And who was it that had begun to give him his love, however small, but He who prepares the will, and perfects by His cooperation what He initiates by His operation? Forasmuch as in beginning He works in us that we may have the will, and in perfecting works with us when we have the will—He operates, therefore, without us, in order that we may will; but when we will to act, He cooperates with us. We can, however, ourselves do nothing to effect good works of piety without Him either working that we may will or co-working when we will."[173]

Grace so acts on the human will that man never does any good which God does not simultaneously effect at the same instance. For God has not only given us the ability and aids it, but He further works in us "to will and to do." It is not because we do not will, or do not do, that we will and do nothing good, but because we are without his help.[174] God does many good things in man which man does not do; but man does none which God does not cause man to do. For, if without Him we are able to do nothing actually, we are able neither to begin nor to perfect, because to begin it is said, "His mercy shall prevent me;" and to finish, it is said, "His mercy shall follow me." And so, it is neither the grace of God alone, nor man alone, but the grace of God in man.[175] Thus it is we that act when we act, but it is God who makes us act, by applying efficacious powers to our will.

The tract *On the Proceedings of Pelagius* reminds us that there are two sorts of aids. Some are indispensable, and without their help the desired result could not be attained. Without a ship, for instance, no man could take a voyage; no man could speak without a voice; without legs no man could walk; without light nobody could see, and so on in numberless instances. Amongst them this also may be reckoned, that without God's grace no man can live rightly. But then, again, there are other helps, which render us assistance in such a way that we might in some other way effect the object to which they are ordinarily auxiliary in their absence. Such are those which I have already mentioned, remarks Augustine, the threshing-sledges for threshing corn, the pedagogue for conducting the child (to school), medical art applied to the recovery of health, and other like instances.[176] The aid, therefore, without which a thing does not come to pass is one thing *(alterum sine quo non)* and the aid by which a thing comes to pass is another *(alterum quo).* For without food we cannot live, and yet although food should be at hand, it would not cause a man to live who should will to die. Therefore the aid of food is that without which it does not come to pass that we live, not that by which it comes to pass that we live.[177]

The first man, Adam, was a special case. For he had a large amount of grace from God, but it was of a different kind. He had no reason to pray to be delivered from evil, nor did he require the blood of the Lamb to absolve him from guilt. The first man did not have that grace by which he should never will to be evil, but he did have the grace in which if he willed to remain, he would never be evil, and without which he could not by free will be good, but which he could freely forsake. Free will is sufficient for evil, but it is too little for good, unless it is aided by omnipotent Good. Adam's grace was such that he could foresake it if he wanted to or continue in it, but it was not such that he would continue in it automatically. That Adam willed not to continue in this grace was his own fault, and if he had, he would have received the merit similar to those holy angels who through their own free will stood, and thus received the fullest of blessings—the fullest certainty of always remaining in the grace of God. By this grace of God there is caused in us the reception of good and the persevering hold of it, not only to be able to do what we will, but even to will to do what we are able. But this was not the case in the first man; for the one of these things was in him, but the other was not.[178]

It follows that there are some graces which are sufficient to achieve their effect, but which actually do not achieve it *(gratia sufficiens)* and there are others which efficaciously move the will *(gratia efficax)*. Augustine holds that God can even change the evil wills of men, whichever, whenever, and wheresoever He chooses, and direct them to what is good. But when he does this, he does it of his mercy.[179] Thus aid is brought to the infirmity of the human will so that it might be unchangeably and invincibly influenced by divine grace, and thus, although weak, it still might not fail, nor be overcome by any adversity. Since God does not tempt any beyond their strength, and can even remove them from this life before they are tempted disastrously, he can also convert the wills of men averse and opposed to his faith, and to operate on their hearts so that they yield to no adversities, and are overcome by no temptation so as to depart from him.[180]

Grace does not destroy man's free will. He who says to God: "Be my helper," confesses that he wishes to carry out what is commanded, but asks help of him who gave the command so that he may be able to do it. God no doubt wishes all men to be saved and to come into the knowledge of the truth, but yet not so as to take away from them free will, for the good or the evil use of which they may be most righteously judged. This being the case, unbelievers indeed do contrary to the will of God when they do not believe his Gospel; nevertheless they do not therefore overcome his will, but rob themselves of the greatest good, and implicate themselves in penalties of punishment, destined to experience the power of him in punishments whose mercy in his gifts they despised.[181] To yield our consent to God's summons, or to withhold it, is the function of our own will. And so it happens, that with an equal amount of grace, one person may say *yes* to God, and the other *no*.

But to do the will of God implies a certain delight. Every man who is attracted to God, is not drawn so much through necessity as pleasure. It is not a matter of obligation so much as delight. We ought boldly to say that a man is drawn to Christ when he delights in the truth, when he delights in blessedness, delights in righteousness, delights in everlasting life, and all of these Christ is. To love, to long for, to hunger after, to travel in the wilderness, to thirst and pant after the fountain of our eternal home, is to know the meaning of the words: "I delight to do thy will, O Lord."[182]

God infallibly knows beforehand how man's free will is about to use a particular grace; if he did not, he would not be God. Our wills have just so much power as God willed and foreknew that they should have; and therefore whatever power they have, they have it within most certain limits; and whatever they are to do, they most assuredly will do, for he whose foreknowledge is infallible foreknew that they would have the power, and would do it.[183] Is God in any way responsible for lack of a good will? No. When the Scripture speaks of darkening the mind and hardening the heart, God is simply letting people alone by withdrawing his aid, and God can do this by a judgment that is hidden, although not by one that is unrighteous.[184] For what is more true than that Christ foreknew who should believe in him, and at what times and places they should believe?

The Pelagians err in saying that grace is the nature in which we were created, so as to possess a rational mind, by which we are enabled to understand—formed as we are in the image of God, so as to have dominion over the fish of the sea, and over the fowl of the air, and over every living thing that creeps upon the earth. This, however, is not the grace which the apostle commends to us through the faith of Jesus Christ. For it is certain that we possess this nature in common with ungodly men and unbelievers; whereas the grace which comes through the faith of Jesus Christ belongs only to them to whom the faith itself appertains.[185] The capacity to have faith, as the capacity to have love, belongs to men's nature; but to have faith, even as to have love, belongs to the grace of believers. Grace totally surpasses the bounds of nature.

Augustine never tires of telling us that grace is a free gift of God. In his letter to Pope Innocent,[186] Vitalus, and others,[187] in his *Expositions on the Psalms*,[188] *On Nature and Grace*,[189] *On the Gospel of Saint John*,[190] *On the Proceedings of Pelagius*,[191] *On Original Sin*,[192] *Against Two Letters of the Pelagians*,[193] *On the Gift of Perseverance*,[194] the essential gratuity of this marvelous gift of divine love is never lost sight of. But this does not mean that we are not to pray for it. When we pray God to give us his help to do and accomplish righteousness, what else do we pray for than that he would open what was hidden, and impart sweetness to that which gave no pleasure? We are to do what we can for ourselves, and to ask his aid in what we cannot do, and this requires on our part a clear discernment of what is possible for us by nature, and what is not possible. Nonetheless, conversion and gift of final perseverance may be obtained by prayer, and these things the church prays for daily. It prays that the unbelieving may believe, says Augustine, therefore God converts to the faith. It prays that believers may persevere, therefore God gives perseverance to the end. But there are some who either do not pray at all, or pray coldly, because from the Lord's own words, they have learnt that God knows what is necessary for us before we ask it of him. It is certain that God sometimes gives the beginning of faith to those who do not ask him, but he never gives the gift of perseverance except to those who do ask it. No one should become lukewarm, for that would stifle prayer and stimulate arrogance.[195]

God's distribution of graces to various individuals is mysterious but at the same time just, despite the inequality involved. We have to remember that even if none were delivered from condemnation, there would still be no just cause for finding fault with God. Why some are called and some are not, some persevere and some do not, remains ultimately in the unsearchable judgments of God. Augustine never tires of saying that God never deserts a man unless God is first deserted by him. None is forced by God's power unwillingly either into evil or good, but when God forsakes a man, he deservedly goes to evil, and when God assists, without deserving he is converted to good. For a man is not good if he is unwilling, but by the grace of God he is even assisted to the point of being willing. When a man is said to be given up to his desires, then, he derives guilt from them because, deserted by God, he yields and consents to them, is conquered, seized, drawn, and possessed by them. From a hidden judgment of God comes perversity of heart, with the result that refusal to hear the truth leads to the commission of sin, which sin is also punishment for preceding sin.[196] Even so, to the most hardened of sinners, sufficient grace is given to all to be converted, if they should so desire.

Not even to infidels, indeed to no one, does God deny sufficient grace for faith and salvation. When the Word became Flesh and dwelt among us, he permitted no man to excuse himself from the shadow of death—the heat of the Word penetrated even to here. Religious salvation has never been lacking to those who were worthy of it, only to those who were not worthy, not worthy by divine grace or predestination. But we must always be careful not to fall into the Pelagian pitfall which asserts that free will vis-à-vis God's grace has such difficulty in its distinctions, that when free will is maintained, God's grace is apparently denied, while when God's grace is asserted, free will is supposedly done away with.[197]

Now the Pelagians are right when they say that if we do not have the will, we commit no sin, nor would God command man to do what was impossible for human volition. But they do not see, that in order to overcome certain things, which are the objects either of an evil desire or an ill-conceived fear, man needs the strenuous efforts, and sometimes even all the energies of the will, and that we only imperfectly employ these in every instance.[198] Augustine calls the Pelagians most bitter enemies of grace when they say that some men exist who by the mere powers of their inborn liberty, are often merciful, modest, chaste, and sober. But what these lack, and makes them ultimately evil, is effectiveness of will to attribute these virtues to the grace of God working within them.[199]

The Semi-Pelagians who think that the beginning of faith and perseverance to the end are in our power and are not God's gifts forget that these are all part of God's predestination which comes solely from him, so that the position of the Semi-Pelagians can be logically reduced back to the original Pelagian position. God works on our thoughts and our wills in such a manner that what we have been given initially as a gift, we may retain through his continuing grace. The saint always comes back to the key words of Saint Paul: "For what hast thou that thou hast not received? And if thou hast received it, why boastest thou as if thou hadst not received it? (1 Cor. 4:7) And it was chiefly by this testimony that I myself also was convinced when I was in a similar error," he continues, "thinking that faith whereby we believe on God is not God's gift, but that it is in us from ourselves, and that by it we obtain the gifts of God, whereby we may live temperately and righteously and piously in this world."[200]

All of this leads us to an examination now of habitual grace.

HABITUAL GRACE

When we are justified before God, we receive a permanent supernatural gift called habitual grace. To those who believe on him, he gives the hidden grace of his Spirit, which he secretly infuses even into infants. Thus the Spirit of grace restores in us the image of God, in which we were naturally created. This baptism gives remission of all sins and takes away guilt; grace perfectly renews man, since it brings him even to immortality of body and full happiness. But while it delivers from sin, it does not deliver from all evil, nor from every ill of mortality by which the body is now a load upon the soul.[201] Man is inwardly renewed by the indwelling of the Holy Spirit. He becomes the adopted son of God, and if adopted sons of God, we have also been made gods, but this is the effect of grace adopting, not of nature generating.[202] Jesus is Son of God by nature; we, by grace.

It rarely happens, says Augustine, that anyone desires to become a Christian, who has not first been smitten with some sort of fear of God. For if it is in the expectation of some advantage from men whom he deems himself unlikely to please in any other way, or with the idea of escaping any disadvantage at the hands of men of whose displeasure or hostility he is seriously afraid that a man wishes to become a

Christian, then, his wish to become one is not so earnest as his desire to pretend to be one.[203] We ought always to dispose ourselves for justification through faith as well as through acts of the other virtues: hope, contrition, love. If, however, being already regenerate and justified, he relapses of his own will into an evil life, assuredly he cannot say, "I have not received," because of his own free choice to evil he has lost the grace of God which he received. Thus habitual grace may be lost through mortal sin. And no matter how great a man's righteousness may be, he ought to reflect and think lest there should be found something blameworthy, which has escaped indeed his own notice, when that righteous King shall sit upon his throne, whose cognizance no sins can possibly escape, not even those of which it is said, "Who understands his transgressions?" (Ps. 18:13). So a man can never be certain if he is abiding in God's grace or not.[204]

Writing to Sixtus, Augustine asks, "What merits of his own has the saved to boast of, when, if he received his just deserts, he would be damned? But, have the just no merits at all? Certainly they have, since they are just; only there were no previous merits to make them just. They became just when they were justified." What merit man has before grace makes it possible for him to receive grace, since nothing but grace produces good merits in us, and what else but his gifts does God crown when he crowns our merits?[205] And since the Lord has given grace, he will also give glory because this is part of the promise which the Lord has bound himself to fulfill. Those who are made just by the grace of God may truly be said to merit eternal life, for eternal life is awarded as if it were the wages which justice deserves, just as death is the wages which sin deserves. And this eternal life (which the denarius in the parable symbolizes) will be equal for all, although through diversity of attainments the saints will shine, some more and some less.[206] "There is henceforth laid up for me," Paul says, "a crown of righteousness, which the Lord, the righteous Judge, shall give me at that day" (2 Tim. 4:8). The crown is called one of righteousness because the grace which preceded it actually justified the ungodly.

Grace itself merits an increase, and the increase merits perfection because God has specifically promised this, provided man cooperates with his free will. An increase in grace presupposes the state of grace to begin with. In all of this, however, Augustine is not in agreement with those Reformers of the sixteenth century who denied that justification actually made a man righteous in the sight of God, enabling him truly to merit eternal salvation and to become an heir to the Kingdom of God.

Saint Augustine: III

THE INCARNATE WORD

Whenever we wish to show to the heathen that Christ was prophesied in the ancient writings, says Augustine, we produce the Old Testament which is in the custody of the Jews, and is not the product of the Christian church.[207] One of the many purposes of these writings is to symbolize various truths subsequently fulfilled in the New Dispensation. For example, animal sacrifices were suitable to ancient people because they indicated the need for purification or the propitiation of God and involved the shedding of blood; the fulfillment of these types is in Christ, by whose blood we are purified and redeemed. This is one of the ways by which Christ and his divine work are predicted in the Old Testament. And, in the fullness of time, the Son of God became incarnate and is none other than Jesus Christ, prophesied in the Old Testament.

If Christ is divine, he is also human, assuming a real, not an apparent, human nature. The Lord Jesus Christ, having come to liberate human beings, including both men and women destined for salvation, was not ashamed of the male nature, for he took it upon himself, or of the female, for he was born of a woman. Besides, there is the profound mystery that, as death had befallen man through a woman, life should be born to him through a woman. By this defeat, the Devil would be tormented over the thought of both sexes, male and female, because he had taken delight in the defection of them both. The freeing of both sexes would not have been so severe a penalty for the Devil, unless man was also liberated by the agency of both sexes.[208]

Possessing a true body from the Virgin and a rational soul makes Christ truly a member of Adam's stock. That God should take upon Himself our own nature—that is, the rational soul and flesh of the man Christ—by an undertaking singularly marvelous, or marvelously singular, because it was never to be feared that the human nature taken up by God the Word in that ineffable manner into a unity of Person would sin by free choice of will, in fact would even have the slightest motion of an evil will![209] Flesh only did Christ derive from Adam, Adam's sin he did not assume. "Let us not heed," says Augustine, "those who say

360

that Our Lord had a body like that of the dove which John the Baptist beheld coming down from heaven, as a symbol of the Holy Spirit, and resting upon Him. Now, the reason why the Holy Spirit was not born of a dove, whereas Christ was born of a woman, is this: The Holy Spirit did not come to liberate doves, but to declare unto men innocence and spiritual love, which were outwardly symbolized in the form of a dove. The Lord Jesus came to liberate human beings, and therefore assumed all the infirmity of human flesh since what was not assumed could not also be healed. And so he was like every other human being, except for the fact that He alone was sinless."[210]

This union of the divine and human nature is a mystery. In writing to Volusianus, the saint remarks that it is a sign of the greatness of God's power not to feel narrowness in narrow quarters; confinement in the Virgin's womb does not prevent him from bettering all mankind without suffering any diminution himself, taking on the humanity of man while at the same time granting him a share of his divinity. The whole explanation of this deed is obviously in the doer.[211] But there are always those who require an explanation of how God is joined to man so as to become the single person of Christ, as if they could themselves explain something that happens every day—how the soul is joined to the body so as to form the single person of a man. But as the soul makes use of the body in a single person to form a man, so God makes use of a man in a single Person to form Christ.

Begotten and conceived, then, without any indulgence of carnal lust, and therefore bringing with him no original sin, and by the grace of God joined and united in a wonderful and unspeakable way in one Person with the Word, the only-begotten of the Father, a Son by nature, not by grace, and therefore having no sin of his own; nevertheless, on account of the likeness of sinful flesh in which he came, was called sin, that he might be sacrificed to wash away sin. Saint Paul says that he who knew no sin was made to be sin for us (2 Cor. 5:21). Augustine implies that the Word was not changed into human nature, nor mixed with it, but took on human nature in such a manner that two distinct natures were somehow joined in a personal union.[212]

Therefore, continues Augustine, the Lord Jesus Christ himself not only gave the Holy Spirit as God, but also received it as man, and therefore is said to be full of grace and of the Holy Spirit. When the apostles in the Book of Acts declare that God anointed him with the Holy Spirit, this does not imply some visible oil, but with the gift of grace which is signified by the visible ointment by which the church anoints the baptized. Nor was Christ anointed at his baptism when the dove descended upon him. He is understood to have been anointed with that mystical and invisible unction, when the Word of God was made flesh—when human nature, without any precedent merits or good works, was joined to God the Word in the womb of the Virgin, so that with it it became one Person.[213]

The precise language which was to characterize such thinkers as Cyril of Alexandria and Pope Leo the Great with regard to the two natures of Christ, the two wills, the theandric operations, is not closely worked out in Saint Augustine. The bishop of Hippo had already been dead twenty years when the great Council of Chalcedon took up the precise formulation of the union of the divine and human natures. This is not to say that Augustine would not have endorsed the formulae pronounced by the council, but his interest is more nearly directed to the nature of man and the necessity of grace. Of the theandric operation, he says that unless the very same were the Son of Man on account of the form of a servant which he took, who is the Son of God on account of the form of God in which he is, Paul would not have said that the princes of this world crucified the Lord of Glory (1 Cor. 2:8). For Christ was crucified after the form of a servant, and yet "the Lord of Glory" was crucified, for that "taking" was such as to make God man, and man God.[214] So in Christ there is a true communication of idioms.

We have already seen that Augustine insists that Christ is the natural, not the adoptive Son of God. There is but one Son of God by nature, who in his compassion became Son of Man for our sakes, that we, by nature sons of men, might by grace become through him sons of God. Christ Jesus is the Mediator between God and men, not in respect to his Godhead, but in respect to his manhood. He was made sin, just as we are made righteousness, which righteousness is not our own, but God's in us.[215]

Christ was full of grace and possessed complete sanctity, which means that he was free from both original sin and personal sin. Hence, he was incapable of sinning since he was righteousness itself. But this is not to say that he was incapable of suffering, for he did possess a real human body subject to human weakness and passions. Christ freely suffered and died. Through no punishment of sin did he lay down his life, because he did not leave it against his will, but because he willed, when he willed, as he willed.[216]

When Adam was created, says Augustine, he, being a righteous man, had no need of a Mediator. But when sin had placed a wide gulf between God and the human race, it was expedient that a Mediator, who alone of the human race was born, lived, and died without sin should reconcile us to God, and procure even for our bodies a resurrection to eternal life, in order that the pride of man might be exposed and cured through the humility of God. Thus, man might be shown how far he had departed from God, when God became incarnate to bring him back; that an example might be set to disobedient man in the life of obedience of the God-man; that the fountain of grace might be opened by the Only-begotten taking upon himself the form of a servant, a form which had no antecedent merit; that an earnest of that resurrection of the body which is promised to the redeemed might be given in the Resurrection of the Redeemer; that the Devil might be subdued by the same nature which it was his boast to have deceived.[217] To those who ask why God could not in his wisdom have found a way to liberate men other than by assuming man's nature, being born of a woman and suffering all the injuries inflicted by the hands of sinners, the saint replies that God could indeed have acted otherwise, but he would have incurred their stupid displeasure just the same. Our Lord's passion shows to what a weakened state man had come by his own fault and how he is liberated from that state by divine assistance.[218] And so, while the Incarnation is a free gift of God, it is also in a sense necessary since Christ chooses to redeem the human race through righteousness rather than through power. Christ held back from doing what was possible for him, that he might do what was more fitting. Hence, it was necessary that he should be both man and God, for unless he had been man he would not have been slain, and unless he had been God men would not have believed that he could do what he did.[219]

Christ did not die for angels, but for men, yet what was done for the redemption of man through his death was in a sense done for the angels, because the enmity which sin had put between men and the holy angels is removed, and friendship is restored between them, and by the redemption of man the gaps which the great apostasy left in the angelic hosts are filled up. The whole purpose of God's coming was to show his great love for man, and since Christ laid his life down for us, we ought also to lay our life down for the brethren. Since he first loved us, it should not be so irksome to love in return. There is no mightier invitation to love than to anticipate in loving; the Lord Jesus Christ, God-man, is both a manifestation of divine love toward us, and an example of human humility with us.[220]

What part does the Devil play in the redemption of man? It is he who holds man in slavery, who slew Jesus Christ and was in turn conquered by his righteousness. In our redemption, the blood of Christ was given, as it were, as a price for us, which by our accepting the Devil was not enriched but rather bound, in order that we might be loosened from his bonds.[221]

Christ restores grace and immortality and thus returns man to his former state before it was lost through the sin of Adam. And so the whole Christian redemption revolves around two men: by one we are sold under sin, by the other redeemed from sins; by the one we have been precipitated into death, by the other liberated unto life; the former has ruined us in himself, by doing his own will instead of his who created him; the latter has saved us in himself, by not doing his own will, but the will of God who sent him: and it is in what concerns these two men that the Christian faith properly consists.[222]

Christ's death offers up for us the one and most real sacrifice; whatever fault there was, when principalities and powers held us fast as of right to pay its penalty, he cleansed, abolished, and extinguished, and by his own resurrection he also called us whom he had predestinated. Now, as men were lying under wrath by reason of their original sin, and as this original sin was more heavy and deadly in proportion to the number and magnitude of the actual sins which were added to it, there was need for a Mediator, that is, a Reconciler, who by the offering of one sacrifice, of which all the sacrifices of the law and the prophets were types, should take away this wrath.[223] Christ is at once both priest and sacrifice, both victor and victim, the object of faith to holy men of old, as well as to us in the present time. Whereas the Gospel of Matthew has in mind the kingly character, and Luke the priestly, they have at the same time both set forth predominantly the humanity of Christ, for it was according to his humanity that Christ was made both king and priest. He is the Priest who offers, and the Sacrifice offered, and he designed that there should be a daily sign of this in the sacrifice of the church, which, being his body, learns to offer herself through him.[224] God has made Christ a sacrifice for our sins, by which we might be reconciled to God. He is made sin (our sins) and we are made righteousness (his righteousness), and the resulting sacrifice reconciles us to God. It is superabundant and it is for all men, and through the Mediator graces are given through him and because of him. The ancients who lived before the Law was given were not saved by nature, but in anticipation of the saving blood of Christ, while the saints of the Old Testament were saved, not by the Law, but in the redemptive merit of Christ, the fulfillment of the Law. So all the saints are saved by the sacrifice of the God-man, regardless of when they happened to live in time. The Pelagians had failed to see that the present is only a point in time, a finite time which stretches back to a beginning, and forward to a future with a specific end.

Christians also firmly believe, Augustine tells us, in the ascension of the Lord, body and soul into heaven, with the implication that at some future time he will return to earth once again.

MARY, VIRGIN AND MOTHER OF GOD

Saint Augustine calls Mary "the Virgin, a true but inviolate Mother, who gave birth to him who became visible for our sake and by whom she herself was created. A virgin conceives, yet remains a virgin; a virgin is heavy with child; a virgin brings forth her child, yet she is always a virgin."[225] Just as Christ passed mysteriously through closed doors after the Resurrection, his birth from the womb of the Virgin is equally mysterious. But Christ is not a branch derived from Adam; flesh only did he derive from Adam; Adam's sin he did not assume. Before she even knew who was to be born of her, Mary had determined to continue a virgin, and chose rather to approve than to command holy virginity.[226] Thus she becomes the new Eve, who plays the role of cooperator par excellence in the mystery of our redemption. In the tract *On Holy Virginity,* Augustine calls her not merely the Mother of our Head, of whom she herself was born after the Spirit, but clearly is also the Mother of his members, which we are, in that she wrought together by charity so that faithful ones should be born in the church, who are members of that Head: but in the flesh, the mother of the Head himself.[227] In fact, the sanctity of the Blessed Virgin was so exceptional that Augustine refuses even to raise the question of sin with regard to her, "out of honor to the Lord," from whom we know what abundance of grace for overcoming sin in every particular was conferred upon her, who had the merit to conceive and bear him who undoubtedly had no sin.[228] Now if we were to assemble together all the holy men and women who have lived and asked them if they had lived without sin while they were in this life, wouldn't they all undoubtedly reply with one voice in the words of the apostle: "If we say we have no sin, we deceive ourselves, and the truth is not in us" (1 Jno. 1:8)? But the Virgin Mary would be the lone exception to this general rule. Her sanctity was exceptional, which implies that she was immaculately conceived; of her bodily assumption into heaven, Saint Augustine says nothing.[229]

THE SACRAMENTS

Sacraments are sacred rites which take their name from the mysteries that they represent. They are signs of divinely bestowed favors, intended either to endow the mind with virtues or to help in the attaining of eternal salvation, the saint writes to Marcellinus. Their observances and performance are exercises of devotion, useful to us, not to God.[230] The sacraments of the New Testament are not the same as those of the Old, for the sacraments of the Old Testament promised a Savior, but those of the New confer salvation. Furthermore, there can be no religious society, whether the religion be true or false, Augustine reminds Faustus the Manichaean, without some sacrament or visible symbol to serve as a bond of union. The importance of these sacraments cannot be overstated, and only scoffers will treat them lightly. For if piety requires them, it must be impiety to neglect them.[231] And he reminds Petilian, the Donatist, that the visible external sacrament can exist in all kinds of men, good and bad, and must therefore be separated from the invisible unction of charity, which is the peculiar property of the good.[232] The ancient church used to offer animal sacrifices in order to draw near to God, and to induce our neighbor to do the same. A sacrifice, therefore, is the visible sacrament or sacred sign of an invisible sacrifice.[233] The spiritual unction is the Holy Spirit himself, of which the sacrament is the visible unction.[234]

A sacrament consists of Christ's word added to some element. What is the baptism of Christ if not the washing of water by the Word; take away the water, and you have no baptism; take away the Word, and likewise there is no baptism. The Word is added to the element and becomes a sacrament, which itself is a kind of visible Word. Water in itself has efficacy when joined to the Word, whose passing sound is one thing, but whose abiding efficacy is quite another. Later theologians were to call the element the *matter* of the sacrament, while the spoken Word would be its *form.*

Even in ancient times the servants of God aided their children by an implicit belief in the Mediator who was to come, for we read of their sacrifices, by which was figured the blood which alone takes away the sin of the world.[235] And in the Old Testament, the first five books of Moses imposed on the Hebrews a servitude in accord with their character and the prophetic times in which they lived. So there were sacraments even before the time of Christ, who also instituted sacraments, very few in number (he writes to Januarius) and very easy to observe.[236]

One of the sacraments of the Old Testament was circumcision, which foreshadowed the sacrament of baptism.[237] At that time it was the sign of the righteousness of faith, and availed to signify the cleansing even in infants of the original and primitive sin, just as baptism in like manner from the time of its institution began to be of avail for the renewal of man.[238]

Sacraments received with some obstacle in the way do not confer grace, although once the obstacle is removed, the sacrament takes effect, and grace is poured into the soul. And some sacraments—baptism, confirmation, and holy orders—imprint a spiritual and indelible sign or mark, which remains even if the recipient no longer remains faithful to Christ and his church, as we shall see when we come to discuss the individual sacraments more in detail.

"It is one Spirit," Augustine writes to Boniface, "that makes it possible for a man to be reborn through the agency of another's will." The Spirit effects the benefit of grace interiorly, loosing the bond of guilt, restoring good to his nature and manifesting what has occurred exteriorly.[239] The sacraments could impart nothing to a man, if the power of the Holy Spirit were not in them. Any sacrament confers grace, therefore, only by the Spirit resident within. It is Christ himself who has instituted these sacraments, not mediately through any other vehicle, but immediately himself. In fact, he is a kind of Ur-sacrament, since he is the author of them, and works through his church, which is likewise a kind of Ur-sacrament. This makes it possible to seek Christ everywhere, says the saint, for when Christ died the spear pierced his side, that the mysteries might flow forth whereby the church is formed. It is Jesus who baptizes through his own power by means of his disciples and his ministers; even those whom Judas baptized were baptized by Jesus, and there was a repetition of baptism only when those who had been baptized by John came to Jesus. In like manner those whom a drunkard baptized, those whom a murderer baptized, those whom an adulterer baptized, if it was the baptism of Christ, were baptized by Christ himself. So the sacraments are morally the actions of Christ, using men as his ministers. It likewise follows that the validity of the sacraments does not depend on who is administering them. After all, who can really have a pure conscience, be he baptizer or baptized? Does that mean that the baptism should be repeated? Hardly, Augustine tells Petilian, the purity of baptism is entirely unconnected with the purity or impurity of the conscience either of the giver or the recipient.[240] But if one is not in the state of grace, it is illicitly administered.

Of course the sacrament has no worth, if one does not intend to receive the sacrament. Certain necessary dispositions are required, at least in the case of adults, who would receive no fruit from the sacrament if their deeds were evil. Thus, the sacrament has validity in the objective order, as well as effectiveness in the subjective. To receive it improperly is to invite condemnation.

In writing to Januarius about the year 400, Augustine refers to the sacraments of baptism and the Eucharist, as well as others in general, and then adds that there are still other observances which all the world keeps that do not derive from Scripture but tradition, and are recommended by the apostles themselves, or plenary councils whose authority is well founded in the church.[241] Commenting on the Gospel of Saint John,[242] Augustine discusses the use of the sign of the cross in the administration of the various sacraments, and in the tract on baptism there is additional comment.[243] In his discussion of the sacraments, Augustine adds his testimony to previous fathers with regard to the arcane discipline of the church. And in addition to the sacraments there are other holy rites or actions which help to sanctify us: prayer, and specifically the recitation of the Lord's Prayer; penance, which helps to blot out venial sins (for there is no one in this life who is without sin); and various works of mercy.

There are frequent references to baptism, which for Augustine clearly surpassed the baptism of John and is a true sacrament instituted by Christ himself. Indeed, baptism is the washing of water by the

Word himself, the essential form of which is the distinct expression of
the one and triune God. While the minister of baptism is usually bishop
or priest, anyone can baptize (and in cases of emergency, should) if he
has the proper matter, form, and intention. So, even heretics may baptize
(we are told in the tract on baptism), and as we might expect, Augustine
cites Cyprian as one who held to the unity of the church in spite of his
disagreement with Rome.

Baptism is necessary for everyone—children as well as adults—for
whoever says that those children who depart out of this life without
partaking of that sacrament will be made alive in Christ contradicts the
apostolic teaching and the universal church, in which it is the practice
to lose no time and run in haste to administer baptism to infant children
who cannot be made alive in Christ without it.[244] The Christians of
Carthage even call baptism "salvation," because without it, according to
earliest apostolic tradition, no one could attain eternal life. Nor let
anyone say, as the Pelagians do, that for unbaptized infants there is
some intermediate state between damnation and the Kingdom of God.
Augustine rules out any tertiary place of eternal abode; it is a case either
of eternal life or eternal death. But the desire for baptism can take the
place of baptism, just as the good thief was admitted to paradise by Our
Lord after he had undergone a change of heart. And unbaptized persons
who die confessing Christ gain the same efficacy for the remission of
sins as if they were washed in the sacred font of baptism. For Christ not
only said, "Except a man be born of water and of the Spirit, he cannot
enter into the Kingdom of God" (Jno. 3:5), but also, "Whoever will
confess me before men, him will I confess also before my Father who is
in heaven" (Matt. 10:32).[245]

Although there were some who seemed to think that children ought
not to be baptized until the eighth day, Augustine appeals to Cyprian's
assertion that a child may be properly baptized immediately after its
birth. The sacrament of baptism is undoubtedly the sacrament of regeneration; so, just as the man who has never lived cannot die, and he
who has never died cannot rise again, so he who has never been born
cannot be born again. Therefore, no one who has not been born can
possibly have been born again in his father.[246] It follows that the effect of
baptism is a spiritual regeneration consisting in the remission of every
sin and its punishment, and an infusion of sanctifying grace. His grace
works (within us) our illumination and justification, for by it he engrafts
into his body even baptized infants, who are not yet able to imitate anyone.
In baptism a full forgiveness of sins takes place; indeed, if a man were
to quit this present life immediately after his baptism, there would be
nothing at all left to hold him liable, inasmuch as all which held him is
released.[247] But baptism is not to be repeated as often as sin is repeated,
but by its one only ministration it comes to pass that pardon is secured
to the faithful of all their sins both before and after their regeneration.[248]

So baptism is the great antidote to original sin, and what our birth imposes upon us, our new birth relieves us from. It is the great act of favor from which man's restoration begins, and in which all our guilt, both of our life from the time that we have the use of reason, provides constant occasion for the remission of sins, however great our advance in righteousness may be.[249]

Confirmation, Augustine calls the sacrament of chrism, and is holy among the class of visible signs, like baptism itself, but yet it can exist among the worst of men, wasting their life in the works of the flesh, and never destined to possess the Kingdom of God. So a distinction must be made between the visible sacrament which can exist with good and bad both, and the invisible unction of charity, which is the peculiar property of the good. In receiving the anointing chrism, the sign of the cross is made upon the forehead, nor is the sacrament of confirmation (or any other) properly received without it. While the sacrament is the visible unction, the spiritual unction is the Holy Spirit himself. Later theologians would call the chrism the remote matter, and the actual tracing of the cross upon the forehead the proximate matter. The effect of confirmation would be to receive more abundant outpouring of the Holy Spirit. Beyond these rather brief comments, Augustine does not go.[250]

The sacrament of the Eucharist is discussed at much greater length. Instituted by Christ, it is a memorial of his Passion and death. The Eucharist is the sign of unity, for the bread (which is truly Christ's body) was made from many grains of wheat joined together by water, and the wine (which is truly Christ's blood) is the result of many grapes crushed together. Through the accidents of bread and wine the Lord wished to entrust to us his Body and Blood which he poured out for the remission of sins. In this way we have a share in the sufferings of Our Lord, in order that we should retain a sweet and profitable memory of the fact that his flesh was wounded and crucified for us.[251] Before the coming of Christ, the flesh and blood of this sacrifice were foreshadowed in the animals slain; in the Passion of Christ the types were fulfilled by the true sacrifice; after the ascension of Christ, this sacrifice is commemorated in the sacrament.[252] Thus, Apostle Paul was able to preach the Lord Jesus Christ significantly, in one way by his tongue, in another by epistle, but perhaps most especially by the sacrament of Christ's body and blood.[253]

In the sixth chapter of John's Gospel, Christ promises to give his body and blood as spiritual food to those who believe in him, not the body which those who heard him speak saw, but a mystery which was visibly celebrated but spiritually understood.[254] To take the words literally, the saint says, would be a crime or a vice; therefore, it is a figure of speech enjoining us to have a share in the sufferings of Our Lord, and that we should retain a sweet and profitable memory of the fact that his flesh was wounded and crucified for us.[255] And so it is the body of Christ which helps us to become the body of Christ, and through the body of Christ to live by the Spirit of Christ. "O mystery of piety! O sign of unity! O bond of charity," Augustine exclaims, after echoing Paul and the *Didache* in comparing the bread composed of many grains of wheat with the many members who go to make up Christ's body, the church.[256] So, while Christ is really present in the Eucharist under the species of bread and wine (or becomes present when the words of institution are spoken) this can really be understood only by the faithful, even though the Real Presence does not depend upon the belief of the faithful.

The reception of the Eucharist is necessary for everyone, even infants, because it is rightly called the sacrament of *life.* Those who do not receive are literally *lifeless,* nor should there be a quibble about Our Lord's words when he says, "Except you eat"—he means everybody, not just those who happened to be listening to him at the time. His words include everybody, and that means infants as well; they are to communicate when sufficiently able. Augustine says that we ought to receive daily, which indicates that in his time it was certainly possible to receive Holy Communion every day.[257] But not to commune worthily is to invite condemnation as the apostle Paul warned the Corinthians.

Fasting preceded the reception of the sacrament, in spite of the fact that the first Eucharist was not received in this way; but is the whole church to be blamed because the sacrament is always received fasting, Augustine asks? Christ's flesh is for the life of the world, by which the faithful themselves become the body and blood of Christ through communion with him. What results is a pledge of resurrection and eternal life, and in this life the fostering of unity, unity between Christ and the individual, and between the various members of Christ's body—the church.[258]

The Mass is a true sacrifice, for while Christ was offered in his Person only once, yet in the sacred mysteries, he is offered for mankind not only on every Easter Sunday but every day. The sacraments have a real resemblance to the mysteries which they represent, and this one represents the sacrifice of Christ on the cross. As both Priest and Sacrifice, he designed a daily sign of this in the sacrifice of the church, which, being his body, learns to offer herself through him.[259] We have already seen that this sacrifice was foreshadowed in the Old Testament, all of which has for its purpose our drawing near to God. Augustine, as we might expect, does not fail to allude to Melchisedech and Malachi's prophecy.

Finally, the saint shows that the holy sacrifice can benefit the souls of the dead when offered by the piety of their friends. Thus, the

Mass serves a propitiatory and impetrative function in addition to being a Eucharistic sacrifice and vehicle of worship. More than this Augustine does not say, for while his doctrine of the Eucharist is complete in its major outlines, he does not give us an elaborated doctrine on this subject.

"Let us not heed those who deny that the Church of God can remit all sins," we read in *On the Christian Warfare*. "Failing to recognize in Peter the 'rock' these unhappy souls have accordingly lost possession of the keys; they are unwilling to believe that the keys of the kingdom of heaven have been given to the Church." Thus it is clear that Christ has given the church the power of remitting or retaining sins, and that this power extends to all sins of any kind committed after baptism. Some think that they only sin against the Holy Spirit when, having been washed in the laver of regeneration in the church and receiving the Spirit, they plunge themselves afterwards into any deadly sin such as adultery, murder, or apostasy, but even these grave sins can be forgiven by the church as long as there is repentance.[260] And in the act of repentance, where a crime has been committed of such a nature as to cut off the sinner from the body of Christ, we are not to take account so much of the measure of time as of the measure of sorrow.[261]

But if all sins can be forgiven by the church when there is true repentance, what about the so-called sin against the Holy Spirit? In writing to Boniface, Augustine explains that Christ did not mean every sin committed against the Holy Spirit by deed or word, but a particular sin—a hardness of heart persisted in until the end of this life, by which a man refuses to accept remission for his sins in the unity of the body of Christ, to which the Holy Spirit gives life.[262] And in writing to Macedonius, Augustine observes that

Vice sometimes makes such inroads among men that, even after they have done penance and have been readmitted to the Sacrament of the altar, they commit the same or more grievous sins, yet God makes His sun to rise even on such men and gives His gifts of life and health as lavishly as He did before their fall. And, although, that same opportunity of penance is not again granted to them in the Church, God does not forget to exercise His patience toward them. . . . It may, therefore, be a careful and useful enactment that the opportunity of that very humble penance be granted only once in the Church, lest that remedy, by becoming common, be less helpful to sick souls, for it is now more effective by being more respected. Yet, who would dare to say to God: "Why do you pardon this man a second time when he has been caught again in the snare of sin after his first penance?"[263]

The ancient church imposed public penance for serious crimes which caused public scandal, but lesser sins were remitted without public penance—through prayer and humility.

Repentance is a true virtue by which man hates sin and is sorry for the insult to God which he intends to repair by some sort of satisfaction. No matter how great the crime, it may be remitted by Holy Church provided one has contrition, which when perfect at once makes a man righteous and can even remove the total punishment due to sin; there is also attrition, which arises from the fear of the punishment incurred and is likewise a good act sufficient for absolution, as long as the desire for sinning does not remain. "For that man is under the law," says Augustine, "who, from fear of the punishment which the law threatens, and not from any love for righteousness, obliges himself to abstain from the work of sin, without being as yet free and removed from the desire of sinning. For it is in his very will that he is guilty, whereby he would prefer (if it were possible) that what he dreads should not exist, in order that he might freely do what he secretly desires.[264] For it is one thing to do good with the will of doing good, and another thing to be so inclined by the will to do evil, that one would actually do it if it could be allowed without punishment. For thus assuredly he is sinning within in his will itself who abstains from sin not by will but by fear."[265]

In the *Commentary on the Gospel of Saint John,* Augustine reminds us that man is compelled to endure, even when his sins are forgiven him, although it was the first sin that caused his falling into such misery. For the penalty is more protracted than the fault, lest the fault should be accounted small, were the penalty to end with itself. On this account it is also, either for the demonstration of our debt of misery, or for the amendment of our passing life, or for the exercise of the necessary patience, that man is kept through time in the penalty, even when he is no longer held by his sin as liable to everlasting damnation.[266] So after absolution, there still remains the obligation of satisfying God's justice.

From the foregoing it is clear that penance is necessary for all, especially those who have sinned seriously, while venial sins can be blotted out through charity, prayer, and good works. Just to say the Lord's Prayer, and especially the line "Forgive us our debts" obliterates the sins of the day. All of us who remain in the weakness of this life commit daily sins, but they are also daily remitted to those who pray in faith and work in mercy.[267] Once again, as in the case of the Eucharist, Augustine contents himself with the main topics of the doctrine of penance, without engaging in elaborate detail.

Augustine says little if anything about extreme unction as a sacrament, and so we turn now to Holy Orders, which he treats in much more detail. In *On the Good of Marriage,* the ordination of clergy, we are told, takes place to form a congregation of people, and even if the congregation does not follow the clergy, there remains in the ordained persons the Sacrament of Ordination; and if, for any fault, any be removed from his office, he will not be without the sacrament of the Lord once for all set upon him, although it continues to his condemnation.[268] The inference from this statement is that the clergy somehow are set apart from the congregations they serve, and that the ceremony of ordination does imprint some special character upon the priest which remains with him throughout life. Augustine does not discuss the three orders of bishops, priests, and deacons, nor does he seem to allude to minor orders, nor discuss the proper mode of ordination of the clergy, nor clerical celibacy as understood in his day, nor the special position of virgins and widows, nor the effects which ordination produces—an increase in grace, an imprint, and the special spiritual powers attached to the priesthood.

Since the Lord came by invitation to a marriage, there is good reason to inquire precisely why it is a good, and why a sacrament. Marriage is more than having children, although that is one of the reasons for it, but it is a natural society itself in a difference of two sexes. Marriages have this good also, Augustine continues, that carnal or youthful incontinence, although it be faulty, is brought to an honest use in begetting children, in order that out of the evil of lust, the marriage union may bring to pass some good. Where the people of God are concerned, the sanctity of the sacrament makes it illegal for a woman who has been separated from her husband to be married to another while her husband is still living. The only thing which can loosen the marriage bond is the death of either the husband or wife.[269]

In marriage, three nuptial blessings should be the object of our love: offspring, faithfulness, and the sacramental bond. Offspring should not merely be born, but born again, for the child is born to punishment if he is not renewed in eternal life. Fidelity should transcend that which unbelievers observe toward one another in their ardent love of the flesh. The sacramental bond, which is lost neither by divorce nor by adultery, should be guarded by husband and wife with concord and chastity.[270]

And God forbid that the nuptial bond should be regarded as broken between those who have by mutual consent agreed to observe a perpetual abstinence from the use of carnal concupiscence; that only makes it a firmer one, whereby they have exchanged pledges together, which will have to be kept by an especial endearment and concord—not by the voluptuous links of bodies, but by the voluntary affections of souls. Therefore, Mary was truly the wife of Joseph because of her first betrothal, although he had no carnal knowledge of her, nor was destined to have.[271] Therefore, even when by common consent married persons maintain their continence, the relations can still remain, and can still be called one of wedlock, inasmuch as, although there is no connection between the sexes of the body, there is the keeping of the affections of the mind.[272]

Matrimony effects an indissoluble bond. Augustine is quite clear on this point, especially in his *On Marriage and Concupiscence* where he says:

It is certainly not fecundity only, the fruit of which consists of offspring, nor chastity only, whose bond is fidelity, but also a certain sacramental bond in marriage which is recommended to believers in wedlock. Accordingly it is enjoined by the apostle: "Husbands, love your wives, even as Christ also loved the Church" (Eph. 5:25). Of this bond the substance undoubtedly is this, that the man and the woman who are joined together in matrimony should remain inseparable as long as they live; and that it should be unlawful for one consort to be parted from the other, except for the cause of fornication. . . . And whosoever does this is held to be guilty of adultery by the law of the gospel; though not by this world's rule, which allows a divorce between the parties, without even the allegation of guilt, and the contraction of other nuptial engagements—a concession which, the Lord tells us, even the holy Moses extended to the people of Israel, because of the hardness of their hearts. . . . Thus between the conjugal pair, as long as they live, the nuptial bond has a permanent obligation, and can be cancelled neither by separation nor by union with another.[273]

Although the sacrament of matrimony carries with it an exclusive bond, we read in the Old Testament that polygamy was sometimes tolerated. It was a work of piety, Augustine says, to beget sons in the carnal sense, but this did not allow a woman to have several husbands even to raise up a large family.[274] However, all of this should be catalogued under "concessions extended because of the hardness of their hearts." As for second marriages (or several, for that matter), they are neither to be condemned nor condoned, we are informed in *On the Good of Widowhood*.[275]

Marriage was instituted by God, and was blessed by him, so that it can hardly be the cause of sin, although sin is transmitted in the natural birth, and atoned for in the new birth. Thus, the Holy Virgin was truly married, even though she always remained a virgin. Therefore, in the widowed state and in virginal continence the excellence of a greater gift is sought for, and when this has been deliberately chosen and offered in the form of a vow, to enter into marriage, or even to wish to marry is a matter of condemnation. So marriage is good, is a sacrament, but virginity is to be preferred.[276] It is indeed true that original sin is perpetuated as long as parents have offspring, but to condemn marriage for this (as Julian of Eclanum did) is simply to make the old Gnostic error of supposing that the root of sin lies in the flesh. The marriage of Christians is lawful and just, despite the fact that the contracting parties bring into the world children of the world who need the laver of regeneration.

THE LAST THINGS

In the twenty-first chapter of *The City of God* the saint tells us that the soul is so connected with the body that it succumbs to great pain and withdraws, for the structure of our members and vital parts is so infirm that it cannot bear up against that violence which causes great or extreme agony. But in the life to come this connection of soul and body is of such a kind that, as it is dissolved by no lapse of time, so neither is it burst asunder by any pain. Death will be eternal, since the soul will neither be able to enjoy God and live, nor to die and escape the pains of the body. The first death drives the soul from the body against its will; the second death holds the soul in the body against its will.[277] Souls after quitting the body are judged before they come to that final judgment to which they must submit when their bodies are restored to them, and are either tormented or glorified in the very same flesh wherein they once lived here on earth. All of this is clearly set forth in the parable of the poor man who was carried to Abraham's bosom, and the rich man who suffered torment in hell.

All souls, when they leave this world, have their different receptions. The good have joy; the evil, torment. But when the resurrection takes place, both the joy of the good will be fuller, and the torment of the wicked heavier, when they shall be tormented in the body. Rest, which is given immediately after death, every one, if worthy of it, receives when he dies.[278] During the time that intervenes between a man's death and final resurrection, the soul dwells in a hidden retreat where it enjoys rest or suffers affliction, in proportion to the merit it has earned by the life it led on earth.

The souls of the dead are benefited by the piety of their living friends, who offer the sacrifice of the Mediator, or give alms in the church on their behalf. But these services are of advantage only to those who during their lives have earned such merit that services of this kind can help them.[279]

In referring to those who are to be saved, yet so as by fire (1 Cor. 3:15), Augustine at the same time prays that he may stand in no need of the cleansing fire, which is hardly to be thought lightly of since it will be more grievous than anything that man can suffer in this life whatsoever. Temporary punishments are suffered by some in this life only, but others after death, by others both now and then, but all of them before that last and strictest judgment. But of those who suffer temporary punishments after death, all are not doomed to those everlasting pains which are to follow that judgment.[280]

The notion of purgatorial fire is not to be taken too literally, it symbolizes the cleansing which must take place for those who have loved the perishable things of this world, and it is in proportion to how much or little sinners have loved these created things. And it is clear that such people can be helped by the suffrages of the faithful. Even the book of Maccabees in the Old Testament makes allusion to this, although the practice of the entire church is of no small authority.[281] And let no one imagine that there are no purgatorial pains before that final and dreadful judgment. Yet even the eternal fire will be proportioned to the deserts of the wicked, so that to some it will be more, and to others less painful, whether this result be accomplished by a variation in the temperature of the fire itself, graduated to every one's merit, or whether it be that the heat remains the same, but that all do not feel it with equal intensity of torment.[282]

Now there are some, indeed many, who make moan over the eternal punishment and perpetual, unintermitted torments of those who are lost, and they say that they do not really believe this. But one must remember that when we speak of God's wrath, this does not mean any disturbed feeling in the mind of God, but it is rather the condemnation of the wicked which they have brought upon themselves. The punishment cannot be assuaged because the condemnation cannot be assuaged, and even though God's wrath remains, his tender mercies likewise remain, which in these cases are of no effect.[283]

Even immaterial spirits may, in some extraordinary way, be really pained by the punishment of material fire, since the spirits of men, which also are certainly immaterial, are both contained in material members of their bodies now, and in the world to come will be indissolubly united to their own bodies. But that hell, which is also called a lake of fire and brimstone, will be material fire, and will torment the bodies of the damned, whether men or devils—the solid bodies of the one, the aerial bodies of the others. One fire certainly will be the lot of both, for that is the way the Truth has declared it.[284]

From the foregoing, it is likewise clear that Augustine believes that the pains of the damned will be eternal, consisting as they do in the loss of the vision of God and the pain of sense, and that both men's souls and the demons themselves will undergo torment. In the life to come, the connection between soul and body is of such kind that it is not dissolved by any lapse of time, nor burst asunder by any pain; the soul cannot live to enjoy God for whom it was created, nor die and escape the pains of the body. The crimes which are punished with these most protracted sufferings, the saint tells us, are perpetrated in a very brief space of time. But the pains of punishment do not occupy the same short time in which the offense was committed, for murder, adultery, sacrilege, or any other crime must be measured by the enormity of the injury or wickedness. Actually eternal life and eternal death are correlative, and to say in one and the same sense that life eternal shall be endless, while eternal punishment shall come to an end is the height of absurdity.[285]

After the resurrection, however, when the final, universal judgment has been completed, there will be two kingdoms, each with its own distinct boundaries, the one Christ's, the other the Devil's; the one consisting of the good, the other of the bad—both, however, consisting of angels and men. The former shall have no will, the latter no power to sin, and neither shall have any power to choose death; but while the former shall live truly and happily in eternal life, the latter shall drag a miserable existence in eternal death without the power of dying; for the life and the death shall both be without end. But among the former there shall be degrees of happiness, one being more preeminently happy than another; and among the latter there shall be degrees of misery, one being more endurably miserable than another.[286] So the degrees of blessedness or damnation will vary with each individual. The mildest punishment of all will fall upon those who had added no actual sin to the original sin they brought with them, and as for the rest who have added such actual sins, the punishment of each will be the more tolerable in the next world, according as his iniquity has been less in this world.[287] Mitigation of these rewards or punishments will be impossible.

Various signs will precede the end of the world. Christ will not come to judge the living and the dead unless Antichrist, his adversary, first comes to seduce those who are dead in soul, although their seduction is a result of God's secret judgment already passed.[288] The dead will rise with their same bodies—the same body which is seen and felt, which needs to eat and drink in order to live, which becomes sick and suffers pain—but there will be no deformity, no infirmity, no languor, no corruption. But what about those consumed by beasts or fire, or have been dissolved into dust or ashes, or have decomposed into water, or evaporated into the air? For the resuscitation and reanimation of our bodies, the omnipotence of the Creator can recall all of these wayward parts.[289]

If a statue of some soluble metal were either melted by fire, or broken into dust, or reduced to a shapeless mass, says Augustine, and a sculptor wished to restore it from the same quantity of metal, it would make no difference to the completeness of the work what part of the statue any given particle of the material was assigned, as long as the restored statue contained all the material of the original one; so God, the Artificer of marvelous and unspeakable power, shall with marvelous and unspeakable rapidity restore our body, using up the whole material of which it originally consisted. Nor will it affect the completeness of its restoration whether hairs returns to hairs, and nails to nails, or whether the part of these that had perished be changed into flesh, and called to take its place in another part of the body, the great Artist taking careful heed that nothing shall be unbecoming or out of place.[290]

Augustine says every soul is subject to two judgments—when it quits this world, and when the resurrection takes place.[291] The first judgment has reference to the soul and is a personal or individual judgment, whereas the judgment at the end of the world is general, final, and is passed upon the body as well as the soul. "Were you really not aware of this?" Vincentius Victor is asked, implying that Augustine is merely stating what the Christian tradition at that time had come to believe.[292]

In Sermon No. 259 Augustine tells us that the eighth day spoken
of in the Scriptures signifies the new life at the end of this world;
the seventh day, the future rest of the saints on this earth. For the Lord
will reign on earth with his saints, as the Scripture says, and he will
have here his Church into which no wicked person will enter, which
will be purged and cleansed from all contagions of iniquity. But any
millenarian idea is explicitly rejected in *The City of God* (No. 20) in
commenting on the evangelist John, who

> . . . has spoken of these two resurrections in the book which is called the
> Apocalypse, but in such a way that some Christians do not understand the
> first of the two, and so construe the passage into ridiculous fancies. For the
> apostle John says in the foresaid book, "And I saw an angel come down
> from heaven. . . . Those, who on the strength of this passage, have sus-
> pected that the first resurrection is future and bodily, have been moved,
> among other things, specially by the number of a thousand years, as if it
> were a fit thing that the saints should thus enjoy a kind of Sabbath-rest
> during that period, a holy leisure after the labors of the six thousand years
> since man was created, . . . And this opinion would not be objectionable,
> if it were believed that the joys of the saints in that Sabbath shall be
> spiritual, and consequent on the presence of God; *for I myself, too, once
> held this opinion.*[293]

God alone is the object of our beatitude: "Thou hast made us for
Thyself, and our hearts are restless until they find rest in Thee."[294]
In the *City of God,* we read that God is the source of our happiness
and the very end of all our aspirations. We elect him, whom, by neglect,
we lost. We offer him our allegiance—for "allegiance" and "religion" are,
at root, the same. We pursue him with our love so that when we reach
him we may rest in perfect happiness in him who is our goal.[295]
Blessedness consists in two things: to enjoy the unchangeable good,
which is God, without interruption; and to be delivered from all doubt,
knowing with certainty that it will eternally abide in the same enjoyment.[296]

Our felicity will be great because it will be tainted with no evil,
will lack no good, and will afford leisure for the praises of God, who
will be all in all. He will be the end of our desires who will be seen
without end, loved without cloy, praised without weariness. There we
shall rest and see, see and love, love and praise. And this will be in
the end which is without end.[297] And although we now see "through
a glass darkly" the reward of our vision will be the face of God, not a
bodily face but rather his manifestation. And whether our bodies are in
motion or in rest, they will certainly be seemly, says Augustine, for
nothing unseemly will be admitted; the body will be where the spirit wills
it, and the spirit shall will nothing which is unbecoming to either spirit
or body.[298]

In the Kingdom of Christ, whose boundaries will be distinct after the final resurrection, the blessed will not have the desire to sin, nor will they be able to; the last state of the blessed will be the felicity of perseverance, not to be able to forsake the good. Beatitude is thus eternal and cannot be lost. For how can that be truly called blessed, Augustine asks, which has no assurance of being so eternally, and is either in ignorance of the truth, and blind to the misery that is approaching, or, knowing it, is in misery and fear?[299] Both the good angels and the blessed share this most certain truth: that they will never fall, and indeed we have already seen that eternal blessedness is parallel to eternal misery in their unchanging, everlasting duration.

Some claim that everyone will rise with the same stature that he died in; Augustine will not dispute this, if it is understood that our glorified bodies will have no deformity, infirmity, or corruption. God himself, the Author of virtue, will be the reward of the blessed, for as there is nothing greater or better, God has promised himself. Then shall we be all equal, and the first as the last, and the last as the first; because that denarius is life eternal, and in the life eternal all will be equal. For although through diversity of attainments *(meritorum)* the saints will shine—some more, some less—yet as to this respect, the gift of eternal life, it will be equal to all. But the many mansions of which the Lord spoke point to the different grades of merit in that one eternal life. This is paralleled by the different degrees of misery suffered by those eternally condemned.

THE CITY OF GOD

To sum it all up, then: two cities have been formed by two loves: the earthly by the love of self, even to the contempt of God; the heavenly by the love of God, even to the contempt of self. The former, in a word, glories in itself, the latter in the Lord. For the one seeks glory from men; but the greatest glory of the other is God, the witness of conscience. The one lifts up its head, in its own glory; the other says to its God, "Thou art my glory, and the lifter up of mine head" (Ps. 3:3). In the one, the princes and the nations its subdues are ruled by the love of ruling; in the other, the princes and the subjects serve one another in love, the latter obeying, while the former take thought for all. The one delights in its own strength, represented in the persons of its rulers; the other says to its God, "I will love Thee, O Lord, my strength" (Ps. 18:1).[300]

Private morality, church and state, and the philosophy of history are thus all wrapped up together, so it will be necessary to separate each of these strands and examine each singly. Beginning with morality, then, the ethical man is he who loves God, and he who loves God loves also

beauty, truth, justice, and goodness. To love God is to unite our will with
his, and to make an act of self-surrender by which we give up our selfish
interests to serve him who is our Creator and Lord. But to love God, and
thus to fulfill his Law, requires grace—God's free gift to every man who
asks it. This necessitates the renunciation of sin, for sin is anything which
separates us from God, and from our fellowmen. Sin is a defect rather
than something positive; it is a nothingness, a blemish, a deficiency, a
non-being, and for this reason it stands directly opposite to him who is
love, truth, and ultimate being. Thus, ethics merges with religion, for
there can be no ethical behavior which is not grounded in God, and the
purpose of ethics is to lead us to God and ultimate blessedness with him
throughout all eternity. Then Augustine sums all this up in the famous
line: "Love, and do what you will."[301]

The human race is therefore distributed into two parts, the one
consisting of those who live according to man, the other of those who
live according to God. The society of the good is predestined to rule
with God forever and ever, while the society of the evil is destined for
everlasting punishment. The City of God is consequently at war with
the city of this world until the end of time. Does Saint Augustine
equate the City of God with the Catholic church? There is a close
parallel, but actually the City of God includes all those from the
time of Abel who have lived righteous lives. It also includes the good
angels and those who are yet to come who will be incorporated in the
mystical body of Christ. Is this to say that the state is equivalent to
the city of this world? The saint is under no illusion about the
fundamental nature of empires, including the Roman Empire which so
mercilessly persecuted the early Christians. Once again, the equation is
not exact, but the cities of this world all look to their original founder
Cain and take their inspiration from the first murderer. Yet there may be
many righteous persons who are in the employ of the state, while there
are churchmen who live for selfish and ignoble purposes and are more
properly identified with the world. Nonetheless, the true Christian will
serve the cause of Christ in his church, and while he is in the world,
will try not at the same time to be of the world. The church is
fundamentally Christian, the world fundamentally secular, and both strive
with each other until the final day. This concept of church and state was
to have enormous consequences for the Middle Ages when it helped to
shape the thinking of medieval Papacy and the Empire.

All of this involves us in a philosophy of history which is enucleated
at considerable length in the closing books of *The City of God*.
Augustine engages in a long analysis of Jewish history and with it,
the secular state—the city of Cain—which has come into being because
administering a kind of rough justice. The saints themselves must obey
of sin, but which nevertheless prevents greater sin and even chaos by

the secular ruler because he holds his authority from God and acts to restrain evil. The state itself, however, is under condemnation, and at the end of the world, the rulers of this world will have their part in outer darkness and eternally with Satan, who is their chief. Until that time, both kingdoms are in the building and are nearing their completion. The City of God realizes itself in the Mystical Body of Christ, which (like the tower in Hermas) embraces all the faithful, until that final day when the work is completed, and "there will be but one Christ loving Himself."[302]

NOTES

The text is in Migne, *Patrologia Latina,* vols. 32-47 (*see* Bibliography).
1. *The City of God* 10. 3.
2. *On the Gospel of Saint John* 106. 4; *On the Usefulness of Believing* 16. 34.
3. *The City of God* 11. 2.
4. *On the Gospel of Saint John* 24. 1.
5. *The City of God* 21. 8.
6. *Concerning Faith of Things Not Seen* 7. 10.
7. *Confessions* 7. 10.
8. *On the Gospel of Saint John* 26. 4.
9. *Reply to Faustus the Manichaean* 18. 4, 6; 19. 11.
10. *Sermons* No. 126.
11. *Expositions on the Psalms* 56. 9.
12. *The City of God* 22. 5.
13. *Expositions on the Psalms* 90. 2.
14. *On the Creed (A Sermon to the Catechumens)* 1. 6.
15. *Expositions on the Psalms* 88. 2.
16. *On Faith and the Creed* 10. 21.
17. *Sermon to the People of the Church of Caesarea* 6.
18. *Against the Epistle of Manichaeus Called Fundamental* 4. 5.
19. *Letter to Vincent* No. 93. (ca. 408).
20. *Against the Epistle of Manichaeus Called Fundamental,* 4. 5
21. *Sermons,* No. 295. 2.
22. *Letter to Generosus* No. 53 (ca. 400).
23. *Against Two Letters of the Pelagians* 2. 3.
24. *Against the Epistle of Manichaeus Called Fundamental,* 5. 6.
25. *Against Two Letters of the Pelagians,* 2. 3.
26. *Letter to Januarius* No. 54.
27. *On the Harmony of the Gospels* 1. 35.
28. *The City of God* 17. 6.
29. *On the Harmony of the Gospels,* 2. 21.
30. *The City of God* 18. 38.
31. *Letter to Jerome,* No. 28.
32. *Letter to Jerome,* No. 82.
33. *Reply to Faustus the Manichaean,* 11. 5.
34. *On the Harmony of the Gospels* 2. 12.
35. Cf. *To Orosius, Against the Priscillianists and the Origenists* 9. 12.

36. *On Genesis* 2. 9.
37. *Reply to Faustus the Manichaean* 33. 6.
38. *On Christian Doctrine* 2. 8.
39. Ibid., 2. 8.
40. Ibid., 3. 27.
41. *Against Julian* 2. 10.
42. *Against the Epistle of Manichaeus Called Fundamental* 5. 6.
43. *The City of God* 16. 2.
44. *Against Julian* 1. 7; 2. 10.
45. *Sermon*, No. 141. 2.
46. *Confessions* 7. 10.
47. *On Genesis* 5. 16.
48. *On the Gospel of Saint John,* 106. 4.
49. Cf. Ludwig Ott, *Fundamentals of Catholic Dogma,* edited in English by James Canon Bastible, D.D., translated from the German by Patrick Lynch, third printing (St. Louis, Mo.: B. Herder, 1958).
50. *Confessions* 11. 4.
51. *On the Trinity* 7. 5.
52. Ibid., 5. 5; 6.4, 7.
53. *On the Nature of the Good* 22.
54. *The City of God* 5. 10.
55. Ibid., 22. 29.
56. *Sermons,* No. 117. 3.
57. *On the Trinity* 5. 1.
58. Ibid., 8. 3.
59. *The City of God* 12. 7.
60. Ibid., 5. 10.
61. *On the Spirit and the Letter* 33. 58.
62. *Against Julian* 4. 8.
63. *On Faith, Hope, and Love (Enchiridion)* 103.
64. *On the Predestination of the Saints* 8. 14.
65. *On Rebuke and Grace* 7. 13.
66. *On the Gift of Perseverance* 7. 15
67. Ibid., 14. 35.
68. Ibid., 17. 42.
69. *On Rebuke and Grace* 10. 28.
70. *On the Gift of Perseverance* 17. 41
71. *On the Gospel of Saint John* 86. 2.
72. *On Rebuke and Grace* 7. 12.
73. *On the Predestination of the Saints* 10. 19.
74. *On the Soul and Its Origin* 4. 11.
75. *On Faith, Hope, and Love* (Enchiridion) 95.
76. *On Rebuke and Grace* 10. 27.
77. *On the Gift of Perseverance* 13. 33
78. *On Rebuke and Grace* 13. 42.
79. *On the Merits and Remission of Sins and on the Baptism of Infants* 2. 17.
80. *On the Soul and Its Origins* 4. 11
81. *Against Julian* 3. 18.
82. *On the Gift of Perseverance* 11. 25.
83. *On the Trinity* 3. 11
84. Ibid., 1. 4.
85. *On the Gospel of Saint John* 14. 7.
86. *On the Trinity* 15. 14.

87. *On the Faith and the Creed* 9. 19.
88. *Letter to Pascentius* No. 238. 2.
89. *On the Trinity* 5. 14.
90. Ibid., 15. 17.
91. Ibid., 15. 26.
92. *On Christian Doctrine* 1. 5.
93. *On the Trinity* 6. 5.
94. *The City of God* 11. 24.
95. Ibid., 11. 6.
96. Ibid., 12. 6.
97. Ibid., 22. 1.
98. *On the Gospel of Saint John* 110. 7.
99. *On Rebuke and Grace* 10. 27.
100. Ibid., 11. 32.
101. *The City of God* 12. 6.
102. *Commentary on Genesis,* passim.
103. *On Faith and the Creed* 10. 23.
104. *Letter to Jerome* No. 166. 2.
105. *On the Soul and Its Origin* 2. 3.
106. *Letter to Vitalus* No. 217. 5.
107. *On the Gospel of Saint John* 3. 4.
108. *The City of God* 14. 26.
109. *On Rebuke and Grace* 11. 29.
110. *On Faith, Hope, and Love* 104.
111. *On Rebuke and Grace* 12. 33.
112. *Against Julian* 4. 3
113. *On the Trinity* 15. 18.
114. *Man's Perfection in Righteousness* 8. 19.
115. *Ten Homilies on the Epistle of Saint John to the Parthians* 8. 1.
116. *Letter to Consentius* No. 120. 1.
117. *On the Gospel of Saint John* 26. 2.
118. *Sermons,* No. 126. 4, 5.
119. *Confessions* 7. 10.
120. *The City of God* 11. 2.
121. *Reply to Faustus the Manichaean* 17. 3.
122. *Letters* No. 194. 3.
123. *On Original Sin* 24. 28.
124. *Against Two Letters of the Pelagians* 1. 7.
125. *Exposition on the Psalms* 72. 32.
126. *Man's Perfection in Righteousness* 8. 19.
127. *On Faith, Hope, and Love* 117.
128. *On the Morals of the Catholic Church* 1.25.
129. *On Christian Doctrine* 3. 10.
130. *On Catechizing the Uninstructed* 4. 7.
131. *On Care to be Had for the Dead* 15. 18.
132. *On the Gospel of Saint John* 11. 3; 118. 5
133. *Our Lord's Sermon on the Mount* 1. 12.
134. *Letter to Jerome* No. 167:24.
135. *Two Souls, Against the Manichaeans* 11. 15; *Disputation Against Fortunatus* 17.
136. *On the Gospel of Saint John* 49. 2.
137. *On Marriage and Concupiscence* 1. 26.
138. *On the Merits and Remission of Sins and on the Baptism of Infants* 34.

139. *Against Two Letters of the Pelagians* 1. 2.
140. *On Marriage and Concupiscence* 1. 23.
141. Ibid., 2. 26.
142. *On Rebuke and Grace* 10. 28.
143. *On Marriage anad Concupiscence* 1. 24.
144. *On the Soul and Its Origin* 1. 9.
145. Ibid., 4. 11.
146. *On the Merits and Remission of Sins, and on the Baptism of Infants* 2. 5.
147. *Against Julian* 4. 3.
148. *On Faith, Hope, and Love* 32.
149. *On Grace and Free Will* 5. 12; 6. 14; 7. 16.
150. *On Corruption and Grace* 11. 31.
151. *On the Gift of Perseverance* 19. 50.
152. *On the Spirit and the Letter* 27. 48.
153. Ibid., 19. 32.
154. *On Faith, Hope, and Love* 117.
155. *On Grace and Free Will* 14. 29.
156. *On the Predestination of the Saints* 5. 10.
157. Cf. *Confessions* 2. 7.
158. *On the Merits and Remission of Sins, and on the Baptism of Infants* 2. 33.
159. *On the Creed: A Sermon to the Catechumens* 1. 7.
160. *On the Merits and Remission of Sins, and on the Baptism of Infants* 2. 6.
161. *On the Spirit and the Letter* 35. 63.
162. *On Nature and Grace* 36. 42.
163. *Man's Perfection in Righteousness* 21. 44.
164. *On Nature and Grace* 26. 29.
165. *On Rebuke and Grace* 12. 38.
166. *On the Gift of Perseverance* 9. 21.
167. Ibid., 13. 33.
168. *Confessions* 2. 7.
169. *Sermons* No. 99.
170. *Expositions on the Psalms* 102. 16.
171. *On the Merits and Remission of Sins, and on the Baptism of Infants* 2. 19.
172. *On Faith, Hope, and Love* 32.
173. *On Grace and Free Will* 17. 33.
174. *On the Grace of Christ and on Original Sin* 25. 26.
175. *On Grace and Free Will* 5. 12.
176. *On the Proceedings of Pelagius* 1. 3.
177. *On Rebuke and Grace* 12. 34.
178. Ibid., 11. 32.
179. *On Faith, Hope, and Love* 98.
180. *On the Gift of Perseverance* 9. 22.
181. *On the Spirit and the Letter* 33. 58.
182. *On the Gospel of Saint John* 26. 4.
183. *The City of God* 5. 9.
184. *On the Gospel of Saint John* 53. 6.
185. *On Grace and Free Will* 13. 25.
186. *Letter to Innocent* No. 177.
187. *Letters* No. 217, No. 194.
188. *Exposition on the Psalms* 70. 2.
189. *On Nature and Grace* 4. 4.
190. *On the Gospel of Saint John* 3. 9; 86. 2.

191. *On the Proceedings of Pelagius* 14. 33.
192. *On Original Sin* 24. 28.
193. *Against Two Letters of the Pelagians* 1. 18.
194. *On the Gift of Perseverance* 13. 33; 21. 55.
195. Ibid., 16. 39.
196. *Against Julian* 5. 3.
197. *On the Grace of Christ and on Original Sin* 47. 52.
198. *On the Merits and Remission of Sins, and the Baptism of Infants* 2. 3.
199. *Against Julian* 4. 3.
200. *On the Predestination of the Saints* 3. 7.
201. *Against Julian* 6. 13.
202. *Expositions on the Psalms* 49. 2.
203. *On Catechizing the Uninstructed* 5. 9.
204. *Man's Perfection in Righteousness* 15. 33.
205. *Letter to Sixtus* No. 194. 3.
206. *Sermons* 87. 4.
207. *Expositions on the Psalms* 56. 9.
208. *On the Christian Warfare* 22. 24.
209. *On Rebuke and Grace* 11. 30.
210. *On the Christian Warfare* 22. 24.
211. *Letter to Volusianus* No. 137.
212. *On Faith, Hope, and Love* 41.
213. *On the Trinity* 15. 26.
214. Ibid., 1. 13.
215. *On Faith, Hope, and Love* 41.
216. *On the Trinity* 4. 13.
217. *On Faith, Hope, and Love* 108.
218. *On the Christian Warfare* 11. 12.
219. *On the Trinity* 13. 14.
220. *On Catechizing the Uninstructed* 4. 7.
221. *On the Trinity* 13. 14.
222. *On Original Sin* 24. 28.
223. *On Faith, Hope, and Love* 33.
224. *The City of God* 10. 20.
225. *Sermons* No. 186. 1.
226. *On Holy Virginity* 4. 4.
227. Ibid., 6. 6.
228. *On Nature and Grace* 36. 42.
229. Ibid.
230. *Letter to Marcellinus* No. 138.
231. *Reply to Faustus the Manichaean* 19. 11.
232. *Against the letters of Petilian, the Donatist* 2. 104.
233. *The City of God* 10. 5
234. *Ten Homilies on the Epistle of Saint John to the Parthians* 3. 5.
235. *Against Julian* 5. 11.
236. *Letter to Januarius* No. 54.
237. *Against the Letters of Petilian the Donatist* 2. 72.
238. *On Marriage and Concupiscence* 2. 11.
239. *Letter to Boniface* No. 98.
240. *Against the Letters of Petilian, the Donatist* 2. 35.
241. *Letter to Januarius* No. 54.
242. *On the Gospel of Saint John* 118. 5
243. *On Baptism* 5. 20.

244. *Letter to Jerome* No. 166.
245. *The City of God* 13. 7
246. *On the Merits and Remission of Sins, and the Baptism of Infants* 2. 27.
247. Ibid., 2. 28.
248. *On Marriage and Concupiscence* 1. 33.
249. *On Faith, Hope, and Love* 64.
250. *On the Gospel of Saint John* 118. 5.
251. *On Christian Doctrine* 3. 16.
252. *Reply to Faustus the Manichaean* 21. 20.
253. *On the Trinity* 3. 4.
254. *Exposition on the Psalms* 98. 9.
255. *On Christian Doctrine* 3. 16.
256. *On the Gospel of Saint John* 26. 13
257. *Sermons* No. 227.
258. *Confessions* 7. 10.
259. *The City of God* 10. 20.
260. *On the Christian Warfare* 31. 33; *Sermons* No. 71. 4.
261. *On Faith, Hope, and Love* 65.
262. *Letter to Boniface* No. 185.
263. *Letter to Macedonius* No. 153.
264. *On Nature and Grace* 57. 67
265. *Against Two Letters of the Pelagians* 1. 9.
266. *On the Gospel of Saint John* 124. 5.
267. *Against Two Letters of the Pelagians* 1. 14
268. *On the Good of Marriage* 24. 32.
269. Ibid.
270. *On Marriage and Concupiscence* 1. 17.
271. Ibid., 1. 11.
272. *On the Harmony of the Gospels* 2. 1.
273. *On Marriage and Concupiscence* 1. 10.
274. *On the Good of Marriage* 17. 19.
275. *On the Good of Widowhood* 12. 15.
276. Ibid., 9. 12.
277. *The City of God* 21. 3.
278. *On the Gospel of Saint John* 49. 10.
279. *On Faith, Hope, and Love* 109.
280. *The City of God* 21. 13.
281. *On Care to Be Had for the Dead* 1. 3.
282. *The City of God* 21. 16.
283. *On Faith, Hope, and Love* 112.
284. *The City of God* 21. 10.
285. Ibid., passim.
286. *On Faith, Hope, and Love* 111.
287. Ibid., 93.
288. *The City of God* 20. 19.
289. Ibid., 22. 20.
290. *On Faith, Hope, and Love* 89.
291. *On the Gospel of Saint John* 49. 10.
292. *On the Soul and Its Origin* 2. 4.
293. *The City of God* 20. 7.
294. *Confessions* 1. 1.
295. *The City of God* 10. 3.
296. Ibid., 11. 13.

297. Ibid., 22. 30.
298. Ibid.
299. Ibid., 12. 14.
300. Ibid., 14. 28.
301. *Ten Homilies on the Epistle of Saint John, to the Parthians* 6. 7.
302. Cf. Herbert A. Deane, *The Political and Social Ideas of St. Augustine* for a fuller account of the saint's thinking in this area, as well as G. Combès, *La Doctrine Politique de Saint Augustin,* and J. N. Figgis, *The Political Aspects of Saint Augustine's City of God.* Deane's work corrects these two classics at specific points, but does not highlight sufficiently, in my opinion, Augustine's philosophy of history. He is too harsh, I think, in censuring the church's attitude toward violence; after all, the early pacifist attitude of the church was very much influenced by the hostile policy of the state, bent on eradicating the new religion.

Bibliography

A BRIEF BIBLIOGRAPHY

HISTORIES OF DOCTRINE

Altaner, B. *Patrology.* Translated by Hilda G. Graef, Freiburg, 1958.
Baur, F. Christian. *Vorlesungen über die Christliche Dogmengeschichte.* Leipzig, 1865.
Burkill, T. A. *The Evolution of Christian Thought.* Ithaca and London, 1971.
Cayré, A. A. *Précis de Patrologie et d'Histoire de la Théologie.* Translated by H. Howitt. Paris, 1935.
Cunningham, William. *Historical Theology,* 2 vols. London, 1862.
Hagenbach, K. R. *Lehrbuch der Dogmengeschichte.* Leipzig, 1867.
Harnack, A. *Lehrbuch der Dogmengeschichte.* 3rd ed. Translated by N. Buchanan. 7 vols. 1894-1903.
Héfélé, C. J. *Histoire des Conciles.* Paris: Letouzey et Ané, 1907.
Kliefoth, Schmid, and Kahnis. *Einleitung in die Dogmengeschichte.*
————. *Lehrbuch der Dogmengeschichte,* 1859.
Loofs, F. *Leitfaden zum Studium der Dogmengeschichte.* Halle, 1890.
McGiffert, A. C. *A History of Christian Thought.* New York, 1932.
Nitzsch. *Grundriss der Christlichen Dogmengeschichte.* 1870.
Ott, Ludwig. *Fundamentals of Catholic Dogma.* St. Louis: B. Herder, 1958.
Pelikan, J. *The Christian Tradition: A History of the Development of Doctrine.* Vol. 1. The Emergency of the Catholic Tradition (100-600). Chicago, 1971.
Quasten, J. *Patrology.* 3 vols. Utrecht and Brussels, 1949.
Ritschl, A. *Der Kirchenglaube historisch genetisch dorgestellt.* 1864.
Seeberg, R. *Lehrbuch der Dogmengeschichte.* Leipzig, 1908. Translated by Charles E. Hay. Grand Rapids, Mich., 1952.
Shedd, W. G. T. *History of Christian Doctrine.* 2 vols. 3rd ed. 1877.
Sheldon, H. *History of Christian Doctrine.* 2 vols. 1886.
Strauss, D. F. *Christliche Glaubenslehre.* Tübingen and Stuttgart, 1840.
Thomasius. *Die Christliche Dogmengeschichte.* Erlangen, 1874.

Thomassin. *Theologica Dogmata*. 6 vols. Paris, 1680-89.

Tixeront, J. *Histoire des Dogmes*. Lyons, 1904. Translated by H. L. B. from the 5th Fr. ed. St. Louis, 1910.

Werner, K. *Geschichte der apologetischen und polemischen Literatur*. Schaffhausen, 1861.

Wiegand, F. *Dogmengeschichte*. 2 vols. 1912, 1919.

TEXTS AND TRANSLATIONS

Ancient Christian Writers: The Works of the Fathers in Translation. Series. Edited by J. Quasten, S.T.D., Walter J. Burghardt, S.J., S.T.D., and J. C. Plumpe, Ph.D. Westminster, Md.: The Newman Press, 1946.

The Ante-Nicene Christian Library: Translations of the Writings of the Fathers to A.D. 325. The Rev. Alexander Roberts, D.D., and James Donaldson, LL. D., editors. Edinburgh: T. & T. Clark, 1873.

The Ante-Nicene Christian Library: Translations of the Writings of the Fathers to A.D. 325. The Rev. Alexander Roberts, D.D., and James Donaldson LL.D., editors (American reprint of the Edinburgh edition). Revised and Chronologically Arranged, with Brief Prefaces and Occasional Notes by A. Cleveland Coxe, D.D. New York: Charles Scribner's Sons, 1889.

The Fathers of the Church. A New Translation. Founded by Ludwig Schopp. Editorial Director: Roy J. Deferrari, Ph.D. Washington, D.C.: The Catholic University of America Press, 1948.

Nicene and Post-Nicene Fathers of the Christian Church. Translated into English with Prologomena and Explanatory Notes under the editorial supervision of Philip Schaff, D.D., LL.D., and Henry Wace, D.D. New York: Charles Scribner's Sons, 1904.

Patrologia Graeca. J. P. Migne, editor. 168 vols. Paris, 1857-68.

Patrologia Latina. J. P. Migne, editor. 222 vols. Paris, 1844-55.

COMMENTARIES AND STUDIES

THE NEW TESTAMENT

The Synoptic Gospels

Literature on the life and teachings of Jesus is voluminous, and so, only a few specific works are cited here below. It has often been pointed out that our only primary source is still the four Gospels.

Adam, K. *The Christ of Faith*. Translated by J. Crick. New York, 1957.

Bonsirven, J. *The Theology of the New Testament.* Translated by S. F. L. Tye. Westminster, Md.: The Newman Press, 1963.

Bultmann, R. *Jesus and the Word.* Translated by Louise P. Smith and Erminie Huntress. New York, 1934.

_____. *Theology of the New Testament.* 2 vols. Translated by K. Grobel. New York, 1951-55.

Case, Shirley Jackson. *Jesus: A New Biography,* 1927.

Cullmann, Oscar. *The Christology of the New Testament.* S. C. Guthrie and C. A. M. Hall. Rev. ed. Philadelphia, 1963.

Dibelius, Martin. *Jesus.* Translated by C. B. Hedrick and F. C. Grant. Philadelphia, 1949.

Durwell, F. X. *The Resurrection: A Biblical Study.* Translated by R. Sheed. New York, 1960.

Garrigou-Lagrange, Reginald. *Christ the Savior.* Translated by B. Rose. St. Louis, 1950.

Goguel, M. *Jesus and the Origins of Christianity.* Translated by O. Wyon. New York: Harper Torchbooks, 1960.

Goodspeed, E. J. *The Life of Jesus.* New York, 1950.

Graham, A. *The Christ of Catholicism.* New York, 1947.

Guardini, R. *The Lord.* Translated by E. C. Briefs. Chicago, 1954.

Knox, John. *The Man Christ Jesus.*

Mascall, E. L. *Christ, the Christian and the Church.* London, 1946.

McCowen, Chester C. *The Search for the Real Jesus.* 1940.

Robinson, J. A. T. *Jesus and His Coming.* London, 1957.

Robinson, J. M. *A New Quest of the Historical Jesus.* Naperville, Ill., 1959.

Schweitzer, Albert. *The Quest of the Historical Jesus.* Translated by W. Montgomery. 1948.

Scheeben, M. J. *The Mysteries of Christianity.* Translated by C. Vollert. St. Louis, 1946.

Scott, E. F. *The Literature of the New Testament.* New York: Columbia University Press, 1936.

Stauffer, E. *Jesus and His Story.* Translated by R. and C. Winston. New York, 1959.

Taylor, V. *The Person of Christ in N. T. Teaching.* New York, 1958.

Tödt, H. E. *Der Menschensohn in der synoptischen Überlieferung.* Gütersloh, 1958.

Saint Paul

Amiot, F. *The Key Concepts of St. Paul.* Translated by J. Dingle. New York, 1962.

Brunot, A. *Saint Paul and His Message.* Translated by R. Matthews. New York, 1959.

Cave, S. *The Gospel of Paul.* London, 1929.

Cerfaux, L. *Christ in the Theology of St. Paul.* Translated by G. Webb and A. Walker. New York, 1959.

Deissmann, Adolph H. *Paul: A Study in Social and Religious History.* New York, 1958.

Dibelius, M. and Kuemmel W. *Paul.* Translated by F. Clark. Philadelphia, 1953.

Dodd, C. H. *The Meaning of Paul for Today.* 1920.

Fitzmyer, J. A. "Pauline Theology" in the *Jerome Biblical Commentary.* Englewood Cliffs, N.J.: Prentice-Hall, 1968.

Glover, T. R. *Paul of Tarsus.* 1925.

Haenchen, E. *Die Apostelgeschichte.* 12th ed. Göttingen, 1959.

Klausner, J. *From Jesus to Paul.* New York, 1943.

Munck, J. *Paul and the Salvation of Mankind.* Translated by F. Clarke, Richmond, 1960.

Prat, F. *Theology of St. Paul.* 2 vols. Translated by J. L. Stoddard. 10th Fr. ed. 2. Westminster, Md., 1958.

Sabatier, A. *The Apostle Paul.* London, 1891.

Sandmel, S. *The Genius of Paul.* New York, 1958.

Schweitzer, A. *Paul and His Interpreters.* 1912.

Scott, C. A. *Christianity According to St. Paul.* Cambridge: The University Press, 1932.

Stanley, D. M. *Christ's Resurrection in Pauline Soteriology.* Anal. Bibl. 13. Rome, 1961.

The Johannine Literature

The Gospel

Barrett, C. K. *The Gospel According to St. John.* London, 1955.

Bernard, J. H. "A Critical and Exegetical Commentary on the Gospel According to St. John" in *International Critical Commentary.* New York, 1929.

Bouyer, L. *The Fourth Gospel.* Westminster, Md.: The Newman Press, 1964.

Brown, Raymond E., ed. *The Gospel According to John, One to Twelve.* Anchor Bible Series, vol. 29. New York: Doubleday, 1966.

Bultmann, R. *Das Evangelium des Johannes.* 13th ed. Göttingen, 1953.

Dodd, C. H. *Historical Tradition in the Fourth Gospel.* Cambridge: The University Press, 1963.

_____. *The Interpretation of the Fourth Gospel.* Cambridge: The University Press, 1960.

Hoskyns, E. C. *The Fourth Gospel.* 2d ed. London, 1947.

Lagrange, M. J. *Etudes Bibliques.*
Lightfoot, R. H. *St. John's Gospel: A Commentary.* Oxford, 1956.
Scott, E. F. *The Fourth Gospel: Its Purpose and Theology.* Edinburgh, 1926.

The Letters

Brooke, A. E. Commentary in *International Critical Commentary.* Edinburgh, 1912.
Dodd, C. H. English translation with commentary in *Moffatt New Testament Commentary.* London, 1946.

The Apocalypse

Allo, E. B. *Saint Jean L'Apocalypse.* 3rd ed. Paris, 1933.
Beckwith, J. T. *The Apocalypse of St. John.* 1919.
Charles, R. H. "A Critical and Exegetical Commentary on the Revelation of St. John" in *International Critical Commentary.* James Hastings, ed., 2 vols. New York, 1920.
Feuillet, A. *L'Apocalypse: Etat de la Question.* Bruges, 1963.
Giet, S. *L'Apocalypse et l'histoire.* Paris, 1957.
Lohse, E. *Die Offenbarung des Johannes.* Das Neue Testament Deutsch II 8th ed. Göttingen, 1960.

THE APOSTOLIC FATHERS

Andriessen, P. "L'Apologie de Quadratus conservée sous le title d'Epître à Diognète" in *Recherches de theologie ancienne et médiévale.* 13. 1946.
Clarke, W. H. L. *First Epistle of Clement to the Corinthians.* New York: Macmillan Co., 1937.
Giet, Stanislas. *Hermas et les Pasteurs.* Paris, 1963.
Grant, Robert M. *The Apostolic Fathers: A New Translation and Commentary.* 6 vols. New York: Thomas Nelson & Sons, 1964.
Harrison, P. N. *Polycarp's Two Epistles to the Philippians.* Cambridge: The University Press, 1936.
Kleist, James A. "Barnabas" in *Ancient Christian Writers.* Westminster, Md.: The Newman Press, 1948.
––––––. "Saint Ignatius of Antioch" in *Ancient Christian Writers.* Westminster, Md.: The Newman Press, 1948.
Lawson, John. *A Theological and Historical Introduction to the Apostolic Fathers.* New York: Macmillan Co., 1961.
Vokes, F. E. *Riddle of the Didache.* London, 1937.

THE APOLOGISTS

Aubé, Benjamin. *Saint Justin: Philosophe et Martyre.* Paris: Thorin, 1875.
Barnard, J. W. *Justin Martyr, His Life and Thought.* Cambridge: The University Press, 1967.
Bonner, Campbell, ed. *The Homily on the Passion by Melito, Bishop of Sardis.* London: Christophers, 1940.
Goodenough, E. R. *The Theology of Justin Martyr.* Jena, 1923.
Gross, Otto. *Die Weltentstehungs—Lehre des Theophilus von Antiochia.* Jena, 1895.
Houssiau, Albert. *La Christologie de Saint Irénée.* Louvain: Publications Universitaires, 1955.
Jalland. *Studia Patristica.* v. 1962.
Kaye, John. *Some Account of the Writings and Opinions of Justin Martyr.* Cambridge, 1829.
Kukula, R. C. *Tatian's sogenannte Apologie.* Leipzig, 1900.
Lucks, Henry A. *The Philosophy of Athenagoras: Its source and values.* Washington, D.C.: Catholic University of America Press, 1936.
Nielsen, J. T. *Adam and Christ in the Theology of Irenaeus of Lyons.* Assen: Van Gorcum & Co., 1968.
Pommerich, Arno. *Des Apologeten Theophilus von Antiochia Gottes— und Logoslehre.* Inaugural dissertation. Leipzig, 1904.
Puech, Aimé. *Recherches sur le discours aux Grecs de Tatien.* Paris: Alcan, 1903.
————. *Les apologistes grecs du 2e siècle de notre ère.* Paris, 1912.

THE SCHOOL OF ALEXANDRIA

Crouzel, Henri. *Origène et la Philosophie Desclée de Brouwer.* Paris: Toulouse, 1960.
Daly, Robert J. "Christian Sacrifice." Unpublished dissertation. Chestnut Hill, Mass., 1973.
De Faye, Eugène. *Clément d'Alexandria: Etude sur les Rapports du Christianisme et de la philosophie Grecque.* Paris: Leroux, 1906.
————. *Origen and His Work.* Translated by Fred Rothwell. London: George Allen & Unwin Ltd., 1926.
Fairweather, Wm. *Origen and Greek Patristic Theology.* New York: Scribner's, 1901.
Kaye, John. *Bishop of Lincoln: Some Account of the Writings and Opinions of Clement of Alexandria.* London, 1835.
Hanson, R. P. C. *Allegory and Event: A Study of the Sources and Significance of Origen's Interpretation of Scripture.* London: SCM Press, Richmond Va.: 1959; John Knox Press.

Tollinton, R. B. *Clement of Alexandria: A Study in Christian Liberalism.* 2 vols. London: Williams and Norgate, 1914.

Von Balthasar, Hans Urs. *Parole et Mystère chez Origen.* Paris: Cerf, 1957.

THE SCHOOL OF NORTH AFRICA

Baylis, Harry James. *Minucius Felix and His Place Among the Early Fathers of the Latin Church.* London: S.P.C.K., 1928.

De Jong, Jakob Jan. *Apologetiek en Christendom in den Octavius van Minucius Felix.* Maastricht: Boosten & Stols, 1935.

Dix, Gregory. *The Treatise on the Apostolic Tradition of St. Hippolytus of Rome, Bishop Martyr.* London: S.P.C.K., 1968.

Fichter, Joseph H. *Saint Cecil Cyprian: Early Defender of the Faith.* St. Louis: B. Herder; London, 1942.

Forget, Jacobus. *De Vita et Scriptis Aphraatis.* Louvain: Valinthout Brothers, 1882.

Harloff, Wilhelm. *Untersuchungen zu Lactantius.* Borna-Leipzig, 1911.

Morgan, James. *The Importance of Tertullian in the Development of Christian Dogma.* London: Kegan Paul, Trench, Tubner, 1928.

Muller, Karl. *Die Bussinstitution in Karthago unter Cyprian in Zeitschrift für Kirchengeschichte.* 16:1-44, 187-219. Berlin.

Musurillo, H. "St. Methodius, The Symposium: A Treatise on Chastity" in *Ancient Christian Writers.* Westminster, Md.: The Newman Press, 1948.

O'Malley, Thomas P. *Tertullian and the Bible.* Nijmegen, Utrecht: Derrer & Van de Vegt, 1967.

Ritschl, Otto. *Cyprian von Karthago und die Verfassung der Kirche Vande.* Göttingen: Vandenhaeck & Ruprecht's Verlag, 1885.

Roberts, R. E. *The Theology of Tertullian.* London: Epworth Press, 1924.

Shortt, C. de L. *The Influence of Philosophy on the Mind of Tertullian.* London: E. Stock, 1933.

Wordsworth, Chr. *St. Hippolytus and the Church of Rome in the Earlier Part of the Third Century.* London: Rivingtons, 1880.

THE TRINITARIAN CONTROVERSY OF THE FOURTH CENTURY

Eadie, John W., ed. "The Conversions of Constantine" in *European Problem Studies.* New York: Holt, Rinehart & Winston, 1971.

Foakes-Jackson, F. J. *Eusebius Pamphili.* Cambridge: W. Heffer & Sons, Ltd., 1933.

Galtier, Paul. *Saint Hilaire de Poitiers.* Paris: Beauchesne, 1960.

Giamberardini, Gabriele S. *Ilario di Poitiers.* Cairo: Franciscan Oriental Seminary, 1956.

Gwatkin, Henry Melvill. *Studies of Arianism.* 2nd ed. Cambridge: Deighton Bell and Co., 1900.

Largent, R. P. *Saint Hilaire.* Paris: Librairie Victor Lecoffre, 1924.

Meijering, E. P. *Orthodoxy and Platonism in Athanasius: Synthesis or Antithesis.* Leiden: E. J. Brill, 1968.

Newman, John Henry. *The Arians of the Fourth Century.* 3rd ed. London: E. Lumley, 1871.

Regis, Bernard. *L'Image de Dieu d'après St. Athanase.* Paris 10, 1952.

Reynolds, Henry Robert. *Athanasius: His Life and Life-Work.* London: Religious Tract Society, 1889.

Véricel, Maurice. *Cyrille de Jérusalem.* Paris: Editions Ouvrières, 1957.

Wallace-Hadrill, D. S. *Eusebius of Caesarea.* London: A. R. Mowbray & Co., 1960.

THE CAPPADOCIAN FATHERS

Cherniss, H. F. *The Platonism of Gregory of Nyssa.* 1930.

Clarke, W. K. L. *St. Basil the Great: A Study in Monasticism.* London, 1913.

Danielou, G. *Platonisme et théologie mystique.* 2nd ed. Paris, 1953.

Fox, M. M. *The Life and Times of St. Basil the Great, as Revealed in His Works.* 1939.

Gallay, Paul. *La Vie Saint Grégoire de Nazianze.* Lyon, 1943.

Lepherz, F. *Studien zu Gregor von Nazianz.* Bonn, 1958.

Newman, J. H. *Historical Sketches.* 3 vols. London, 1872-3.

Ruether, Rosemary R. *Gregory of Nazianzus. Rhetor and Philosopher.* Oxford: Clarendon Press, 1969.

Völker, W. *Gregor von Nyssa als Mystiker.* Wiesbaden, 1953.

CHURCH AND STATE IN THE FOURTH CENTURY

Baur, Chrysostom, O.S.B. *John Chrysostom and his time.* 2 vols. Translated by Sr. M. Gonzaga, St. Joseph Mercy Hospital, Ann Arbor, Michigan. London: Sands & Co., 1960.

Cavallera, Ferd. *Saint Jérôme: Sa Vie et Son Oeuvre.* Louvain and Paris, 1922.

Dudden, F. Homes. *The Life and Times of St. Ambrose.* 2 vols. Oxford: Clarendon Press, 1935.

Morino, Claudio. *Church and State in the Teaching of St. Ambrose.* Translated by M. Joseph Costelloe, S.J. Washington, D.C.: Catholic University of America Press, 1969.

Moxon, Rev T. Allen. *St. Chrysostom on the Priesthood.* London: S.P.C.K., 1907.

Murphy, Francis X. C.S.S.R., *A Monument to Saint Jerome.* New York: Sheed & Ward, 1952.

Neander, Johann. *The Life of St. Chrysostom.* Translated by C. Stapleton. London: Seeley-Burnside, 1845.

Thierry, M. Amédée. *Saint Jérôme.* 2 vols. Paris: Didier et Cie, 1867.

SAINT AUGUSTINE

Bardy, G. *Saint Augustin.* 6th ed. Paris, 1946.

Bourke, V. J. *Augustine's Quest of Wisdom.* Milwaukee, 1945.

Boyer, C. *Christianisme et néo-platonisme dans la formation de saint Augustin.* Paris, 1920.

————. *Essais sur la doctrine de saint Augustin.* Paris, 1932.

Combes, G. *La Doctrine politique de saint Augustin.* Paris, 1927.

Deane, Herbert A. *The Political and Social Ideas of St. Augustine.* New York: Columbia University Press, 1963.

Figgis, J. N. *The Political Aspects of St. Augustine's City of God.* London, 1921.

Gilson, E. *Introduction à l'étude de saint Augustin.* 2nd. ed. Paris, 1943.

Grabmann, M. *Der göttliche Grund menschlicher Wahrheitserkenntnis nach Augustinus und Thomas von Aquin.* Cologne, 1929.

Hessen, J. *Augustins Metaphysik der Erkenntnis.* Berlin, 1931.

Le Blond, J. M. *Les conversions de saint Augustin.* Paris, 1948.

Martin, J. *La Doctrine sociale de saint Augustin.* Paris, 1912. *Saint Augustin.* (2nd ed.) Paris, 1923.

Mausbach, J. *Die Ethik des heiligen Augustinus.* 2 vols. 2nd ed. Freiburg, 1929.

Messenger, E. C. *Evolution and Theology.* London, 1931.

Switalski, B. *Neoplatonism and the Ethics of St. Augustine.* New York, 1946.

Index